MINORITIES, WOMEN, AND THE STATE IN NORTH AFRICA

MINORITIES, WOMEN, AND THE STATE IN NORTH AFRICA

Edited by
Moha Ennaji

THE RED SEA PRESS
TRENTON | LONDON | CAPE TOWN | NAIROBI | ADDIS ABABA | ASMARA | IBADAN

THE RED SEA PRESS
541 West Ingham Avenue | Suite B
Trenton, New Jersey 08638

Cover design by Lemlem Tadesse
Book Typeset by SpiralUp Solutions (P) Ltd

Library of Congress Cataloging-in-Publication Data

Minorities, women, and the state in North Africa / edited by: Moha Ennaji.
pages cm.
Includes bibliographical references and index.
ISBN 978-1-56902-404-1 (hardcover) -- ISBN 978-1-56902-405-8 (pbk.)
1. Minorities--Civil rights--Africa, North. 2. Minorities--Legal status, laws, etc.--Africa, North. 3. Africa, North--Ethnic relations. 4. Women--Africa, North--Social conditions. 5. Women--Legal status, laws, etc.--Africa, North. I. Ennaji, Moha, editor of compilation.
DT193.M56 2014
305.0961--dc23
2014022889

CONTENTS

INTRODUCTION: CONTEXTUALIZING MINORITIES, WOMEN, AND THE STATE IN NORTH AFRICA

Moha Ennaji

Since the second half of the twentieth century, North African societies have become increasingly complex and diverse. Ignored in the past, minority and women's rights have gradually started to acquire a new dimension in the aftermath of the so-called Arab Spring, and demands for respect of cultural diversity, minority and women's rights have become stronger.

Colonialism and the ensuing postcolonial governments were the major enemies of minorities and their cultural rights. Instead of recognizing and celebrating the richness of diversity, successive governments in most North African countries have worked hard to curb cultural and political pluralism. Colonial powers adopted the divide and rule approach by playing one group against the other, and totalitarian regimes established after independence have followed the same centralized unifying trend in the name of nationalism and national unity (Benrabah 2014; Boudraa and Krause 2007, 9; Ennaji 2005, 21). More than fifty-two years have elapsed since independence and more than three years after the Arab Spring; many changes have occurred that reflect the internal shifts that have affected women on the one hand, and minority populations such as Jews, Copts, Berbers, and Tuaregs on the other hand. Undoubtedly, no major works have been undertaken to analyze the recent hot debates between Islamism, secularism, religious minorities, women, and the Berber culture revival highlighted in part by the recent uprisings.

The political unrest that has cascaded back and forth across North Africa over the past four years has opened up new possibilities and new challenges in many states. Their public spheres—political and social—are increasingly contested, even in those countries that have not experienced regime change. In particular, the demands of ethnic and religious minorities for recognition, the concomitant promotion of political pluralism and democratization, the demands for women's rights, and the variety of challenges these pose to the political and social order are now prominent features of the region's political discourse (Ennaji 2009; Zuhur 2014).

North Africa, particularly Tunisia, is the place where the so-called Arab Spring all began, back in December 2010. This volume addresses the common themes and variety of experiences in the five states commonly understood as constituting the core of the Maghreb—Libya, Tunisia, Algeria, Mauritania, and Morocco—plus Egypt. As is clear from the informed studies in this volume, their trajectories differ from each other, and thus the outcomes vary accordingly.

Facts about the Arab Spring

The year 2011 saw dramatic changes in the Arab world. Unprecedented popular demonstrations in Tunisia, Egypt, and Libya led to the overthrow of autocratic rulers in North Africa. These uprisings, demanding end of corruption and dictatorship, freedom of expression, social justice, democracy, and dignity, have resonated across the region in Algeria, Morocco, Jordan, Yemen, Syria, Bahrain, Saudi Arabia, Sudan, and so on.

The Arab Spring was a big shock to everyone. No one thought Tunisia was on the verge of an eruption, or that the upheaval would spread from Tunisia to Egypt, or that the shocks would reverberate around the Middle East. The old regimes themselves were surprised by the force and speed of the uprisings. Traditional political parties in the region were at first absent or hesitant after the uprisings started. Even the Western powers were taken by surprise.

The protesters were from different ages, genders, and trends: women, men, children, old, young, liberal, democrat, Islamist, communist, socialist,

Muslim, non-Muslim, educated, non-educated, Arab, non-Arab, white, colored, and so on (Ben Jelloun 2011a, 2011b).

No particular ideology was behind the uprisings. It was a social revolution for social justice, gender equality, and human rights, which had no particular leadership, as it was mostly spontaneous and organized by angry mobs. As mentioned above, the first protest was held in Tunisia on December 18, 2010, which ultimately led to the ouster of Ben Ali. But as of November 2012 four regimes have been overthrown.

Many governments in North Africa had a low or a zero tolerance for the protestors; many of the latter were injured and hundreds killed in the region by the police and military brutality, especially in Tunisia, Libya, and Egypt.

Here are some of the main reasons for the uprisings. First, according to the World Bank, food prices rose by 15% between October 2010 and January 2011, which was 29% above its level a year earlier.[1]

Second, low wages, poverty, and the high unemployment rates especially among the youth reaching 30% in countries like Egypt (Tadros 2014). Many youth had been able to go to university, but after graduation, they faced the harsh reality of unemployment. Third, there was the frustration with closed, corrupt, unresponsive political systems. Fourth, the increasing inequality and gap between the haves and the have-nots, as most of the gains were amassed by a wealthy few. Fifth, the dictatorial systems characterized by human rights violations and government corruption had become intolerable and outdated.

On another level, social media and communication technologies proved to be a new and powerful political tool. They helped increase the intensity of the protests and their spread across the region. The youth became "a real threat to the regimes in mid-2010, when social media facilitated their collective mobilization against entrenched regimes" (Bayat 2011, 3). A large contribution was made by the new "Internet-savvy youth" who wanted change. Sites such as Twitter and Facebook helped support and organize protests. The Tunisian Ben Ali government and Qaddafi did whatever they could to block these sites to the public through the use of malicious malware.

If it had not been for the social media, a lot less people would have been aware of the protests going on or would have had enough courage to participate in them. Thanks to the spreading out of social media, young protesters had an unparalleled chance to converse, rally, and express their democratic demands on the public scene. Today, a revitalized new generation, armed with a fresh political ambition and the tools for realizing it, has emerged and is ready to protest for change and reforms.

The Moroccan Francophone writer Tahar Ben Jelloun calls it "the fall of another Berlin Wall." The uprisings motivated him to write two books: *Par le Feu* and *Le Printemps Arabe au Cas par Cas* (both published in June 2011), in which he praised the youth in the region, stating, "we trust our youth." The younger generation are more Internet literate and for that alone, they have the upper hand.

Overall, the use of the social media helped in the spread of protests, as well as ways to inspire others from all over the world to join in virtually through the media even if they were unable to do so in real life. The impact of satellite TV channels, especially *Al-Jazeera*, *Al-Arabiyya*, and CNN was so significant, as they informed and reported on events on the ground on a daily basis sometimes in real time.

The Impact of the Arab Spring

The Arab Spring has had a significant long-lasting impact on politics, democracy, and human rights. One of its major effects is the fact that religious discourse has relatively decreased, even though the overall population is deeply religious. In Tunisia, like other affected North African countries, protesters' central objective was to establish a democracy, not to Islamize society.

Similarly, in Egypt, the revolution demanded "change, freedom, and social justice" and was broadly secular. In fact, the major religious groups did not initially back the revolution; the Islamists joined reluctantly and late (see Bayat 2011; Zuhur, this volume).

During the Libyan revolution, there was no sign of the Islamist leadership, as most protesters demanded democracy, respect of dignity, and human rights. The protesters included secular and moderately religious people, as Qaddafi's oppressive regime had eradicated the Islamist movement. A new constitution had been voted, but what was urgent was state building, stability, and security to curb ethnic and regional clashes (see Sawani, this volume).

Islamists have been the greatest beneficiaries of the Arab Spring on account of their superior organizational abilities, and because of the support they have received as victims of authoritarianism.

Having long supported Ben Ali and Mubarak as shields against a rising tide of radical Islam, some Western governments now fear that

Islamist groups are poised to take over (Goldstone 2011). Polls, however, have shown that the Turkish model (secular, democratic, Western-friendly) engages the imagination of Arab public opinion in a way that Iran's does not (Tadros 2014; Zuhur 2014). Many tend to consider Turkey a vibrant democracy and a dynamic economy led by Islam's equivalent of Christian Democrats. This favorable attitude has started to be tainted by the corruption charges and the repression engaged by the current Islamist government in Turkey.

Whereas a revolution produced regime change in Tunisia, Morocco underwent peaceful reforms that left the monarchy in place: a new constitution shifts executive power from the king to the prime minister, guarantees separation of powers and gender equity, and recognizes Berber as an official language. The prime minister is appointed from the party that wins majority seats. Tunisia has now a new constitution that stipulates gender equity, freedom of speech and faith, separation of powers, and respect for diversity. But to what extent this new constitution will be adequately implemented is unknown for implementation is always a problem (Ennaji 2012).

Yet, these post–Arab Spring governments have much work to do, namely, job creation, encouraging foreign investment, and a crackdown on the corruption that has plagued their countries' economies. Both the ruling al-Nahda in Tunisia and the Party of Justice and Development (PJD) in Morocco have taken a pragmatic stance, and Western investors and professionals in both countries have received strong government assurances that business will continue as usual. Having started to lose supporters, the Islamist ruling parties in the region have, for the most part, become moderate and realistic.

Democratic Transition: Between Authoritarianism and Islamism

Islamism has recently begun to lose its appeal considerably, and the Iranian model of revolution has lost much of its attractiveness. As Bayat (2011, 2) states "Al Qaeda's violence, moreover, had caused a backlash against ordinary Muslims, who found al Qaeda's practices abhorrent to the true spirit of Islam." Post-Islamism emerged as a frame within which religious politics could become more inclusive. As the Turkish case illustrates, "Muslims could confidently remain Muslim but also have a democratic state" (Bayat 2011, 3).

We notice a shift in the rhetoric of Islamism (from religion and national identity to economic issues), abandonment of the implementation of *Shari'a* (Islamic law), neutralization of the mosque, and acceptance of the civil state: citizenship, women, and minority rights (Brown and Shahin 2010, 29; Entelis 1997, 37).

The experience of North Africa shows that a vote for Islamists is often a vote of protest instead of a vote for Islamist principles, which foreshadows the rise of other political strains. The collapse of military and police regimes presents a unique opportunity to establish democracy in the region.

Political Islam, as an ideological movement that seeks to create social change in Muslim-majority societies on the basis of Islamic values and beliefs, has suffered a serious blow in Egypt and, as a consequence, in the region, after the Islamists lost power.

Political Islam has proved to lack a clear economic and social road map. In Tunisia, the Islamist al-Nahda party in power, which was inspired by the Muslim Brotherhood, now faces mass protests against its rule, the latest sparked by the assassination of two prominent opposition figures Mohamed Brahmi in July 2013 and Choukri Belaid in February of the same year.

In Morocco, the Islamist ruling party has proved weak and inept because it could not lead any reforms, nor implement the constitution regarding the new official Berber language, nor respond to the impatient demands of the impoverished masses for a better life. Protests have recently expressed dissatisfaction and pointed out the decline in the economy and education performance under the PJD rule.

To achieve the separation of Islam and politics and strengthen sustainable development, North African Muslim countries should work on several fronts: democratization, reforms of education, judiciary, and administration, consolidating women's and minority rights, fight against corruption, poverty, illiteracy, and substandard housing, and so on. These are the real issues.

The uprisings have changed the postcolonial political landscape in the region and have immensely impacted the daily life of North Africans. Just before the Arab Spring occurred, it seemed improbable that authoritarian regimes ruling North African countries would be toppled down or radically transformed and that there would be any foremost change in the status of minorities. Today, however, thanks to the Arab Spring, change is there, for good or bad. The new elites emerging in Tunisia, Libya, and Egypt may establish a form of democratic pluralism in which minorities and women have a respectable place, or they may drift into a type of fanatical Islamist regime that is even more unreceptive to the Copts or the Nubians than Mubarak, and more hostile to the Tuareg and the Berbers than Qaddafi.

These issues necessitate serious scientific debates and objective academic research in order to analyze various experiences, the challenges to democratization in each country and the roles played by civil society, media, women, and minorities.

Minorities at Risk in North Africa

All countries are bound by international law to recognize and to protect minority rights. It is important to stress the multiple identities that characterize multicultural North Africa, which includes Jewish roots, Christian, Arab, Berber, Muslim, African, European, and Andalusian legacies, that are still strong and dynamic today (Ahlstrand and Gunner 2009; Bengio and Ben-Dor 1999; Shatzmiller 2005).

Nevertheless, there is a sturdy tendency against being called a minority, because the Christians and the Berbers in the region, for example, prefer to be regarded as major elements of national identity. The Copts in Egypt underline their Egyptian citizenship. In 1994, Pope Shenouda III turned down the use of the word minority to refer to Egyptian Copts (Ennaji 2014, 8).

Likewise, the Berbers in Morocco and Algeria are reluctant to be called minorities. The Berber cultural movement underscores that historically North Africa was a Berber land, but unlike in Iran and Afghanistan, the advent of Islam to this region in the eighth century led to the Arabization of the indigenous populations (see Chaker 1998; Ennaji 2005, chap. 1).

During the French colonization, in the first half of the twentieth century, the Moroccan and the Algerian populations have been split, following the divide and rule policy, into two ethnic groups, "Arabs" and "Berbers." However, today, these terms are not to be used in a racial sense, for they now refer to communities that have been raised in the Arabic or Berber language and culture respectively. From a cultural perspective, one should avoid opposing "Arab culture" to "Berber culture" for the simple reason that customs, values, and beliefs are often similar across the two countries (see Dourari, this volume; Ennaji 2014, 9).

Minorities across the Arab world face increasing risks to their lives following the 2011 revolutions. Libya, Egypt, Tunisia, Algeria, Morocco, and Mauritania have all suffered incidents of violence against minorities since then.

"If 2011 will be remembered as the year of the Arab Spring, then 2012 could become the year the revolutions soured," said Minority Rights Group Executive Director Mark Lattimer.[2]

The remarkable changes taking place across the region, while increasing hopes for democratization, represent for both minorities and women perhaps the most dangerous period since the end of the cold war (Batha 2012).[3]

As a case in point, in post-Qaddafi Libya, former rebels and militias still hold up to 6,000 people arrested during or after the revolution. Around half of them are sub-Saharan migrants or black Libyans, and some have been tortured to death.[4]

Additionally, violent repression continues against black Libyans from the town of Tawergha, which Qaddafi had used as a base to shell the coastal city of Misrata. Although they deny charges that they collaborated with the Qaddafi regime, they have been forced to leave their hometown, and thousands nowadays still live in displacement camps.

In Egypt, increasing numbers of Copts are reported to be leaving their country following attacks on churches and intimidation (Tadros, this volume). Activists' euphoria at the downfall of the Mubarak regime has been supplanted by mounting fury at the arbitrary detention and torture practiced by the Supreme Council of the Armed Forces against minorities. The political rise of the Muslim Brotherhood and of Salafist groups is also viewed with apprehension by other religious and ethnic minorities, including the Shi'a Muslims, and the Baha'i.[5]

Cultural differences between Sunni and Shi'a, Muslims and non-Muslims, Arabs and non-Arabs are all expressions of an internal diversity in the region that is usually ignored and which depends on mutual respect. These differences must be appreciated and respected, and must not be exploited as risk factors for violence and oppression.[6]

The transition from revolution to rights-respecting democracy is primarily a task for the North African states and peoples, but other democratic governments should exercise significant influence. However,

Western powers' support for human rights and democracy in the region has been erratic when interests in oil, military bases, or Israel are at issue.

North Africa's new leaders will need to show righteous willpower in order to improve human rights in a region that has long resisted democratic change. "And they will need consistent and unwavering support from influential outsiders," Kenneth Roth, executive director of Human Rights Watch declared.[7]

Women's Rights in the Aftermath of the Arab Spring

Although women across North Africa participated actively in the Arab Spring uprisings, their rights remain neglected, even in countries where revolutions toppled oppressive regimes. Indeed, the Islamist governments now in power in countries such as Tunisia and Morocco seem determined to keep women out of politics.

In conducting interviews with women in the region, I was shocked by their overall pessimism. They fear the loss of their rights and feel increasingly vulnerable. Female political participation in parliaments and governments after the Arab Spring has been either absent or weak. As a result, women feel a great deal of concern that Islamists in power will enact backward and gender-biased policies. In Egypt, for example, the Freedom and Justice Party claims that a woman cannot become president. Egyptian women took an active part in the revolution that toppled down former President Hosni Mubarak in 2011, yet they have been mostly excluded from any executive decision-making responsibility after the uprisings.

In Morocco, while there were eight women in the previous cabinet, today there is only one in the Islamist-led government. Women's political representation in parliament also decreased, especially in Egypt, where women held less than 1% of seats in the 2012 Egyptian parliament against 12% in the previous regime. In Libya, a first draft of the electoral law reserved 10% of seats in the constituent assembly for women, but the quota was later abandoned.

In Tunisia, 49 women won seats into the 217-seat Constituent Assembly in the 2011 elections. But the vast majority of these women were members of al-Nahda party, which considers *Shari'a* the source of legislation (Ennaji 2013).

The recent assassinations in Tunisia, mentioned above, have raised the stakes for women there. The assassinated leaders were very supportive of women's rights, and the threat of political murder will loom on those who back up secularism and gender equality for all Tunisians.

Salafists and other Islamist forces in the region constantly attack women at times of political unrest. In Tunisia, one of the most Westernized and modernized of the Arab countries, women have been attacked at universities and schools, and are forced to wear the veil. A woman who was raped by two policemen in September 2012 was indicted for public indecency when she took the matter to court.

Similarly, in Egypt, women protesters were more criticized than men, and those detained by the military during the anti-Mubarak uprisings had to undergo virginity tests as a form of terrorization. Across North Africa, conservative forces have harassed, arrested, and tortured women pro-democracy activists.[8]

These countries should eradicate gender-based discrimination and violence and protect and consolidate women's rights as a way to reinforce democratic ideas and culture. The hope for women's emancipation is truly a hope for a civilized society in which development for all is achievable.

Organizations such as the United Nations Development Program have repeatedly issued reports demonstrating the connection between economic decline and oppression of women. Simply put, Middle Eastern and North African countries will not succeed unless women are fully integrated into political and economic life.

Theoretical Approach, Themes, and Objectives of the Book

Approach

This book seeks to offer a pioneering theoretical and empirical approach to minorities and women in North African states, especially ethnicity and women's rights in the light of the Arab Spring. In line with Kymlicka (1996), the book argues that women and minority rights should be protected in order to promote equality, and societies need to become more inclusive than they are currently in respect of group rights. I also adopt the theory of intersectionality that underlines the intersection of domains of domination such as class, politics, gender, religion, language, ethnicity, education, media, and so on (Belleau 2007; Collins 2000; Crenshaw 1989).

The recent developments and the impact of the uprisings on the construction of democracy, power relations, and social equity have not been sufficiently dealt with by many publications in English.

Minorities, women, and the impact of conflicts on the construction of democracy, power relations, and social equity have not been tackled by many publications in English. The existing books have not focused on Islamic countries, and have not sufficiently discussed the theme of minorities and power-sharing in North Africa.

The effects of modernity and the international convention of human rights on this issue have not been amply dealt with either. Given the fact that Islam is practiced by the vast majority of North Africans and by over a billion people the world over and that fifty-seven countries have Muslim-majority populations, the tensions stemming from Islam's clash with cultural modernity impacts other peoples and the rest of the world (Tibi 2009).

Themes discussed

There are three important themes tackled in this book. The particular strong point is that it seeks to provide ample space to elaborate on the variety of Berber experiences in the Maghreb states—an important component in the promotion of diversity and democracy. The second issue is the part devoted to women's rights after the Arab Spring, with their status being a lightning ride in the cultural and political wars of post-revolution North Africa. The third involves the chapters on the Copts and other minorities in Egypt, who often get lost in the shuffle of analyzes of tumultuous post-revolution Egypt.

Objectives

This volume aims to unravel the problems and injustices suffered by minorities and women and focuses on the strategies adopted in each country to integrate their populations and to respect cultural diversity. The book equally seeks to discuss the role played by the state and civil society organizations on the ground to combat discrimination and totalitarianism. It examines in depth the interconnection of gender, nation, citizenship, and language.

The lack of serious academic scholarship on minority politics and minority policies in the Arab world is a glaring problem. It seems unclear how the new movements for democratic reform relate to minority struggles for recognition. The evidence from other regions suggests that while democracy is good for minorities in the long run, the first stages of democratic transitions can often be dangerous for minorities (see *From Voting to Violence: Democratization and Nationalist Conflict* by Jack Snyder 2000, for the Eastern European case). But we know little about the attitudes of reformers toward minorities, or of minorities toward democratic reform, in the Arab world.

The Structure of the Book

The book includes six parts: "Conceptualization and Anthropological Overview," "The Berber cultural movement in Algeria and Morocco," "Islamism, Women, and Media in Tunisia and Morocco," "Women, "Copts, and Other Minorities in Egypt," "Minorities and Sociocultural Change in Libya," and "Democratization, Race, and Cultural Diversity." All in all, the book comprises fourteen chapters, with each chapter providing a particular perspective and addressing specific minorities or groups.

Part I: Conceptualization and anthropological overview

This part includes a chapter by Kevin Dwyer, which provides conceptual and anthropological insights into the problematic of "value conflict" and "cultural confrontation" that is especially relevant now after the Arab Spring in the region, as individuals and groups compete in this new context and offer conflicting visions of the present and future. The chapter, focusing on divergent views of human rights, debates how to reach some form of mutual understanding. Dwyer sees "culture" not as a self-contained entity, but as "constructed out of the diverse actions" and behaviors, and therefore open-ended.

Part II: The Berber cultural movement in Algeria and Morocco

This part comprises four chapters. The first one by Abderrezak Dourari deals with Berbers as a linguistic minority in Algeria. It underscores the setback of Berbers, which is exacerbated by the necessity to modernize the state, which converges in favor of the French. The nation-state model has failed as an alternative political system because it was exclusive.

The second chapter by Mathew Andrews and Moha Ennaji, on "Language Policy and Social Cleavage in Algeria and Morocco," provides a historical comparative background to the issue of Berbers and their language since independence. The chapter argues that leaders in both countries manipulate linguistic divides during political liberalization to gain constituents, during economic liberalization for special concessions and perks, and during periods of social liberalization (or conservatism) to promote specific societal agendas.

The third chapter on "Berbers in Morocco: From the Margins to the Core" by Moha Ennaji reveals that there are many historical, political, and socioeconomic causes of the marginalization and exclusion of the Berber populations. Drawing on both historical and up-to-date accounts, the chapter shows that Berbers strategize and react to this marginalization by various forms of militancy, which differ according to their context and to the sociopolitical situation. Thanks to their activism and to the state's will to integrate Berbers in public life, Berber language and culture are more included today in many sectors than ever before.

Abderrahman El aissati's chapter on Amazigh language and culture in the era of social media in North Africa focuses on the role of the Internet in making discourse on Amazigh language and identity more visible than in the past. In addition to giving an account of the online environments where Amazigh is thriving, the chapter discusses the importance of these new avenues to the Amazigh language and culture in the way they help set up new communities and strengthen ties between social network users reinforcing discourse on language and identity in the offline world.

Part III: Islamism, women, and media in Tunisia and Morocco

Part three highlights the sociopolitical implications of Islam and media in relation to the hegemony of the state apparatus, and the effects of Islamist and Salafist discourses on women in Tunisia prior to and after the revolution. Lilia Labidi takes us to the nineteenth and twentieth century to explore and analyze, on the basis of a corpus of 300 biographies of women from Tunis, who, between 1881 and 1961, were active in the struggle for freedom and against gender-based discrimination. She concludes that women's marginalization before and after the Tunisian revolution of January 2011 thrust us to investigate the devastating ramifications of "neglect" and its consequences. She also discusses the new developments concerning the situation of women in Tunisia and shows that the fight for women's rights is an ongoing struggle, one that should recognize its roots in the actions of its historical figures.

Khedija Arfaoui's chapter "What Future for Women in Tunisia?" analyzes the situation of women, three years after the revolution. Arfaoui compares the privileged women's status in Bourguiba and Ben Ali regimes, as a significant factor in maintaining an image of a modern Tunisia. Tunisian women suffered a blow after the Islamists took power in the country with the intention to re-Islamize Tunisia and impose *Shari'a* law, which is harsh on women and restricts freedom. The chapter illustrates the resistance of the Tunisian women to this new regime and the positive impact it had on the final draft of the new Constitution, which is thought to be progressive (Ben Jelloun 2014).[9]

Fatima Sadiqi's chapter on "The Marginalization of Moroccan Women in Society and Media" discusses the images and effects of media on women. It provides an overview of the social status of women and the media in Morocco, and deals with the interaction between media and women in Morocco. The chapter shows how important it is to listen to the voices of women who are struggling to improve their lives.

Part IV: Women, Copts, and other minorities in Egypt

Sherifa Zuhur's chapter, titled "Egypt's Revolution Reshapes Women's Rights Advocates and Their Aims," reveals that the Muslim Brotherhood and its political party, Freedom and Justice, the Salafist parties, and many Egyptians demonstrated significant antipathy to Egypt's feminists and women's rights. Following the June 30, 2013, "corrective" revolution, some measures were taken to counter the lackluster approach, or even sidelining of women under the Morsi government. The chapter argues that there is a sense of greater support for women and minorities under the new government, despite continuing political divisions. Zuhur underlines that feminist movements recognize that they must work independently, as well as influence future governments.

The chapter by Marlyn Tadros argues that the recent rise of the Muslim Brotherhood to power in Egypt has revealed underlying tensions not only in the relationship of the Brotherhood vis-à-vis the liberal and secular community but also vis-à-vis religious minorities, among whom are the

Copts who constitute the largest minority in the Arab World. The chapter provides a historical overview of the conflict between the Brotherhood and the Coptic community and explains why the relationship between the two continues to be one of mistrust, discord, and apprehension.

Part V: Minorities and sociocultural change in Libya

Part five goes deeper into the concepts of minority and democracy by analyzing the social, political, and cultural ramifications of the Arab Spring in Libya. The chapter by Dirk Vandewalle, titled "Libya after the Revolution: Identity and Nation-Building," underscores that post-Qaddafi Libya faces numerous obstacles. Its major challenge is to move from a political system where neither minorities within the country nor democratic principles were tolerated toward a new social contract for the country's population that will allow for diversity while promising inclusiveness, allowing for political rights for groups that had been kept on the margin for over four decades. The author also focuses on the institutional deficiencies left by the Qaddafi regime, and argues that the creation of a new and more inclusive social democracy that can integrate the country's minorities will, for a number of historical and institutional reasons, prove extremely tough.

The chapter by Youssef Sawani analyzes the democratic process launched in Libya through the first free and fair elections in post-Qaddafi Libya, which will indisputably be seen in retrospect as a very vital but fairly simple stride to take in the long road toward democracy. This chapter, while providing an analysis of the ethnic fabric of Libya, attempts to understand why multiculturalism was not considered as an approach for managing diversity in contemporary Libya. The chapter further explores the potential for the adoption of a multiculturalist approach in Libya after the revolution.

Part IV: Democratization, race, and cultural diversity

This part starts with the chapter by Chouki El Hamel on "Blacks and the Making of the Arab Majority in Morocco." The chapter argues that the construction of race in Morocco is different from that of its American counterpart. It analyzes how racial segregation became not only an ideology of enslavement but also a structure based on patterns of color and cultural prejudice.

"Multiculturalism and Minorities in Mauritania" is the title of Madina Touré's chapter. It provides a historical overview of the Black presence in this vast North African country. The aim is to see the impact of this ethnic diversity among its population. The chapter studies the different ethnic groups that were inherited through historical exchanges and their minority status as a result of their country's joining of the Maghreb.

All these chapters emphasize the close links between democratization, human rights, cultural diversity, and rights of minorities and women in North African states. Minorities and women's rights are addressed in connection with their impact on democracy as political and cultural practice.

The book does not pretend to have covered all minorities in the region, nor to have discussed all women's woes and issues, but it has attempted to include different perspectives and put together several interesting cutting-edge contributions from scholars in the region and in the West.

Notes

1 See details about the rise of food prices according to the World Bank Website: http://www.worldbank.org/foodcrisis/food_price_watch_report_feb2011.html, accessed March 2, 2014.
2 For more details, cf. this URL: http://www.trust.org/item/?map=minorities-at-risk-following-arab-spring-rights-group/, accessed March 1, 2014.
3 Ibid.
4 Ibid.
5 See more at: http://www.minorityrights.org/11338/press-releases/minorities-face-attack-as-revolutions-sour-in-middle-east-and-north-africa-says-new-global-peoples-under-threat-survey.html#sthash.OwjIdZXY.dpuf, accessed March 2, 2014.
6 See details in this link: http://www.minorityrights.org/11337/peoples-under-threat/peoples-under-threat-2012.html, accessed March 1, 2014.
7 See this report with quotes from Kenneth Roth, Executive Director of Human Rights Watch: http://www.hrw.org/news/2013/01/31/world-report-2013-challenges-rights-after-arab-spring, accessed March 1, 2014.
8 See Ennaji's (2013) entire article in this URL: http://www.project-syndicate.org/commentary/women-in-politics-after-the-arab-spring-by-moha-ennaji#vsPV5zxKgyvgOk7j.99, accessed February 28, 2014.
9 Read this article by the Moroccan Franchophone writer Tahar Ben Jelloun: http://www.lepoint.fr/invites-du-point/tahar-ben-jelloun/ben-jelloun-la-nouvelle-constitution-tunisienne-est-revolutionnaire-22-01-2014-1783017_1921.php, accessed April 16, 2014.

References

Ahlstrand, K., and G. Gunner, eds. 2009. *Non-Muslims in Muslim Majority Societies.* Eugene: Pickwick Publications.

Batha, E. 2012. "Minorities at Risk Following Arab Spring—Rights Group." Thomson Reuters Foundation, May 24. Accessed March 1, 2014. http://www.trust.org/item/?map=minorities-at-risk-following-arab-spring-rights-group/.

Bayat, A. 2011. "The Post-Islamist Revolutions: What the Revolts in the Arab World Mean." *Foreign Affairs*, April 26. Accessed March 2, 2014. http://www.foreignaffairs.com/articles/67812/asef-bayat/the-post-islamist-revolutions.

Belleau, M.-C. 2007. "'L'intersectionalité': Feminisms in a Divided World; Québec-Canada." In *Feminist Politics: Identity, Difference, and Agency*, edited by O. Deborah et al., 51–61. Lanham: Rowman & Littlefield.

Bengio, O., and Gabriel Ben-Dor. 1999. *Minorities and the State in the Arab World.* Boulder: Lynne Rienner.

Ben Jelloun, T. 2011a. *Le Printemps Arabe au Cas par Cas*. Paris: Gallimard.

Ben Jelloun, T. 2011b. *Par le Feu*. Paris: Gallimard.

Ben Jelloun, T. 2014. "la nouvelle Constitution tunisienne est révolutionnaire." *Le Point*, January 22. Accessed April 16, 2014. http://www.lepoint.fr/invites-du-point/tahar-ben-jelloun/ben-jelloun-la-nouvelle-constitution-tunisienne-est-revolutionnaire-22-01-2014-1783017_1921.php.

Benrabah, M. 2014. "Tensions between Berberophones and Arabophones in Algeria." In *Multiculturalism and Democracy in North Africa*, edited by M. Ennaji, 57–80. London: Routledge.

Boudraa, N., and J. Krause, eds. 2007. *North Africa Mosaic*. New Castle: Cambridge Scholars Publishing.

Brown, N., and E. E. Shahin, eds. 2010. *The Struggle over Democracy in the Middle East*. London: Routledge.

Chaker, S. 1998. *Berbères aujourd'hui*. 2nd ed. Paris and Montréal: Éditions L'Harmattan.

Collins, P. H. 2000. *Black Feminist Thought: Knowledge, Consciousness, and the Politics of Empowerment*. New York: Routledge.

Crenshaw, K. 1989. "Demarginalizing the Intersection of Race and Sex: A Black Feminist Critique of Antidiscrimination Doctrine, Feminist Theory and Antiracist Politics." *University of Chicago Legal Forum* 140:139–67.

Ennaji, M. 2005. *Multilingualism, Cultural Identity, and Education in Morocco*. New York: Springer.

Ennaji, M. 2009. "Multiculturalism, Citizenship, and Education in Morocco." *Mediterranean Journal of Education Studies* 14 (1): 5–26.

Ennaji, M. 2012. "The Maghreb's Modern Islamists." *The Project Syndicate*, February 16. Accessed February 23, 2014. http://www.project-syndicate.org/commentary/the-maghreb-s-modern-islamists.

Ennaji, M. 2013. "Arab Women's Unfinished Revolution." *The Project Syndicate*, February 28. Accessed May 29, 2014. http://www.project-syndicate.org/commentary/women-in-politics-after-the-arab-spring-by-moha-ennaji.

Ennaji, M. 2014. "Contextualizing Multiculturalism and Democracy in North Africa." In *Multiculturalism and Democracy in North Africa*, edited by M. Ennaji, 1–14. London: Routledge.

Entelis, J. P. 1997. *Islam, Democracy, and the State in North Africa*. Bloomington: Indiana University Press.

Goldstone, J. A. 2011. "Understanding the Revolutions of 2011: Weakness and Resilience in Middle Eastern Autocracies." *Foreign Affairs*, May/June 2011 Issue.

Kymlicka, W. 1996. *Multicultural Citizenship: A Liberal Theory of Minority Rights*. Oxford: Oxford University Press.

Shatzmiller, M. 2005. *Nationalism and Minority Identities in Islamic Societies*. Montreal, QC: McGill-Queen's University Press.

Snyder, J. 2000. *From Voting to Violence: Democratization and Nationalist Conflict*. New York: W.W. Norton.

Tadros, M. 2014. "The Not-So-Silent Minority: The Case of Egypt's Coptic Minority in Post-Arab Uprising Egypt." In *Multiculturalism and Democracy in North Africa*, edited by M. Ennaji, 203–22. London: Routledge.

Tibi, B. 2009. *Islam's Predicament with Modernity: Politics, Religious Reform and Cultural Change*. London: Taylor & Francis.
Zuhur, S. 2014. "Claiming Space for Minorities in Egypt after the Arab Spring." In *Multiculturalism and Democracy in North Africa*, edited by M. Ennaji, 246–74. London: Routledge.

PART I

CONCEPTUALIZATION AND HISTORICAL OVERVIEW

This part provides insights into the notions of "value conflict" and "cultural confrontation" that are especially relevant in post–Arab Spring in North Africa, as individuals and groups compete in this new context and offer conflicting visions of the present and future. The chapter in this part focuses on divergent views of human rights and debates how to reach some form of mutual understanding.

This part also discusses the concepts of cultural diversity, minority and women's rights, intercultural and inter-faith dialogue, and democratization. It shows that democratic culture fosters respect of women and minority rights and equal cultural rights. It contributes to the debate on multiculturalism and its interface with identity concerns and democracy.

The chapter in this section highlights the challenges, benefits, and role of multiculturalism in the integration of minorities and women. However, the conservative right and critics of multiculturalism argue that fostering cultural diversity may provoke domestic conflicts and tensions in society.

Three relevant issues are brought to the fore, particularly the topic of human rights, nation-building, and the role of intercultural dialogue. Important theoretical aspects that are related to cultural anthropology are also debated in the hope of understanding the recent evolution in North Africa in the aftermath of the Arab Spring.

1

MULTICULTURALISM, HUMAN RIGHTS, AND THE METAPHOR OF INTERCULTURAL DIALOGUE

Kevin Dwyer

This chapter, although written before turbulence spread across the region following the December 2010 Tunisian uprising, addresses issues of "value conflict" and "cultural confrontation" that are especially relevant now, as individuals and groups compete in this new context and offer conflicting visions of the present and future. The chapter, focusing on divergent views of human rights, poses the central question: how may we envisage movement toward some form of mutual understanding and, in the best of cases, agreement, in situations where human groups believe many different things and behave in many different ways and where people, when they do not actually try to dominate one another, often show little tolerance for the beliefs and behavior of others?

I look for answers to this question, first, by seeing "culture" not as a self-contained entity with clear boundaries and transmitted relatively consistently from generation to generation, but as constructed out of the diverse actions and dispositions of a variety of individuals and social groups, sometimes in opposition to one another, and sometimes working together, with a result that is inherently open-ended.

Second, in seeking a process that might lead to productive encounters in situations dominated by different constructions of culture, by "value conflict," I re-examine the notion of "dialogue," moving beyond its usual meanings of "conversation" or "negotiation" and toward seeing it as a "wager," predicated upon some faith in success, admitting the risk of failure, and recognizing that any action's success depends upon forces beyond the actor's control. This strengthens the view that the actor or social group must come to some accommodation with a world of larger forces, even while contributing to these forces, and requires approaching an encounter as potentially a learning and innovative experience, avoiding a self-certain and self-righteous tone, adopting a vocabulary and stance characterized by tentativeness and circumspection, recognizing risk and the possibility of failure, maintaining a willingness to hear criticism and to engage in self-criticism, and remaining open to one's own vulnerability and to contradiction by the other.

In no way are these considerations meant to provide a recipe, for such a recipe, were it to exist, would have to emerge from the forces currently in play or on the horizon. We can only hope that the new forces unleashed in the region since December 2010—forces that have provided so much hope to so many, but also reasons for disappointment and cynicism and, for some, despair—will find ways to deal with one another, which explicitly or implicitly recognize principles of the sort I have been suggesting, and to fulfill the promise of mutual accommodation, agreement, and enrichment.

Let's consider two episodes, each based on my own experience. The first is a meeting between Amnesty International (AI) representatives and a delegation of the world's jurists, the subject being "the death penalty." AI's position is clear: the organization is unconditionally opposed to the imposition of the death penalty in all conceivable cases. A delegate from the United States expresses another view, "Our studies show that fair and impartial application of the death penalty contributes to lowering the rate of serious crime and also provides closure for those aggrieved by the victim's death." A delegate from Al-Azhar offers his view, "There are cases clearly indicated in the Qur'an where, if certain conditions are met, capital punishment must be applied as a sacred duty." At the end of a day-long discussion, the outcome is clear: the positions remain exactly as they were at the outset.

The second episode concerns an anthropologist who embarks upon fieldwork, leaving New York to arrive in a small village in Morocco, with only a rudimentary knowledge of the local Arabic dialect and having only the introduction of an itinerant vegetable marketer to help ease his entry. How does the effort to reach a common understanding with people of a "different culture" proceed? The outcome in this episode is that during his two years in the field, the anthropologist, having reflected on the encounter between members of different cultural groups, has become unwilling to advance "essentialist" versions of Moroccan "culture," despite the fact that this is precisely what he has been trained to do.[1]

In both these situations, the different parties to the interaction face a similar problem, a problem in "value conflict," in "cultural confrontation." While value conflict is one of anthropology's fundamental problems, it is not *only* an anthropological problem, as the first incident demonstrates. The question I want to ask is, in situations where human groups believe many different things and behave in many different ways and where people, when they do not actually try to dominate one another, often show little tolerance for the beliefs and behavior of others, how may we envisage movement toward some form of mutual understanding and, in the best of cases, agreement?

To explore this question, I will focus on the domain of human rights. In the first section, "Difference," I will present, as examples of value conflict, a number of objections that are frequently raised to international human rights notions. In the second section, "Accommodation," drawing on some insights from anthropology, philosophy, and discourse theory, I will explore how confrontation between different cultural values might be re-imagined, with a view toward constructing processes that encourage accommodation.

Difference

Differences in general

For convenience, we might divide criticisms of human rights into "substantive" ones that address the content of human rights, and "procedural" criticisms. Substantive criticisms come in two forms: an "internal," "friendly" criticism that accepts the "goodness" of human rights even while disagreeing, sometimes quite strongly, with the way they are formulated, and an "external" or "hostile" form that rejects or, at best, remains skeptical about the "goodness" of human rights.

A substantive, friendly critique is the Marxist/socialist criticism that human rights, in focusing on the individual, concentrates only on "bourgeois" freedoms—of speech, association, conscience, religion, and so on—and, as such, merely promotes the ideology of capitalism without attacking the essence of social injustice. (Criticism from this quarter led to international conventions that formulated second-generation human rights—i.e. economic, social, cultural rights).[2]

Examples of substantive, hostile criticism include the "cultural" ones that human rights notions are not appropriate for particular cultural traditions; other varieties invoke "reasons of state," or a "development imperative," to challenge the relevance of human rights.

The "procedural" criticism may also take two forms: one that calls into question the way in which contemporary human rights notions and international human rights law have been elaborated, and a second that questions the way they have been wielded. In the first, we find challenges to the way in which human rights conventions have construed the state as the primary moral agent, or to the way in which the Universal Declaration of Human Rights (UDHR) was elaborated[3]; in the second, some may claim that human rights notions are used as political tools by powerful nations to bring less powerful ones into line, and that "double-standards" are one clear symptom of this.

Another contrast in views regarding human rights is between what might be termed the "trumps"[4]—"where there are rights, the rights decide the issue, rendering thoughts of consequences null and void" (Dancy 1991, 227)—versus consequentialist views, which argue that the consequences (economic, social, cultural) of upholding rights must be taken into account in considering their normative worth.

Amartya Sen (1995) has phrased his consequentialist argument in the following terms: "Advocates of moral rights often see them as unconditional and uncompromising requirements—independently of consequences. Insisting on these rights independently of consequences may appear to make such rights more powerful. I shall argue that this is often not the case. The political and social acceptability of a moral right—and of course its effectiveness—must depend to a considerable extent on its ability to be persuasive. Cutting the consequential link can reduce—rather than enhance—its status as well as its following, and also compromise its reach" (p. 203).

Sen (1995) does not deny that safeguarding rights is important in itself—he does not therefore take the strict utilitarian position—but he argues that "the fact that importance is attached to safeguarding these rights does not automatically entail that they must prevail in an overall moral or political evaluation. Civil rights can be—and have been—justifiably violated to prevent greater harm, such as a consequential eruption of a communal riot in which thousands may perish . . . This is the arena of balancing of different consequences that would have to be invoked in evaluating the controversy over civil and political rights in poor economies in need of development" (p. 208).

Sen (1995) is not arguing that democratic rights, or free choice, are inherently barriers to economic development. To the contrary, he has taken pains to show that "No case against democratic rights can be established on the basis of their allegedly negative effects on economic growth." But he adds, "Nor, of course, can a case for political rights be based primarily on their role in promoting economic growth" (p. 209). In essence, then, he insists on the importance of "not neglecting happiness, misery and other consequences in evaluating the case for and against a moral right" (p. 212).

Any particular criticism of human rights notions may combine several of these aspects, and, in one form or another, in one context or another according to the particular conjuncture, these kinds of criticisms have been voiced not only in the West but by citizens of southern Mediterranean countries and the Middle East, as well as by those from other parts of the world, and not only by state representatives but also by grassroots organizations, intellectuals, and others.

Accommodation?

We have already seen some ways in which the concept of human rights has been challenged. It is clear that to argue effectively the defense of a "right," one must do more than simply hurl one absolute claim at another absolute claim. However, in a world where members of different communities refer to very different absolute values and sources of authority, it is far from evident how we can go beyond situations where apparently contradictory absolutes confront one another, and whether such conflicts can ever be rationally settled. In an effort to see how such conflicts might be ameliorated, I want to delve more deeply into the two key concepts that underlie our notions of value conflict or "cultural confrontation"—the concepts of "culture" and of "confrontation/conflict" in relation to "dialogue."

Culture

The notion of culture has a long and complex history that I cannot discuss at length here.[5] Let me simply start with one of the standard classical formulations: "Culture is the way of life of a people.

It consists of conventional patterns of thought and behavior, including values, beliefs, rules of conduct, political organization, economic activity, and the like, which are passed from one generation to the next by learning—and not by biological inheritance" (Hatch 1985, 178). In this definition, certain aspects are usually highlighted: (1) "the patterns which both guide and define thought and behavior are learned"; (2) "a large component of culture is below the level of conscious awareness"—for example, language; and (3) cultural patterns are not simply forms of behavior but "structure both thought and perception" (p. 178).

This view certainly takes us some way beyond the earlier uses of the term which equated it with "high" civilization (in fact, this newer view took hold around the turn of the nineteenth/twentieth century in reaction to those earlier ideas); it also has the clear merit of providing us with notions that give pride of place to diversity, encourage us to look at societies and social groups on their own terms, and do not lead inevitably to determinations and ranking of superior and inferior.[6]

However, this view also tends to abstract a population's shared symbolic representations from material social relations and conditions, and reinforces the opposition between culture and material social relations that is a foundational principle of modern social consciousness.[7] Just as importantly, this view also went hand-in-hand with the view that cultures were self-contained, relatively impermeable, and composed of comparatively stable entities such as rules, values, and beliefs that persisted from one generation to another. Ernest Gellner (1995) has put this view in lapidary form saying, "A collectivity united in a belief is a culture" (p. 6). This has been called, aptly, the "billiard-ball" theory of culture. Among the many issues this view has had difficulty treating is the question of cultural change: if cultures are largely unconscious, transmitted from one generation to another, and are incompatible and incommensurable, how then would they ever change and what would happen when they encountered one another?

Whether this view was ever well-suited to a phenomenon as complex and dynamic as culture is arguable, but certainly today it is no longer fitting in a world of significant population movements, growing global integration, glaring distinctions within societies, and where many people speak not only their native language but other dialects and languages as well, where "by some calculations, more than 99 percent of the world's peoples live in states containing more than one ethnic group" (Zimmerman 1996, 13).

Although the billiard-ball view is no longer intellectually defensible, this has not stopped its being used effectively to advance tactical political goals. For example, as one anthropologist has recently written, "the standard anthropological definition of culture as constituting a way of life and a 'peoplehood' is now being used by reactionary political forces to justify social prejudice and nativism. Immigrants and their descendants are condemned as 'not belonging' by this opportunistic use of the concept of cultures and cultural relativism" (Fox 1995, i). Another anthropologist has argued that, in the context of European attitudes toward Third World immigrants, "a perceptible shift in the rhetoric of exclusion can now be detected. From what were once assertions of the differing endowment of human races there has risen since the seventies a rhetoric of inclusion and exclusion that emphasizes the distinctiveness of cultural identity, traditions, and heritage among groups" (Stolcke 1995, 2). This, she suggests, is different from racism because, although "[t]here may be occasional references to 'blood' or 'race', there is more to this culturalist discourse than the idea of insurmountable essential cultural differences or a kind of biological culturalism . . . , namely, [there is] the assumption that relations between different cultures are by 'nature' hostile and mutually destructive because it is in human nature to be ethnocentric; different cultures ought, therefore, to be kept apart for their own good" (Stolcke 1995, 5). An extreme and extremely well-publicized formulation of this assumption is found in Samuel Huntington's 1993 article, "The Clash of Civilizations?," which argues that, in the foreseeable future, "[t]he great divisions among humankind and the dominating source of conflict will be cultural."

As Edward Said (in an afterword to his now classic *Orientalism*) has asked, "What is *another* culture? Is the notion of a distinct culture (or race, or religion, or civilization) a useful one, or does it always get involved either in self-congratulation (when one discusses one's own) or hostility and aggression (when one discusses the 'other')?" (Said 1979, 325).

As a remedy for some of the paramount deficiencies of the billiard-ball view, a different vision has gained currency, a vision that sees cultures as "overlapping" (people may find themselves positioned variously with regard to a number of different cultural groups), "interacting" (globalization leads to growing influence and interchange across geographical boundaries), and "internally negotiated" (meanings and practices are not given once and for all, but are a product of the interplay of the various forces and constituencies both within and outside the unit).[8]

While undeniably an improvement over the previous formulation and constituting a more faithful representation of the world we live in, this more recent formulation leaves aside, or does not sufficiently emphasize, at least two crucial aspects: first, that the construction of the notion of "culture" and of a particular "culture" as having certain characteristics is just that—a *construction*—from a particular perspective, and second, as a "situated" construction, the notion becomes "self-reflexive"—it opens to question both the situation of the construction's proponent(s) and the relationship between this situation and the sociopolitical implications of the notion.

Placing the emphasis on cultures as "constructed" entities, and insisting on interpreting these reflexively, we might then see a "culture" (or a "tradition") as constructed out of the diverse actions and dispositions of "individuals within social groups who inevitably have different perspectives, different psychological and physiological profiles, different points of view. . . . [a 'culture' is] a more or less coherent construction of these historically and geographically situated differences, a simplifying construction of course, but it too situated historically and geographically" (Dwyer 1996, 78). To move in this direction helps us see competition between groups promoting particular cultural visions as open-ended, reminding us of the unpredictability of the future and of the fact that any construction is inherently "unstable, vulnerable to being called into question by other constructions, . . . [and] its domination at any given moment and in any given place is not a forecast of its future domination" (Dwyer 1996, 78). Moreover, viewing these terms as situationally constructed and self-reflexive pushes us to question not only particular boundaries and the processes behind their construction but, at the same time, the "we" that works to construct them.

I hope these remarks may help us see the dangers of certain kinds of usages and may go some way toward enabling us to avoid them. It is to these ends that I suggest we try to keep topmost in our minds the principles I have highlighted: that "cultures" overlap and interact; their meanings are negotiated; these meanings and the very notion of "culture" that these meanings presuppose are "situated," elaborated from particular perspectives, in particular situations, implying particular programs; that use of these terms should encourage self-reflexivity—any particular interpretation calls for questioning the stance of the interpreter and the kinds of boundaries the interpretation constructs.

With these principles in mind, let us return to the incidents with which I opened this discussion. In the first, the Amnesty official was asserting a moral value, the "right to life" as a trump, in opposition to the US delegate's "consequentialist" view, and both these positions were distinct from the Al-Azhar representative who asserted a religious variety of "cultural" value. Yet, all these people were representatives of cultures that overlapped and interacted: they were all meeting in one place, and they were all quite aware, before the meeting, of the counter-arguments they were likely to face. Also, the positions they articulated had been "internally negotiated": (1) the Azhari knew full well that other Muslims, and very likely other Azharis (one thinks of many who follow in the footsteps of the Azhari Taha Hussein,[9] for example, as well as those who see the *Qur'an* as providing fundamental principles rather than strict prescriptions), would differ with him on what terms such as "clearly indicated" and "certain conditions" referred to, to say nothing of some of his fellow Egyptians who might stress the merciful rather than the punitive themes in the *Qur'an*, those who might challenge the applicability of Islam to public policy, and his Coptic fellow citizens who might have similarly complicated relationships to their very different sacred obligations; (2) the US delegate was also promoting one vision among many and no doubt was well aware that many studies in the United States showed, contrary to those she or he referred to, that capital punishment was not a deterrent at all, and that the issue of capital punishment was a very contentious one in the United States; (3) the Amnesty official, too, although presenting the right to life as a "trump," an absolute, was radically simplifying his own organization's history and stance on this issue, since the organization had adopted its position only after it had settled on its primary mandate and then only after very heated debates. If someone present had pushed the various interlocutors to confront and historicize their own positions by bringing such complexities to the fore, might they have been willing to question their rigid positions and might stalemate have been avoided?

The anthropologist in Morocco certainly constructed a kind of mutual understanding, but this understanding was inevitably partial, incomplete, and situated culturally and historically. Having encountered Moroccans of different generations, different sexes, who had pursued a variety of occupations and had a wealth of life experiences impossible to summarize, how could the anthropologist hope to provide, in such a context, a sketch of Moroccan "culture" that would portray it as somehow self-contained, with clear boundaries, and transmitted relatively consistently from generation to generation.[10]

Confrontation and dialogue

Keeping in mind such striking, or sometimes subtle, cultural differences, but armed with a revised concept of culture, how can we conceive of people with different values encountering one another, entering into what we may term "cultural confrontation"?[11] This confrontation between the new and the old, conceived of as a question of communication across cultural difference, is often framed utilizing a metaphor of "cultural dialogue."

There is something about dialogue that is fascinating. We need not go as far back as Plato, nor even as far back as Diderot's use of fictionalized dialogues to discuss philosophical issues or Goethe's *Conversations with Eckermann*, to see this. An important contemporary playwright claims to write plays simply "because dialogue is the most respectable way of contradicting myself" (Tom Stoppard, quoted in Tynan 1977, 44). The use of dialogue has on occasion even been elevated to civilizational significance as in the Irish cultural critic Terry Eagleton's view that "dialogue [becomes] . . . an instrument for exposing hidden authoritarianism in the institutions of Western societies" (Kelly 1992, 45), or where it is seen as a challenge to dominant expressive traditions—one commentator argues that the "dialogism" used by the Irish writers Wilde, Yeats, Joyce, "modeled on that of those classic Greek authors whom Wilde revered . . . [and reflecting] Wilde's philosophy of 'both/and' rather than 'either/or', is one of the many features that places him in a tradition of Irish as opposed to English writing" (Kiberd 1991, 384).

On the contrary (as any self-respecting, soliloquizing, dialectician might say), there is another view, one that derides dialogue, treating it as raw material, brute transcriptions, "tape-recorder literature." A somewhat deeper criticism has been formulated by Gilles Deleuze:

> C'est très difficile de "s'expliquer"—[dans] une interview, un dialogue, un entretien. La plupart du temps, quand on me pose une question,

> même qui me touche, je m'aperçois que je n'ai strictement rien à dire. Les questions se fabriquent, comme autre chose. Si on ne vous laisse pas fabriquer vos questions . . . si on vous les "pose," vous n'avez pas grand-chose à dire. L'art de construire un problème, c'est très important . . . Rien de tout cela ne se fait dans une interview, dans une conversation, dans une discussion. . . . Les objections, c'est encore pire. Chaque fois qu'on me fait une objection, j'ai envie de dire: "D'accord, d'accord, passons à autre chose." (Deleuze and Parnet 1996, 7)

And then there is the hackneyed official trope of "dialogue among civilizations" often used in international gatherings and serving as a kind of "empty signifier."[12]

So, simply invoking "dialogue" does not move us much closer to understanding how various sorts of dialogue may be more or less likely to lead to mutual comprehension and perhaps even agreement, in situations of value conflict. To move in this direction I would like to go somewhat beyond our ordinary use of this term—"a conversation between two or more people; an exchange of views in the hope of ultimately reaching an agreement" (Kirkpatrick 1983)—and examine more specifically what constructing dialogue across cultural boundaries entails.

Let me begin by drawing a distinction among several different kinds of dialogue. Consider, first, what we might call "the everyday dialogue," where individuals, in a relatively unreflective way "choose to live with a spirit of openness and good neighborliness . . . the other is welcomed fraternally, with his cultural or religious difference." Second, there is what has been called "the committed dialogue . . . where people from different milieus . . . decide to work together to perform a service that goes beyond them . . . here too difference is recognized and assumed, but the aim is not to clarify or specify this difference." Third, there is the "intellectual dialogue [which] is a matter for specialists . . . indispensable for getting to know and understand the thought of the other." And finally, "the existential dialogue," practiced by those "[who] believe that the other possesses . . . qualities that may renew, deepen, and illuminate their own being . . . to the extent that the other calls me into question . . . this is where the existential dialogue is situated" (Levrat 1993, 48–49).[13]

I think we can see that there are a number of traits here that tend to contribute to productive interchange in situations of value conflict. In particular, the last three types of dialogue, with the emphasis on people from different milieus working together, getting to know and understand the thought of the other, with an awareness that the other may force a questioning of the self's own being and sense of certainty, may have something to contribute to our understanding of the *kind* of dialogue we are searching for.

But still, we have learned little about what might be involved in that kind of dialogue, what might be its rules. It may perhaps help us to understand dialogue better if we first contrast it with two other terms: conversation and negotiation. When dialogue is compared to conversation, the latter "is freer, more spontaneous. It leaves room for the unexpected, permits a mixing of genres, of tones, it is essentially composite . . . whereas dialogue, in its desire for a respectful hearing and its effort to elucidate, goes beyond the usual conventions, the routine, the habits, opens new perspectives" (Levrat 1993, 42–43).

When dialogue is compared with negotiation—beyond the similarity that people in both seek agreement—differences exist on a number of points: (1) negotiation takes place as a contest between rivals, in a context of differential power and interests and does not exclude bluff, threats, exaggeration, or manipulation; and (2) whereas dialogue should be a confrontation "between people who treat one another . . . as partners . . . [with] the other equal to oneself. It abstracts itself from the field of power" (Levrat 1993, 44). It should also be noted that the kind of accord looked for differs: in negotiation, the accord is meant to be precise and limited, whereas dialogue "has no time limit, it remains always open. It seeks to make better understood the place from which one speaks, to share profound convictions, to elaborate with the other a meaning, a significance" (Levrat 1993, 45).

We can find further discussion of this issue in the field of discourse theory, in which the German philosopher Jurgen Habermas is a major figure.[14] In essence, Habermas argues that in situations of value conflict among different groups, we cannot know beforehand the correct position on the issue under dispute, and we can only learn this as the product of a rational discussion taking place in what he refers to as an "ideal speech situation," leading to a consensual outcome.

Some efforts have been made to specify in a general way what the characteristics of an "ideal speech situation" might be: for example, according to the German philosopher Wolfgang Kuhlmann (1985), one would choose "to cooperate as equal partners, acknowledging and treating each other in the course of argument as possessing equal rights . . . that in the course of argument each participant is accorded the same right to contradict, to interrupt, to begin afresh, to demand that the argument continue, to put questions, to insist that points are justified, to adduce fresh viewpoints, etc." (p. 198, cited in Wellmer 1993, 185).[15]

But the notion of "ideal speech situations" remains somewhat if not distantly removed from the particular problems of political and economic dialogue, as these problems manifest themselves in the contemporary situation and, in particular, in situations where the parties have vastly unequal power. This critique has been phrased by Albrecht Wellmer (1993), among others, who argues that we may postulate about moral imperatives "if *ideal* conditions for achieving agreement could be assumed. But of course this still says very little about how we should act in real conditions of communication" (p. 155). In such situations, he goes on, "[t]he ideal communication community would have passed beyond error, dissent, non-understanding and conflict, but only at the price of freezing language, of the extinction of its productive energies, and thus of suspending the very linguistic and historical life-form of humanity" (Wellmer 1993, 176). Edward Said (1989) says this more muscularly, that this "kind of scrubbed, disinfected interlocutor is a laboratory creation, with suppressed, and therefore falsified, connections to the urgent situation of crisis and conflict that brought him or her to attention in the first place" (p. 210, cited in Tully 1995, 138).

For Wellmer (1993), rather, the very constitution of an ideal speech situation, and the meaning of a rational consensus, is not a clear ideal or end-point, but "can only be conceived as a process of learning and innovation . . . the point of reference for this process is not an ideal communication community conceived as situated in the future, but the present with all those pathologies, irrationalities, psychological blocks and inhumanities which may be empirically observed" (p. 224).

I find it helpful in raising this question: what are the dialogical traits that might encourage accommodation—to recall Lucien Goldmann's discussion of the wager, a discussion that takes Pascal's seminal text as point of departure. For Goldmann, the constituent elements of all human action are "risk, the possibility of failure, the hope of success and the synthesis of these three in the form of a faith which is a wager." Furthermore, all individual action is necessarily tied to the wider world since it depends, for its success, on forces in the wider world that go beyond the control of the individual: "a wager on the success of one's own action . . . [is consequently a wager] on the existence of a force which transcends the individual" (Goldmann 1964, 301). I have argued elsewhere that there is a crucial distinction to be made between a Pascalian wager [where the wager is on an external reality independent of the wager (as in a wager on the existence of God or, more prosaically, on a particular horse at the race track or a favorite football team in a match)] and one that operates more dialectically, as in a poker game, where the wager may influence the behavior of other players and thus change the reality on which the bet is made.

To view human action as this second sort of wager challenges views that see action and positions as invulnerable and immune to criticism—a view underlying the absolutist formulations of "universal" human rights and also communal visions that construe (some version of) society or "culture" as beyond criticism. Conceiving of action as such a wager argues instead that action must assume the risk of failure while recognizing that it can only be initiated on the basis of some faith in success, on some vision of a possible future state of affairs. And by virtue of this perspective, recognizing that any action's success depends crucially upon forces beyond the actor's control establishes and prolongs a vision that the actor (or social group) must envision and come to some accommodation with a world of larger forces, while contributing in some way to these forces.

Action and discourse in the field of human rights have emerged as part of the effort to reach a common understanding about certain aspects of human behavior, to reach a moral vision of the proper relations between the various instances of human society. Discourse and action in this field, if they are to remain true to, rather than deny, their wager nature, must strive to avoid the self-assured, self-certain tone of much of the current human rights discourse, whether it be voiced by individuals, social groups, associations, international organizations, or by states and governments. Embedded in its cultural and historical moment—especially in the contemporary moment of conflicting appeals to absolute value by different institutions and/or populations—and attesting to a "faith" in a future where, if not agreement, at least accommodation on disputes over values would be possible, a human rights discourse can only build toward this future with a vocabulary and stance characterized by tentativeness and circumspection, recognition of risk and the possibility of failure, and an openness to dialogue and contradiction by the other.

Constructing such a discourse has little to do with applying a taken-for-granted blueprint where, like an architect's plan, the future is given in the present, but is more like embarking on "a quest [which] is always an education both as to the character of that which is sought and in self-knowledge" (MacIntyre 1984, 219).

Conclusion

I have not tried to provide a recipe for conducting intercultural dialogues that would lead to mutual understanding—in fact, the implication of much of what I have said is that there is no such recipe, and that to claim to have one would be to foreclose discussion on one of the key matters where agreement, however provisional, needs to be reached interculturally. But I have suggested what some of the traits of such a dialogue are likely to be, even if we cannot presume to know through what mechanism these might be reached.

Consequently, the dialogues that are most likely to be productive in this situation should be entered into as a *learning and innovating experience*, one where each participant certainly has goals in mind but where these goals may be called into question, revised, even rejected by oneself and by others; second, that a central element in such learning is the willingness to hear criticism and to engage in self-criticism; and third, that this process is necessarily open-ended. All of these elements come together when one is willing to put oneself, the presuppositions one carries, and even the sociocultural context within which one lives, at risk.[16]

Notes

1 This story is told at some length in a book I wrote in the 1980s that has recently been translated into Arabic in Morocco. In English, *Moroccan Dialogues: Anthropology in Question* (Baltimore: Johns Hopkins University Press, 1982); in Arabic: *Hiwaaraat Maghribiyya* (Casablanca: Al-NajaH Al-Jadida, 2008).

2 Another example would be a "post-modern" or "deconstructive" critique that sees the key postulates of the Enlightenment (rationality, man as the center of creation, progress) as composing just one among many possible narratives. When this post-modern perspective is turned on human rights discourse, we find the category of "foundational truth," the transcendental concept of man, and government claims to rational legitimacy, among other presuppositions, called into question. This criticism does not so much dispute the "goodness" of human rights as challenge its universality, limiting its relevance to those traditions within which it provides a convincing story. There are also critiques that are feminist, psychoanalytical, utilitarian, and so on.

3 For example, only ten Islamic countries were members of the United Nations at the time the Universal Declaration of Human Rights (UDHR) was elaborated: Egypt,

Iran, Iraq, Lebanon, Syria, Turkey, Pakistan, Afghanistan, Saudi Arabia, and Yemen. Of these ten, eight voted for the UDHR, Yemen was absent, and Saudi Arabia abstained. The other Islamic countries were colonized or not yet formed (and several of those listed above were under colonial control or influence at the time). In response, it has been argued that one Muslim (an Iranian) was present on the drafting committee, but this answer far from settles the issue.

4 A view associated with the American legal philosopher and ethicist Ronald Dworkin.

5 As Raymond Williams has pointed out, whereas "culture in all its early uses was a noun of process: the tending of something, basically crops or animals . . . a decisive change of use [occurred] in [Johann Gottfried] Herder . . . [who argued that it was necessary] to speak of 'cultures' in the plural: the specific and variable cultures of different nations and periods, but also the specific and variable cultures of social and economic groups within a nation." (It is interesting to note, as Williams does, that Herder's innovative usage was closely tied to his attacks on both "the assumption of the universal histories that 'civilization' or 'culture' . . . was what we would now call a unilinear process," and on "what he called the European subjugation and domination of the four quarters of the globe.") Williams goes on to say, "This sense was widely developed, in the Romantic movement, as an alternative to the orthodox and dominant 'civilization.' It was first used to emphasize national and traditional cultures, including the new concept of folk-culture" [Williams 1983, 87–89, referring to Herder's *Ideas on the Philosophy of the History of Mankind* (1784–1791)].

6 For an interesting discussion of the notion of "culture" that in many respects rejoins my own, see the work of Mohsen Lahsen Khukhu (2009). Also, see Abdou Filali-Ansary's contribution to the World Congress in 2009 for a more general argument supporting the need to exercise "epistemological prudence" toward concepts like "culture" or, in the specific example he adduces, "nationalism"—concepts that operate more like ideals, aspirations, or directions, than like objective realities.

7 For an anthropological example of this argument, see Turner (1995, 18).

8 This formulation, as well as the term "billiard-ball" theory of culture, comes from the political philosopher James Tully (1995, 10), who adopts it from the anthropologist Michael Carrithers (1992).

9 See Osman (2009).

10 The partial, incomplete, historically situated mutual understanding that did emerge between the anthropologist from New York and a diverse community of Moroccans, and the unfolding of this encounter, can be seen in Dwyer (1982/2008).

11 I am using the term "confrontation" here as Gadamer does, that "[e]very experience is a confrontation. Because every experience sets something new against something old and in every case it remains open in principle whether the new will prevail, i.e. will truly become experience, or whether the old, accustomed, predictable will be confirmed in the end" [Gadamer (1975) 2006, 350]. I would just question his "either/or" formulation.

12 Three examples taken both temporally and geographically at random: the meeting of l'Association pour le dialogue islamo-chrétien in December 1990 in Strasbourg; the international conference on "Le dialogue entre la culture arabe et les autres cultures," held in Tunisia in 1997, under the auspices of Arab League Educational, Cultural and Scientific Organization (ALECSO) and the Tunisian Ministry of Culture; the international conference on "Le dialogue des civilisations et la diversité culturelle," held in Kairouan, Tunisia in June 2009, under the joint auspices of Islamic Educational, Scientific and Cultural Organization (ISESCO), Organisation internationale de la Francophonie (OIF), and the Tunisian government. For an interesting summary of some positive results emerging from intercultural dialogue, including an emphasis on the importance of self-criticism in religious discourse, see Ennaifer's (2009) discussion of an experience in Islamo-Christian dialogue.

13 The distinctions in this paragraph and those following are adapted from Levrat (1993).

14 Habermas (1990), borrowing and reworking many of the major contributions from philosophy, anthropology, and sociology, has tried to (1) take the most "progressive" aspects of Kantian ethics—the view that it may be possible to construct moral visions on the basis of reason alone, a quality all human beings are taken to share; (2) transform its "monological" aspect—such reason is presumed universal in content—to a "dialogical" one where "rather than ascribing as valid to all others any maxim that I can will to be a universal law, I must submit my maxim to all others for the purposes of discursively testing its claim to universality. The emphasis shifts from what each can will without contradiction to be a general law, to what each can will in agreement to be a universal norm" (p. 67); and (3) move the discussion to the plane of procedure rather than substance. Discourse theory has resonated in philosophy, literary criticism, ethics, and legal theory. It is, of course, not without its critics, some of whom we shall hear from shortly.

15 The German legal philosopher Robert Alexy (1995) summarizes his systematic book-length attempt to formulate the rules for an ideal speech situation in the following words: with

> their aim [being] the impartiality of the discourse . . . to be realized by securing the freedom and equality of the argumentation [the most important rules are]
>
> 1 Everyone who can speak may take part in discourse.
>
> 2 (a) Everyone may question any assertion.
>
> (b) Everyone may introduce any assertion into the discourse.
>
> (c) Everyone may express his or her attitudes, wishes, needs.
>
> 3 No speaker may be prevented from exercising the rights laid down in 1 and 2 by any kind of coercion internal or external to the discourse (p. 22)

16 I have dealt with some of the implications of dialogue as this kind of "wager" in Dwyer (1982/2008, 255–88).

References

Alexy, R. 1995. "Discourse Theory and Human Rights." In *Proceedings of the 17th IVR World Congress*, vol. 2, 22–28. Bologna, June 16–21.

Carrithers, M. 1992. *Why Humans Have Cultures: Explaining Anthropology and Social History*. Oxford: Oxford University Press.

Kirkpatrick, E. M., ed. 1983. *Chambers 20th Century Dictionary New Edition 1983*. Edinburgh: Chambers.

Dancy, J. 1991. "An Ethic of Prima Facie Duties." In *A Companion to Ethics*, edited by Peter Singer, 219–29. Oxford: Blackwell.

Deleuze, G., and C. Parnet. 1996. *Dialogues*. Paris: Flammarion.

Dwyer, K. 1982. *Moroccan Dialogues: Anthropology in Question*. Baltimore: Johns Hopkins University. Arabic version *Hiwaaraat Maghribiyya* (Casablanca: Al-NajaH Al-Jadida, 2008).

Dwyer, K. 1996. "Arguments moraux et projet universel." *Prologues: Revue maghrebine du livre* 5 (Winter): 76–81.

Ennaifer, H. 2009. "Dialogue pour un nouveau langage religieux." *Prologues: Revue maghrebine du livre* 38 (printemps): 33–44. Rabat: Editions Marsam.

Filali-Ansary, A. 2009. "Identités collectives et idéal démocratique." Paper delivered at the World Congress on the theme, "Multiculturalism and Democracy in the Islamic World," Fes, Morocco, July.

Fox, R. 1995. "Editorial." *Current Anthropology* 36 (1): i–ii.

Gadamer, H.-G. (1975) 2006. *Truth and Method*. London: Continuum Books.

Gellner, Ernest. 1995. "Anything Goes." *Times Literary Supplement*, June 16, 5–6.

Goldmann, L. 1964. *The Hidden God*. Atlantic Highlands, NJ: Humanities Press.

Habermas, J. 1990. "Morality and Ethical Life." In *Moral Communication and Communicative Action*, edited by Jurgen Habermas, 195–215. Cambridge, MA: MIT Press.

Hatch, E. 1985. "Culture." In *The Social Science Encyclopedia*, edited by Adam Kuper and Jessica Kuper, 178–79. London: Routledge.

Kelly, A. 1992. "Revealing Bakhtin." *New York Review of Books* 39 (15): 44–48.

Khukhu, M. L. 2009. "Hawla al-thaqaafaat: mulaaHadhaat naqdiyyat." *Prologues: Revue maghrebine du livre* 38 (printemps): 23–27. Rabat: Editions Marsam.

Kiberd, D. 1991. "Introduction to "From: Intentions (1891)." In *The Field Anthology of Irish Writing, vol. 2*, edited by S. Deane, 1109–16. Derry, Northern Ireland: Field Day Publications.

Levrat, J. 1993. *Du dialogue*. Casablanca: Horizons Méditerranéens.

Kuhlmann, W. 1985. "Reflexive letztbegründung versus radikaler fallibilismus." *Journal for General Philosophy of Science* 16 (2): 357–74.

MacIntyre, A. 1984. *After Virtue*. Notre Dame: University of Notre Dame Press.

Osman, T. 2009. "The Islamic World, the United States, Democracy: Response to Shadi Hamid." *openDemocracy*, May 15. Accessed January 27, 2015. http://www.opendemocracy.net/article/idea/the-islamic-world-the-united-states-democracy-response-to-shadi-hamid.

Said, E. 1979. *Orientalism*. New York: Vintage.

Said, E. 1989. "Representing the Colonized: Anthropology's Interlocutors." *Critical Inquiry* 15 (2): 205–25.

Sen, A. 1995. "'Legal Rights and Moral Rights: Old Questions and New Problems.' Proceedings of the 17th IVR World Congress, Bologna, June 16–21." *European Journal of Law, Philosophy and Computer Science* 2 (1995): 203–14.

Stolcke, V. 1995. "Talking Culture: New Boundaries, New Rhetorics of Exclusion in Europe." *Current Anthropology* 36 (1): 1–13.

Tully, J. 1995. *Strange Multiplicity: Constitutionalism in an Age of Diversity*. Cambridge: Cambridge University Press.

Turner, T. 1995. "Comment." *Current Anthropology* 36 (1): 16–18.

Tynan, K. 1977. Profiles: Withdrawing with Style from the Chaos. *The New Yorker*, December 19, 41–111.

Wellmer, A. 1993. "Ethics and Dialogue: Elements of Moral Judgement in Kant and Discourse Ethics." In *The Persistence of Modernity*, edited by A. Wellmer, 113–231. Cambridge, MA: MIT Press.

Williams, R. (1976) 1983. *Keywords*. London: Fontana.

Zimmerman, W. 1996. "Last Chance for Bosnia?" *New York Review of Books*, December 19, 10–13.

PART II

THE BERBER CULTURAL MOVEMENT IN ALGERIA AND MOROCCO

This part comprises reflections and studies on Berbers as a linguistic minority in Algeria and Morocco and underscores the setback of Berbers, which is exacerbated by the nation-state model that has failed as an alternative political system because it was exclusive.

It provides a historical comparative background to the issue of Berbers and their language in both countries since independence and reveals that leaders in the region manipulate linguistic and cultural diversity to promote specific political and societal agendas.

This part argues that there are many historical, political, and socioeconomic causes of the marginalization and exclusion of the Berber populations. The Berbers strategize and resist this marginalization by various forms of militancy that differ according to their context and to the sociopolitical situation at hand.

In addition, this part debates the role of social media and the Internet in raising consciousness about Berber identity and in enhancing the demands of the Amazigh movement for the promotion of their language and culture and for the socioeconomic integration and development of Berber zones across North Africa.

2

AMAZIGHS (BERBERS) IN ALGERIA: AN ETHNIC MAJORITY YET A LINGUISTIC MINORITY

Abderrezak Dourari

> North Africa is like an island located between the Mediterranean and the Sahara. Waves of human encounters and interactions have swept ashore and shaped the "island's" rich cultural and historical morphology. Accordingly, extraordinary peoples and histories have fashioned an impressive transcultural legacy.
>
> Naylor (2009, 21)

It goes without saying that one of the most obvious components of identity customarily referred to by ethnographers and anthropologists is language. If it is an unquestioned criterion for them, it is even more irresistible for the layman in multilingual societies. In fact, identities are circulated according to the languages that are spontaneously spoken. In the multilingual Algeria of today, a citizen is said to be Kbayli, Chaoui, Mzabi, Targui, Chelhi, or Chenoui (Amazigh) when he or she speaks any one of these corresponding varieties of Tamazight (Berber), and similarly, one who speaks Algerian Arabic is declared an Arab. Moreover, people assign identities according to regional origins, namely, Jijelis (from Jijel, East of Algeria), Kbayli (from Kabilya), Stayfi (from Setif, East of Algeria), Sahrawi (from the Sahara regions), and Wahrani (from the western regions of Algeria) and pretend they have a clear cut idea of them so well that they would be able to predict their behavior.

From this point of view, the Algerians perceive their identity today as an intricate fabric mixing different languages, accents, colors, and regions, but nonetheless recognizable altogether as Algerians. In parallel with this, the laws as well as the official discourse do not go beyond general statements on Amazighness while heavily insisting on the Arab and Islamic components, although the revised Algerian Constitution in 2002 cites Tamazight as a national language besides Arabic.

Amazighs in Algeria and the Maghreb: Continuity since Prehistoric Times

The official frontiers of modern Algeria were a creation of the nineteenth-century French colonialism, cut in an ancient Amazigh territory stretching from East to West from Egypt (the Siwa Oasis) to the Canary Islands, and from North to South from the Mediterranean to the Sahara desert (Nigeria, Niger, Mali, Mauritania). These frontiers correspond, however, roughly to those it had during the reign of the Aguellid Massinissa by the end of 2nd century BC when the Maghreb was divided into three kingdoms.

The Amazigh space was divided into the *Massyle* kingdom, extending from Oued Cheliff (West) to Thugga (East), the *Massesyles* from Oued Cheliff (East) to the Moulouya (West), and then the *Maures* from the Moulouya (East) to the Atlantic Ocean (West), whereas the Getules lived in the South. The most important personalities were the *aguellids* Syphax for the Massesyles, Massinissa for the Massyles, and Bocchus for the Maures.

Keeping this fact in mind, we understand easily that the historic Amazigh population of this country could not have been dispersed to be replaced by an entirely new incoming Arab population. The immigrations into these territories, however big, could not be all that overwhelming to submerge the existing population who had been there for many centuries.

The history of immigration into these territories—from centuries BC up to now and passing through the Arab conquest and the Berber dynasties of the Middle Ages, until the modern history with the arrival of the Turks—does not provide evidence for anything like a tsunami of incoming Arabian population to give substance to the hypothesis of an ethnic Arabization by overpopulation. Gabriel Camps (2007, 142) summarizes this situation by saying,

> The history of this ethno-sociological transformation of a many million population of Berbers by some ten thousands of Bedouins is a strange and a truly marvelous one.

Subsequently, we are bound to conclude that often, in the kaleidoscopic Maghreb, language doesn't truly show the way to historic identity. In fact, it generally manifests a resulting linguistic and cultural superstructure characterizing the society today, but revealing no clear-cut clue about its origins. Philip C. Naylor (2009) observes that

> Studying North Africa offers . . . an exceptional opportunity to appreciate the formative and transformative role of historical transcultural relations.

Due to the consequential conjunctures of humans, cultures, and languages, the resulting society often makes out a fuzzy representation of it and builds up a perceived fantastic identity, partially reflecting the traces of the violently imposed one by the official hegemonic discourse, and partially that of its own true complex history.[1]

"Algeria" in Prehistoric Times

A brief outline of the prehistoric central Maghreb[2] (current Algeria) shows that the ancestors of Algerians left traces during the Paleolithic era (2,000,000 years before this era). The *Homo habilis* left round stones in the archeological sites of Ain Hnech near Setif and El-Eulma. The *Homo erectus*[3] was present one million years later near Oran, the Sahara oases, the Hoggar, and the Tassili n Ajjer epitomized by the so-called *Man of Tighennif* near Mascara. Then the *Homo sapiens* left traces between 100,000 and 40,000 years BC in the Sahel, Tipaza, Mostaghanem, and the region of Bir al-Ater in the Nememcha region (called thereafter the *Aterian,* a Neanderthaloid group). Around 22,000 BC, the *Man of Mechta Afalou* (between Bedjaïa and Chelghoum al-Aid) appeared and was also present near Maghnia. This Paleolithic culture reached its climax around 10,000 years BC.

At the beginning of the 8th millenary BC, the *Capsian* (from Gafsa, Tunisia) culture appeared. Scholars think that the fundamental composition of the current Maghrebi population is made of the Mechta Larbi (Ibero-Maurusians or Oranians) and the Capsian peoples (Mesolithic). The latter may have come from Egypt between 7000 and 5000 BC and settled in the east of present-day Algeria.

The Neolithic revolution began between 8000 and 4000 BC. The cave engravings and sculptures in the Saharan Atlas (Djebel Amour, M'zab,

Djelfa, and Tassili n Ajjer) are testimonies of this era. There comes the Bovidian era (5000 years BC), followed by the Cabbalian (2000 years BC), and then the Camelian ones.

The Getules, who lived in the south of nowadays Constantine, became horse riders at the threshold of history. The Garamantes (of Djarma) of the central Sahara gave birth to the nowadays Tuaregs. The Libyan characters appeared around the 5th century BC in the site of *Azib n Ikis* and in the 2nd century BC in Thugga [see Thugga Stone, engraved in two columns, one in Libyan and the second in Latin characters, now exposed in the Tunisian Chimtou (Simitthus) museum, near the town of Thugga, which is an archeological site of a Numidian sanctuary seemingly dedicated to Massinissa by Micipsa (149–118 BC)].

Herodotus thinks that the Amazigh population, which might have given present-day Algeria, is constituted of Libyans and nomads who lived down an imaginary line constituted by the Algerian and Tunisian salt lakes (chotts), and sedentary populations living in the north of it.

Many legends would draw the North African population from oriental origins. Salluste, compiling the Punic books ascribed to the Amazigh king Hiempsal (2nd century BC), derives the origins of Amazighs from the myth of Hercules and the Medes people (erroneous transliteration of Mazighs, Amazighs?); the Greek geographer Strabo thinks they come from India led by Hercules. But Saint Augustine, an Amazigh church Father born in Taghast, states that rural people (*rustici*) contend they are from Canaanian descent (the legend goes on to state that the Hebrew king Joshua chased them out around the 13th century BC before the foundation of Carthage by mythical queen Elisa in 814 BC). Jean Perier (2013 [1870]) reports the very words Saint Augustine uttered when he asked the inhabitants of Hippon (present Annaba) about their origins:

> Unde interrogati rustici nestri quid sint, Punicè respondentes Chanani, corruptà scilicet, sicut in lalibus solet, und litterd, quid aliud respondent quam chananoei?

Al-Bakri, an Egyptian historian, Al-Mas'oudi, an Iraqi, as well as Ibn Khaldoun, a Maghrebi one, claim that the Amazighs are the sons of Mazigh, son of Canaan, son of Cham, son of Noah.

The Yemeni origin is still defended by the Arabist ideologues in Algeria and the Maghreb despite the fact that Ibn Hazm Al-Andalusi, a famous Arab genealogist, asserts straightforwardly that the presence of

Himyarites in the Maghreb exists nowhere else than in the lies of the Yemeni historians (Dourari 1993).

These legends, assigning an Oriental origin to all civilizations, are common to that period of time. Based on genealogies, rather than on the study of territories and peoples' localizations, these legends skip the fact that all these migrations to the Maghreb did not find a space empty of people but, on the contrary, had to combat them arduously before being able to settle.

Overview of Berber Dynasties in Central Africa after the Arab Conquest until the Arrival of the Turks

It took the Arabs more than half a century to straighten out their domination over the Amazighs. They first appeared in Ifriqya in 647 where the battle of Sufetula (Sbeitla) took place; then Oqba ibn Nafi, an Arab general during the Umayyad dynasty from Damascus, who began the Islamic conquest of North Africa, founded Kairouan in 670. Koceila, a Moslem Amazigh, followed by Queen Dihiya (after his death), seemingly a Jew, led the Amazigh resistance against the Arab conquerors and failed.

From then on and until the Turks penetrated into the Maghreb in 1514, when Baba Aroudj captured Djidjelli, then Algiers, in 1516, and except from the Aghlabid dynasty (led by Arabs) that governed the one and only Ifriqya province between 800–909, a succession of Amazigh dynasties have dominated the Maghreb.

The Amazighs were expelled out of history only when, in the 16th century, the Turks took over the Maghreb.

However, three main events disrupted the population of ancient North Central Africa to a certain extent: the first involves the manifestation of nomad camel tribes in the south-east of the Roman Africa at the beginning of the fourth century; the second event concerns the military conquest by the Arabs in the seventh century; and the third, and certainly most determining, is the storming in of many Arab Hilalian nomad tribes who did not go back like their Arab predecessors.

The Amazighs were constituted of different groups. The Zenata group, however, is not from Numidian or Maures descent, and their Tamazight language bears linguistic peculiarities. They settled in the places of the Getules and mingled among them through time. There have been so many rivalries between the Sanhadja group and the Zenata, the ones who were the first Amazigh group to be Arabized. But the Tamazight languages, still spoken by the nomad Tuaregs, belong to the Sanhadja group.[4]

The Arab Moslems made many consecutive military raids against the Maghreb that did not aim, in the beginning, to colonize the region (bring population settlements) but were limited to plundering and making of booty.

Ten years after the death of Prophet Mohammad, the Caliph's army occupied Egypt and Cyrenaica. In 643, they penetrated into Tripolitania. Ibn Saâd, the foster-brother of Caliph Othman, led an army against Ifriqya in the time of disarray between the Byzantines and Amazighs. The unraveling of the wealth of the country as well as its weak spots encouraged the constitution of waves of Arab troops according to historian An-Nuweiry. The army began in Medina with 5,000 men, but it grew to 20,000 troopers in Egypt. It confronted Patrice Gregory, leader of Byzantines, in Sbeitla (Tunisia) and killed him. Having gathered a fantastic booty, the Arabs went back in 648.

Caliph Moâwiya sent a troop commanded by Moawiya Ibn Hodeidj in 666. Three years later, Oqba ibn Nâfi' founded Kairouan, the first Islamic city in the Maghreb. After a certain time, he went to Tiaret and then to Tangier, where he had been convinced to subdue the Amazighs of the Sous depicted as "savages." He made slaughtered terribly and took with him a great number of Amazigh women renowned to be very beautiful. This episode is described similarly by the Arab historiographer Ibn al-Athîr al-Djazari in his *al-Kâmil fî t-târîkh*.[5] But when Oqba was on his way back, Koceila confronted him, killed him in the village of *T'huda* near Biskra, and then took over Kairouan.

Koceila was killed in 686, Carthage was subdued in 693, and Tunis was founded in 698. Thereafter, Dihya, of the Djerawa Amazigh tribe, resisted the Arab troops between 695 and 700 before being slaughtered after her defeat, thus putting a term to the Amazigh resistance to the Arab successive invasion attempts. The conversion of her sons to Islam seems to have accelerated the Arab domination.

In 711, an Amazigh leader *Tariq Ibn Ziyyâd*, a client of *Mûsa ibn Nuçayr*, crossed the Mediterranean with an Amazigh Maures' army to conquer Spain under the pennant of Islam. After the domination of North Africa by the Arabs had been completed, many tribes built up genealogies that hinged them to Arab origins. During the Almoravid period (eleventh century), the Maghreb "*grew up forests of genealogy trees*" claiming descent from noble Arab origins, according to Mohammed Chafiq (see Chafiq 1989; Schatzmiller 1983).

The Amazighs adopted Khâridjism because this school of Islam professes a kind of democratic doctrine: any person, whatever his or her origin or the color of his or her skin can attain high governmental posts if he or she is competent and honest. Khâridjism gives an outlet to the indigenous people to occupy higher functions in society and was preferred by Amazighs. It dominated the whole of eighth and the ninth century.

The Amazigh Botr and Zeneta have, through time, occupied the higher plains, while the other branch, the Sanhadja, kept the mountainous territories of central and oriental Algeria. The Ketama tribe brought a missionary, Abu Abdellah, who advocated the coming back of the Mahdi. He built an Amazigh army and freed Obaïd Allah who was kept prisoner in the far away Sidjilmassa in 909. He built a capital called Mahdia in Tunisia in 916 and sent Ketama troops to Sicily, and then to Egypt, which they dominated and later built Cairo in 973. The dynasty of Obaid Allah, the Fatimid, dominated the whole Maghreb for a certain time. But Khâridjism was still practiced there under the leadership of Abou Yazid who created trouble.

The Fatimids left the Maghreb territories to their Amazigh lieutenant Bologhin Ibn Ziri; but in 1045, El-Moezz rejected Shi'ism and proclaimed allegiance to the Abbasside Caliph provoking in return, as a punishment, a flow of the Hilalian army and population (see below).

While the Sanhadja kingdoms of the Zirids and the Hammadids, in the central Maghreb, were declining, another Sanhadja branch from the Maghreb al-aqsâ emerged with a new religious ideology: the Almoravids. The nomad Sanhadja tribe of the Lemthouna (al-*moulathamoun*, or "the veiled," from Western Sahara) built a huge empire extending from Spain to Senegal and from the Atlantic Ocean to Algiers' meridian guided by Ibn Yacin, a religious reformer. He gathered his followers in a *ribât*—a fortified monastery—where they were trained for military and religious actions by Youcef Ibn Tachfin. They took over Morocco and the majority of what is now Algeria and Spain.

In less than three generations, the Almoravids were destroyed by the Almohads religious reformers. The Almohads are another Sanhadja tribe—the Masmouda from the High Atlas. The initiator of this reform is Ibn Toumert, proclaimed *mahdi*, from the Amazigh Hergha tribe, pretending to be an Ali descent. His successor was Abdelmoumen from the Amazigh Koumia tribe (Nedroma). They took over Fes, Tlemcen, and Marrakech in 1147, extending the tribal traditional law to their empire and were helped by Andalusian vizirs. In their Andalucian royal court, they had the support of philosopher Ibn Rochd. They fought the Hilalian tribes (it was not a racial war), subdued them, and then adopted them as auxiliaries and so did their successors, who were the Zenata Merinids. The Abdelmoumen dynasty disappeared in the late thirteenth century, and Ifriqya became an independent kingdom governed by the Almohad Abu Hafç (around thirteenth century).

The long period of Sanhadja domination (Hammadid, Almoravid, Almohad) was then closed and replaced by the Arabized Zeneta Abdelwadid in Tlemcen, and the Beni Merin (other Zenata branch) in Morocco, who lived in constant competition, a tripartite division of the Maghreb that continues to date.

As Islamic ideology was declining in the Maghreb, there were many colonization attempts undertaken by the Portuguese or Spanish conquerors under the pennant of crusades. The Spanish outposts (*presidios*, similar to Ceuta and Melilla) on the Mediterranean coast stand testimony to this. It was time for the Turks to come and dominate the Maghreb for a long time excluding the Amazighs from history.

This brief overview gives us an idea of how modest the Arab immigration to the Maghreb was and how less influential they were as a population rather than in language and religion.

The Tamazight Identity Denial in an Amazigh Independent State: A Story of Self-Hatred

As one can observe clearly, actual history goes one way, and representations go the opposite way. In fact, history is rational whereas representations are emotional; that's why the latter determine more decisively a person's attitudes. The violent controversy within political parties in the 1940s, the PPA-MTLD,[6] between partisans of the "Algérie Arabe" and the "Algérie Algérienne," pervaded the Algerian national identity contests giving birth to a long-lasting political and cultural unease. In fact, this is a domain where linguistic, cultural, ideological, and political factors overlap (Dourari 2005).

Historically, Algeria has always been multilingual. One can hardly imagine a country as big as Algeria with such dispersed human groups who miraculously kept speaking the same language in an epoch where communication means were rudimentary!

Classical Arabic penetrated this space early among some townsmen elites but not any larger social tissue. The Arab conquest under the cover of Islam succeeded after many trials, yet Arabs made no population colonization and generally relied on their Amazigh clients to run their local interests.

The Banu Hilâl, the Banu Soleim, and the Banu Ma'qil (who arrived in 1051 century) came to the Maghreb after their eviction from Egypt by the Fatimid Caliph. After the foundation of Cairo in 973, the Fatimid dynasty remembered the help that Ziri, leader of the Sanhadja tribe, rendered to counter the threat of the Kharedjit "Man with the donkey," Mahlad Ibn Kaydad (Abu Yazid), as well as his support in the conquest of Egypt itself. But the Zirids later loosened their links with the Fatimids, and El-Moezz, the leader of the Zirids, proclaimed in 1045 the supremacy of the Sunni Abbassid Caliph, infuriating the Fatimids who sent the Hilalians (Djochem, Atbedj, Zoghba, Riyah, Rebia, and Adi tribes) to punish the Zirids.[7]

The conflicts between the Amazigh cousins, the Zirids and the Hammadids, gave the Hilalians the opportunity to make alliances with one or the other cousin to combat the opposition.

In fact, there was no systematic war between Amazighs and Banu Hilâl Arabs. They had conflicts but also alliances with the Amazigh fractions, tribes, and dynasties throughout history. The Amazigh princes resorted to using them as an efficacious ready Bedouin military force, and so did the Zirids, the Hammadids, and later the Almohads.

The Hilalians settled in such small numbers, tens of thousands according to Gabriel Camps (1996), that they likely could not change profoundly the indigenous demography nor revert it. Their language has spread since the 13th century BC for sociolinguistic reasons.[8]

For Camps,

> This Maghrebi Arabic derives from the Bedouin language introduced in the 11th Century by the Hilalian Tribes; it is them who effectively Arabized a great part of the Berbers. (Camps 1996, 56, authors' translation)

The author underlines later that

> the successive population contributions of the Beni Soleim, then of the Mâ'qil who settled in the Moroccan Sahara, did not bring the population of Arab origin to more than one hundred thousand individuals who penetrated North Africa in the 11th Century. (Camps 1996, 57)

The hypothesis of an exclusive Arabic origin of the Maghrebi is contested by Abdou Elimam (2003), who thinks that it derives from Punic. Our hypothesis is that because of the diversity of the Tamazight varieties, communication and transactions were rendered difficult. The need for a common language would have made of the Hilalians' Arabic a *lingua franca*, which shared the linguistic family with Punic and Tamazight and helped prevent cousins' jealousies due to the symbolic values attached to the social position of the holder of the norm.

The Hilalians' language, mixed with Tamazight and Punic, may have given birth to the Algerian Arabic (or Maghrebi), now spoken by a majority of Maghrebis. This native language worked as an identity marker throughout time. Scholarly Arabic[9] and French have become, for symbolic and historical reasons, the formal domain languages, while the native languages (Tamazight varieties and Algerian Arabic) are overwhelming in the domain of interpersonal relations and popular art (theater, songs, folk tales, etc.).

With time, Maghrebi Arabic became a kind of vehicular language in all the main countries of the Great Maghreb where Tamazight varieties used to be the major languages.

Marcel Cohen (1971, 44) supports this idea and draws a kind of aphorism:

> In history, we can undoubtedly observe cases of a language overlapping another one, but of the same origin however . . . Arabic has expanded over other Semitic languages domain (South Arabic, Aramaic) or over other Hamitic-Semitic languages (Egyptian Coptic, Berber).

Gabriel Camps, amazed by this apparently paradoxical identity and linguistic situation in the Maghreb, observes,

> In fact we can find today no Berber language, in the sense that this language would be the reflection of a community conscious of its

> unity, neither a Berber people and even less a Berber race . . . and however the Berbers exist. (Camps 1996, 57)

The Tamazight Quest in the Context of the Anti-colonial Struggle

Tamazight, and all that is related to it, is so controversial in the Maghrebi states and societies that we can say it is one of the most keenly discussed issues. An overview of the recent historical contexts in which its controversial sharp debate evolved may render the idea of its future progression clearer, notably in Algeria.

The first plain demand of Tamazight-speaking Algerians for the recognition of the Algerian people—with an autonomous identity, history, culture, and territory— occurred in 1949 within the Algerian revolutionary PPA-MTLD. Asked to prepare a document on the Algerian people's authentic history and culture to be presented to the United Nations Organization (UNO) as a cogent proof of the existence of the Algerian people (distinct from French Europeans), the MTLD sent an official memorandum in which Algeria is said to be "Arab" to which frustrated Tamazight speakers responded through a document called *Idir al-Wataniy*, written by five scholars, containing a historical and cultural argumentation.

The radical MTLD aimed at the independence of the "Algerian Republic." Algeria was then referred to by the official MTLD as "Algérie arabe," to make clearer the contrast with "Algérie française" defended by both partisans of assimilation and colonialists. In this confrontation between colonial plans and those of revolutionaries, the Tamazight identity had to be sacrificed for the sake of invoked unity. In the same move, the revolutionaries wanted to oppose the colonialists' purported identity (French and Christianism), with something equal in prestige (Classical Arabic and Islam).

The memorandum sent to the UNO by the end of 1948 began with the following statement:

> The Algerian nation, Arab and Muslim, exists since the 7th century . . .

Consequently, there was no nation before the seventh century! No trace of Amazighs!

The issue was blatantly clear in the minds of the revolutionary Tamazight speakers. They felt their identity was being denied completely and illegitimately. Subsequently, one trend of the PPA-MTLD defended the slogan of "Algérie Algérienne" and wrote a manifesto called *Idir Al-Wataniy* with the subtitle "L'Algérie libre vivra." This was, according to one of its authors (Yahia Hennine, barrister), to counter the interrogation of Leon Blum: "L'Algérie vivra-t-elle?" [can Algeria survive?] This document had been written by Ali Yahia Said, Belhocine Mabrouk, Henine Yahia, Hadjeres Sadek, and Si Said Oubouzar and was to be sent to the Central Committee of the PPA-MTLD by Ould Hammouda Amar.

One immediate consequence was that in April 1949, the PPA-MTLD Federation de France was struck by a thunderstorm opposing the followers of the "Algérie Arabe" and the partisans of the "Algérie algérienne."

The *Idir al-Wataniy*[10] is meant to respond to this psychologically anguishing question. Having been completed in June 1949, after the death of Ould Hammouda (who was poisoned), discussions of identity and language matters had become impossible within the party. The document had been edited secretly from both the colonial authority and from the MTLD leadership. The promoters of this brochure all joined the National Liberation Front (FLN) by 1955.[11]

Here lies the main foundation of the long-lasting struggle of Tamazight speakers for the recognition of the Amazigh identity of Algeria, an identity founded on historical, linguistic, and cultural facts and not upon ideological grounds of Arabism and Islamism.

This document, rejected by the charismatic leader of Algerian nationalism at that time, Messali Hadj, as well as by the party leadership, triggered what later came to be called the "Berberist crisis," despite the fact that the term "Berber" had never been mentioned in the brochure.

During the 1949 crisis, partisans of "Algerian Algeria" and partisans of "Arab Algeria" came to grips. The *Idir al-Wataniy* brochure, produced in the heart of the Algerian nationalism, expresses the Algerianist stand:

> The linguistic factor has also contributed to the making of our national conscience; the spoken language, as well as the classical one . . . the Algerian person, Arabic or Berber speaker, uses nowadays his own mother tongue proudly and feels less the desire to speak otherwise, in French for example. He seeks, on the contrary, to study classical Arabic to know Islam and the Islamic culture to which our people have contributed. (Belhocine 2001, 17)

The accusation of Berberism and separatism went even further and built a putative Kabyle party (PPK). Ferhat Ali (treasurer of the PPA-MTLD) declared in the newspaper *Alger-Républicain* (August 21–22, 1949):

> A Party for the Kabyle People has never existed. For the mere reason that there exists only one Algerian people, whose components are nevertheless different in origin and language, who lives brotherly united and animated by the same will of national liberation . . . As for me, I have always thought that Algeria is neither Arab, nor Berber, and could not be anything else than Algerian and that in our homeland, all the cultures as well as all the components of our common heritage deserve respect and free development.

This brochure, however, provided, whether consciously or not, the doctrinal basis and the framework for the Tamazight claim all along the Algerian recent history (1980 crisis, 1990's opening horizons, and Kabylia citizenship movement in 2001–2003). The Amazighs felt an unfathomable injustice that independence had sharpened over the exclusive Arab-Islamist language and cultural policy uncompromisingly conducted by the successive Algerian governments.

Algerian Language Policy in the Aftermath of Independence

The Algerian language policy has completely been determined by the ideological and political controversies of the colonial period that put to grips the advocators of "Arab Algeria" and advocators of "Algerian Algeria." The FLN elites in power since independence, mentally shaped in this ideological and political humus, imposed ruthlessly a monolingual policy on a historically multilingual society.[12]

The linguistic policy of Arabization was meant, surreptitiously, to uproot the Tamazight languages as well the expansion of the Islamist ideology to contain leftist remarkable influence and thought. The spread of Islamic ideology (over the sacredness of classical Arabic) was intended to make milder the merciless oppression of Tamazight languages. Statements such as "I am an Amazigh arabized by Islam" are recurrent in that trend of political speech.

But if this negative attitude of revolutionary elites toward native languages and cultures, particularly Tamazight varieties, could be tolerated to a certain extent by Tamazight speakers in the context of resistance to colonialism, how would it be after independence? How could the Kabyles accept the outlawing of a simple lecture by Mouloud Mammeri, a Kabyle well-known scholar, on ancient Kabyle tales in Tizi-Ouzou University in April 20, 1980?

The interdiction entailed brutally crushed riots (called thereafter *Tafsut Imazighen*, Imazighen's spring). This contestation mainly demanded democracy, free expression of individual and collective opinions, free political organization, and the recognition of Tamazight as national language along with Arabic (the classical and the Algerian one) within a united Algerian State.

Opening horizons after 1989: Lack of constancy

The imposition of the pan-Arabist ideology conjoined to a conservative perception of Islam as unique cultural references led through time to political and ideological crystallizations that transformed the linguistic query into a vital confrontation where the educative and the cultural policies became the favorite battlefields perpetuating the fundamental cleavage lines of the 1949 crisis.

After 1989, the superficial multipartism was spoiled by a disincarnated monolingualism. The 1976 presidential ordinance, affirming the necessity of total Arabization, was reinforced by the 1996 one imposing the immediate and total Arabization under penal sanctions if any other language came to be used.

The novelty, however, was the establishment of two Tamazight language and culture university departments in Tizi-Ouzou, in 1990, and in Bedjaïa, in 1992. The popular slogan *tamazight di lakul* (meaning Tamazight at schools) was implemented in 1995 after the creation of the Higher Authority for Amazighness (HCA)—consequence of the "school bag strike" that rattled Kabylia in 1994.

Yet, the introduction of Tamazight in the educative system was hasty: with no standardization, no dictionary, no pedagogical program, no reader's book, and no trained teachers, it was a big challenge.

The April 2001 *tafsut taberkant* [black spring] contestation held by citizens' organizations and the Aarouch[13]—that lasted three years for reasons of unpunished crimes committed by the police against young protesters; perceived as a crowning of cultural, social, and economic disarray; and complicated by lack of democracy and corruption—resulted in the promotion of Tamazight to a recognized national language in the Constitution amended in 2002, while the two Kabyle-based parties Front des Forces Socialistes (FFS) and Rassemblement pour la Culture et la Démocratie (RCD) boycotted the parliament voting.

By virtue of this amendment, the polynomial Tamazight acquires, after twenty-three years of dire struggles, what it naturally had by virtue of history and territory. But the obsession of total unity cultivated by the leaders of the state was not buried yet.

Standardization Institutions of Tamazight

Tamazight is now in the constitution, in school, the media, and political discourse. Three university institutes for teaching and research are dedicated to it, and the Ministry of National Education has created the National Pedagogical and Linguistic Center for Tamazight Teaching (CNPLET)[14] after the HCA. The Ministry of Higher Teaching and Research publishes National Research Program calls for tender in the domain of Tamazight.

These institutions suffer from diverse handicaps such as the lack of researchers, as in the CNPLET, or lack of a head, as in the HCA, which has been functioning without a head since the death of Mohand Idir Ait-Amrane in 2004.

Tamazight now faces, after extending to some aspects of formal domains, qualitative demands: it's a polynomial language and is still taught with an appalling methodology. The teachers of Tamazight, who are graduates from the Tamazight departments of the university, have no training in the field of pedagogy. The language is not standardized, and each teacher operates intuitively from his or her stock of knowledge of his or her mother variety using numbers of repulsive neologisms. Above all, there is no agreement between advocates of the Arabic, Latin, and Tifinagh alphabets over the script to use. The scholarly Arabic specialists look down on Tamazight but would prefer that it be written in Arabic script; the French specialists, who have been supporting Tamazight since the seventies, would like it to keep the French script, rejecting viscerally the Arabic alphabet; the Kabyle speakers constitute the elite in the Tamazight demand of recognition and symbolic elaboration, but they refuse that their language be written in Arabic script; the Chaouia and the Mozabites speakers prefer in a certain way the Arabic scripts and the Tuaregs prefer the Tifinagh one!

On which criteria can this issue be decided so as to gain the users' acceptability and that of the society in general?

In this context, Habib Allah Mansouri[15] states,

> They are surprised [the Oran Algerian Arabic speakers] that the Tamazight speakers use the French scripts to write their language; these scripts rid this language of any historic legitimacy and would link it to a foreign civilization sphere.

There was another crucial concern for the teachers: are we to teach Tamazight for Algerian Arabic speakers as well as to Tamazight speakers? What variety is going to be taught and to whom? Will that be obligatory or optional?

All these unthought-of endocentric issues undermine the planning of the linguistic corpus (codification) on scientific bases and bring up a fuzzy presence of Tamazight in the societal landscape.

Under pressure of urging demands, the Tamazight manuals are actually full of unauthentic texts, generally French texts (badly) translated into Kabyle for the mere sake of fitting in a specific typology. Translations comprise a plenty of frustrating neologisms due to the different encyclopedia backgrounds of the source and the target languages.[16]

Otherwise, recourse is made to the Kabyle folk tales whose rural and pastoral semantics are unfit for the present cultural context of pupils who are, moreover, confronted with the French and English modern methodologies and pedagogical contents.

In a study conducted by the CNPLET in 2009, the issue is presented as follows:

> The teaching of Tamazight has been introduced in the educative system syllabus since 1995. A teacher's textbook was handed over to the teachers and learners in 1997/98. Since then, three types of textbook have been edited. The last type in use was the one elaborated by the GSD members (inspectors and teachers) of the MNE (Ministry of Education). Up to now, all the stages from the primary school 4th year to the secondary school 3rd year have had textbooks of this type. [. . .] In the programs the aims of the teaching of Tamazight as well as the competences and the learning contents are

> specified. The accompanying document contains details as to the way the textbooks must be used and how to construct a lesson. [. . .] Even before the beginning of the teaching of Tamazight at school, there existed pedagogical aids . . . .

In addition, the Tamazight contestation has caused collateral psychological leftovers of the aggressive governmental propaganda that presented Tamazight as a "colonial plot to disintegrate the nation" and as "a backward language and culture that deserve no consideration."

Othman Saadi, one of the most resolute ideological denigrators of Tamazight, proclaims straightforwardly that the Amazighs don't even exist, because they are indeed original Arabs,[17] when everyone knows that even the Hashemite Prophet Mohammad is not considered an original Arab.[18]

He derives the Tamazight lexicon from Arabic! "Tamettuth" (*woman* in Tamazight)[19] is said to be derived from "Tamath" ("menstrual" in classical Arabic). He skips over these logical questions: did the Amazighs have a name for their women before the Arabs came to North Africa? Why didn't the Arabs call their women that way! Wasn't it easier to borrow the Arabic word rather than create a new one out of a different Arabic root?

This is how self-hatred was officially cultivated reaching nihilism. If any self-esteem had to survive, the introduction of Tamazight in the educational system had severely undermined it because of its messy presence in the societal scene causing disenchantment.

Weak Institutional Framing

Scholarly Arabic benefits from the full support of the government which allocate a large budget for its development: an academy, a superior council, and many research centers within the ministry of higher education and research. Tamazight—the second national language—receives crumbs. The academy project was abandoned after being accepted by the council of the government; the HCA has had no higher commissioner since 2004; there is no research center under the administration of the Ministry of Higher Education, despite the fact that this language is direly in need of normalization institutions.[20]

The teaching of Tamazight began in Algeria during the colonial period at the university level in the nineteenth century. Initiated by an Arabic speaker Belkacem Bensedira,[21] this course was continued by his Kabyle student Said Boulifa. The teaching of Tamazight continued until the end of the sixties as a chair for Tamazight at the Algiers University, held by the late Mouloud Mammeri. Apart from the endeavors of the Tamazight civic associations, the introduction of the Tamazight teaching within the Algerian institutions began in 1995. This raised great enthusiasm and hopes for the future; however, people were quickly disenchanted because of the shrinking space where it was taught.

In a survey of the CNPLET,[22] the decrease in the number of teachers was observed in the following districts:

- Algiers: where the number was eight in 1995/1996, but evolved to ten the year after, and then decreased to three in 2002 and zero in 2007
- Batna: nine teachers in 1995/1996, then eight in 1996/1997, and then zero in 2002. But there was resumption in 2007 when twenty-one teachers were recruited
- El Bayed: one in 1995/1996, then zero in 2002, and in 2007
- Ghardaia: twelve in 1995/1996, then one in 2007
- Illizi: three in 1995/1996, then zero in 2002
- Khenchela: six in 1995/1996 to one in 2007
- Oran: two in 1995/1996, then zero in 2002. No change till now
- Oum El Bouaghi: six in 1995/1996 to thirteen in 1997/1998, then to five in 2002 and eight in 2007
- Sétif: three in 1995 to eight in 2000 and four in 2002, then five in 2007
- Tipaza: eleven in 1995/1996, then zero in 2007

We also notice the feeble growth of the number of pupils and teachers in the primary, the middle, and the secondary schools. The reports of the general inspection of the Ministry of Education (MNE) do not mention such data.[23]

In March 1990, in a colloquium held by the University of Oran on dialects in Algeria, the idea to teach each variety of Tamazight by itself was defended. It was suggested that an academy would implement the language planning of this polynomial language, and that the teaching contents, the textbooks, and the dictionaries would be made available, as great efforts were needed from the whole nation to recover its historic identity and to avoid recoiling in morbid self-loving.[24]

The setback of Tamazight in "the linguistic market," following Bourdieu (1982) and "the stock exchange of languages" of Calvet (2002), is exacerbated by the necessity to modernize the state, which converges in favor of the French, because it is well anchored in the national fabric. On the contrary, the Arabization policy, the semantic content of which and references are well entrenched in conservatism,[25] has completely failed because of its functional inappropriateness to modernity and to the populations' expression needs.

The nation-state model of the twentieth century has also failed as an alternative political system. But one political principle is necessary for building a modern democratic state: the respect of citizenship, democracy, and individual and collective liberties, which must be at the very foundations of this state in order to cope with the kaleidoscopic differences within society.

Conclusion

The Algerian Amazigh populations, which used to be a majority before the arrival of the Arabs, have continued to practice their language (as a minority language), due to the strong influence of Arabic and French, but have adopted colloquial Algerian Arabic that they use as a vehicular, now native, language.

Today, neither the Berberist particularism nor the mythical Arab-Islamic transnationalism can truly encompass the rich and multifarious resulting anthropological, social, cultural, and linguistic reality of Algeria. The Algerian constitution, influenced by the genealogist point of view common to the Arab thought, features the identity components, namely, Amazighness, Islam, and then Arabness, as if they were geological layers that one could excavate as such in the Algerian soil.

But, in fact, the identity of Algerians can also be defined on the basis of nationality and territory: Algerianity, leaving any other dimensions to Algerians' individual and collective liberties and representations.

Notes

1 We mean symbolic violence as Pierre Bourdieu (1982) puts it, but surely physical violence as well.
2 G. Camps, *Les Berbères* (Paris: Edisud); G. Meynier, *L'Algérie des origines, de la préhistoire à l'avènement de l'Islam* (Alger and Paris: La Découverte, 2007).
3 "*Homo erectus* (meaning upright man) is an extinct species of hominin that lived throughout most of the Pleistocene, with the earliest first fossil evidence dating to around 1.9 million years ago and the most recent to around 70,000 years ago. It is believed that the species originated in Africa" (http://en.wikipedia.org/wiki/Homo_erectus).

4 See Ag KhammadineDida Badi, *Les Touaregs de Tassili n Ajjer, Mémoire collective et organisation sociale*, Mémoires du CNRPH, Nouvelle série no. 17 (Alger: Centre National de Recherches Préhistoriques Anthropologiques et Historiques, 2012).

5 *al-Kamil fi' t-tarikh* is a classic history book written by Ali ibn al-Athir, composed in ca. 1231. It is considered by historians one of the most important Islamic historical works.

6 PPA-MTLD: Parti du Peuple Algérien, Mouvement pour le Triomphe des Libertés Démocratique, at that time the leading Algerian nationalist party. The crisis took place in 1949.

7 Camps, *Les Berbères*, 140–41.

8 See G. Camps, cited supra; W. Marçais, "Comment l'Afrique du Nord a été arabisée?" in *Annales de l'Institut d'Etudes Orientales d'Alger*, Tome iv, 1938 et tome xiv, 1956.

9 Scholarly Arabic is a modern derivation of the classical one formerly used in the field of religion, law, grammar, and poetry.

10 *Idir* is a proper name of a person, which means "will live" in Kabyle, and is generally used by families who have lost a lot of new born male babies.

11 This is roughly the point of view of Belhocine Mebrouk, one of the authors of the *Idir Al-Wataniy* brochure.

12 Abderrezak Dourari, "Politique linguistique en Algérie: entre le monolinguisme d'Etat et le plurilinguisme de la société," in *Synergies Pays germanophones*, Coordonné par Peter Cichon et al., *Les politiques linguistiques implicites et explicites en domaine francophone*, Revue du Gerflint, Berlin, 2012, p. 75 sq.

13 See for the misleading term of *'Aarch* or tribe A. Dourari, "Réponse à Camille Lacoste-Dujardin," Internet Site Algeria-interface, *Les Malaises de la société algérienne, crise de langues, crise d'identité*, Casbah Ed., 2003, p. 125 *sq.*; A. Dourari, "Pratiques langagières effectives et pratiques langagières postulées en Kabylie, à la lumière des événements du 'printemps noir' 2001," in *Insaniyât*, Oran, no. 17–18, Mai–Décembre, 2002.

14 CNPLET, created in 2005, see website http://cnplet.net/, accessed February 4, 2015.

15 Habiballah Mansouri is now a Tamazight inspector at the Ministry of Education; he conducted a research on the Oran population with regard to the Tamazight scripts.

16 See *Timsal n Tamazight*, no. 1–3, September–October 2011; September 2012, Magazine edited by the CNPLET/MEN, Algeria

17 Othman Saadi, *al-amazigh 'arabun 'âriba* . . . He is a Chaouia Amazigh from the East of Algeria, a well-known member of the FLN party and once an Algerian ambassador to Syria: "*arab 'âriba*," as opposed to "*'arab musta'riba*" (original Arabs/Arabized Arabs).

18 Cheikh Ahmad Al-'Iskandarî and Cheikh Mustafâ Annâni, *Al-Wassît fi l-'adab al-'arabî wa târîkhih*, 6ème edition (Ed. Matba'at al-ma'ârif, 1927), 6–8.

19 "*Tamettuth*" is derived from the Tamazight verb "*Tedh*" (root ***TD*** = "*suck*"), in the passive form meaning "*the one who is sucked.*" The phonetic assimilation process makes the link between the two words less clear.

20 See A. Dourari, "Interview to the Daily National Newspaper," *La dépêche de Kabylie*, March 21, 2009, accessed February 4, 2015, http://www.depechedekabylie.com/propread.php?id=68156&;ed=2069.

21 Belkacem Bensedira is the author of the *Cours de langue Kabyle, grammaire et version* (Alger: A. Jourdain, 1887), CCXIII. See for more, O. Ould-Braham, "Belkacem Bensedira et son cours de langue kabyle 1887" *Etudes et documents Berbères* 21 (2003): 149–90

22 Namely, Akbal-Ibri Saliha, Imarazen Moussa, Sabri Malika, Berdous Nadia, and Chemakh Said (*A Study of the Profile of the Tamazight Teachers of the Districts of Béjaïa, Bouira, Boumerdes and Tizi-Ouzou*).

23 See document entitled "l'Enseignement de Tamazight, Etat des lieux" [The teaching of Tamazight, inventory of the fixtures], 2007, p. 14.
24 See. A. Dourari (S/d), Actes du colloque international du CNPLET, *Tamazight langue nationale en Algérie: Etats de lieux et problématique d'aménagement*, Sidi Fredj, 05-07/12/2006; and international colloquia in partnership with the Laboratoire paragraphe de l'Université Paris 08: *Tamazight dans le système éducatif algérien, problématique d'aménagement*, 2007; *Workshop sur la normalisation, la numérisation et le e-learning, 2008*; *Tamazight, Les TICE et les méthodes d'enseignement/apprentissage des langues*, 2009; *La dictionnairique des langues de moindre diffusion, le cas de tamazight, 2010 . . .*).
25 Dourari, "L'impéritie de la lexicographie/lexicologie arabe." Revue *Langues et langages*, 32 (December 2013): 59–77.

References

Belhocine, M. 2001. *Idir al-wataniy, l'Algérie libre Vivra*. Alger: Le combat algérien.

Bensedira, B. 1887. *Cours de langue Kabyle, grammaire et version*. Alger: A. Jourdain.

Bourdieu, P. 1982. *Ce que Parler Veut Dire*. Paris: Fayard.

Calvet, L.-J. 2002. *Le marché aux langues. Les effets linguistiques de la mondialisation*. Paris: Plon.

Camps, G. 1996. *Les Berbères*. Paris: Edisud.

Camps, G. 2007. *Les Berbères Mémoire et identité*. Alger: Actes Sud-Barzakh.

Chafiq, M. 1989. *Lamha 'an Thalâtha wa thalâthîn qarnan min târikh al-Amazîghiyyîn*. Rabat: Dâr Al-Kalâm.

Cheikh Ahmad Al-'Iskandarî and Cheikh Mustafâ Annâni. 1927. *Al-Wassît fi l-'adab al-'arabî wa târîkhih*. 6ème ed. Cairo: Matba'at al-ma'ârif.

Cohen, M. 1971. *Matériaux pour une sociologie du langage*. Paris: Petite collection Maspero, Tome II.

Dida Badi A. K. 2012. *Les Touaregs de Tassili n Ajjer, Mémoire collective et organisation sociale*. Mémoires du CNRPH, Nouvelle série no. 17. Alger: Centre National de Recherches Préhistoriques Anthropologiques et Historiques.

Dourari, A. 1993. "Le discours idéologique arabe contemporain." Doctoral thesis, Sorbonne University.

Dourari, A. 2002. "Pratiques langagières effectives et pratiques langagières postulées en Kabylie, à la lumière des événements du 'printemps noir' 2001." In *Insaniyât*, Oran, no. 17–18, Mai–Décembre.

Dourari, A. 2003. "Réponse à Camille Lacoste-Dujardin." Internet Site Algeria-interface, *Les Malaises de la société algérienne, crise de langues, crise d'identité*, Casbah Ed., p. 125 *sq*.

Dourari, A. 2005. "Choix épistémologique et enjeux sociolinguistiques." In *Insâniyyât*, 21–27. Oran: CRASC.

Dourari, A. 2012. "Politique linguistique en Algérie: entre le monolinguisme d'Etat et le plurilinguisme de la société." In *Synergies Pays germanophones*, Coordonné par Peter Cichon et al., *Les politiques linguistiques implicites et explicites en domaine francophone*, Revue du Gerflint, Berlin, p. 75 sq.

Dourari, A. 2013. "L'impéritie de la lexicographie/lexicologie arabe." *Revue Langues et Linguistique* 32:59–77.

Elimam, A. 2003. *Le Maghribi alias ad-dârija, la langue consensuelle des Maghrébins*. Oran: Dâr al-Gharb.

Marçais, W. 1938. "Comment l'Afrique du Nord a été arabisée?" *Annales de l'Institut d'Etudes Orientales d'Alger* iv:1–22.

Marçais, W. 1956. "Comment l'Afrique du Nord a été arabisée?" *Annales de l'Institut d'Etudes Orientales d'Alger* xiv:6–7.

Meynier, G. 2007. *L'Algérie des origines, de la préhistoire à l'avènement de l'Islam.* Alger and Paris: La Découverte.
Naylor, P. C. 2009. *North Africa: A History from Antiquity to the Present.* Austin: University of Texas Press.
Ould-Braham, O. 2003. "Bensedira, B. et son 'Cours de langue kabyle.'" *Etudes et documents Berbères* 21:149–90.
Perier, J. 2013. *Familles berbères, esquisse sur l'origine et l'ethnologie des Berbères, étude.* Paris: Belles lettres, first edition in 1870.
Schatzmiller, M. 1983. "Le mythe d'origine berbère, aspects historiographiques et sociaux." *Revue de l'Occident musulman et de la Méditerranée* 35 (35): 145–56.

3

BERBER IDENTITY AND SOCIAL CLEAVAGE IN ALGERIA AND MOROCCO

Mathew Andrews and Moha Ennaji

Between 1945 and 1960, three dozen protectorates and colonies in Africa and Asia achieved independence from their European rulers.[1] Yet, the end of colonial rule did not guarantee the smooth transition to stable and legitimate regimes. New leaders faced the arduous task of state building and developing bonds of nationhood between groups and populations with different cultural, linguistic, and religious backgrounds. In the grab bag of state policies that followed, imposition of a national language in the government and in education became the principal means of drawing the nation together.

While many minority language speakers adopted the nationalist narrative, others refused to let their native tongues die. In some countries, minority languages took on significance of a magnitude never considered earlier and began to play a principal part in people's self-definition. Rather than one means of communication among many others, language became an important source of social cleavage. The question therefore arises as to why some minority language speakers not only seek to protect their language in the face of assimilationist pressures but even develop a consciousness that divides societies along linguistic lines.

Introduction

The emergence of the Berber/Amazigh culture movement in Morocco and Algeria provides a unique opportunity for such analysis due to the countries' similar economic, political, and social development. Both

Morocco and Algeria experienced French colonial rule, maintained state-centered socialist economies after independence, and are predominately inhabited by followers of Islam (see Ennaji 2005, chap. 1). Colonial policy in both countries sought to solidify French rule vis-à-vis separating Berber speakers from Arabic speakers and cultivating the former through greater government representation and application of different legal doctrines (Maddy-Weitzman 2001). Most importantly, both countries promoted Classical Arabic as the principal language in the government and in education as a means of cementing national identity.

Despite these similarities, Berber language provides a significantly greater source of social cleavage in Algeria than in Morocco. In 1980, an official decision to ban a lecture on Berber poetry at Tizi-Ouzou University in Kabylia coincided with protests and several days of unrest and clashes with police that left between thirty and fifty persons dead and hundreds wounded (see Maddy-Weitzman 1998). The event, later known as the "Berber Spring" (a reference to the Prague Spring in 1968), served as a "political watershed" and "marked the spreading of notions of Berber/Kabyle consciousness from the Kabyle intelligentsia to ordinary Kabyles and subsequently increased interest in Kabyle culture, history, and identity amongst the Kabyles themselves" (Willis 2008). According to one Berber activist, "the 1980 insurrection [. . .] was by far the most important, perhaps most revolutionary event to take place in Algeria [. . .] the population of Algiers took to the streets to demonstrate its massive opposition to colonial rule" (cf. Mezhoud 1993). While Berber cultural organizations developed in Morocco, language failed to take on the same social and political significance for Moroccan Berber speakers and a similar "Berber Spring" never occurred.

This chapter analyzes the development of the movement that led to the Algerian "Berber Spring." While many scholars such as Madani (2003) describe this movement as a cultural backlash against Algerian Arabization policies, Moroccan Berber speakers should have been equally active in protecting their cultural practices. The existence of Arabization policies in both Algeria and Morocco illustrate that attacks on cultural and linguistic practices do not independently lead to significant sources of social cleavage. As Hatoss (2002) argues, "success of language maintenance in minority groups is highly dependent on the vitality that minority group members attach to their language." Another variable must exist to make language a much more important factor for

Algerian Berber speakers than Moroccan ones. While traditional explanations attribute the factor to the legacy of French rule in Algeria, the centralized structure of the Algerian government, and the geographic concentration of Algerian Berber speakers in the region of Kabylia, these explanations provide too blunt a tool to dissect the intricate relations between Berber and non-Berber speakers in Algeria. Arabization schemes, combined with the legacy of French educational policy in Kabylia, aimed to push Kabyle Berber speakers out of educational and government positions. As these Berber speakers began to see their cultural, political, and economic interests threatened, a movement around linguistic and cultural rights provided the most effective means of challenging exclusion.

This chapter begins with a discussion of Berber identity and the distribution of Berbers in Morocco and Algeria. Then, it discusses Moroccan and Algerian policy toward Berber speakers following independence in each country. Next, it will discuss competing theories for social cleavage in Algeria, which include the success of French policies in creating a Berber "ethnic" identity, the use of centralized strategies of direct-rule by the Algerian government, and the geographic concentration of Berbers into one area in Algeria. It will also discuss the impact of Arabization policies on Berber speakers and how impediments to attaining educational and government positions served as an important catalyst for protests during the Berber Spring. Finally, the chapter will discuss the positive impact of the "Arab" Spring on the recognition and promotion of Berber language and culture.

The Berbers

The "Berber" movement provides an especially challenging object of analysis. "Berber" describes members of a cultural/linguistic group rather than a group composed by a host of factors, such as physical features and religious belief. The idea that someone can be "Berber" implies a linguistic distinction making the leap to a source of identity, social cleavage, and even political demands. For the native speakers, *Amazigh* is preferred, plural *Imazighen* (the Berbers). This word means "free man." The word "Berber" is a little stigmatizing to Berber natives because it stems from the Roman word *Barbar*, which designated an alien language or people (see Ennaji 2014). As Crawford (2005) notes,

"Simply being Berber in North Africa is a political act—at least for some" (p. 178). The trend of some Algerian Berber speakers to define "Berber" as an ethnicity has only increased the sensitivity of the issue. The move closely relates to the promulgation of an "Amazigh" ethnicity "used to signify a pan-Maghreb historical, cultural and linguistic identity" (Goodman 2004) However, ethnic identity implies certain rights under international norms and the idea that language does not represent a choice but rather an integral part of an identity that people are born into. The Algerian and Moroccan regimes and the majority of non-Berber speakers, thus, remain opposed to the use of ethnic distinctions.

Berber speakers additionally fall outside the simple secular/Muslim dichotomy, as fundamentalist Islamist movements and secular democratic parties both include Berber leaders (Willis 2008).[2] However, the vast majority of people claiming Berber identity are Muslims, "most of whom are devout observers of the faith" (Layachi 2005, 202). Geographic separation and dialectical diversity further complicates discussion of a uniform "Berber" identity. Moroccan Berbers, constituting more than 40% of the population (Maddy-Weitzman 1998, 33), live in three rough linguistic blocks centered in the mountains of the south, the Middle Atlas, and the Rif mountains (Crawford 2008, 172). While dialects in theory imply mutual intelligibility (Salzmann 2006), "rural Imazighen (Berbers) only sometimes claim that they can understand other people from other regions" (Crawford 2008, 173). Algerian Berbers, 25% to 30% of the population by official estimates, share similar circumstances, divided into four distinct geographically separated communities with differing dialects. While each region in Morocco contains roughly the same number of Berber speakers, "approximately two-thirds of Algerian Berbers live in the Kayblia mountainous region southeast of Algiers" (Maddy-Weitzman 1998, 33). The second largest group, slightly less than one-third of the Berber-speaking population, lives in the mountainous region of Aures, while the remaining two Algerian Berber groups reside in Mzab and the Sahara Desert.

Post-independence policy toward Berber speakers

In 1956, Morocco gained its independence from France and Spain and brought the question of who would rule to the fore. Two forces dominated the independence movement: the Istiqlal, an Arab nationalist movement in support of a figurehead King, and the monarchy of Mohammed V. Both parties possessed considerable prestige at independence; however, the Istiqlal maintained dominance during the first four years of independent rule (see Byman 1997, 324).

The Istiqlal government "welcomed Berbers only to the extent that they put aside their particularist identity as a relic of the colonial past" (Maddy-Weitzman 2001, 30). During the 44 years of colonial rule, French authorities in Morocco pursued a strategy of divide-and-rule by strengthening the division between "Berbers" and "Arabs" (Maddy-Weitzman 2001, 29). The extent to which this distinction existed prior to the French rule remains a hotly contested topic among scholars, Berber activists, and Arab nationalists[3]; however, parties generally agree that even if Berber language served as a distinguishing factor, it was "one of more ambiguous and subsidiary importance" (Maddy-Weitzman 2001, 29). The sharp reaction to the infamous French policy of 1930, which implemented Berber customary law rather than Shari'a law in predominately Berber areas, from non-Berber *and* Berber speakers illustrated the weakness of linguistic/cultural factors in the formation of Moroccan identity.[4]

The Istiqlal party nevertheless remained strongly influenced by this colonial legacy and sought "to impose their dominant Arab nationalist identity on the Berber parts of Morocco . . . [filling] all the local leadership posts with French-speaking Istiqlal supporters, almost all of whom were Arab and urban" (Byman 1997, 325). These replacements alienated traditional leaders in Berber-speaking areas, who saw the Istiqlal's appointments as a threat to their status positions and to their communities' ways of life. As Maddy-Weitzman (2001) argues, "tribal revolts . . . constituted not so much a challenge to the new state as [. . .] an assertion of Berber tribal prerogatives against the domineering, patronizing ways of a 'modern,' Istiqlal party-dominated administration" (p. 29).[5]

Mohammed V quickly capitalized on these social divisions to strengthen his control vis-à-vis political alliances with Berber notables (see Willis 2008, 233). The monarch complemented these alliances with appointments of Berber speakers to the majority of posts in the main royalist party, the Mouvement Populaire (MP), the military, and two of the four positions in the Throne Council (an advisory body similar to a President's Cabinet; see Maddy-Weitzman 2001, 30; Byman 1997, 330).

Despite these alliances, the MP never developed a Berber agenda and eventually served as part of the governing coalition that introduced

Arabization in Morocco in 1965 (cf. Willis 2008, 233). Additionally, Mohammed V vigilantly suppressed any explicit articulation of Berber identity through cultural and political movements (Maddy-Weitzman 2001, 331). Following the death of Mohammed V in 1961, Hassan II adopted his father's carrot-and-stick approach to governance. The new king divided Berbers into local communities under traditional leaders and continued the use of political patronage (Byman 1997, 334). Hassan II complemented these practices with authoritarian security measures, hundreds of forced disappearances, stringent censorship, and police brutality. The government regularly suppressed peaceful gatherings and arrested activists for acts such as publishing articles on Berber history (Byman 1997, 332).

While repression and accommodation prevented the formation of Berber political organizations, Arabization policies (including recognition of Arabic as the national official language and promotion of classical Arabic as the sole language of educational institutions) did galvanize the formation of Berber cultural associations (cf. Ennaji and Sadiqi 2008; Aslan 2007). However, these organizations maintained only a limited following and "avoided antagonizing the regime by functioning solely in the cultural arena, such as the collection of Berber oral poems and stories, making documentaries on the Berber culture, and recording Berber music" (Aslan 2007, 9).

As in Morocco, Algeria also confronted the question of who would rule after independence in 1962. Two forces dominated the scene: the Front de Liberation National (FLN), led by Ahmed Ben Bella and Houari Boumedienne, and the Forces des Fronts Socialistes (FFS), led by Kabyle leader Hocine Ait Ahmed. While the FLN garnered support from multiple regions of Algeria, the FFS drew mainly from Kabylia (Maddy-Weitzman 2001, 37).

While armed skirmishes between the political contenders ended with a power-sharing agreement in September 1962, tensions grew over the next year (see Quandt 1972). The Kabyle leaders who once accepted Ben Bella's leadership quit their government posts and called for a rejection of Ben Bella's Constitutional Referendum. Ben Bella, Algeria's first president after independence, was based in Cairo at the outbreak of the Algerian War in 1954, and thus was influenced by the Egyptian President Gamal Abdel Nasser's Arab nationalist ideology. Once in power, Ben Bella promoted Arabic and eradicated Berber language and culture in Algeria. Open conflict resumed in September

1963, when Ben Bella formed a new government and banned the FFS. According to Maddy-Weitzman (2001), "at least some of the new ruling hierarchy were convinced that the Kabylians were secessionists, and favored a policy of isolation of the region and then afterward destruction" (p. 38). Such fears, although politically motivated, also had to do with the legacy of French colonialism.

The concentration of two-thirds of Algerian Berbers in Kabylia led French authorities to concentrate their efforts in the region. Preferential policies included the promotion of Berber language over Arabic, provision of greater educational and professional opportunities, favoring Berber speakers for migration to France as laborers, and attempting to instill in them the belief of European ancestry. While Kabyles provided "the fiercest resistance to French colonialism and some of the bravest nationalists," many Algerians remained suspicious of the FFS's motives (Layachi 2005, 202).

Fighting lasted just over a year, ending with the defection of Kabyle military commander, Mohand oul Hadj, and Ait Ahmed's arrest in October 1964. In the following years, the Ben Bella and Boumedienne governments passed a series of charters and codes centralizing their administrative power. The Code of the Wilayas, the official text regulating regional institutions, "rejected notions of local autonomy in making explicit that there should be no 'scattering of revolutionary power'" (Baduel 1991, 347; Charrad 2001, 180). The 1976 Algerian National Charter further elaborated that "the Revolution aims not only to eliminate all these relics (tribal, patriarchal and quasi-feudal structures), but also to prevent their return. Basically, it is a matter of making Algerians conscious citizens of a modern nation" (Charrad 2001, 180).

Yet, the policies of governments and the texts they claim to follow often fail to align. As Charrad (2001) argues, "At the same time that its texts called for their eradication, the Algerian state that emerged with national independence integrated kin-based forms of association into the political and administrative systems of the country" (p. 181).

The FLN, far from being a highly organized and coordinated party, suffered from extensive factionalism that forced the leadership to draw power from local and regional ties. Lack of administrative resources further forced the administration "to tolerate the retention of substantial autonomy on the part of kin-based forms of association" (Charrad 2001, 180).

The Algerian government, thus, paid special attention to avoiding moves that might alienate Berber speakers. Ben Bella filled five out of nineteen minister positions with Berber speakers (Charrad 2001, 182). When Boumedienne came to power following a coup in June 1965, the new administration continued accommodating Berber speakers by providing important positions in the central government "in proportion to the percentage of Berbers in the population at large, about 20 percent" (Charrad 2001, 182).

Accommodation coincided with severe repression of overt acts of Berber cultural activism and the establishment of Arabization policies. As Evans and Phillips (2008) note, "any sign of Berber assertiveness was immediately denounced as the work of the neo-colonial fifth column" (p. 87). The Algerian government regularly shut down cultural events (Goodman 2004, 73), replaced Berber singers with Arab singers during annual festivals (Maddy-Weitzman 2001, 39), and imprisoned peaceful protestors (Stone 1997, 205). At the same time, the Algerian government promoted Arabic as the sole language in schools and universities and mandated knowledge of classical Arabic as a prerequisite for government jobs (Schulze and Azodi 2002, 170).

Because of their exclusion and marginalization, the Berbers have clashed with Algeria's central government since the country won its independence from France in 1962. "A clique of generals and power brokers, called 'Le Pouvoir' (The Power), has ruled the country since then, behind a civilian façade," as Spencer (2001) put it. For decades, the Berbers have fought for the official recognition of their language and struggled against state-sponsored cultural discrimination.[6]

Algeria and Morocco, thus, implemented nearly identical policies of accommodation and repression during the decades after independence. Yet, while Berber activists in Morocco operated quietly within the cultural sphere, Berber speakers in Algeria grew increasingly confrontational with the Algerian regime throughout the 1970s. Riots erupted at an annual Kabyle festival in 1974 and during a national football championship featuring a Kabyle team in 1977, both requiring suppression by troops and police (Maddy-Weitzman 2001, 39). As 1980 approached, Kabyle Berber speakers increasingly viewed the Algerian regime as out of touch with their needs and realities. However, the question remains as to why in the presence of identical cultural and political polices the Algerian Berber speakers attached such significance to their language while their Moroccan counterparts did not.

Traditional explanations for social cleavage

Scholars generally identify three differences between Algeria and Morocco in explaining social cleavage along Berber/non-Berber lines: the experience of more than a century of direct and brutal French rule, the inflexibility of a "Jacobin-like" regime seeking to "mold society under a single state socialist Arab-Islamic banner," and the concentration of the majority of Algerian Berbers in Kabylia (Maddy-Weitzman 2001, 36–37). However, these arguments fail to take into account the multilayered (and often contradictory) relationship between the Algerian government and Berber speakers.

Proponents of the first approach rely on the importance of colonial rule in engineering the ideological differences and social cleavages in postcolonial nations. This model, articulated by Laitin (1986) in his study of politicization in Yorubaland, stresses "the importance of key historical periods [. . .] unlike both social systems and rational choice theories, the model of hegemony assumes that hegemonic forging of alliances occurs rarely, and is a function of historically peculiar circumstances [. . .] but once a hegemonic order is created, its consequences are long-lasting" (p. 168). While Morocco remained a French Protectorate for only 44 years, French rule in Algeria lasted 132 years. Scholars, therefore, argue that colonization in Algeria uniquely and heavily shaped Algerian Berber communities (Laitin 1986, 168). According to Layachi (2005), the French policy "succeeded in creating a serious and lasting schism between the people of the Greater Kabylie and the rest of the population" (p. 202). Despite heavy Kabyle participation in the nationalist independence movement, the conceptual divide left over from the French rule ensured that significant social cleavages along Kabyle–non-Kabyle and Berber–Arabic lines would inevitably occur. The post-independence revolts of the FFS, therefore, attest to such deeply rooted divisions between the Kabyles and the rest of Algerians (Quandt 1972). While scholars concede that "Berber–Arab distinctions were never as important as other factors in explaining intra-elite cleavages" (Maddy-Weitzman 2001, 37), the existence of a distinct "Kabyle" identity served as the foundation for the development of a future Berber consciousness, as the majority of Kabyles are Berber speakers.

This approach, however, simplifies the structure and intent of the Kabylia uprisings. The FFS failed to mobilize a substantial number of local Kabyles, and half of the Kabyle deputies in Algeria's national assembly condemned the party's actions (Gellner and Micaud 1972, 436). Moreover, rather than the FFS pursuing a separatist agenda or Kabylian rights, demands focused on greater representation and integration in the Algerian government. The French colonial legacy, thus, failed on the onset of independence to create a unified Berber or Kabyle movement. As Quandt (1972), a key proponent of this theory, concedes, "Kabyles fought one another almost as passionately as they fought Arab rivals for power [. . .] only rarely were leaders paid deference because of their acknowledged regional backing" (p. 287).

The second explanation for social cleavage focuses on state strategies of governance. According to Hechter (2000, 42), in his study on nationalism and state formation, national governments may administer countries in two separate ways: indirectly and directly. While indirect rule incorporates traditional structures of governance (e.g. tribal or regional) into a countrywide political framework, direct rule replaces local institutions with national bureaucracy and centralized decision making. Indirect rule makes localities feel they are ruled by "their own" elites and allows rulers of small governance units to easily thwart collective action (Hechter 2000, 28). Groups lack the incentive and ability to mobilize on a large scale around certain social divisions. In contrast, direct rule erodes traditional political systems and throws localities' ways of life into question. As Hechter (2000) argues, "The growth of direct rule provides local authorities with a strong interest in mobilizing populations dependent on them to protect their extensive rights and prerogatives" (p. 28).

Scholars, thus, argue that while the Moroccan government pursued more "nuanced" policies of indirect control by co-opting traditional leaders into the regime, the Algerian government sought to stamp out regional power structures as a threat to national unity and incited the rebellions it sought to contain. As Maddy-Weitzman (2001) argues, "the regime's efforts to centralize authority and promote national integration [. . .] produced a simmering backlash" from Berber speakers (p. 38). However, this explanation only takes into account the laws and codes of the Algerian government and not their implementation. As noted by Charrad (2001), the FLN remained highly fragmented after independence and relied heavily on regional power structures for the administration of political affairs.[7] The texts of the Algerian government only elaborated an ideal among national leaders, not a reality.

Proponents of the final approach explain the difference in terms of geography. According to Ben-Dor (1999), "compact minorities [. . .] occupy a well-defined geographical territory that makes up only a small amount of the state and constitute a comfortable majority in the region" (p. 7). This geographical concentration leads to a sense of cultural distinctiveness, since inhabitants only interact with others of the same language and customs, as well as removing barriers to communication. When such compact groups come under cultural attack, they maintain a sufficient "cultural consciousness" and low enough costs of mobilization to effectuate effective social movements. While the heavy concentration of Berber speakers in Kabylia resembles the situation of compact groups, Moroccan Berbers live in equally distributed and geographically dispersed communities. Moroccan Berbers, thus, suffer from the political ineptitude of a group that has no single center, as "their numbers do not make them really important; their voting rights are not important either, as voting in general does not make a real difference, and they lack the political punch of either a strong regional base or a strong connection with the instruments of power (such as the military)" (Ben-Dor 1999, 10).

However, Moroccan Berbers occupied many important positions in the government and military. Furthermore, if geography were such an important factor in the development of ethnic consciousness, residents of Kabylia should have maintained a "Kabyle" consciousness long before the French arrived in Algeria. At the very least, the FFS uprisings in Kabylia should illustrate the development of such a consciousness, which appears to be entirely absent during the event. As Layachi (2005) argues, "Contiguity is not always a necessary condition for the birth and development of an ethnic and national consciousness and cohesion, notably since ethnic and national communities are mostly imagined and not always the result of direct social interaction" (p. 213).

Representation, Arabization, and the Berber Spring

The Berber cultural and political movement that led up to the Berber Spring resulted from two important and mutually reinforcing factors: the unique impact of French colonialism on Kabyle education and Arabization policies requiring literacy in classical Arabic as a prerequisite for teaching and public service. These conditions combined in Algeria to prevent Kabyle Berber speakers from attaining government and educational positions (even as Berbers received proportional representation in government). As Kabyle Berber speakers felt increasingly marginalized and their interests overlooked, they began to mobilize around linguistic and cultural rights.

While French rule failed to engineer the intended "ethnic" differences between Kabyles–non-Kabyles and Berber–Arabic speakers, it did significantly impact Kabylia in one way that was different from other regions in Algeria and Morocco: Kabyle Berbers spoke extremely poor Arabic after independence. According to Michael Brett and Elizabeth Fentress (1996), "French policy [. . .] emphasized the importance of education in French rather than Arabic for the Berber areas [. . .] while these had been refused in the Mzab for religious reasons and ignored in the Aures for economic ones, they had slowly taken hold in Kabylia" (p. 272). Berber communities in Morocco rejected French education out of similar concerns as those voiced in Mzab and Aures (Brett and Fentress 1996, 276). After independence, Kabylia Berbers constituted the country's (and perhaps the region's) most accomplished francophones and disproportionately served in Algeria's educational and administrative structures (which were still conducted in French; cf. Willis 2008, 230).

Arabization policies in Algeria uniquely impacted the professional opportunities for Kabyles relative to other Algerian Berber speakers, whose grasp of Algerian Arabic led them to quickly adopt Modern Standard Arabic. For Kabyle Berber speakers, the confrontation over Arabization was never about Berber versus Arabic, but *French* versus Arabic. However, as Brett and Fentress (1996) point out, it was politically impossible "to lead the popular battle for French: Arabic is the language of Islam, and French remains that of the colonizer. The battle lines had to be drawn between the natural languages of the country—Berber and Algerian Arabic—and standard, classical Arabic" (p. 274). As Kabyle representation in government and educational structures declined during the 1970s, "all sections of the Kabyle middle class—the teachers and liberal professionals, the civil servants and officials, and the traders, proprietors, entrepreneurs and salaried executives of the private sector"—began to see their material and cultural interests threatened (Roberts 1980, 118).

While teachers and civil servants facing unemployment would naturally have reason to protest, the relationship between government jobs and private business remains less apparent. Until the 1990s, Algeria (unlike Morocco) maintained a state-centered, socialist economy (Posusney 2004). The growth of the state sector reduced private activity and forced entrepreneurs to depend on state enterprises for contracts (Roberts 1980, 118). The government further required businesses to have licenses for a host of economic activities and controlled the distribution of supplies of raw materials and components. If private entrepreneurs wanted to prevent state firms from taking the most lucrative projects or ensure the public sector would use their firm for subcontracting, they had to depend "upon the degree and quality of their representation, via patronage networks of friends and relations, in the administrative apparatus of the state and the public sector" (Roberts 1980, 231). By contrast, Morocco has never been a socialist country; its economy was state-controlled, yet the government has encouraged the private sector since independence, which has become relatively strong after the structural adjustment measures of the 1980s.

The opposition to Arabization further transcended class lines. Family and wider kinship links formed the principal building blocks of Kabylian society and served as "the single most important avenue of access to the administration, whence all things [flowed]" (Roberts 1980, 119). All Kabyles benefited from a presence in the state apparatus and an awareness of this interest began to develop across class, familial, and tribal lines.[8] While this "awareness" did not exist among all Kabyles before the Berber Spring, the protests and clashes no doubt played an important role afterward in spreading concern among all segments of the Kabyle society and creating a sense of common identity.

However, material concerns cannot solely explain the importance of representation at the national level. First, access to government jobs meant "career aspiring individuals knew that, by working hard, they could advance toward significant positions in the central government" (Wang 2001, 188). Desire for such advancement may arise from the honor entailed, the power involved, or the chance to better one's society. Arabization policies made obtaining central government positions less about merit and more about the languages that Algerians grew up with. In the absence of a pure meritocracy, politically motivated Kabyles had to appropriate traditional symbols and grievances as a means of gaining political following. Thus, language and culture became powerful tools for social mobilization in the hands of a frustrated, politically astute leadership.

Second, without an effective political voice at the center, the Kabyles could not "rest assured that their interests would not be neglected [. . .] and that their grievances would be heard and remedied" (Wang 2001, 188). Concerns covered a host of measures outside of material issues, such as family laws and penal codes propagated by conservative Islamists (an issue also present in Morocco; cf. Sadiqi (2008a, 2008b). Thus, even ordinary Kabyles began to see the efficacy of mobilization.

Third, representation served as a safety valve for dissent and ensured that concerns would be voiced within the political apparatus and according to its rules. Berber speakers faced high opportunity costs of mobilization and dissent because a disaffected Algerian regime could respond with *total* political exclusion. However, as Kabyle Berber speakers increasingly lost their positions at the political center, the calculated costs of mobilization shifted.

These conditions set the stage for protests during the "Berber Spring." While the government pursued Arabization of the educational system since the 1960s, the changeover proceeded only incrementally due to a lack of teachers of standard, classical Arabic (Ruedy 2005, 182). Thus, the decision of an official commission in December 1979 to increase the pace of Arabization in the entire educational system (from primary to university level) only magnified the concerns of the French- and Berber-speaking faculty (Maddy-Weitzman 2001, 40).

On March 10, 1980, Kabyle intellectual Mouloud Mammeri was scheduled to give a public lecture on the role of poetry in traditional Kabyle society at the University of Tizi-Ouzo in Kabylia. While a crowd of more than a thousand gathered to listen, Mammeri never arrived. He was stopped at a police roadblock, brought before the regional governor, and informed that an official commission had canceled the event as there was the "risk of disturbing the public order" (Goodman 2004, 71). While the affront sparked intense student protests leading up to April 20, it was not the motivating factor for protests outside the university. According to Goodman (2004), "the cancellation itself was hardly newsworthy: it was not the first Berber cultural event to be shut down by the state [. . .] it was not initially reported to the press [. . .] it did not spark immediate public outrage [. . .] no one beyond Tizi-Ouzou seemed terribly interested in what was happening" (p. 73). The ban instead galvanized students and teachers to take advantage of university organizations to cooperate with other Kabyle groups and coordinate protests against the

Algerian government. As the movement grew, other Kabyles adopted the students' demands for equal cultural and linguistic rights as a means of achieving their own diverse concerns. The presence of demands for "an end to dictatorship and the establishment of a pluralist political system" (Roberts 1980, 116) illustrates the fusion of the student agenda with the agenda of Kabyles concerned with lack of government representation. By April, opposition widened to a general strike across the whole of the Kabylia region (cf. Evans and Phillips 2008, 122). In the early hours of April 20, antiriot police began cracking down on students and workers and sparked five days of violent clashes.

The scope of the protests, the nature of their demands, and the ensuing crackdown ensured that the Berber genie could not be put back into the bottle. While in the past, government crackdowns fractured the tentative alliances made between Kabyles, the Berber Spring gave birth to a powerful ideology that linked the diverse concerns of Kabylia's Berbers and gave them a common voice. Thus, when the government responded with troops, it had to cut off all of Kabylia and further "enhanced the region's internal unity" (Mezhoud 1993, 151).

Activists continue to unofficially commemorate the Berber Spring every year in Algeria since 1980. While the ethnic designation Amazigh circulated among intellectuals in the 1970s, it did not form part of the vocabulary of most Kabyles at the time. According to (Goodman 2004, 62), the Berber Spring became "one of the key sites through which a discourse of Amazigh identity [circulated]" and frames much of the relationship between Berber activists and the Algerian state (Goodman 2004, 61). The incident signaled a rewriting of the historical narrative of Kabylia and the progressive reworking of Kabyle Berber speakers' identity.

Impact of the "Arab" Spring

The year 2011 brought an end to decades of political stagnation in North African countries, raised citizens' expectations, and brought about new political dynamics. Citizen demands focused on constitutional amendments, empowering parliament, strengthening local government, holding freer elections, setting up independent national commissions, and easing restrictions on Berbers' political and civic participation. The Arab Spring's dramatic popular support for political change in North Africa showed that democracy is a governance model that people of all cultures yearn for.

The recent uprisings show that the authoritarian regimes in the region have been taken back. Islamist forces have risen to the center of political life. Liberal and democratic forces are present throughout the region and, though weak and disorganized, are relatively influential. Tunisia is thought to be on the way to attain a democratic political system, emphasizing the importance of continued democratization in a way that would ensure the protection of women and minority rights and the rule of law, but it will not be without painstaking hard work and a long transition with setbacks that can disappoint expectations (see Ennaji, forthcoming).

As the Arab Spring swept through the region in 2011, Berbers in every country in North Africa took advantage of the new climate of freedom to push forward their own long-simmering demands.

In post–Arab Spring, the Berbers now had political momentum, demanding for more rights and political space as communities. The Amazigh movement is stronger, as it is raising populations' awareness about the important place of Amazigh language and cultural identity, which should no longer be marginalized or underestimated.

In Tunisia, the small Berber community has formed its first cultural associations and is once again speaking its forbidden language. In Libya, the Berbers were a key part of the rebel force that overthrew Qaddafi. In Mali, the Tuareg, another Berber people, have armed themselves and are declaring a homeland in large swatches of the north. Yet the same Arab Spring has also brought to power Islamist parties that traditionally have seen the Amazigh as a threat (see Sawani, this volume; Ennaji, forthcoming).

At the social and political levels, and taking into account that democratization is a long process, one can conclude that the inclusion of Berber identity in public space and democracy are gradually taking shape and that North African countries are steadily learning democratic principles, and accumulating experiences with cultural diversity patterns and practices.

Although the 2011 uprisings led by the youth movement called the 20 February Movement in Morocco have failed to achieve all their aims and to impose radical change, they provoked significant reforms, the most fundamental of which is the official recognition of Amazigh language in the constitution amended in July 2011.

However, to date, there is no real common strategy shared by all components of the Amazigh Movement in Morocco and Algeria. This is due to the divisions that exist within the Berber cultural movement, but also due to the repression of freedom of expression by the state.

Several political reasons prompted the decision to recognize and promote Berber: (1) to appease Berber activists and protestors, (2) to show the West that the state is serious about the democratization process, and (3) to weaken the Islamist movement that had started growing since the 1990s.

The promotion of Berber and its official recognition, which is unique in the region, are also meant to please the Western countries and critics, because this move will polish the image of the state inside and abroad, and allow the building of a multicultural society that includes Imazighen, a project that will have overarching effects on the whole of North Africa (Crawford 2005, 189).

Conclusion

Since 2011, the "Arab" Spring has galvanized and strengthened the Berber movement in North Africa. Oppressed by their own political systems for decades, Amazigh communities have surged to the center of the political scene not only in Morocco and Algeria but also in Tunisia, Egypt, and Libya. The post-Qaddafi power struggle in Libya is a good case in point. In Libya, Tunisia, and Egypt, Amazigh civil society associations have organized vast campaigns to secure recognition of their language and culture. The Amazigh movement in North Africa is an ongoing process that has not been placated by long overdue reforms and concessions hastily granted by their governments in the aftermath of the Arab Spring. It will continue growing and participating in the debate about cultural identity, democracy, human rights, peace-building, and democratization.

The development of the Berber/Amazigh cultural movement in Morocco and Algeria poses unique theoretical difficulties and opportunities due to the considerable similarity of the two countries' political, social, and economic development. French rule failed to create its intended divides between Arab and Berber speakers. The post-independence regimes faced challenges from Islamist movements, maintained state-centered socialist economies, pursued strategies of indirect rule, and promoted large-scale Arabization policies. Yet, only Algeria experienced the convulsions of the Berber Spring.

This chapter contends that the criticism of Arabization policies is only half correct. If cultural repression provided the catalyst for social cleavages along linguistic lines, then events similar to the Berber Spring should have occurred in Morocco as well. The legacy of French colonialism on the educational system of Kabylia combined with Algeria's Arabization policies to exclude francophone Kabyles from the government and teaching positions. While Kabyles' proficiency in French ensured that they disproportionately occupied these jobs during the early years of independent rule, they could not compete with other Algerian Berber speakers once literacy in classical Arabic became a requirement for teaching and public service. Thus, although laws ensured Berber political representation in proportion to the percentage of Berbers in the population at large, Mzabs and Aures progressively replaced Kabyles in the state apparatus.

Decreasing representation threatened the material, cultural, and political interests of all segments of the Kabyle society and provided a common grievance that transcended family, tribe, and class lines. As the battle lines could not be drawn in terms of French versus Arabic, a "cultural" movement aimed at protecting the Berber language became the next best option. When students at Tizi-Ouzou University began demonstrations for cultural and linguistic rights, Kabyles adopted their grievances and linked them to demands for political liberalization and equal representation. While only portions of Kabylia joined the activists at first, interest grew among all portions of the Kabyle society as protests intensified. The ensuing military crackdown only furthered Kabyle Berber speakers' sense of common identity and the importance of language in forming group boundaries.

While the past cannot explain every contour of the present, it does provide a lens though which analysis can proceed. The Berber Spring heavily influenced Algerian Berber activists and their political agendas. After the Algerian government changed the constitution to allow political parties in 1989, two Kabyle-based parties monopolized the votes in the region, the Rally for Culture and Democracy (RCD) and the re-formed FFS (Layachi 2005, 205–6). While only the RCD articulated a specific "Berberist" agenda, both failed to gain support outside of Kabylia and illustrated the social divide between the Kabyle Berber speakers and the rest of Algerians (Layachi 2005, 205–6). Political representation further failed to quell the concerns of the Berber activists, as the formation of political parties led the leadership of the RCD to manipulate linguistic social cleavages and conflate them with ethnicity. Thus, Berber activists and government officials now face a new round of confrontations with even less room for concessions.

While Morocco opened up its political system in 1992, linguistic cleavages failed to become a significant force of social friction, and cultural movements remained markedly apolitical (Crawford 2005, 164). In 2001, King Mohammed VI announced the creation of the Royal Institute of Amazigh Culture and the introduction of Berber in educational institutions. While the results of the royal *decision* remain to be seen, it appears that Moroccan Berbers do not see themselves as sufficiently discriminated against to bridge cultural practices with political and social divides.

These outcomes illustrate a final point: once language, or any other factor, becomes a significant source of social cleavage, this division poses a tenacious and resilient opponent (or ally) for reformists. Leaders may manipulate linguistic divides during political liberalization to gain constituents during economic liberalization for special concessions and perks, and during periods of social liberalization (or conservatism) to promote specific societal agendas. If Algerians hope to smooth the tensions between Berber speakers and their Arabic-speaking counterparts, all sides must be wary of the opportunistic leaders who hope to capitalize on social strife and ideological divide.

In Morocco, the Berber activists fear that the Islamists now controlling the government may try to rollback the progress they have made since the Arab Spring. Although the new Moroccan constitution now recognizes Amazigh as an official language, its actual implementation in schools is slow, and the bureaucracy awaits an organic law that has to be written by Benkirane's government—which Berbers fear will fall short of their goals.

Notes

1 US Department of State, "Decolonization of Asia and Africa, 1945–1960," http://www.state.gov/r/pa/ho/time/cwr/98782.htm.
2 Willis (2008) states, "Many leading Islamists are Berber speakers themselves, most notably the leaders of Morocco's two largest Islamist organizations. In Algeria, the leadership of both the FIS and some of the armed groups (including the extremist GIA) included Kabyles" (p. 236).
3 For proponents, see the statement of Amazigh writer Kateb Yacine in Crawford (2005): "We are a majority which quickly becomes aware now of the Arab-Islamic affliction throughout the world . . . wherever people are alienated, betrayed, drowned in the name of race and religion" (p. 168). Also see Shatzmiller (2000). For opponents, see Saad (2000) and Gellner and Micaud (1972).
4 For discussion of the Berber response to the policy, see Hart (1997).
5 For more details, see Maddy-Wietzman, (2001, 29), citing Hart (1997, note 23), and Waterbury (1970, 242).

6 See more at: http://www.culturalsurvival.org/publications/cultural-survival-quarterly/algeria/algiers-joins-berbers-protest#sthash.dPkCGVWF.dpuf, accessed February 6, 2014.
7 See footnote 47.
8 Ibid.

References

Aslan, S. 2007. "Negotiating National Identity: Kurdish and Berber Rights Activism in Turkey and Morocco." Paper presented at Annual Meeting of the American Political Science Association, Chicago, August 30–September 2, pp. 8–9.

Baduel, P. R. 1991. "Etat, Pouvoir et Territoire." In *L'Etat du Maghreb*, edited by L. D. Lacoste and Y. Lacoste, 344–49. Paris: La Découverte.

Ben-Dor, G. 1999. "Minorities in the Middle East." In *Minorities and the State in the Arab World*, edited by O. Bengio and G. Ben-Dor, 3–18. Boulder: Lynne Rienner Publishers.

Brett, M., and E. Fentress. 1996. "*Berbers and Berberism*," *The Berbers*. London: Blackwell Publishers.

Byman, D. L. 1997. "Preventing the Recurrence of Ethnic Conflict: Lessons from the Middle East." PhD diss., Amherst College.

Charrad, M. 2001. *Elite Divisions and the Law in Gridlock, Algeria, States and Women's Rights: The Making of Postcolonial Tunisia, Algeria, and Morocco*. Berkeley: University of California Press.

Crawford, D. 2005. "Amazigh Identity and the Moroccan State." In *Nationalism and Minority Identities in Islamic Societies*, edited by M. Shatzmiller, 164–94. Montreal: Mc-Gill-Queen's University Press.

Crawford, D. 2008. *Moroccan Households in the World Economy: Labor and Inequality in a Berber Village*. Baton Rouge: Louisiana State University Press.

Ennaji, M. 2005. *Multilingualism, Cultural Identity, and Education in Morocco*. New York: Springer.

Ennaji, M. 2014. "The Berber (Amazigh) Movement in Morocco: Local Activism, the State, and Transnationalism." In *Multiculturalism and Democracy in North Africa*, edited by M. Ennaji, 93–112. London: Routledge.

Ennaji, M. 2015. How the "Arab Spring" Boosted Berber Language and Culture in North Africa. In *Proceedings of the Conference in Honor of Professor Jilali Saib*. Rabat: Publication of the Faculty of Letters.

Ennaji, M., and F. Sadiqi. 2008. "Morocco: Language, Nationalism, and Gender." In *Language and National Identity in Africa*, edited by Andrew Simpson, 51–69. Oxford: Oxford University Press.

Evans, M., and J. Phillips. 2008. "*The Berber Spring*," *Algeria: Anger of the Dispossessed*: New Haven: Yale University Press.

Gellner, E., and C. Micaud. 1972. *Arabs and Berbers: From Tribe to Nation in North Africa*: New York: Lexington Books.

Goodman, J. 2004. "Reinterpreting the Berber Spring: From Rite of Reversal to Site of Convergence." *The Journal of North African Studies* 9 (3): 62–82.

Hart, D. 1997. "The Berber Dahir of 1930 in Colonial Morocco: Then and Now (1930–1996)." *The Journal of North African Studies* 2 (2): 11–33).

Hatoss, A. 2002. "Identity Formation, Cross-Cultural Attitudes and Language Maintenance in the Hungarian Diaspora of Queensland." Paper presented at In Cultural Citizenship: Challenges of Globalisation: An Interdisciplinary Conference, Melbourne, Australia, December 5–7.

Hechter, M. 2000. *Containing Nationalism*. New York: Oxford University Press.

Laitin, D. D. 1986. *Hegemony and Culture: Politics and Religious Change among the Yoruba*. Chicago: University of Chicago Press.

Layachi, A. 2005. "The Berbers in Algeria: Politicized Ethnicity and Ethnicized Politics." In *Nationalism and Minority Identities in Islamic Societies*, edited by M. Shatzmiller, 202–15. Montreal: Mc-Gill-Queen's University Press.
Madani, B. 2003. "Arabization of the Amazigh Lands." *International Journal of Francophone Studies* 6 (3): 211–13.
Maddy-Weitzman, B. 1998. "The Berber Question in Algeria: Nationalism in the Making?" In *Minorities and the State in the Arab World*, edited by O. Bengio and G. Ben-Dor, 31–52. Lynne Rienner Publishers.
Maddy-Weitzman, B. 2001. "Contested Identities: Berbers, "Berberism" and the State in North Africa." *The Journal of North African Studies* 6 (3): 23–47.
Mezhoud, S. 1993. "Glasnost the Algerian Way." In *North Africa: Nation, State, and Region*, edited by G. Joffe, 143–56. London: Routledge.
Posusney, M. P. 2004. "From Economic Policies to Public Perceptions: Theirs and Ours, and Its Implications for the Discipline." *Contemporary Conflicts*, March 26. Accessed March 1, 2014. http://conconflicts.ssrc.org/archives/mideast/posusney.
Quandt, W. 1972. "The Berbers in the Algerian Political Elite." In *Arabs and Berbers*, edited by E. Gellner and C. Micaud, 285–303. Lexington: D.C. Heath.
Roberts, H. 1980. "Towards an Understanding of the Kabyle Question in Contemporary Algeria." *The Maghreb Review* 5 (5–6): 115–24.
Ruedy, J. D. 2005. *Modern Algeria: The Origins and Development of a Nation*. Bloomington: Indiana University Press.
Saad, S. 2000. "Interpreting Ethnic Quiescence: A Brief History of the Berbers in Morocco." In *The Arab-African and Islamic Worlds*, edited by R. M. Coury and R. K. Lacey, 167–81. New York: Peter Lang.
Sadiqi, F. 2008a. "Facing Challenges and Pioneering Feminist and Gender Studies: Women in Post-colonial and Today's Maghrib." *African and Asian Studies Journal* 7 (4): 447–70.
Sadiqi, F. 2008b. "The Central Role of the Family Law in the Moroccan Feminist Movement." *British Journal of Middle Eastern Studies* 35 (3): 325–37.
Salzmann, Z. 2006. "Idiolects, Dialects, and Styles." In *Language, Culture, and Society*, edited by Z. Salzmann, J. Stanlaw, and N. Adachi, 175–76. Boulder: Westview Press.
Schulze, R., and A. Azodi. 2002. *A Modern History of the Islamic World*. London: I.B.Tauris.
Shatzmiller, M. 2000. *The Berbers and the Islamic State*. Princeton: Markus Wiener.
Spencer, K. 2001. "Algiers Joins Berbers in Protest." Accessed February 21, 2015. http://www.culturalsurvival.org/publications/cultural-survival-quarterly/algeria/algiers-joins-berbers-protest.
Stone, M. 1997. *The Agony of Algeria*. New York: Columbia University Press.
Wang, Y.-K. 2001. "Toward a Synthesis of the Theories of Peripheral Nationalism: A Comparative Study of China's Xinjiang and Guangdong," *Asian Ethnicity* 2 (2): 188–99.
Waterbury, J. 1970. *Commander of the Faithful*. London: Weidenfeld and Nicolson.
Willis, M. J. 2008. "The Politics of Berber (Amazigh) Identity." In *North Africa: Politics, Region, and the Limits of Transformation*, edited by Yahia H. Zoubir and Haizam Amirah-Fernandez, 231–43. London: Routledge.

4

THE BERBERS IN MOROCCO: FROM THE MARGINS TO THE CORE

Moha Ennaji

This chapter argues that there are many historical, political, and socio-economic causes of the marginalization and exclusion of the Berber populations (see Dourari, this volume; Ennaji 2014).

Drawing on both historical and up-to-date accounts, the chapter shows that the Berbers strategize and react to this marginalization differently according to their local and national environments. In Morocco (which is the focus of this chapter), Berber identity is defined through linguistic and cultural behaviors, land usage, and orality. Unlike in Algeria, where the demands for the recognition of Berber have been at times violent (the Berber Spring of 1980 led to dozens of deaths), in Morocco, these demands are peaceful and cultural because Morocco has the largest Amazigh population in the region, and the broader political climate is Amazigh-friendly and less brutal than in Algeria (see Andrews and Ennaji, this volume).

The data for this chapter were collected on the basis of my own readings of the literature, documentary research, official statistics, mass media products, diaries, letters, and government reports, in addition to historical and contemporary records. This chapter is organized as follows. The first section gives an overview of the link between the Berber language and ethnic identity. The second provides a historical background of the Berbers in North Africa. The third section debates the causes and consequences of the social and political exclusion of the Berbers and their culture. The fourth section discusses the ramifications of this exclusion for Berber language and identity. The last section discusses the inclusion of the Berbers through integration into development and through identity formation.

This chapter argues that language, ethnicity, and identity are affected by the context in which they are shaped. Following Fishman (2010), I illustrate how language, ethnicity, and identity are erratic and unstable. I view the Berber linguistic minority and ethnic identity through the lenses of sociolinguistics, cultural anthropology, politics, and economics.

Berber Language and Ethnicity

There has been little research devoted to the subject of ethnicity, and there is even less consensus among social scientists and theoreticians on the definition of the word "ethnicity" (see Ennaji 2010; Fishman 1977; Fishman and Garcia 2010). Ethnicity was regarded as marginal by the classic masters of sociology such as Karl Marx (1818-1883), Emile Durkheim (1858-1917), and Max Weber (1864-1920), perhaps because they were Eurocentric in their approaches, and no one predicted the role and importance that ethnicity would assume in the twentieth and twenty-first centuries (Berlin 1992). Max Weber was one of the most outstanding sociologists who extensively studied group behavior. However, Weber has been criticized by many researchers for overlooking minorities and ethnic groups. Yet, other scholars have revealed that there is "implicit reference" to racial and ethnic groups and conflicts in Weber's works, which led to the development of a new approach to minority and ethnic group formation (Stone 1995). Hitherto, the whole notion of ethnic groups is extremely complex and so fuzzy that it might be good to deal with it with skepticism.

Dominant ideologies and authoritarian governments arbitrarily determine and influence what constitutes an ethnic group. An ethnic group may be defined as a group of people who share the same language, culture, history, religion, and values, and which adopts a certain lifestyle to distinguish itself from other ethnic groups. The Berber (Amazigh) language has often been an element by which Berber ethnicity is defined. Race, color, political affiliation, and social class are not as central as language in determining ethnicity or minorities in the Maghreb, especially in Morocco and Algeria. It is not viable to tell apart an Amazigh from an Arab on the basis of race. Additionally, Amazigh and Arab people alike belong to various political and ideological trends and social strata. The historical and cultural environments do not help one to differentiate correctly one ethnic group from another. Historically, many Arabic-speaking tribes were Berberized (e.g. Lemtuna, Ketama), and many Amazigh ones were Arabized over the centuries (e.g. Beni Yazgha, Chawiya, Ouardigha; Sadiqi 1997, 21). The language dynamic is, however, a key component in the development of an ethnic group. It is plausible to affirm that Berber speakers constitute an ethnic group, since non-Berbers seldom speak Berber (cf. Boukous 1995; Ennaji 1991, 1997; Sadiqi 1997). The struggle between the Berbers, who are a linguistic minority, and the Arabs, who are the majority, is fundamentally a struggle for power and representation; it is far more than a mere conflict between the use of Arabic versus Berber as an indigenous language.

Before the French colonization, it was relatively simple to distinguish the Arabs from the Berbers in the Maghreb because each linguistic community spoke its own language only; for example, there were very few Arabic–Amazigh bilinguals. Nowadays, most Amazighs are bilingual, as they also speak colloquial Arabic, because of education, media, social mobility, intermarriages, and socioeconomic exchanges.

Accordingly, in the Maghreb, one can speak of two major ethnic (linguistic) groups: the Arabic-speaking group and the Amazigh-speaking one (Benrabah 2014). The Berbers (Imazighen for the natives) constitute a distinct ethnic group that has been marginalized and socially and politically excluded in North Africa. Adopting the theory of intersectionality, which underlines the intersection of domains of domination such as class, politics, gender, religion, language, ethnicity, education, media, and so on (Kimberlé Crenshaw 1989; Patricia Hill Collins 2000; Marie-Claire Belleau 2007), and using history and a comparative approach, I analyze the causes and consequences of this exclusion and the interconnection between marginalization and demands for the preservation and promotion of Amazigh cultural identity.

The Berbers of North Africa: A History

The Berbers may be defined as the indigenous populations of North Africa. In the first century AD, North Africa came under Roman occupation. Based on previously existing kingdoms, the Romans created quasi-states and controlled newly acquired territory through increased stability. They co-opted Berber leaders to act as facilitators of Romanization and colonization, though some clans refused to accept the Roman rule.

Subsequent to the Romans and the Byzantines, North Africa experienced a process of reunification through the Arab conquest and the religion of Islam. The Berbers took advantage of the Arabic language and of this newfound Islamic identity to conquer Spain and France, joining forces with Arabs to triumph over Europe (Dourari, this volume).

In history, the Berbers were the first inhabitants of North Africa, and the Arabs came from the Arabian Peninsula in the seventh century and brought with them the Arabic language and Islam (see Sadiqi 1997, 20; Dourari, this volume). Because Classical Arabic is associated with Islam, and has a great literary tradition, it has been proclaimed the official language. The Islamization of the Berbers went through many phases, starting from the seventh century until the eleventh. Unlike other Muslim countries such as Iran, Afghanistan, and Pakistan, in North Africa, Islamization has engendered Arabization of the indigenous Berber populations (Fitouri 1983).

Although it was met with a lot of resistance at the beginning, Islam eventually became a popular religion while Classical Arabic evolved into the language of the literate and the learned. While Muslim Berber dynasties ruled Morocco since antiquity, Moroccan identity has constantly been defined in terms of its links to the Arab and Islamic civilization (Chafik 1989). The Berbers adopted Arabic as the language of administration, and soon their own language was relegated to a minority status. The widespread idea of Arabic as a superior language (among Arabists) continues today, and Berber as an indigenous language remains endangered.

Becoming a linguistic minority in their own land, the Berbers had to negotiate power with the Arabs who brought with them a new religion, a strong language, and economic know-how, which transformed North Africa and the Mediterranean into a hub of cultural and economic exchanges and prosperity. Islamic faith and economic interests changed social relations between the two ethnic groups as both put aside their cultural and social specificities.

The French rulers understood the Berbers to be moderately Islamized, intensely independent, probably candidates for French education, perhaps citizenship, definitely in need of protection from Arab-Islamic hegemony, particularly the Kabyle Berbers in Algeria (Dourari, this volume). The French strictly defined the minorities and ethnic groups in ways that served their agenda in North Africa (see Andrews and Ennaji, this volume). They attempted to marginalize and to isolate the Berbers into their own category, once again in opposition to the Arab identity in order to control the region.

In an effort to contextualize the Berbers' identity and to find out why they were excluded and how their strategies and struggle for the integration of their language and culture have evolved over the past few years, I argue that the marginalization of Berbers in Morocco is not solely a cultural one, for it has created class structures and an urban/rural divide that shapes identity. The evolution of the Berber cause is related to the ways in which national and ethnic identities intersect, while social, political, and cultural factors intermingle.

In the following section, I discuss the major causes and consequences of the social and political marginalization of Berber language, culture, and populations, the forces that shape their social exclusion, particularly the political context, historical factor, and economic context.

Causes and Consequences of Exclusion

Causes

The reasons for the exclusion of the Berber component and the linguistic, social, and political contexts involved are subtle and highly complex. Some of these factors have to do with the fact that the Berber language was considered a dialect until 2002. Other factors are political, having to do with government policy, or historical, such as the way the Berber language was excluded from the state sphere over the centuries.

At any rate, there are several historical, social, economic, political, and cultural causes for the exclusion of the Berber communities in North Africa, some of which go back to ancient and contemporary history. Even before the Arab conquest, Berber was never an official language of the state (for example, during the Roman period, the Berbers took Latin as their official language), and its domains of use, as the language of the masses, were limited to the Berber people's homes, the market place, and other informal settings. With the advent of Arab-Islamic civilization, as mentioned earlier, the Berber language continued to be excluded from public life, as Arabic became the official language of the state and Islam its religion (see Ennaji 2014). During the French occupation, the Berbers remained marginalized, although the French allowed the teaching of the Berber language only in one high school (Lycée franco-berbère d'Azrou), and used Berber ethnicity to divide and rule North Africa. The Berber

Dahir ("decree") of May 16, 1930, was enacted to separate Morocco into Arab and Berber zones; however, the nationalists (Arab and Berber alike) joined forces to reject this law.

After independence, North African governments used the Berbers as scapegoats and considered them ex-French collaborators although they had actively fought, and many had died, for independence (see Andrews and Ennaji, this volume; Dourari 2014).

State-building was also used as an alibi to exclude minorities such as the Berbers because, for authoritarian traditional regimes, minorities were a taboo and a threat to the security and unity of the nation-state. The Berbers were considered divisive and it was believed, by the state, that they could become dangerous if recognized and integrated in the politics and in the public sphere in general. Until very recently, most states in the region were totalitarian, and the nation-state discourse emphasized "a holistic approach: one language (Arabic), one religion (Islam), one God (Allah), and one people (Arab)," one culture (Arab-Islamic), one nation, and one leader, and rejected diversity, women, and minority rights (Ennaji 2014; Lewkowicz 2011; Maddy-Weitzman 2011).

The Arabization policy, the implementation of which began in the 1960s to strengthen state-building and to assimilate the Berbers, led to the exclusion of the Berbers for decades. It aimed not only at replacing French with Arabic in all walks of life but also at Arabizing the Berber populations across North Africa (Benrabah 2014).

Furthermore, the impact of Arab nationalism, which was championed by President Gamal Abdel Nasser in Egypt, was extremely strong between the 1960s and 2000s. Its main role was to unite Arabs against Israel and to consolidate the union of the Arab countries. However, Arab nationalism was detrimental to minorities such as the Berbers in North Africa and the Kurds and other ethnic groups in the Middle East, as they saw their languages and cultures not only ignored but also banished from the public space, mainly from schools and administration (see Ennaji 2014; Maddy-Weitzman 2011).

Modernization and urbanization also led to the marginalization of Berbers and other minorities. In their pursuit of modernity and efficacy, the Moroccan government rejected the Berber language and culture on the grounds that they were primitive, under-developed, anachronic, and pointless. The newly independent state encouraged the Berbers to leave behind their "customs" and "traditions" in the countryside and integrate into the growing urbanized and modern zones.

Rural exodus, which increased between the 1980s and 2010s, led to more urbanization of the Berbers, which means that many urbanized Berbers have lost their mother tongue (because all transactions in urban zones are carried out in Arabic), and have failed to transmit it to their children. As a result, a regression of the Berber language in urban areas, and a low interest in it among urbanized Berbers, is perceptible (see Ennaji 1997).

Similarly, the exclusion of the Berber language from schools since independence until 2002 contributed to its regression and marginalization. Berber was not taught as a language, and even the Azrou Berber course was discontinued after Morocco's independence on account of the fact that it was part of a colonial policy by the French colonizers to divide Moroccans.

Another factor that led to the exclusion of Berbers was the impact of the two military coups (of Skhirat on July 10, 1971, and Sale on August 16, 1972), which were instigated mostly by the Berber generals of the like of Mohammed Oufkir and Mohammed Medbouh, which nearly led to the overthrow of the monarchy.[1] After the failure of the two putsches, the Berbers were further excluded from decision making, with the Berber language being banned from public space, and even research on the language and culture was disallowed and discouraged.

Another reason for the exclusion of Berbers is that while they were stripped off their land by the French, after independence, their land was confiscated by the state or by the rich land-owners, and as a consequence, the Berbers never recovered their lost property. Today, with the revival of the Berber language, there are strong demands for the recovery of their land, now called "collective land" or *aradi aljumuu* (Maddy-Weitzman 2011). However, the state denies them any claim to legal ownership of their ancestral lands.

Consequences

Many significant consequences permeate from the exclusion of Berbers. First, there is a high illiteracy rate among the Berbers, especially those living in rural areas (more than 50% according to official statistics)[2]; second, a high unemployment rate is attested in these regions (ranging from 14% to 25%).[3] Third, Berber zones have suffered from socioeconomic deprivation and from lack of infrastructure and services, such as roads, schools, and health centers. Fourth, the Berbers were excluded from decision-making positions as a result of which most Berbers were farm workers, shop assistants, or soldiers in the army. Very few were land-owners, businessmen, entrepreneurs, or had key positions in the government. Fifth, a regression of the Berber language was noticeable in the public space, and Berber culture was referred to as folklore or popular culture, rather than as a major component of Moroccan identity. Sixth, there was an unfavorable attitude toward the Berber language and culture until very recently. Finally, the exclusion of the Berber language led to its absence in schools, administration, and media, particularly until 2002 (Spencer 2001).

For all these reasons, the Berber movement's demands were not only about linguistic and cultural rights but also about economic opportunity, democracy, and respect for human rights and dignity. As a matter of fact, the Berber movement has been struggling for the past five decades against authoritarianism, favoritism, corruption, poverty, and marginalization, using the language and culture element (considered symbols of Amazigh ethnicity) as the mobilizing political tool to make the voice of Imazighen heard.

The Berber movement in Morocco, which has been militating for the inclusion and revival of the Berber language since the late 1960s, has not claimed any form of self-government nor has it evolved into a type of nationhood. The only nation the Berbers are attached to is Morocco, and hence they emphasize that the Berber component should be recognized as an essential element of Moroccan identity. I argue that since the Berber movement struggles for a political system that is more democratic and inclusive, it is a civic, democratic, secular, and patriotic movement (Ennaji 2014).

Making Sense of Economic and Social Exclusion

I use "congruence procedure," which consists of examining the similarities and differences between constant and dependent variables. The constant variable resides in the local and national environments in which the Berbers live, while the dependent variables are social marginalization and identity formation (cf. Lewkowicz 2011). With this method, I make observations of values across a range of facts in order to compare values through national contexts.

I also use the method of "process tracing," which assumes that facts and historical events impact decision making and results (see Lewkowicz

2011). By observing historical events, we can verify the previous circumstances, or causes, that affected outcomes and interests. Through a thorough sociocultural survey of the Berbers, it is possible to account for the fact that history, politics, economy, and society shaped a context that was favorable to their marginalization and exclusion.

Socioeconomic exclusion and identity formation are useful in negotiating power mechanisms that determine Berber identity, as they illustrate and reveal the factors shaping the marginalization of the Berbers, and why the Berbers react differently from one context to another.

The marginalization of Berbers has widened the gap between rural and urban zones and the gulf between the wealthy Arabs of the urban bourgeoisie and the poor Berber rural populations. As a result of their social and political exclusion, the Berbers have suffered from discriminatory policies and practices, a systematic denial of citizenship, and linguistic and cultural exclusion for a long time.

Ethnic Berber identity is essentially constructed through language use and land structures. Identity can be formed both in contrast to and together with the national identity. It is precisely the contradictions that result between the imposed national (Arab-Islamic) identity and the Berber identity that cause marginalization and social exclusion. Political and cultural links to the rest of the Arab world foster connections between Morocco and its Arabo-Islamic heritage (see Hoffman 2008, Chap. 1). This relation is emphasized in majority national identity formation and influences social exclusion.

Inclusion through Integration in Development and Identity Formation

Thanks mainly to the hard work of Berber militants and activists such as Mohammed Chafik, Mahjoubi Aherdan, Brahim Akhiyat, and Ali Sidki Azaykou, official and unofficial attitudes and discourses have become favorable to the Berber language since the 1990s. To pacify the protests in Errachidia, south of Morocco, demanding the recognition and integration of the Berber language, the late King Hassan II took a politically significant initiative by deciding, on August 20, 1994, to include Berber in primary education. This step was much hailed, particularly by those involved in the Berber cultural movement. On October 17, 2001, King Mohammed VI created the Royal Institute for Amazigh Culture

(IRCAM), the chief purpose of which is to promote Berber in all sectors, namely, in education, culture, and media. Today Berber is taught in thousands of primary schools and in five universities in Morocco (Sadiqi 2014). These remarkable measures symbolize both a "co-optation and a kind of liberation" (Crawford 2005, 189) and also represent a way of building a multicultural state that includes the Berbers, a project which will have overarching effects on the country of Morocco and on the whole of North Africa.

The inclusion of Berber as an official national language can be explained by the fact that Berber demands for its recognition have become vigorous in the last three decades apart from the following four main reasons: (i) the advent of a young king, Mohammed VI, to power in 1999; (ii) the end of Arab nationalism and the rise of Islamism after the invasion of Iraq; (iii) the growing role of ethnicity and minorities in the region and the world over; and (iv) the political resolve of the monarchy to open up to all layers of Moroccan society and to democratize the country. The recognition of Berber is also linked to the increase of Muslim fundamentalism in North Africa and the Middle East since the 1980s; Berber has been used as an instrument by liberal politicians and secular groups to counter Islamists and to keep them out of power because the Berber language is not based on any holy book, unlike Arabic, and its culture is secular. Being secular, the Berber movement has been fighting against the Islamist fundamentalists who have a different vision and societal project, their goal being the Islamization of the whole society.

In response to the Arab Spring uprisings that reverberated across North Africa, the Moroccan government took pre-emptive actions to placate the Berbers and alienate them from the broader discontent percolating the region. On July 1, 2011, Morocco amended its constitution and declared Amazigh an official language alongside Arabic. But some Berber activists, such as Ahmed Adghirni, a founder of the "Parti Démocratique Amazigh" in 2005, stated that the law will do little to integrate the Berbers into the national socioeconomic and political fabric. His party was dissolved by Morocco's judiciary in 2008, on the ground that the constitution prohibits ethnic political parties.

With the establishment of more inclusive policies, the Berbers today demand the implementation of the new constitution, development initiatives in their zones, job creation for the youth, and political representation. Although official channels of exclusion have been removed, the Berbers remain on the margins of the economy, pursuing completely separate lifestyles from the increasingly connected and modern urban areas. Although the Moroccan government is pushing an agenda to integrate the Berbers in sustainable development and celebrate their cultural heritage, these measures may in fact maintain their status as folkloric, rural, marginalized, and exotic. Urbanization and economic development may be at the expense of cultural preservation, for it can dangerously lead to the "fragmentation of Berber communities, villages, and homes" (Lewkowicz 2011). In an increasingly global market economy where income is tied to individualism and self-worth, the Berbers may become apprehensive as the world changes around them, eventually leading to the marginalization of their language and culture unless much is done to preserve them from oblivion.

Construction of a national identity

Today's Moroccan identity is Arab-Muslim and Berber, with a lot of openness onto the West and modernity. The overriding discourse regarding Moroccan identity has started to change, however, as the current Moroccan government is trying to distance itself from the Arab issues and focus on Morocco's needs.

King Mohammed VI has initiated significant reforms to change the dominant discourse regarding Moroccan national identity in favor of an inclusive pluralistic approach in which the Berbers and their culture are a major component of this identity. In 2001, he delivered the Ajdir speech, in which he stressed that Amazigh language and culture are a national heritage pertaining to all Moroccans. In July 2011, following the uprisings in the region, the king announced an amended constitution in which Berber is considered, for the first time in Moroccan history, an official national language side by side with classical Arabic. Through policy changes as well as language usage, such as referring to indigenous Berber groups as part of the Moroccan identity, the king set an example that emblematically valorized this culture and pushed people to hold attitudes favorable to the Berber language.

Today Berber culture is celebrated as part and parcel of the national identity, although the Berbers remain economically and socially marginalized, as many Berber zones lack in drinking water, sanitation, electricity, roads, health services, and other amenities (Ennaji 2014). Many critics and activists such as Ahmed Assid (2010) consider that though the aforementioned reforms and policies are significant and eliminate institutional discrimination against the Berbers, they are merely a symbolic signal to appease Berber demands and please the international community.

The reforms are also a response to global Islamism and to the rise of Islamic fundamentalism in the region. Morocco's official strategy marginally shifts the focus away from Islamic tradition toward modernity and toward other elements of Moroccan history such as the Berber heritage, as part of a Moroccan policy in the "war on terror" (cf. Silverstein and Crawford 2004). These policies provide a polished good image of Morocco as a democratizing and modernizing nation. However, they symbolically foster cultural diversity and accommodate alternating interpretations of national identity. Although such policies are beginning to change decades of discrimination and exclusion, reality on the ground is reminiscent of the fact that Moroccan national identity is modern, Muslim, and Arab. Islam strongly shapes Moroccan society today by prescribing behavior and conditioning the public not to subvert the status quo in which some groups (such as the Berbers) are ignored while others are favored.

Conclusion

Marginalization has impacted on the Berber conception of self, as well as on attitudes toward the Berbers, for whom tensions between tradition and modernity create social stress. Because the society emphasizes Arabic, modernity, and development following the Western model, the Berbers are "caught in a greater struggle to participate in a broader, globalized movement without necessarily having the means to do so" (Lewkowicz 2011). The Berbers seek to become modern, developed, and connected with the global economic community, while preserving their cultural heritage and lifestyle. It is, then, the responsibility of the state to help the Berbers to navigate the modern way of life while maintaining their identity. This puts many young Berber people in a contradictory situation in which they self-identify as Moroccan but are viewed by other Moroccans as the "Other." Young activists identify with Berber culture more than with Arab, Muslim, or Western culture, and seek to integrate their cultural traditions into the modern world.

The Amazigh movement in Morocco has been pushing for greater rights and recognition of Berber identity through peaceful means (mainly protests, demonstrations, media reports, etc). Consequently, since 2002, the Berber language has made great headway, especially with its introduction in primary schools. After decades of exclusion and marginalization, Berber is no longer limited to the confines of the home, close friends, and rural areas. The recent official recognition of Berber in Morocco has opened doors for reflection and debate. The current strategy is to work on the organic laws that will allow the use of Berber in public life, and on its standardization and its integration into the education system.

Thus, the status of Berber has changed from a spoken non-recognized language to a written recognized national official language thanks to the activism of the Amazigh cultural associations, the state's new will to integrate Amazigh into development, the work of the intelligentsia, and the globalization changes in favor of democracy, minorities, and human rights. Discourses and attitudes toward the Berbers have also improved since the last two decades. Most politicians and decision makers have started to include Berber as a means for fostering diversity and democracy. The official inclusion of Berber communities is, thus, an essential (and much-demanded) step in Morocco's efforts to strengthen its democratic credentials.

Notes

1 See this informative link: http://philippepoisson-hotmail.com.over-blog.com/article-le-complot-de-skhirat-au-maroc-10-juillet-1971-37910761.html (accessed February 6, 2014).
2 See the figures provided by the "Haut Commissariat au Plan" in their website: http://www.hcp.ma/Analphabetisme_a413.html (accessed February 7, 2014).
3 Ibid.

References

Assid, A. 2010. *Siyassat tadbir achaâne alamazighi fi Al Maghrib* [Language Planning of Amazigh in Morocco]. Rabat: Publication of Observatoire Amazigh des Droits et des Libertés.

Belleau, M.-C. 2007. "'L'intersectionalité': Feminisms in a Divided World; Québec-Canada." In *Feminist Politics: Identity, Difference, and Agency*, edited by O. Deborah et al., 51–61. Lanham: Rowman & Littlefield.

Boukous, A. 1995. *Société, Langues et Cultures au Maroc* [Society, Language and Cultures in Morocco]. Rabat: Publications de la Faculté des Lettres, Rabat.

Benrabah, M. 2014. "Tensions between Berberophones and Arabophones in Algeria." In *Multiculturalism and Democracy in North Africa*, edited by M. Ennaji, 57–80. London: Routledge.

Berlin, I. 1992. *The Crooked Timber of Humanity*. New York: Vintage.

Chafik, M. 1989. *An Overview of Thirty Three Centuries of Berber History*. [In Arabic]. Rabat: Dar El Kalam.

Collins, P. H. 2000. *Black Feminist Thought: Knowledge, Consciousness, and the Politics of Empowerment*. New York: Routledge.
Crawford, D. 2005. “Royal Interest in Local Culture: Amazigh Identity and the Moroccan State.” In *Nationalism and Minority Identities in Islamic Societies*, edited by M. Shatzmiller, 164–94. Montréal: McGill-Queen’s University Press.
Crenshaw, K. 1989. “Demarginalizing the Intersection of Race and Sex: A Black Feminist Critique of Antidiscrimination Doctrine, Feminist Theory and Antiracist Politics.” *University of Chicago Legal Forum* 140:139–67.
Dourari, A. 2014. “Algeria: Cultural Multiplicity and Unity Dialectics.” In *Multiculturalism and Democracy in North Africa*, edited by M. Ennaji, 35–54. London: Routledge.
Ennaji, M. 1991. “Aspects of Multilingualism in the Maghreb.” Sociolinguistics of the Maghreb, Special Issue, *International Journal of the Sociology of Language* 87:7–25.
Ennaji, M. 1997. “The Sociology of Berber: Change and Continuity.” Berber Sociolinguistics, Special Issue, *International Journal of the Sociology of Language* 123:23–40.
Ennaji, M. 2010. “The Arab World: Maghreb and the Near East.” In *Handbook of Language and Ethnic Identity Disciplinary and Regional Perspectives*. Vol. 1, 2nd ed., edited by J. A. Fishman and O. Garcia, 407–21. Oxford: Oxford University Press.
Ennaji, M. 2014. “The Berber (Amazigh) Movement in Morocco: Local Activism, The State, and Transnationalism.” In *Multiculturalism and Democracy in North Africa: Aftermath of the Arab Spring*, edited by M. Ennaji, 92–112. London: Routledge.
Fishman, J. A. 1977. “Language and Ethnicity in Intergroup Relations.” In *Language and Ethnicity in Intergroup Relations*, edited by H. Giles, 16–53. London: Academic Press.
Fishman, J. A. 2010. “Sociolinguistics: Language and Ethnic Identity in Context.” In *Handbook of Language and Ethnic Identity Disciplinary and Regional Perspectives*. Vol. 1, 2nd ed., edited by J. A. Fishman and O. Garcia, xxv–xxxv. Oxford: Oxford University Press.
Fishman, J. A., and Garcia, O., eds. 2010. *Handbook of Language and Ethnic Identity Disciplinary and Regional Perspectives*. Vol. 1, 2nd ed. Oxford: Oxford University Press.
Fitouri, C. 1983. *Biculturalisme, Bilinguisme et Education*. Paris/Neuchatel: Delachaux & Niestlé.
Hoffman, K. 2008. *We Share Walls: Language, Land, and Gender in Berber Morocco*. Malden: Wiley-Blackwell.
Lewkowicz, K. 2011. “Exclusion, Marginalization and Identity Formation: The Berbers.” Research Paper. Accessed February 7, 2014. http://web.colby.edu/oak/student-involvement/oak-research-organization/.
Maddy-Weitzman, B. 2011. *The Berber Identity Movement and the Challenge to North African States*. Austin: Texas University Press.
Sadiqi, F. 1997. *Grammaire du Berbère* [A Grammar of Berber]. Paris: L’Harmattan.
Sadiqi, F. 2014. “Berber and Language Politics in the Moroccan Educational System.” In *Multiculturalism and Democracy in North Africa*, edited by M. Ennaji, 81–91. London: Routledge.
Silverstein, P., and D. Crawford. 2004. “Amazigh Activism and the Moroccan State.” *Middle East Report*, Winter.233. Accessed February 8, 2014. http://works.bepress.com/david_crawford/14.
Spencer, K. 2001. “Algiers Joins Berbers in Protest.” Accessed February 21, 2015. http://www.culturalsurvival.org/publications/cultural-survival-quarterly/algeria/algiers-joins-berbers-protest.
Stone, J. 1995. “Race, Ethnicity, and the Weberian Legacy.” *American Behavioral Scientist* 38(3):391–416.

5

AMAZIGH LANGUAGE AND CULTURE IN THE ERA OF SOCIAL MEDIA IN NORTH AFRICA

Abderrahman El Aissati

This chapter is an attempt to give an overview of the current situation of Amazigh language and culture in North Africa, with particular focus on the role of the Internet in making discourse on Amazigh language and identity more visible than ever before. In addition to giving an account of the online environments where Amazigh is thriving, I will also try to explain the importance of these new environments to the Amazigh language and culture in the way they help set up new communities and strengthen ties between social network users reinforcing discourse on language and identity in the offline world. This focus on the Internet is motivated by the massive changes brought about by this medium in the North African sociopolitical, linguistic, and cultural scenery. After a brief presentation of online ethnographic research in sociolinguistic literature, I will proceed to a description of the North African online landscape with focus on Amazigh language and identity in this part of the world. After that, I will provide an account of the recent developments in the sociopolitical scene that have had undeniable influence on the use of Amazigh and on the discourse on Amazigh identity, both in online and offline modes.

The main contribution of this chapter is twofold. On the one hand, it endeavors to establish a strong relationship between modern communication (especially social media) and social movements, exemplified by the demands of the Amazigh cultural movement. On the other hand, it looks at the discourse on Amazigh itself, and analyzes it in terms of ideology and practice. That is, in addition to providing a descriptive approach to the discourse on Amazigh culture and language (regardless of which position one takes), it subjects the very discourse on Amazigh, especially the one promoting the Amazigh cause, to a detailed analysis by looking at how it manifests itself on the Internet. Questions that will be addressed in this regard are as follows: "do social media offer extra possibilities for the visibility of Amazigh discourse?" Since the answer is obviously in the affirmative, the following question becomes necessary: "what modalities are used to advance the visibility of Amazigh on the Internet, that is, what means are used to achieve this? What do these modalities have in common with "offline" modes of communication? By answering these questions, we will have a clear picture of the Internet scenery and where Amazigh is situated in this scenery. However, this is not enough to understand the intricacies of the Amazigh discourse, which like any other discourse, is subjected to—and formed by—the interaction of various power relations. These relations are themselves undertaken as a function of interest—symbolic or material—at a given time. An activist fighting for the recognition of Amazigh as an official language will probably take a different stand if that officialization is granted by a government sensed to be "an enemy," in that it has stood against the very thing one is trying to get. To elaborate on this example, the same militant would probably shift his or her focus from demands for officialization to demands for a given script, or a given spelling. This in itself is not "contradictory" and simply illustrates a standard path of a militant. However, in other cases, an individual or organization may stand behind some demand, but once acquired will not make use of it. This is interesting in that it shows the discrepancy between ideology and practice, which might seem contradictory, but in depth is very consistent with the individual's perception of his or her identity. The demands are mostly an act of establishing one's position in a symbolic market where political activists are highly valued and attributed certain prestige by their "allies."[1]

Online Ethnography

Any attempt to deal with the Amazigh sociocultural space in North Africa is an oversimplification by definition. The large number of Amazigh varieties and the communities that use them necessitate a detailed account of the practices and ideologies of these communities to avoid overgeneralization and to uncover the power relations that govern the communities in question. Such a detailed account will have to rely on people's voices as a guide for the interpretation of their discourse. Ethnographic studies are necessary in such an enterprise. The present chapter is a modest contribution in this direction, in that it looks at the Amazigh culture and identity through the lenses of online ethnography (for a discussion of the uses and limitations of sociolinguistic ethnographies of online discourse, see Androutsopoulos 2008; for examples of online sociolinguistic studies, see Androutsopoulos 2006a, 2006b; Siebenhaar 2006). I will focus mainly on the presentation of a number of interactions and manifestations illustrating the online linguistic landscape, adding to these my own interpretations as an active participant in a number of these interactions. My goal here is to introduce the reader to an updated version of the sociocultural scenery in North Africa, more than a detailed and critical analysis of the various stands taken by relevant actors on this scenery. (For a similar relatively detailed account, see El Aissati, in print; for previous accounts of the sociolinguistic scenery in North Africa, see, for example, Boukous 1977, 1995; El Aissati 1993, 2001; Ennaji 1997, 2005.)

As pointed out above, any attempt to deal with the sociocultural and sociopolitical scenes in North Africa cannot ignore the new spaces provided by online communication. This new communication medium (also referred to as computer-mediated communication, see Thurlow, Lengel, and Tomic 2004) has proven to be a powerful instrument for ideologies proclaiming social change in the North African territory recently and elsewhere in the world (see, for example, Larémont 2013). Although the Internet right from its start has been described as a revolutionary medium and praised for the changes it can bring around, it is more the new era of social media that has caused a much more radical change in the way people communicate. The second generation of websites, known as Web 2.0, has made it possible to have an interactive Internet, with synchronous communications and various graphic enhancements, as well as video postings (see, for example, Anderson 2007). The Internet has thus become a very rich arena for discourse on politics, culture, and religion, as well as a place for all sorts of mundane everyday discourse and sociocultural practices, thanks to its interactive nature that allows anyone to voice one's opinion, make a statement, or express oneself in general.

Social media can provide valuable data on these discourses and practices, by virtue of their being an open space, and their power in archiving massive amounts of information. However, a note of caution is in place here. Despite the relatively high presence of North Africans on social media and Internet in general, large groups of people remain unconnected and as such their voices on the Internet are not heard. But again, if one thinks of literate people as the most likely agents in social change, then the Internet can be considered of tremendous value in that it reflects whatever issues are being dominant in the public discourse in a given society.

As such, a major credit of social media is the affordance of spaces for all kinds of voices to express themselves, whether this concerns political preferences, religious convictions, language ideologies, or artistic expressions (e.g. YouTube), and so on. Another credit of the Internet is that it provides complementary information to the traditional sociolinguistic accounts that usually link speakers to geographic areas. The mobility of speakers/users in the "offline world" does not—necessarily—affect their presence on the Internet, but it does render sociolinguistic accounts obsolete rather quickly. The Internet, provided it is spread out and used extensively, can restore the links between groups and communities, which were broken due to their geographical dispersal. It also allows the establishment of contact between small groups, which were restrained in their use of a "minor" language, due to the presence of a more valued and more powerful competitor language (e.g. Arabic in the North Africa case). As early as 1963, Penchoen pointed out the fragile sociolinguistic situation enhanced by the geographical dispersion of the Amazigh speakers [Pencheon [1968] 1983 cited in Gabsil 2011, 141]. This is not to say that the Internet is the savior of Amazigh, but simply means that there are now more possibilities to be connected, knowing that such connections will always have a social meaning that will reflect the value given to the languages as communication media (see Bourdieu 1982).

As pointed out above, one of the greatest merits of the Internet is providing platforms for voices that were previously not valued enough to be listened to. In a society classified as high on power distance (an index of 63/100, the cultural dimensions index of Hofstede 2009), communication on important issues is sensed to be coupled with a power position in society (or at least in the context where the communication is taking place). Being active on the Internet allows the individual to choose an identity, as well as to defy roles dictated by the social codes defined by power relations and social conventions in a society. Any individual can say anything he or she chooses, and address anybody he or she wants, without being submitted to any form of sanction, legal or otherwise, provided he or she stays anonymous where necessary. Next to anonymity, distance can provide a safe haven for the Internet user. A Moroccan citizen living in the United States can address various audiences on the Internet, without the fear of being harassed by Moroccan authorities, or being subjected to social constraints that apply in Morocco, since the social context where he or she is now provides for a high degree of freedom of speech.

Amazigh Presence on the Internet

I will sketch some background information on social media use in North African countries in order to give an idea of the role of these media in making data on Amazigh culture and politics more accessible than ever. This accessibility calls for updating the knowledge we have of the situation at hand, and provides opportunities for looking at the Amazigh discourse from digital lenses (Zouhir 2011).

The Internet has opened up spaces for the publication of various topics related to Amazigh language and culture, ranging from serious academic papers and discussions to unmoderated (artistic or otherwise) expressions in Amazigh. For ease of understanding, I will start with referring to three types of websites. The first type is illustrated by websites that are partly in Amazigh, such as amazigh.nl (the Netherlands), mondeberbere.com (France), anavad.org (website of the self-proclaimed Kabyle Republic, France), tawalt.com, amazighworld.org, and so on. A second type is illustrated by those that are entirely in languages other than Amazigh, but proclaim a clear Amazigh identity. The following websites fall within this category: nadorcity.com (Arabic), dalil-rif.com (Arabic), agraw.com (English), amazightimes.com (Dutch), and amazightv.net (Dutch). A third category is exemplified by a very limited number of websites that are completely in Amazigh, such as nadorama.com (Tarifit variant of the Amazigh language), imyura.net (Kabyle), and ayamun.com (also Kabyle). These websites offer spaces for readers' comments, and these come usually in the language of the website, but occasionally in different languages, including Amazigh.

Another distinction can be made along the lines of the type of content posted on the websites. A large number of websites act as news-spreading points, with content ranging from issues that have to do with Amazigh culture and language (such as coverage of demonstrations, publication of communiqués from pro-Amazigh organizations, interviews with Amazigh activists, etc.), such as amazighworld.org and amazigh.nl. A second category, probably the most popular in terms of number of visitors and number of websites, is the news portals, where Amazigh is almost by definition less visible, such as nadorcity.com, dalil-rif.com, midar.info (entirely in Arabic, with the exception of the name in Tifinagh transliterating "midar infu").

Another example of the availability of new online spaces for Amazigh language and culture are discussion forums. However, these environments are generally in languages other than Amazigh. Forums explicitly dealing with Amazigh but using other languages are a reflection of the limited spread of Amazigh writing (regardless of the script chosen).

Back to Orality?

The limited spread of literacy in Amazigh does not hinder communication in Amazigh on the Internet. It is ironic that that written text was the basic medium used when the Internet just started, and that only at a much more advanced stage of its development was Internet able to incorporate speech in different environments. The possibility for direct chat came much later than text-based chat, just the reverse of what happened in human language evolution.

The problem posed by the lack of familiarity with Amazigh writing disappears in "chat modes" such as those provided by Paltalk: a synchronous chat environment where anyone can set up an account, invite people to the created chat room(s), and accept or reject applications to join the discussion. Users are usually anonymous (but don't have to be). The Paltalk environments are popular among Amazigh militants. The only equipment needed is a computer with a microphone and an Internet connection. Paltalk offers the possibility of audio and/or video chats.

Other environments such as Google hangouts (where people can talk to each other using videoconferencing) are also used, but it is difficult to know the extent of such use among Amazigh speakers. Skype is also a popular medium for chatting in audio only or in audio and video mode. As will be discussed below, Facebook has now the lion share in practically every aspect of informal online communication, although businesses are also increasingly making use of this medium (mostly to advertise their products).

Facebook

A more pervasive medium that has changed the communication landscape is Facebook, undoubtedly the most revolutionary medium in terms of connecting individuals, groups, and organizations that choose to use it (see usage statistics below). A basic but powerful property of Facebook is that it allows anyone with an account to "friend" anyone who agrees to a friendship request, join groups, make groups, share pictures, videos, and so on. The possibility of creating groups is accompanied with different privacy settings. Groups can be secret (seen only by members of the group), private (only members can see the posts of the group, but the group is visible to non-members), or public (practically a website that anyone can visit and see all content). In such an environment, individuals are not constrained by social considerations when choosing a language for their interactions, which provides more opportunity for the use of Amazigh.

In addition to group settings, Facebook provides the possibility of posting hyperlinks to content from other websites, again making it possible for previously unseen texts, pictures, or videos to be visible and to get a second life. The importance of hyperlinks can be appreciated if we compare electronic versions with paper versions of texts. In the past, the latter could be spread only by making photocopies and handing them or mailing them to others, with all the needed costs and time to undertake such an operation. With the use of hyperlinks, not only the costs are reduced, but the speed with which the sharing happens increases tremendously.

The graphic advances in Facebook have also increased the visibility of Amazigh language and culture. Pictures and videos are very easy to share, and in a culture characterized as a rather collective one with a preference for high-context communication, graphics are very important (for cultural dimensions, see Hofstede, Hofstede, and Minkov 2010, and for studies of cultural differences between websites see Marcus and Gould 2000; for high- and low-context communication see Hall 1976). Anyone with a Facebook account can post pictures and videos from one's own computer, link to other pictures or videos on the Internet, or make one's own picture or video (using one's own equipment, such as a computer with a camera and a microphone, a smartphone, a tablet, etc.). It is hard to think of any Amazigh event in recent years that has not been posted on Facebook.

YouTube

Despite the popularity of Facebook and the possibility it offers to upload videos directly from one's smartphone or computer, YouTube remains the place to be when one needs to watch a video. YouTube offers more possibilities in customizing one's videos, namely, adding meta information (e.g. on the maker of the video, the description of content), editing the videos, turning one's videos into revenue-generating products through advertising, and allows anyone with a YouTube account to have a personal channel where all the videos can be stored and viewed, with the proper statistics of visitors and the length of time that a video was watched.

Amazigh events and happenings are abundant on YouTube. A simple search on the YouTube website with the term "Amazigh" yields about 250,000 videos/hits, while a search with the term "Berber" yields 178,000 hits.[2] A large number of these videos are in Amazigh and feature music videos, speeches, lectures, comedy, and so on. Posters of events dating back to as early as twenty years ago are also posted as fond memories. Videos on YouTube can be for fun; for serious lecturing, for example, by religious figures using Amazigh; or for any other purpose. More research is needed to see what type of discourse is popular among viewers and why. A few examples showing type of discourse and popularity are in place here. A popular Imam, Tarik Ibn Ali, who has been aware of the power of videos and YouTube for some time now can be heard giving directions to cameramen while he is giving a talk. All of his talks/sermons are in Amazigh (Tarifit) and have acquired immense popularity. His YouTube channel "TarikIbnAli" has 3,974 subscribers who are notified each time he adds a video to his channel, and has 693 uploaded videos. He can show the viewers that he really does what he preaches: in a video, viewers can watch him take a dive in the swimming pool of his rented vacation villa, and witness him getting ready to barbecue! Through the comments on his videos, one can see the admiration viewers have for this YouTube user. Many of these comments are in Amazigh, which most likely implies that viewers understand that Amazigh is highly valued in this context, since the Imam himself is using it, and proceed to converge to the medium used in the video they are watching (see example of the absence of Amazigh and its significance below).

Despite this relatively broad description of the presence of Amazigh voices on the Internet, one would not do justice to the crucial role of social media if one does not deal with the possibility these media offer to build and, perhaps more importantly, to sustain communities. Comments posted on any space on the Internet usually call for more comments, in a recursive way that leads to threads of comments, not necessarily enriching the "discussion," but certainly allowing the identification of partners or adversaries, with potential of future "get together," or any other conceivable outcome. The point being made here is that this interactivity is similar to the offline interactivity, and inevitably plays a role in strengthening or weakening ties in a community.

By now it must have become clear that the presence of Amazigh on the Internet in North African countries and in immigration countries in Western Europe cannot be ignored, and one can easily discern a collateral increase of Amazigh voices in the "offline" world. More demonstrations are being organized and more protests can be witnessed, which are all constantly "fed" by comments, invitations to join a protest, articles on the reasons behind the protest, and so on, on the Internet. People can form secret groups on Facebook and communicate in a relatively free environment (for a case study of the use of social media in the Egyptian revolution, see Aly 2011). While in the pre-Internet era any activist could be stopped from undertaking certain actions, nowadays such an act would only fuel more protest, and help spread the message of the activist, in addition to the difficulty of tracing down authors of any text (or post) undesired by the authorities.

Free Internet and Self-Censorship

The massive use of Internet also uncovers a less rosy side of Amazigh culture and language: the voluntary refrain of Amazigh speakers from using Amazigh when addressing Amazigh audiences. This is exemplified by numerous websites, especially news portals, which are very local in nature; carry local news, which are mostly meant for local audiences; feature ads for local companies; and carry names of local communities, such as midar.info, aroui24.net, nadorcity.com, dalil-rif.com, and so on. With no exception, these websites all post news in Standard Arabic. In many cases, they conduct interviews in Arabic with individuals who clearly speak Amazigh. An example of the absence of Amazigh in a local public event can be provided by a video report on a meeting about public transportation in Arouit, a village twenty-eight kilometers south of Nador. The video is twenty-six minutes long and shows fifteen oral interventions, and a fragment of a video that was shown to the public during the event. None of the interventions was partly or completely in Amazigh (Tarifit), and most of them were in Standard Arabic. The video fragment that was shown to the public was in Standard Arabic, eight interventions were exclusively in Standard Arabic, three used a mix of Standard Arabic and Moroccan Arabic, four were only in Moroccan Arabic. The village Arouit is part of the province of Nador, where according to the census of 2004, 86.8% of the population speaks Amazigh.

This is a clear indication of the low value of Amazigh on the symbolic market as contextualized here (for a context where the use of Amazigh remains of high value, see comment on the videos of Tarik Ibn Ali discussed above). It would have been insightful to ask the participants who were present at the meeting discussed above why they did not speak in Amazigh. An answer to be expected here—based on previous similar experiences—is that there might be people who don't understand Amazigh. It is very significant that seldom are those who do not understand Arabic taken into consideration. However, the situation is more complex than it seems, especially when one asks the same question to an Amazigh speaker who addresses another Amazigh speaker in a different language. This brief review of the YouTube video report should not raise wrong expectations. In other situations, such as interviews with local farmers in Midar, a village about seventy-three kilometers west of Nador, the language used with the interviewees was exclusively Tarifit[3] (see the website of Midar.info and videos embedded there). Also on the website of Arouit24.net, there are a number of videos in Amazigh. This rich sociolinguistic landscape calls for more detailed ethnographic analyses that would help shed light on the meaning of language choice, language preference, and language use.

As will be pointed out below, Algeria and Tunisia also have a relatively high number of Internet users. Since the number of Amazighophones is much higher in Algeria than in Tunisia (see below), one would expect more websites dealing with Amazigh language and culture in Algeria than in Tunisia. This can be confirmed by a quick search on the Internet. A number of Algerian websites devoted to Amazigh issues can be found on the Internet, but the majority of these are hosted abroad (e.g. kabyle.com, tiziri.net).

The official website of Tizi Ouzou, a wilaya (province) of 1,119,646 inhabitants in 2008, is exclusively in French, and the Facebook page to which it links has fifty-six friends, a very small number.[4] A Facebook group named "tiziouzou," very likely created by non-officials, has 249 friends, and features information on Amazigh-related issues (such as the recent violent clashes in Gherdaya in the Mzab area). The prevalent language of this Facebook group is French. The Facebook page of Radio Tizi Ouzou has 12,134 friends, and at the time of consulting it, there were about 1,000 people talking about it (as indicated by the Facebook statistics, on February 10, 2014). Again, the language of this group is French. The discrepancy between the website of the wilaya and the Facebook page of the radio is indicative of the desire of Internet users to express themselves, more than to consume news of the wilaya through reading.

It remains difficult to distinguish websites that are run locally from those run from outside of North Africa. For example, the website tiziri.net deals with everything local in Tizi-Ouzou, but the person in charge lives in Germany. This difficulty in itself indicates that the geographical boundaries in the Internet era have become obsolete, at least as far as communication is concerned.

While sometimes speaking Amazigh can lower the prestige of the speaker, which does not necessarily lead to economic loss, in other situations avoiding the use of Amazigh is necessary in order to secure a financial revenue. The websites presented above all depend on advertising for their income, and as such, they try to address as many visitors as possible. A website in Amazigh will not be consulted by many people, seeing the high degree of illiteracy in this language, and its relatively new history in writing, compared to Arabic and French (on the Moroccan market).

A second factor that might help explain the scarcity of websites in Amazigh is the fear of making spelling "mistakes," which are inevitable in the absence of clear standards. A primarily collectivist culture places high value on expertise and certification. Any writer in Amazigh is exposing himself or herself to criticism from the outside, an act that would lead to lowering one's prestige.

The Impact of the Internet on the North African Sociocultural Landscape

To help the reader get an idea of the importance the Internet plays in the lives of North Africans, I will introduce some figures to this effect. The information reported below on Internet users in North African countries is taken from internetworldstats.com.[5]

The number of Internet users in Algeria was estimated at 5,230,000 as of June 30, 2012, or 14.0% of the population, and the number of Facebook users was estimated at 4,111,320 at the end of 2012, with a 11% penetration rate (the population was 37,367,226 at that time).[6] Regardless of the double accounts that people might have or fake accounts, this remains a sizable amount of Facebook users, confirming the impact of the Internet that I have pointed out above.

In Morocco, sources cite a much higher number of Internet users: 16,477,712 in June 2012, which is equivalent to 51.0% of the population (total population was about 32,309,239).[7] This makes Morocco the country with the highest penetration rate of Internet in Africa, and the third in terms of absolute numbers of Internet connections (after Nigeria and Egypt, which have penetration rates of 28.4% and 35.6%, respectively). The number of Facebook users reached 5,091,760 on December 31, 2012, with a 15.8% penetration rate (http://www.internetworldstats.com/).

Tunisia has a relatively large number of Internet users. With a population of about 10,732,900 in 2012, the number of Internet users on June 30, 2012, was approximately 4,196,564, or 39.1% of the population. The website internetworldstats.com indicates that there were 3,328,300 Facebook subscribers on December 31, 2012, with a 31.0% penetration rate.

Libya seems to be lagging behind with regard to Internet usage, which is not surprising seeing that prior to the fall of Qaddafi in 2011, no free Internet was available to its citizens and filtering content was common procedure.[8] The figures reported by internetworldstats.com are the following: out of a population of 5,613,380 in 2012, there were 954,275 Internet users as of June 30, 2012, with a penetration rate of 17.0%. There were 781,700 Facebook users on December 31, 2012, with 13.9% as a penetration rate. There are no more recent statistics on Libya, but there is reason to believe the percentages will grow exponentially.

In all these countries, it is easy to see that the number of Internet users is quite close to the number of Facebook users, which is an indication of the popularity of social media in the countries in question. It is also clear from the review presented so far that the countries where Amazigh is widely spoken, namely, Morocco and Algeria, are the countries with high percentages of Internet users. Although the Internet is accessible to a large number of people, the use of Amazigh on the Internet remains minimal, compared to Arabic and French that are dominant, and in environments defined as Amazigh, such as discussion Forums and Facebook pages devoted to Amazigh issues. This could be an indication that modernity reinforces the ideological discourse on Amazigh, which is more of a symbolic nature, while traditional environments, such as the countryside, are places where Amazigh still thrives.

"Back to Earth"—Amazigh in the Offline World

We have so far seen that Internet use is an important part of the lives of North Africans, regardless of their ethnicity or language. We have also seen that Amazigh language has made use of the extra space afforded by the Internet. To have a bigger picture of Amazigh language and culture in North Africa, we will proceed to an examination of the changes at the sociopolitical level that have affected the position of Amazigh language and culture. Since education is an essential part of the social landscape in any modern country, I will start with a brief review of recent developments in this area. After that, we will move to a brief consideration of the changes that are taking place in the traditional media landscape.

Amazigh at School

Algeria was the first North African country to have introduced Amazigh in public education. The first classes started in 1995 in the Amazighophone areas (Kabylia, Mzab, and Aures) in sixteen wilayas (provinces). In 2010–2011, the number of children learning Amazigh at school was about 240,000 (Boukhlef 2010), 95% of whom were in the Kabyle area alone. Such a high concentration and low number of children learning Amazigh at school contradicts the ambition of Algeria in making Amazigh a national language in 2002.

Since its introduction in primary schools in Morocco in 2003, Amazigh has (re)gained more territory in Morocco, by being officially acknowledged as a school language. There have been many obstacles for a successful teaching program of Amazigh, which have to do with the number of hours not exceeding three a week, the shortage in school materials and teachers, added to the unwillingness of a number of educational institutions to actively encourage and provide for the teaching of Amazigh [personal communications with a number of researchers at the Royal Institute of Amazigh Culture (IRCAM), Rabat]. A decade after the introduction of Amazigh in the public education system, about 500,000 Moroccan pupils have followed classes in Amazigh language, according to a statement of the Moroccan Minister of Education in 2012[9] (aujourdhui.ma). The same source also mentions the presence of 5,000 teachers of Amazigh and 300 specialized inspectors (for a detailed study of Amazigh at school, see El Aissati, Karsmakers, and Kurvers 2011).

The presence of Amazigh in the school system has been accompanied by the publication of a number of school manuals and other support materials, both on paper and in electronic form.[10] A number of works on Amazigh culture, history, language, and so on have been published, and some of them are available in electronic form on the website of the IRCAM.

Regarding Libya and Tunisia, there is no information available on teaching Amazigh. It is very likely that there are some Amazigh cultural associations that would take this initiative. These cultural associations have been very active in Morocco.

Thanks to financial and logistic support from the IRCAM, hundreds of cultural associations were able to organize Amazigh study days and cultural events in the last decade in Morocco. These events have inevitably spread more awareness of Amazigh history and culture, but perhaps even more importantly, they have helped in removing a certain taboo that was associated with publicly proclaiming an Amazigh identity.

By considering the detailed official statistics of 2004 in Morocco, one can only notice that the traditional accounts of where Amazigh is spoken are rather outdated. The statistics indicate that a mere 28.3% of the Moroccan population speaks Amazigh, which amounts to a sizable figure of 8,404,479 (14.6% Tashelhit, 8.8% Tamazight, 4.8% Tarifit).[11] Regardless of whether this percentage is reliable, one can see a wide distribution of Arabic in areas traditionally Amazighophone.[12] For example, the province of Nador has 13.2% speakers of Arabic only (out of a population of 726,520), Agadir Ida Ou Tan has a percentage of 31.3% speakers of Arabic only (out of a population of 486,048), and so on. Major cities such as Casablanca and Rabat have sizable amounts of Amazighophone, namely 12.3% (Province of Casablanca with a total number of 2,936,874 residents) and 14.8% (Province of Rabat with a total of 620,996 residents). Although these statistics can give an idea about the importance and spread of Amazigh in Morocco, more research is needed in order to understand the position of this language in modern Morocco, and its role in the sociocultural and political reality of this country.

Similar to Morocco, ethnographic research on Amazigh in Algeria is very hard to find. Questions relating to how Amazigh speakers deal with the other languages they use, how they engage in negotiations on which language to use in which situation, how they deal with public administration, what their attitudes are toward the different varieties of Amazigh and toward a common Standard Amazigh, and so on are not widely dealt with in research on the languages and cultures of North African countries.

The literature on the sociolinguistics of Algeria commonly emphasizes the large size of Amazigh-speaking populations, with the Kabyle variant being the most widely spoken. Estimates have put the number of Amazigh speakers at about 25% of the population, equivalent to about seven or eight million speakers (Chaker 2004), but no solid data can be found to back this up, since no Algerian official statistics are available on the Algerian languages.

Amazigh in Tunisia

Before the revolution of 2011, Amazigh was not very visible in Tunisia. The number of speakers was put at about 50,000 people, especially in Djerba and a few small villages (Chaker 2004). The events of 2011, which culminated in the removal of president Ben Ali and the instauration of a transitional government, have brought some change. The Internet has helped make visible and audible the voices of Amazigh by providing safe and efficient ways of expressing one's identity. An example of such an environment is Facebook.[13] However, the presence of Amazigh in Tunisia remains very weak, which explains its weak presence on the Internet.

Amazigh in Libya

Libya was considered home to a few Amazigh speakers, a percentage as low as 1% of the population, mainly in the areas of Nefussa. During the 42-year rule of President Qaddafi, which ended in August 2011, Amazigh remained a taboo in Libyan society. Qaddafi has made his stand clear at a number of occasions, when he referred to Amazigh as "a group of tribes which are now extinct [*sic*]."

During the Libyan revolution, Amazigh tribes played a major part in bringing down President Qaddafi. Amazigh flags were raised in different parts of the country, and constant references to Amazigh culture and language could be found on the Internet. Pictures showing the Amazigh flag being raised on the former residence of the president are an indication of the importance of Amazigh identity and its visibility in Libyan society. Numerous websites from different countries and in different languages have featured articles on Libyan Amazighs.[14] The YouTube channel ImazighenLibya has posted 871 videos and has 1,996 subscribers as of January 2014.[15]

It is practically impossible to give a complete and updated view of the presence of Amazigh on the Internet, but a word on the importance and effect of posting news and videos on the Internet is in place. Because Internet is a rich medium, offering the possibility of adding images and videos to text, of hearing voices with their real physical characteristics (like intonation), of hearing voices from the surroundings, and so on, the effect of these media on viewers can be very significant, much more than an article in a paper version of a newspaper. Also for research purposes, a careful observer of all the relevant materials posted on the Internet can use them as data sources.

The impact of the Internet on social order was already apparent during the Egyptian revolution, during which different types of social media were extensively used, next to traditional communication instruments (see Aly 2011 for a study of the Egyptian case).

Concluding Remarks: Amazigh in the Era of the "Arab" Spring: Old Voices, New Spaces?

Undoubtedly, the groundbreaking decision to include Amazigh as an official language in the Moroccan constitution has brought many changes with it, but these remain mainly symbolic. Similarly, the decision of including Amazigh as a national language in Algeria in 2002 has done little more than boosting the prestige of this language. The new Libyan and Tunisian constitutions do not refer to the Amazigh constituents at all. Demands for more rights are constantly voiced on the Internet, protests shown in videos on YouTube, and events discussed in comments or lengthy articles in different platforms, mainly on Facebook. Despite the lack of figures, one can state that most of the discussions that are taking place on the Internet on issues relating to Amazigh identity are voiced through the vehicle of languages other than Amazigh. This leads us to interesting questions about the relationship between identity claims as ideological constructs, and the act of living an Amazigh identity, through using the Amazigh language.[16] The Internet has uncovered this discrepancy between ideology and practice, by providing numerous spaces to express oneself, and to accent any identity one chooses to enact on the Internet. It is most likely that the intellectual discourse on Amazigh identity refers more to a symbolic level, where one is recognized as "Amazigh," but not necessarily having to "perform" one's Amazighity, through, for example, language, or clothing, and so on. Perhaps the major drive behind identity claims will lose its effect once the demanding party gains political and economic control.

It is conceivable that in some cases Amazigh speakers would resort to the constitution to underline their right to use Amazigh in a given context, for example, in a court of law. However, more than two years after it was made second official language of the kingdom, there are still no laws regarding its use and status. Amazigh activists will undoubtedly continue voicing their demands, whether through traditional or modern means. Being part of a broader sociopolitical movement, increasingly asking for more freedom and democracy, the Amazigh discourse is entrenched in the overall struggle for these rights, and a careful analysis of its ideology and practice will reveal tendencies observed in other societies where there are similar demands from minority language (and culture) groups such as the Kurds in the Middle East. The Internet provides extraordinary opportunities to observe policy and practice in this respect, since it has lowered the threshold for "ordinary" citizens as well as intellectuals and members of the elite to express themselves.

Notes

1 See Canagarajah (2005) for a detailed analysis of ideology and practice in the case of Tamil.
2 Search conducted on youtube.com on January 28, 2014.
3 Interview with local farmers: http://www.youtube.com/watch?v=_lurscDHygk, accessed February 4, 2014.
4 tiziouzou-dz.com, accessed February 12, 2014.
5 As one can read on the website itself: "Internet usage information comes from data published by Nielsen Online [http://www.nielsen.com/content/corporate/us/en.html], by the International Telecommunications Union [itu.int], by GfK [*Gesellschaft für Konsumforschung* (Society for Consumer Research [gfk.com]), local ICT Regulators and other reliable sources."
6 Internetworldstats.com, accessed February 1, 2014.

7 http://www.internetworldstats.com/africa.htm#ma, accessed February 4, 2014.
8 https://opennet.net/research/profiles/libya, accessed February 10, 2014.
9 Aujourdhui.ma: http://www.aujourdhui.ma/maroc-actualite/actualite/el-ouafa-la-suspension-de-la-circulaire-autorisant-les-enseignants-du-public-a-donner-des-cours-dans-les-etablissements-prives-est-irrevocable--97998.html, accessed February 4, 2014 (Source: MAP 2012-09-14 N°: 2765).
10 See website of IRCAM (www.ircam.ma) for online courses to learn the basics of the Amazigh language.
11 These are the figures provided by the Moroccan official census of 2004, see: http://www.hcp.ma/Recensement-general-de-la-population-et-de-l-habitat-2004_a633.html, accessed February 12, 2014.
12 Researchers have given higher estimates of the percentages of Amazigh speakers, see Ennaji 1997 and Boukous 1995.
13 See the page https://www.facebook.com/tunisieberbere for example, accessed February 5, 2015.
14 See, for example: http://www.mediarabe.info/spip.php?article1960; http://www.theatlantic.com/international/archive/2011/11/berber-revivals-first-big-sell-convince-libyans-theyre-all-berbers/249100/; http://tamazgha.fr/Kadhafi-menacerait-d-exterminer.html http://www.youtube.com/watch?v=YBBZaKBO8JQ (video report on Amazigh fighters in Libya); (all links accessed on February 6, 2014).
15 http://www.youtube.com/user/ImazighenLibya?feature=watch, accessed February 5, 2015.
16 For a detailed account of Ethnic minority linguistic rights and practices of the elite, see Canagarajah (2005).

References

Aly, S. 2011. "21st Century Revolutions: Facebook Messages Mightier Than the Sword?" Master thesis, Tilburg University.

Anderson, P. 2007. "What Is Web 2.0? Idea, Technologies and Implications for Education." JISC Technology and Standards Watch, February. Accessed February 2, 2014. http://21stcenturywalton.pbworks.com/f/What+is+Web+2.0.pdf.

Androutsopoulos, J. 2006a. "Introduction: Sociolinguistics and Computer-Mediated Communication." *Journal of Sociolinguistics* 10 (4): 419–38.

Androutsopoulos, J. 2006b. "Multilingualism, Diaspora, and the Internet: Codes and Identities on German-Based Diaspora Websites." *Journal of Sociolinguistics* 10 (4): 520–47.

Androutsopoulos, J. 2008. "Potentials and Limitations of Discourse-Centred Online Ethnography." *Language at Internet* 5. Accessed February 1, 2014. http://www.languageatinternet.org/articles/2008/1610.

Arouit24.net. Accessed February 4, 2014. http://www.arouit24.net/?p=24374. (Video on YouTube: http://www.youtube.com/watch?v=i2Eoi6DTOEc#t=52).

Boukhlef, A. 2010. "Algérie: Tamazight entre volonté et réalité." Accessed February 5, 2014. http://fr.allafrica.com/stories/201004200474.html.

Boukous, A. 1977. *Langage et culture populaires au Maroc: essai de sociolinguistique*. Casablanca: Les imprimeries Dar El Kitab.

Boukous, A. 1995. *Société, langues et cultures au Maroc: Enjeux symboliques*. Rabat: Faculté des Lettres et des Sciences Humaines.

Bourdieu, P. 1982. *Ce que parler veut dire: L'économie des échanges linguistiques*. Paris: Fayard.

Canagarajah, S. A. 2005. "Dilemmas in Planning English/Vernacular Relations in Post-colonial Communities." *Journal of Sociolinguistics* 9 (3): 418–47.

Chaker, S. 2004. "Langue et littérature berbères." Clio. Accessed February 4, 2014. http://www.clio.fr/BIBLIOTHEQUE/langue_et_litterature_berberes.asp.

El Aissati, A. 1993. "Berber in Morocco and Algeria: Revival or Decay." *AILA Review* 10:88–109.
El Aissati, A. 2001. "Ethnic Identity, Language Shift and the Amazigh Voice in Morocco and Algeria." *Race, Gender and Class: An Interdisciplinary and Multicultural Journal* 8(3): 57–69.
El Aissati, A. 2014. "Script Choice and Power Struggle in Morocco." In *African Literacies: Ideologies, Scripts, Education*, edited by K. Juffermans, Y. M. Asfahaand, and A. Abdelhay, 147–77. Newcastle-upon-Tyne: Cambridge Scholars Publishing.
El Aissati, A., S. Karsmakers, and J. Kurvers. 2011. "'We Are All Beginners': Amazigh in Language Policy and Educational Practice in Morocco." *Compare: A Journal of Comparative and International Education* 41 (2): 211–27.
Ennaji, M., ed. 1997. "Berber Sociolinguistics." *International Journal of the Sociology of Language* 123:23–40.
Ennaji, M. 2005. *Multilinguallism, Cultural Identity, and Education in Morocco*. New York: Springer.
Hall, E. T. 1976. *Beyond Culture*. New York: Anchor Books.
Hofstede, G. 2009. *Culture's Consequences: Comparing Values, Behaviors, Institutions and Organizations across Nations*. London: Sage.
Hofstede, G., G. J. Hofstede, and M. Minkov. 2010. *Cultures and Organizations: Software of the Mind*. 3rd ed. New York: McGraw-Hill.
Larémont, R. R., ed. 2013. *Revolution, Revolt and Reform in North Africa: The Arab Spring and Beyond*. London: Routledge.
Marcus, A., and E. W. Gould. 2000. "Crosscurrents: Cultural Dimensions and Global Web User-Interface Design." *Interactions* 7 (4): 32–46.
Pencheon, T. G. (1968) 1983. "La langue Berbère en Tunisie et la scolarisation des enfants berbérophones." In *Language in Tunisia*, edited by R. M. Payne, 23–34. Tunis: The Bourguiba Institute of Modern Languages.
Siebenhaar, B. 2006. "Code Choice and Code-Switching in Swiss-German Internet Relay Chat Rooms." *Journal of Sociolinguistics* 10 (4): 481–506.
Thurlow, C., L. Lengel, and A. Tomic. 2004. *Computer Mediated Communication: Social Interaction and the Internet*. London: Sage.
Zouhir, G. 2011. "Attrition and Maintenance of the Berber Language in Tunisia." *International Journal of the Sociology of Language* 2011 (211): 135–64. Accessed February 2, 2015. http://tamazight-officielle.com/Signataires.html (list of signatures for officializing Amazigh in Algeria).

PART III

ISLAMISM, WOMEN, AND MEDIA IN TUNISIA AND MOROCCO

Part three highlights the sociopolitical implications of Islam and media for women in Tunisia and Morocco. Drawing on comparative studies, this part explores and analyzes the situation of women in the region after the Arab Spring and their ongoing struggle for freedom and gender equality.

This part shows that women's rights have suffered a regression after the Islamists took power in North Africa, who intend to re-Islamize society by imposing the *Shari'a* (Islamic) law, which is harsh on women and restricts freedom. It points out the resistance of women to this new trend and to their marginalization in society and media. The chapters in this part show how important it is to listen to the voices of women who are struggling to improve their lives.

6

HISTORIC WOMEN FIGURES AND WOMEN'S DAILY STRUGGLES IN TUNISIA: NEGLECT AND SOCIETAL RESPONSIBILITY

Lilia Labidi

Two developments, one occurring before and one after the Tunisian revolution of January 2011, push us to explore the impact of neglect and its consequences. First, in November 2008, an article titled "The philosophy of couples" ("*La philosophie des couples*") in the Tunisian newspaper *Le Temps* strongly attacked women philosophers teaching at the university and married to philosopher colleagues.[1] These women were called, among other epithets, "frivolous," "females," or "a bitch in heat" ("chienne mordue"). One philosopher wife was accused of "inhibiting" her husband and one of these philosopher couples was said to have a handicapped child, another was genetically sterile, and a third had a child with DNA problems.

The second development concerns women who immolated themselves and about whom there has been very little discussion. Some psychiatrists in the country spoke of a suicidal compulsion for these cases in 2011 when, between January and June, 111 cases of suicide were recorded, with thirty-one of the suicides by women[2] with sixty-nine of the suicides by self-immolation.[3] Now, suicide by self-immolation is not a new phenomenon in Tunisia. In all, 15.1% of the burn cases recorded between 1992 and 1995 in the burn center of the Aziza Othmana Hospital in Tunis were self-immolation cases, thus constituting a serious public health problem.[4]

The press reported seven cases of self-immolations by women in 2011. All were between sixteen and seventy years old and lived in the North West (Sidi Bouzid, Bousalem, Beja) or the Center East (Jammel, Monastir). Whereas Farhana Ali and Yoran Schweitzer find personal motives to be the basis for women's self-immolation in Afghanistan,[5] we find, in the Tunisian situation, that the majority of cases denounce social policy (unemployment, crumbling homes, the absence of medical support for a husband with a long-term disease, etc.). These women chose to express their despair over a political system unable to improve their inhuman situation; they commit the act, as men do, in front of a public building (provincial office, police station, etc.).

Yet, despite the shocking nature of these cases, there was no collective outcry, no call to understand what was happening inside the heads of these women.[6] The absence of a public and collective response to such events reflects the lack of a broad expression of solidarity with women who were suffering.[7] This raises questions about notions of justice and collective responsibility that are central to the research we will be presenting here, which concerns historic women figures in Tunisia struggling against colonialism and for their rights, as well as women, young girls, and adolescents from rural or poor urban milieus fighting for improvements in their lives. The experiences and emotions of these individuals have been systematically neglected by social/political institutions in Tunisia and by the public at large.

The neglect we will be discussing here echoes the public neglect experienced by some well-known historic women figures in the region. Jamila Bouhired, a symbol of the Algerian struggle against colonialism, speaking in 2005 to a correspondent of the Arab magazine *Al-Mar'aa Al-Youm*, voiced her regret at not having this conversation with a journalist from her own country, which would enable her compatriots to discover who she was and what she had done. And she also confided how a forest of thorns had supplanted her memories.[8] And when the Tunisian woman Rafia Bornaz, who had been sentenced in 1952 by a French court martial to two years in prison, was questioned by a journalist, following a ceremony in which several women militants were given decorations by the Tunisian head of state in 1989, she answered in a few phrases: “AI have been forgotten. I have forgotten.”[9] During the decade of the 2000s, in constructing biographies of some 300 historic Tunisian women, I uncovered similar images and poignant metaphors among women political militants in a variety of Tunisian regions. My meetings with these women, and/or with their relatives and witnesses, were often marked by the women’s tears, or by the strong feelings and/or anger of their relatives and friends in cases where the women themselves had already passed away.[10]

The absence of reaction on the part of civil society and government departments to support women whose private lives were publicly attacked is very surprising. We are also intrigued by the audience response to films such as *The Season of Men* (*Maussim al-rijal*) and *Clay Dolls* (*3ara’is al-Tin*), directed during the early 2000s by, respectively, Moufida Tlatli and Nouri Bouzid. Despite the artistic qualities of these films, both of which won prizes in international festivals abroad, they were poorly received in Tunisia and quickly taken off the screens.[11] As in the cases of self-immolating women, both productions deal with women who struggle in their daily lives: on the one hand, those who are looking for new kinds of man–woman relationships, for another kind of dialogue within the couple, and on the other hand, creative young girls and adolescents who imagine new life paths but who, taken from their original milieus, will serve as maids in bourgeois households.

Moufida Tlatli was criticized for her insults to the “national image” of women—an image that basks in the halo of the Tunisian Personal Status Code (PSC), which, since its promulgation in 1956, gave rights to women far beyond those seen elsewhere in the Arab world, even until today. She was accused of having made a film to satisfy the expectations of the West and the needs of her financial partners from the North, of producing “postcard” images.[12] Nor did Nouri Bouzid’s film, which stigmatized the failure of the state of law, a failure of which the filmmaker himself had been a victim,[13] gain a wide audience. These films, produced as Tunisia approached the fiftieth anniversary of the PSC’s promulgation and casting a critical look at women’s condition in today’s Tunisia, raise several questions. Do the moral emotions that are generated by these two situations contribute to a confrontation between *Sitr* (hiding) and *Tajahur* (revealing)? Why are political/social institutions neglecting the social marginalization of women? Why is the public remaining silent regarding their political marginalization?

We are here in the presence of two different situations but the responses on the institutional level, on the one hand, and by the public, on the other, seem to be well aligned. As a consequence, our discussion will concern the impact on the public of the institutionalized repression of historic women figures' participation in the struggle,[14] and the public's neglect of the daily struggles of women, young girls, and adolescent girls—what Amartya Sen has called their agency role.[15] This discussion will also examine the meaning of justice both for institutions and for the public and how the contribution of Tunisian feminists of the 1980s, who gave visibility to the political history of women, restored to these women militants their self-respect and self-esteem (*3azzit al-nafs*).[16]

Historic Figures

Our corpus, which comprises women who, between 1881 and 1961, were active in the struggle against colonialism and for their rights, comprises 300 biographies of women from Tunis, from the northern and southern suburbs of the capital, and from rural and poor urban areas in Téboulba, Tazarka, Nabeul, Djebel Bargou, Nefza, Beja, Tajerouine, Dahmani, Le Kef, Tatouine, Remada, Kebili, Tozeur, Metlaoui, Redeyef, Nefta, Sfax, Sousse, Remada, Degueche, Kairouan, Gabès, and Bizerte. In this chapter, we will look closely at five women from rural or poor urban areas who were active in this struggle. We met three of them in person; for the other two, who had passed away, we met their family members. We have also chosen these figures because they experienced barbaric treatment rarely seen in more favored urban areas and because they testify to types of militant action that have been rarely documented elsewhere.

(a) The search for legitimate historic figures from rural and poor urban areas who engaged in the struggle for independence

In filiation with the work of Abu Abdur-Rahman as-Sulami (d. 1021), who collected more than eighty biographies of Sufi women who lived between the eighth and eleventh centuries, we have searched for the name, title, or the name by which these women were known in their region, their characteristics, the nature of their achievements, the names of women and men with whom they were associated, as well as the names of whoever related the information.[17] Beyond this information, we have tried to take into account the societal representations that concern them, such as their subjectivity in the construction of identity and their particular life path.[18]

For our discussion here, we will be focusing on five women who were, in their way, reformist figures, and where political acts dominate. Our discussions with Tahar El-Matoussi, only son of Mdalla Bent Mohamed Ben Belgacem Ben Hourria El-Matoussi, and with close relatives of Fatma Bent Amor Ben Abidi, known as Mama Gannoucha, were all marked by strong emotions where our interlocutors, their voices choked up, related the stories of these women. The son spoke of the pain of the child whose mother was torn away from him while he was still feeding at her breast, how she died under torture a week after her arrest, and how he still cries at her memory. Those who were close to Mama Gannoucha spoke of the courage of this woman who, despite the death sentence pronounced on her son and his being removed from his region, did not renounce her struggle.

Among the three other women whom I will be discussing here, there was Habiba al-Nabli, wife of Mansour Trabelsi, who shortly after our telephone conversation was hospitalized, and explained her hospitalization by saying that the conversation stirred up memories that had been blocked and that caused her much agitation. In the presence of several of her descendents and other women, Fatma Bent Boubaker Ben Ahmed al-Meherzi (wife of Belgacem Bouhjar al-Bargaoui) cries as she describes in great detail her rape by the colonial army, committed in front of her family who were unable to provide her with any assistance. Sometime later, her co-wife, who was also raped, managed to flee from the region. She herself has never been able to forget her rape, nor the deaths of her three children that occurred shortly thereafter. And then the third woman we met, Hafsia al-Abrougui, recounts how, after the colonial soldiers had separated the women from the men, she was raped in the presence of the women of her family, without their being able to come to her aid. Later, she married her cousin, who had himself been raped by the colonial army, on the very same day she had suffered her ordeal. But this provided very poor consolation in a society where honor is measured by the woman's virginity.

(b) Testimony relating to two women political militants outside of history

Mdalla Bent Mohamed Ben Belgacem Ben Hourria El-Matoussi (from rural area of Medjez El-Bab)

Present at her husband's trial, in 1941, she and other women ululate when the judge sentenced him and his comrades, as a way to encourage the men in their struggle. She enters into contact with Chadlia Bouzgarou, the niece of Habib Bourguiba who was well-known for her commitment to the anti-colonial struggle, and she continues her husband's struggle. Aware that children were rarely searched when they visited prisoners, she frequently hid messages for her husband on her infant, Tahar el-Matoussi.

On one occasion, she brought back from Tunis a bag full of pamphlets covered by vegetables. A few minutes after she reached home, colonial soldiers entered to search her home and discovered leaflets that the nationalist Neo-Destour party had given her to distribute to the people. She fought her arrest, slapping one of the soldiers, and was led away by force, leaving behind her a son of four months.

When her husband was released from prison where he was one among many, including Rachid Driss, he was surprised to find his wife not at home. Learning from the family that she hasn't been seen since her arrest and trying to uncover her trace, he found her name on a hospital register in the capital, indicating that she had died from torture one week after his arrest.

Fatma Bent Amor Ben Abidi, known as Mama Gannoucha (from the small town of Degueche)

Born in 1881, died in 1977, daughter of Amor Ben Abidi Aicha Bent Mohamed Ben Belgacem, Fatma Bent Amor Ben Abidi had two sons and a daughter from her two marriages. Carrying a pistol at her waist, she worked her palm groves on her own.

Very conscious of the injustices of colonialism, in 1934, she became the first woman to follow the political discussions that were open only to men, listening to them from behind the doors and then relaying them to the other women. She was noticed by Youssef Rouissi who came to depend on her to transmit his political messages to the women and, after 1938, when he was engaged in actions outside the region, she continued participating in the scout and youth meetings, as well as in the men's political meetings. She worked for the introduction of a new educational system of which Hasnia Bent Othman Ben Salha, who entered what was formerly an all-boys school in 1936, was the first female beneficiary.

She encouraged women to participate along with their husbands and sons in the struggle against colonialism, arguing that the men would be even more effective when supported by their wives and mothers. Given responsibility for propaganda, she brought women to meetings, distributed pamphlets she carried in her shopping bags, going as far as organizing a false "little marriage" (the circumcision of her young son Ahmed) to provide an occasion for distributing pamphlets to the guests. She collected memberships for the movement, called upon merchants to participate in strikes, and disdained those who did not share the anti-colonial ideal.

She brought suit against the colonial authorities when her son, Mouldi Horchani, born in 1904 in Tozeur, was arrested for having led the November 10, 1940, demonstration, having killed a gendarme, and carrying a gun without authorization. Dressed in men's clothing, she visited her son in prison and told him, "you are a lion and your mother is a lioness, you will defeat them!" When she learned that her son had been executed by a firing squad, in 1941, she disappeared for several days into the oasis region, her face covered in ashes and an earthenware plate (*tajine*) hanging from her neck. Sequestered in Jugar, her role was taken up by Hafsia Debeza. After her release, she continued the struggle until independence. And when Habib Bourguiba, visiting Degueche, moved to recognize her sacrifice, she responded, "Mouldi is a martyr."

(c) Meetings with three historic women figures and their stories.

Habiba al-Nabli, wife of Mansour Trabelsi.

Born in 1932, daughter of Ahmed al-Nabli and Aziza Guathoum, she was from a poor urban community in Kairouan, married, with several children.

During the month of Ramadan 1953, French soldiers burst into her home, demanding she turn over the explosive device she possessed. Her family, having no idea of her activities, is astonished to see her turn the device over. She is imprisoned with other militants B Khomais Ouhada, Mohamed Mojraba, Mustapha Ben Abdelkarim, Ali Trabelsi, Mohamed Essid, Ben Khoud, Habib Landoulsi, Hédi Tebib, and Tahar Halillou.

After several days of detention in the Kairouan jail, where she sleeps on the cement floor while the French police come and go as they please and show no respect for the women's modesty, she is put into the prison of Sousse and is photographed—something she finds shocking. Refusing to accept being put among women imprisoned for offenses to morals, she begins a hunger strike that she continues until she is transferred to prison in Tunis.

In the Tunis prison, she again meets Chadlia Bouzgarou and other women. Although Yamina Zouaoui, an elderly woman, takes her under her wing, Chadlia Bouzgarou refuses to accept her among the political prisoners. And, although the police insist on her status as political prisoner, Habiba al-Nabli herself refuses to accept this term from them, for the term "political" in popular speech means "false, hypocritical." Finally, after having been interrogated by Chadlia Bouzgarou and other elderly women, the group agrees to accept her and to begin the adoption ritual. She is placed in the center of a circle formed by Rafia Bornaz, Kmar Ghliss, Fatma Jerbi, Asma Belkhodja, Oum Saad, Yamina Zouaoui, and numerous other women, covered with a flag, and the women then sing patriotic songs and ululate. After this, Chadlia Bouzgarou justifies her earlier reluctance by her fear of a mole infiltrating the group.

After she leaves prison, many people come to celebrate her release, some touching her and looking at her closely, to see whether, under torture, she may have lost her hair, her breasts, and so on. However her father, believing that his daughter Habiba had been led into these supposedly bad actions by her brother-in-law, refuses to permit the celebration of her marriage.

> Fatma Bent Boubaker Ben Ahmed al-Meherzi, born in 1919, sister of the anti-colonial militant Abdelwahed Ben Boubaker, from the rural area of Djebel Bargou, and wife of Belgacem Bouhjar al-Bargaoui

Dressed in mourning clothes during the battle of Djebel Bargou, without jewelry, her face covered in ashes, she prepared meals for the fighters and washed their clothes. She hid an anti-colonial fighter and procured regional dress for him, enabling him to move throughout the region. The colonial army, avenging the killing of two of its soldiers, cut telephone lines, sequestered all village men in one place, sacked the barns, mixed flour and wheat into the foodstuffs, and then doused this in water and, finally, raped Fatma, her sister-in-law, and Shaghaira Bent Ali, her co-wife, in front of their crying children. Several weeks later, her son and two of her daughters died.

Hafsia al-Abrougui, born in 1933, the daughter of Ahmed Ben Mohamed al-Abrougui and Gamra Bent Zaghdoudi

From the rural area of Tajerouine, she was the wife of AbdAllah al-Abrougui. Orphaned early in life, she was raised by her uncle Hafaiedh al-Abrougui, a political militant. She married her cousin AbdAllah in 1956, after both had been raped by the colonial army. In the early 1950s her family was regularly attacked by the colonial army, which set fire to provisions and destroyed work equipment as punishment for the support the family furnished militants who were carrying out sabotage operations and cutting electrical power wires.

One day, the colonial army directly attacks the family. Separating men from women, some soldiers target the women, others the men. Oum Hénia Bent Hafaiedh, her cousin, manages to flee but Zina al-Abrougui, her uncle's wife, has her clothes stripped off in front of her relatives and, suffering from shock, dies on the spot. Three soldiers attack Hafsia al-Abrougui, still a virgin. One of them drags her by the hair into a room, saying, "with blue eyes like that she can't be an Arab"; two others, undressed, rape her. While she struggles to free herself, she is struck in the face and on the leg with a gun, and is seriously injured. Her grandmother, in tears and immobilized by the soldiers' violence, is unable to come to her aid.

Her cousin AbdAllah al-Abrougui, stripped of his clothes, is raped in front of the other men. Then he and his father are brought to the Kef prison, then to Teboursourk camp and finally to Mahdia prison, while other militants from the region are sent to Ben Guerdane. The only militants who were able to avoid being arrested were Ali Ben Issa, Dr Salah Ben Majed, and a third, known under the name of Salah of Tala. In 1956, members of her family were providing aid to the Algerians struggling for their freedom and again found themselves the target of French colonial soldiers.

(d) Undocumented forms of militant activity.

The memories of these militants are not free from distortion, deformations, concealment, or simply errors. The presence of other women who heard these stories repeatedly, or who were witnesses to the actions depicted, enabled the militants to re-discover certain details. Other women or men who were witnesses during this period and/or who participated in the events were able to provide complementary information during our meetings. And, in other cases, some witnesses have called into question particular versions. In addition, during these meetings, the women themselves or the witnesses to their stories expressed these women's ardent desire to defend their country against colonialism and to stand up against oppression.

What should we take from these accounts that evoke moments when women who had not received formal education and perhaps only some modest instruction in the Quran in a family context, who may have been married or single at the time of these events—who were the epitome of grassroots activists—who demonstrated, in their adherence to reformist ideals, women's resilience in the face of both patriarchy and colonialism? These biographical selections are important for many reasons. Among these reasons are that they show us

- undocumented forms of militant activity;
- the networks among which these women militants were active;
- that the political participation of women was not limited to urban areas where it involved mostly women members of the same family or extended family and/or of the same age group, as was the case in the cities of Tunis and Sfax;
- the ways they reacted to humiliation and brutal physical aggression in many forms, including rape, constituted a challenge to the barbarism that was meted to them[19];
- women displaying great autonomy with regard to their families and the centralized structures of the struggle.

Yet, these historic figures have yet to find a place in the school books of the nation or in the names of streets in their localities. In the communities where they were active, fewer and fewer are the people who remember their roles. The biographical notes presented here show the agency and subjectivity of these women, how they lived through their rebellion against colonial domination and patriarchal authority, and also show happy moments and those that were less so, dimensions systematically undiscussed in official history. These biographical notes are not abstract descriptions of actions carried out by women engaged in the anti-colonial struggle but moments where the reader can discover the emotions that suggest the sources of power these women showed in struggling against domination, condemning repression, and protesting against the arrests of militants, against the destruction of their possessions, and against their humiliation. And how, in the course of these struggles, some were raped, others killed. These notes also show us that such sacrifices were not in vain, for they prepared the ground for further actions by women in their communities.

However, despite their significant role in the independence struggle, during the decades since independence, they have not been recognized for their achievements and remain unknown to today's citizens.[20] Against this silence that contributes to cultural and historical amnesia, the life stories justify their historic will to oppose oppression, as Shahrazade struggled against death through her story-telling activity.

Cinema: Witness to the Postcolonial Condition of Tunisian Women

After independence, a number of governmental programs in education, health, and labor were instituted, to the benefit of urban women. The two films we will be analyzing here—*The Season of Men* (*Maussim al-rijal*, Moufida Tlatli, 2000) and *Clay Dolls* (*3ara'is al-Tin*, Nouri Bouzid, 2002)—were both produced almost fifty years after independence and suggest the malaise of women living outside the cities and far from central authority.

Moufida Tlatli, born in 1947 in Sidi Bou Said, a graduate of Institute for Advanced Cinematographic Studies (IDHEC) in Paris, belongs to the first generation of Tunisian filmmakers. She directed her first film, *Samt el-Qusur (Silences of the Palace)* in 1994 and her second film, *Maussim al-rijal (The Season of Men)* won a number of prizes abroad, including the grand prize at the Institut du Monde Arabe in Paris. She was Minister of Culture in the first government following the January 14 revolution, under Prime Minister Mohamed Ghannouchi, from January 17–27, 2011. Nouri Bouzid, who was born in Sfax in 1945, studied cinema in Brussels. From his period of imprisonment for his political opinions (1973–1979), he created two autobiographical films, *Man of Ashes (L'homme de cendres,* 1986) and *Golden Horseshoes (Les sabots d'or*, 1988), and has made several films following these.

(a) For a different dialogue within the couple

In the two films directed by Moufida Tlatli, *Silences of the Palaces* and *The Season of Men,* we are in the presence of two groups of women:

those who don't work (members of the bourgeoisie), and those who do. Of modest origins, her heroines work in kitchens and in textile workshops. We will focus on her second film, *The Season of Men*, which is set in the post-independence period and examines the vision of women whose husbands leave them in order to work abroad or in Tunisian coastal cities (including the capital city of Tunis). The film begins with scenes of Aisha in Tunis, thinking about her life. Flashbacks allow Moufida Tlatli to construct parallels between Aisha's life in the past and the lives of her children today. And the failures in her daughters' relationships with men—one of her daughters is in a marriage that has not been consummated, another is having an affair with her music teacher, himself already married—push her to confront her own failures.

Was Tlatli using Aisha's autistic son to symbolize the lack of communication within the couple, the man's failure to separate himself from his mother? In this context, Aisha takes the decision to return to Djerba to live with her autistic son, interrupting her life with her husband because she realizes that, in fact, this couple has never really been one. And the return to Djerba is for her a way to condemn, simultaneously, men's infidelity, their whims, and their vices. Where Aisha wanted to construct a relationship built upon exchange and sharing, with a man who might resemble her daughter's teacher for whom she had some tender feelings, her husband Said threw himself into the arms of other women, of prostitutes. And this also provides the filmmaker with the opportunity to show that the women's preparations for the men's periodic return were as important as the actual encounter between woman and man, for they constituted moments of solidarity among women who shared the experience of suffering in similar ways.[21]

The language of Aisha and another woman, Zeineb, whose situation is similar to Aisha's, is very Freudian.[22] Through their bodies, they draw upon the unconscious to express their frustrations. Zeineb is waiting for her husband who, since having left her in the days following their marriage, has never returned. Aisha waits expectantly for eleven months for the moment when *The Season of Men* arrives. When, in her desire to reach the city, gain her freedom, and escape from the authority of the family and of her mother-in-law,[23] Aisha asks her husband to sell the carpets that she is weaving and to take her with him, Said offers in response an appeal to tradition—that she give him a son, an allusion to the fact that, up until this point, she has only given birth to girls. Also, whereas we witness scenes of Aisha weaving, nowhere do we see Said handing to her the profit from the sale of her work. With regard to this son, named Aziz (the loved one), Moufida Tlatli says that Aisha "desires this son who will free her and enable her to go to Tunis but, at the same time, she doesn't want this child because he also signifies the superiority of males over females."[24] Tlatli also shows the husband's parents forbidding their daughter-in-law from going to the doctor, from going out, from visiting those close to her, just as the mother-in-law physically disciplines the daughter-in-law. Aisha's husband allows her no say over the money from the carpets she weaves, which he sells in Tunis.[25] These women undergo psychological suffering. Whereas Aisha deals with her own psychological suffering, disappointments, anxieties, and conflicts, her difficulties seem to be reflected by her children, all of whom display some symptoms of psychological disturbance.

If a few researchers during the 1970s focused on emigrant workers, a very small minority of these showed any interest in the wives. And this lack of attention was even more acute in the case of those women whose husbands, while having left the household, emigrated internally and did not cross national boundaries. Therefore, Moufida Tlatli's film manages not only to partially fill this gap but also constructs images where silence has taken the place of history. Her film renders well the affective deprivations endured by the women who remain alone in their regions.[26]

(b) "Creative women" in the service of the bourgeoisie of the capital

Nouri Bouzid's film *Clay Dolls* treats the phenomena of sacrificed children, and the gulf between the urban and rural, between the wealthy and the poor. The director approaches these via the case of a middleman who provides maids to the new rich and who vouches for the virtue of the young maids. These domestic workers usually come from rural villages,[27] most of them from the northwest and central-west regions of the country.[28] The film presents us a man, Omrane, who himself grew up as a domestic worker for a family living in the capital. Afterward he became a middleman between families seeking employment for their daughters and the families that hire them. He returns to the village monthly with the wages of the employed girls, giving these wages to the parents, while also looking for new recruits. In the course of this search he comes upon Feddha, a young girl aged eight, and asks her whether she wants to go to the city. Her response is immediate and positive, with her face lighting up at the thought. With her parents' approval and carrying the clay she plays with, she gets on Omrane's motorized tricycle and together they travel toward the city. In a scene where they have great difficulty pushing the vehicle in the hilly new Tunis suburb of En-Nasr, we get a feeling for the suffering of these children who are pulled out of their own universe.

Putting Feddha in an attic, Omrane goes to look for Rebbeh, a girl in late adolescence, whom he doesn't find at her employer's home because, having been sexually abused by their son, she has fled. Rebbeh is, for her part, also looking for Omrane, and she walks through the streets at night, stopping at cafes that serve alcohol and are frequented only by men seeking to forget their misery. When they finally do meet, we come to understand that each feels some tenderness toward the other. Rebbeh meets Feddha, her alter-ego through whom the director portrays the earlier experiences of Rebbeh. When young, Feddha made dolls out of clay in her village; now, in the city, she is ushered into a family where her main task will be watching over a sick man—a symbol here of the current state of the bourgeoisie. Feddha is shocked by this world so different from the one she knows and her clay, with which she made the traditional clay dolls and which comforted her, is confiscated by the mistress of the house. She too then flees, wanders the streets, and finally finds Omrane. We discover in the course of the film that he too has been a victim of an employer's sexual violence.

Nouri Bouzid wants to show that whereas men, traditional and modern, construct women according to their own vision, the women and men who have understood the role of patriarchy, because they have suffered under it, struggle against these visions to construct their own personalities, their own representations, on the basis of their own choices, analyses, and subjectivity. The women and girls, all the Rebbehs and Feddhas, work on clay and make dolls as they imagine them and as they imagine themselves to be since their uprooting, that is to say, as broken dolls. Here, too, the city has been unable to provide a welcome for these artists with their traditional artistic skills.

The living situation in rural areas throughout the independence period has been very difficult. Up until the 1990s, medical coverage was minimal,[29] with mobile medical teams, vaccination campaigns, programs to combat diarrhea and respiration problems, and so on, serving this "second Tunisia." In 1980, the Tunisian population numbered 6,369,000 of which 823,000 were classified as poor—that is, 13% of the total population. In the northwest, 188,000 people of a population of 1,068,000 had household budgets under the poverty threshold. The children of the northwest, deprived of minimum needs, lived in areas having the lowest employment rate in all Tunisia and also the lowest schooling proportions and the worst living conditions (dwellings, equipment, etc.).

Poor rural families have, over the four decades that followed independence, placed their daughters as workers in urban families. It wasn't uncommon to see many cars on the roads and fields, with passengers on the lookout for that special girl who knew how to cook, clean, iron, take care of the children, and so on. At the outset, the wages these girls earned was symbolic and placing them in urban families was one way to assure their nourishment, since conditions in rural areas were so difficult. Just a few bills of paper money given to parents in the northwest would get them to close their eyes to the behavior of the host family. Nor was it rare for the young girl's work to provide the funds permitting a brother to attend university, or the father to finish repairing the roof of the house, or to offer medical care for the sick mother.

A foreign journalist, who investigated the situation of working children in the Third World, noticed "maids ten years old, coming from the rural areas to be employed by a bourgeoisie that wants to be served in the same style as the former colonizers or the ex-pachas, but doesn't have the money to treat themselves to real domestic help."[30] Therefore, girls like Rebbeh/Feddha, having arrived at a very young age in the city, learn to reject a rural world they no longer know, no longer want to know, and the values they no longer appreciate.[31] Ilhem Marzouki interviewed fifty domestic workers (twenty-five currently and twenty-five formerly employed) together with twenty-five mistresses of the house, and confirms what we have argued. The workers told her: "I don't like to go home because our home is isolated and it has no conveniences"; "I don't like going home—after two days I've had enough and I prefer what has become my new family"; "I don't like my home because I no longer like my father."[32]

From house to house, these young women domestic workers also swell the ranks of the unmarried—a woman, after having spent many years in one family raising three children from birth to adulthood, was suddenly dismissed from her position because she dared to say that she hoped she wouldn't be forgotten when the time came to apportion the family's inheritance. They may join the ranks of those who rebel,[33] or become prostitutes,[34] or become single mothers, or even commit suicide.[35] One widely discussed case involved a young girl who had been raped by an employer who managed to have the matter hushed up by giving the father five dinars to state that his daughter was not a virgin when she entered service. Revolted by such an action, the young girl broke with her father and found a job as a hospital attendant in a neighborhood rife with prostitution, to which she eventually succumbed.[36] Much of the time, when these prostitutes are arrested by the police, they are put in reeducation centers.[37]

Despite their differences, both *The Season of Men* and *Clay Dolls* have, nonetheless, a common point in the manner in which the two film-makers approach their subject, putting the accent on experience, pain—on emotional life and sexuality. Moufida Tlatli focuses on Aisha, who looks back on a life filled with frustration and a succession of failures: marital, educational, her son's autism as symptom of a couple unable to communicate, and Aisha's return to Djerba after numerous struggles in the city. Nouri Bouzid explores the exploitation of creative girls who become domestic workers and who, thrown onto the streets, have no future and have lost their dreams.

Whereas Tunisian cinema has for a long time concerned itself with social and political questions, it now seems to be becoming an explorer of the social psyche.[38] When Moufida Tlatli explores Aisha's suffering, she represents a woman suffering in a society where men, dominated by the mother, are unable to achieve a humanizing sexuality. Nouri Bouzid, whose political commitment is evident in all his films, puts Rebbeh/Feddha and Omrane in opposition to the employers/the rich. Unlike in Moufida Tlatli's films, Bouzid shows that the differences between the sexes diminish once it is a question of their experiences. They share the same pain. When the husband rejects his wife, and when the masters do violence to their employees Rebbeh and Omrane, and when the mistress of the house tears the clay away from Feddha, they deprive their victims of their words and of their dreams. Damaged, they are no longer able to create, to live.

Whereas the institutions and spectators who may be expressing the same attitude of *sitr* (don't see/don't show)—a cultural value signifying a refusal to take pleasure in viewing others' unhappiness, in the poverty and sexual misery of women[39]—to choose, today, to ignore women's struggles, yesterday against colonialism and for their rights, today for new forms of communication and relations within the couple and for new dreams, is to work against the truth, against *Tajahur* (public revealing).

Diverse Situations, One Response

The psychological phenomena of repression and repetition compulsion can help us understand why the experiences of historic women figures in their fight against colonialism, and of young and adult women in their daily struggles for dignity, have been neglected by social/political institutions and by the public. *Sitr* (keeping things hidden, protecting privacy), usually a value protecting an individual's intimacy, in this particular context, operates against women, hiding their participation in battling for an improvement in the quality of life. At the moment of Tunisia's exaltation at its liberation from colonial rule, *sitr* worked to the advantage of the "Supreme Combatant's" charisma to promote a "masculine feminism"—that is, where decisions and visions are determined by the country's masculine leadership. The promulgation of the Personal Status Code in 1956, which owed much to the legitimacy of Habib Bourguiba, was accomplished while silencing women's contribution to the country's liberation. In this context, the dominant powers and their ideology manipulated with great success the notions of identity, while historic figures, relegated to a subordinate level, began themselves to forget the roles they played. Rafia Bornaz, very weakened, was one who forgot her role, saying, "AI was forgotten. I forgot." The repression of women's contributions repeats itself several decades later, when the public fails to empathize, in films such as Tlatli's *The Season of Men* and Bouzid's *Clay Dolls,* with women characters who struggle to promote new situations, to realize new dreams.

Our resuscitating such experiences operates here like a return to consciousness, rescuing women militants from neglect and rehabilitating women, young girls, and adolescent girls, in their true dignity. Bringing to the forefront women's struggles against oppression, as was done during the 1980s by feminist researchers whom we will discuss below, can work against the repetition compulsion of psychological wounds, and gain for these women resisting oppression the respect they deserve, as noted by Ann E. Cudd.[40]

In his *Theory of Justice*, Rawls discusses how Kant argues that not acting in accordance with the law gives birth to feelings of shame, and how, by acting in an unjust manner, the individual fails to express human beings' rational nature and their free and equal relationship to one another, thus leading to a loss of self-respect.[41] These authors are referring to behavior that is also central to the concept of social justice in Islam, characterized by integrity, honesty, and virtue—notions that, under the regimes of Bourguiba and Ben Ali, lost all their meaning, with the Tunisian public, after the revolution of January 2011, realizing the extent of Ben Ali's mockery of them.[42]

The Arabic word for justice, *3adl*, is used as both a noun and adjective; as noun it means "justice" and as adjective it means "straight, just, balanced," applies to people and to things, and is a basis for legitimacy in the exercise of power. Mawardi sees *3adl* as a state of moral and religious perfection; for Ibn Rushd, it consists in not committing major sins and avoiding minor ones. Although *3adl* and *3adala* have the same root, the first means the justice system, and the second refers to social justice. Here, it is interesting to note that violations of *3adala* are termed *jarh* (wound, injury).[43] For the contemporary author Salâh al-Din al-Munadjid, morals in Islam refer to the virtue that stops one from attacking the rights of others and from allowing oneself to engage in bad acts.[44] With this in mind, the lack of recognition given to the experiences and emotions of women by political and social institutions has implications with regard to notions of justice, in situations where the public appears uninterested in women's psychological wounds and abandons its social responsibility. Bartky's work shows us, in this context, how the political order may force groups to interpret life from the perspective of the dominant social group, generating among the dominated groups feelings of deficient abilities and denial of value.[45] For Amartya Sen, states (or, we might say, social and political institutions) that are satisfied with looking at their populations only in terms of needs have "a meager view of humanity."[46]

Here, we would like to turn to the experience of feminists of the 1980s, which shows how feminist research, the work of creative artists, and civil society constituted a response on the level of social responsibility to the legitimate expectations of women. This is consonant with what Amartya Sen calls the "agency role" that is "central to recognizing people as responsible persons: not only are we well or ill, but also we act or refuse to act, and can choose to act one way rather than another."[47] Feminist researchers raised questions about the situation of women and devoted particular attention to women's history.[48] In the political domain, they privileged oral history,[49] socio-historical research,[50] archival studies[51] cinema.[52] Collective works were also published by associations such as Association des Femmes Tunisiennes pour la Recherche sur le Développement (AFTURD) and by centers such as Centre de recherche et d'étude pour la diffusion du français (CREDIF).[53] These studies and others brought forward the actions of women and the birth and growth of women's movements during the first half of the twentieth century, and dealt almost exclusively with women figures from urban areas.[54]

They show how women's involvement in the struggle against colonialism and for their rights created a favorable climate for the promulgating in 1956 of a Personal Status Code that enhanced women's rights, outlawing polygyny, making divorce follow a judicial process, establishing equality of salary for both sexes, prohibiting stoning as a punishment for adultery, and expanding women's inheritance rights. These studies have also shown how these women organized women's associations and how, with many unaffiliated women intensifying pressure in this direction, they all contributed to establishing a republican form of government and to subsequent social, cultural, and political developments as well. They also have had the effect of shedding new light on the discussion over women's rights in Tunisia. In addition, they have enabled the autonomous feminist movement of the 1980s to see its links to the historic women figures. Educated women who were active in women's circles in the 1950s were encouraged in this context to publish their autobiographies.[55] They showed a renewed taste for this genre and a number of them published their own autobiographies.[56] In addition, some families were motivated to publish family documents reflecting women's actions—some published letters,[57] others tributes,[58] others press articles,[59] all bringing forward the contribution of women in the social, cultural, and/or political fields.

Conclusion

To conclude, can we say that this interest in women's history and women's contribution to the construction of democracy have succeeded in conquering institutional resistance and disinterest on the part of the public? Not completely. On the one hand, the lack of written and oral archives in this area today remains very striking and, in addition, the interest of the families in such publications, and the interest of institutions as well, remains problematic. Of course this varies from family to family, but it also varies from region to region and according to the political situation as well.[60] For example, films treating activist women are very rare in Tunisia.[61] The political history of women has no specific place in any of the university departments of history, nor is there a civil society association devoted to preserving the memory of politically active women.[62] On the other hand, this discussion, which had its apogee during the 1980s, encouraged, in the variety of its forms—publications, expositions, roundtables, the magazine *Nissa*, public presentations of published works, debates—a passion for knowledge regarding historic women figures and for a recognition of the experiences and emotions of women, as a way to defend society's achievements against the attacks on the PSC in the 1980s and, again, in 2011–2012.

The policy of "yes . . . but"—of giving women rights but always within limits—explains why over more than a century the women's question has remained a political issue every time society experiences a cultural transition, as was the case in the 1950s and as is the case since the January 2011 revolution. Will the current situation take into account the appeal of those women who immolated themselves as a way to denounce their marginalization? The law on political parity adopted in 2011 by the High Instance for the Realization of the Objectives of the Revolution, of Political Reform, and of the Democratic Transition (which was formed in March 2011), meant to ensure greater presence and participation of women in writing the new constitution, should encourage significant progress in the discussion over women's participation in formal politics. This law opened the door for women, especially those of the Nahdha party—the party that had suffered from discrimination under the various Tunisian regimes—to take seats in the Constituent Assembly after the October 2011 elections.

Those who have been elected, and the various political parties, have they heard what the women who immolated themselves were saying? Are they attentive to what Alia, the protagonist of *The Silence of the Palaces*, or Aicha in *The Season of Men,* are saying about relations between men and women and within the couple during the 1960s as well as during the 2000s? Do they hear what Feddha and Rebbeh, characters in the film *Clay Dolls*, are saying about their uprooting from the rural world and their situation as maids in urban bourgeois families?

Article 28 in the draft for the new constitution was adopted by the Commission for Freedoms and Rights, the majority of which is composed of Nahdha party members who won in the October 2011 elections. This article provoked a heated controversy. The notion of "complementarity," which article 28 employed, raised fears, during the summer of 2012, that Tunisia's PSC might suffer the same setbacks as occurred when the new Algerian family code was adopted in 1984. For Tunisian feminists and civil society, this notion recalls the logic of master and slave, attacks women's achievements, puts forward a paternalistic approach, and refuses to recognize women's right to citizenship as equal to men's, among its other failings. Nahdha party members' declarations, as well as their having signed an agreement in 1988 affirming their support of the PSC, were not enough to allay the fears. The ATFD (Tunisian Association of Democratic Women) demanded that article 28 be withdrawn and jurists proposed that equality between men and women be part of an agreement on human and citizen rights that would be submitted by referendum to the population and would have a legal value superior to the constitution. The choice that many Algerian families had made for exile following the new 1984 family code, that they would not accept living under discriminatory laws, was still strong in the minds of Tunisians and demonstrations were organized in a number of Tunisian regions. Following this controversy, a number of figures of the political elite left their political parties to join the newly formed Nida Tounis political party, which presented itself as defending women's rights.

This new dynamic, similar to the one during the 1950s, pushed the Joint Committee of the Constituent Assembly, responsible for ensuring coherence in the work of the assembly's various commissions, to respond to the controversy by modifying article 28, replacing "complementarity" with "equality" between men and women and equality in their professional opportunities, so that women might no longer feel it necessary to engage in extreme forms of protest, like self-immolation, to denounce social injustice. Now, this equality must also be extended into other areas of social life and into all of Tunisia's regions.

This controversy, as well as other developments, shows that the struggle for women's rights has not led to irreversible achievements, but that this is an ongoing struggle, one that should recognize its roots in the actions of its historical figures. The women who immolated themselves following the January 2011 revolution are among the new figures of Tunisian feminism, and their story remains to be written. My discussion here has shown, I hope, how important it is to listen to the voices of women, whether they be historic figures or women today struggling to improve their lives—the struggles of all these groups are joined together.

Notes

1 Salah Musbah, "La philosophie des couples," *Le Temps*, November 17, 2008. However, Salah Mosbah, head of the philosophy department at the Faculty of Human and Social Sciences of the University of Tunis, denied authorship of this article in a "right of reply" published in *Le Temps* (November 21, 2008), claiming that his identity had been stolen, that he had never been in contact with the publisher of *Le Temps*, and he expressed his solidarity with his colleagues and reserved the right to initiate a legal case against the author of the original article.
2 Mona Gamra, "111 cas de suicides, depuis le 14 janvier 2011, dont 69 par immolation par le feu," *Le Temps*, June 16, 2011.
3 Rym Ghachem, Afif Boussetta, Ahmed Benasr, and Nejla Oumaya found, among the patients in the psychiatric hospital between 1994 and 2005, a rate of 2% by self-immolation, 58% cases of suicide by hanging, 10% by ingestion of medicines, and 10% by poisoning. In all, 82% were men, 50% suffered from psychoses, 65.8% were unmarried, 76.3% were unemployed, and 84.2% lived in poor socioeconomic circumstances. In "Suicide et pathologie à Tunis: étude rétrospective sur 12 ans à l'hôpital Razi," *L'information psychiatrique* 85, no 3 (March 2009): 21–23.
4 See Messadi et al. (1988).
5 Cited by Carole André Dessornes, "Les shahidas—Femmes kamikazes dans le monde arabo-musulman," *Geopldia*, October 2008, accessed May 29, 2013, http://www.geopoldia.org/index.php/fr/component/content/article/6-articles/22-les-shahidas.
6 There were a few individual challenges: Zyed Krichen in "La philosophie en Tunisie et ses adversaires" called the article a public "lynching" (*Réalités*, no. 1196, November 27–December 3, 2008); Tahar Ben Guiza in "De la philosophie des couples aux couples de la philosophie" denounced the article's defamatory nature, wondering "How long are we going to have to tolerate this type of buffoonery and defamation . . .?" (*Réalités*, no. 1202, 8–14 January 2009).

Table 1 Number of Entries during the First Five Weeks in the Theaters in Tunis and the Rest of the Country.

Week	*The Season of Men*	*Clay Dolls*
1	5,200 (3 days)	4,618
2	10,466	3,930
3	8,368	2,626
4	3,220	1,788
5	2,361	1,325 + 303 (week 6 in one theater)
Total	29,615	14,590

Note. I would like to thank Mme Hayet Lejeri-Abassi of COTUDIC and Mr Mondher Farhat of APOLLO for having provided me with these figures. Film distributors in Tunisia estimate that a film must reach 90,000 entries to be considered profitable, a number attained by some Egyptian films (such as those featuring the stars Muhammad Heneidi and Adel Imam) and certain films from the West, such as James Cameron's *Titanic*.

Table 2 Types of Women Militants' Acts and Their Consequences.

Item	*Mdalla*	*Fatma (from Degueche)*	*Habiba*	*Fatma (from Djebel Bargou)*	*Hafsia*
Militant act	Liaison; pamphlet distribution.	Liaison; propaganda, pamphlet distribution; raising women's political consciousness; encourages merchants to support strikes; initiates complaints against the colonial authorities.	Hides a bomb.	Provides support for militants (washes their clothes, cooks, hides a militant, and procures regional dress for him).	Provides support for militants.
Consequence	Sentenced to a prison term.	Her son is executed by the colonial army; she is sequestered in the Jugar camp.	Interrogated at the police commissariat; arrested in Sousse; tried in Tunis; and sentenced to a prison term.	Her goods are destroyed; she is raped in front of her children; her son and two daughters die shortly after the rape.	Raped in the presence of her grandmother.

Table 3 Characteristics of Women Militants and the Relatives with Whom They Acted.

Item	*Mdalla*	*Fatma (from Degueche)*	*Habiba*	*Fatma (from Djebel Bargou)*	*Hafsia*
Born–died	? –1941	1881–1977	1932–	1919–	1933–
Education	Qur'anic school	Qur'anic school	Qur'anic school	Qur'anic school	Qur'anic school
Civil status at time of militancy	Married with one child	Divorced and remarried with children.	Engaged to be married.	Married with children.	Unmarried
Region	Medjez-al-Bab	Degueche	Kairouan	Djebel Bargou	Tajerouine
Date of political activity	1952	1934	1953	1954	1952
Relatives who were also militants	Husband	Son	Brother-in-law	Brother and husband	Father-in-law and cousin

7 Ii is not the first time that women university professors have been attacked by male colleagues, often below them in rank and age, without administrative sanction or public response.
8 See Al-hamami (2005).
9 See Ben Sassi (2009).
10 The repression of women's participation in the construction of the nation is also evoked in *Fatma 75*, a film directed by Selma Baccar on the occasion of the 1975 International Women's Year, which mixed documentary and fiction and was seen as calling into question this aspect of the dominant discourse, leading to the film's being censored.
11 See Table 1.
12 Reem Saad, "Shame, Reputation and Egypt's Lovers: A Controversy over a Nation's Image." *Visual Anthropology* 10 (1998): 401–12. Saad discusses a similar controversy in Egypt over what images of a nation are appropriate representations and who should control their distribution.
13 Hédi Khelil writes that "the audaciousness of filmmaker Nouri Bouzid [lies in his taking] as main characters individuals who are wounded and vulnerable, whose status as men is called into question by those around him" [AMatière, "mémoire et regard," *Sociétés. Revue des Sciences Humaines et Sociales*, no. 28 (1990): 27–30, with this citation from p. 27].
14 See Cudd (2006).
15 Sen (1999: 115–16).
16 John Rawls, *Théorie de la justice* (Paris: Editions du Seuil, 1997), 473. Rawls considers self-respect, one of the primary goods, to occupy a central position in the moral psychology that is at the foundation of the theory of justice as equity.
17 See As-sulami (1999).
18 Cf. Golley (2003).
19 See Table 2.
20 See Table 3.
21 Cf. Barlet (2000).
22 The scarcity of hospitals and official care-givers contributes to the fact that many women seek recourse with traditional healers. In the Er-Razi hospital, there were twelve psychiatrists in 1972, twenty in 1979, and thirty-one in 1985. In the year 2000, the number of psychiatrists reached 130. See Tunisian Ministry of Public Health/Tunis: Institut National de Santé Publique, *Trente ans au service de la santé. Un engagement, une éthique*, Collectif (Tunis: Ministry of Health Publication, 1986), 82 et 142.
23 See Karoui (1989, 69).
24 Barlet, "Interview with Moufida Tlatli."
25 See Belhassine (2002) and Labidi and Hamza (1983).
26 In "De la solitude des femmes du Sud," I discussed how women whose husbands have emigrated to work dress in mourning clothes during the eleven months the husbands are absent: clothes were worn inside out and house decorations were taken down (*Le Temps*, August 8, 1980); Fadhila Bergaoui, "AAvez-vous entendu parler de Boujilda?," *La Presse*, June 20, 2002.
27 The province of Jendouba had been the target, since the 1970s, of massive family planning programs. It is reported that, in 2004, the region obtained the best figures in Tunisia for natural population growth, at 1.02%, compared with a national figure of 1.08% (see Unsigned article. "AJendouba—Planning familial. Des résultats Positifs," *La Presse*, February 25, 2004).
28 Naima Karoui shows how, in the interior and rural areas of the country, the raising to seventeen of the minimum age at marriage for girls led to an exodus from rural areas of underprivileged groups who, unable to support their daughters for this

longer period, were obliged to look for work in the cities and to seek employment for their daughters. Karoui, "ALe couple en Tunisie: du discours à la réalité," 59–73, especially 67.

29 Women had to travel long distances in order to reach a healthcare facility. In addition to the scarcity of official healthcare institutions, doctors for a long time systematically refused to work in poor areas of the country. After independence, in order to increase medical presence in these areas the government trained large numbers of midwives, with a course of study much shorter than that for gynecologists and obstetricians, and also attracted doctors from Eastern Europe and China.

30 A study carried out by *Le Monde* (December 27–30, 1979) on working children in the Third World, cited by Ilhem Marzouki in her "Le travail des enfants: cas des employées de maison" (master's thesis, Faculté des Sciences Humaines de Tunis, 1982).

31 The representation of settings outside the capital city of Tunis in telefilms as well as in the Tunisian theater systematically devalues these settings. During Ramadan 2010, the Tunisian television series *Nsibti laâziza* (*My dear mother-in-law)* showed characters speaking with a caricature of the Sfax dialect, which led to controversy and a petition requesting that the series be discontinued.

32 Marzouki, "Le travail des enfants."

33 Young men from impoverished areas also suffer from this deprivation. The countries north of the Mediterranean have become a kind of Eldorado for the youth of the south. With legal entry increasingly restricted, those wanting to emigrate often have to take serious risks, putting themselves in small boats and setting off on a journey described, in everyday language, as *Al-Harqa* (burning), with their families describing the emigrants as *fallagha* (guerrilla fighters). This phenomenon has figured importantly in films from the Maghreb, such as Merzak Allouache's *Harraga* (2010) and Mahmoud Ben Mahmoud's *La Traversée* (1982). For a discussion of the importance of emigration to Europe in Morocco and Moroccan cinema, see Kevin Dwyer, *Beyond Casablanca* (Bloomington: Indiana University Press, 2004).

34 Christelle Taraud (in *La prostitution coloniale. Algérie, Tunisie, Maroc (1830–1962)*, Paris: Payot, 2003) relates that prostitutes often found refuge in the *zawiya*-s during the colonial period.

35 Sleim Ammar [in "Le suicide, problème de santé mentale," *Tunisie médicale*, no. 2 (March–April 1972): 99–120] shows how, starting in 1970, the number of suicides among women bypassed that of men. Since then, further studies show that this trend has been maintained. A group of medical studies on suicide carried out in the final decade of the twentieth century show a large proportion of such acts committed by women, unmarried persons, youth, and individuals who reached secondary school. Hanging and drowning gave way to medicines as means. Aside from psychiatric cases, the reasons that appear to motivate such acts are family environment, unemployment, or a recent death.

36 Lorna Durrani [in "Tensions and Role Conflict in the Tunisian Family," *Maghreb Review* 2, no. 3 (May/June 1977): 13–17] discusses how a pregnant girl, abandoned by her family, might easily be tempted by prostitution as a way to earn a living and provide for the needs of her child (p. 16).

37 L. Pruvost, *La prostitution des mineures*, Mémoire en Sciences Criminelles (Tunis: University of Tunis, 1973).

38 Hédi Khelil relates, in "Salah Abou Seif: entretiens de Hachem Nahhass. L'oeuvre passée au crible," *La Presse*, November 1, 2003, how the critic H. Nahhass wrote that the Egyptian filmmaker Abou Seif chose social commitment, trying to be the most faithful mirror of the concerns of the poor and middle classes. And if Abou Seif was able to move the public in the Arab world, it's because he "mastered the art of cinematic language and the techniques of narration."

39 Mustapha Nasraoui, "Les réactions des tunisiens non pauvres à la vue des pauvres," in *Les déterminismes socio-culturels de la pauvreté* (Tunis: CERES, 1994, Série Sociologique no. 23, 241–258, especially 247, 248, 258) concludes that ideas about poverty are dominated by notions of charity and sympathy, rather than leading to imagining solutions involving social or political-economic measures.
40 Cudd, *Analyzing Oppression*, 163–65.
41 Rawls, *Théorie de la justice*, 292.
42 TAP, "Tunisie—Bilan des biens confisqués de la liste des 114 du Clan Ben Ali," *Businessnews.com*, accessed January 1, 2014, http://www.businessnews.com.tn/Tunisie—Bilan-des-biens-confisqu%25C3%25A9s-de-la-liste-des-114-du-Clan-Ben-Ali,520,31654,3.
43 Robert Brunschvig, *Encyclopédie de l'Islam*, vol. 1 (Paris: Maisonneuve et Larose, 1975), 215–16.
44 See al-Munadjdjid (1982, 103–104).
45 See Bartsky (1990, 22–32).
46 See Sen (2009, 250).
47 See Sen (1999, 288).
48 Among the works discussing women's political activity in the Maghreb, we find Alison Baker, *Voices of Resistance: Oral Histories of Moroccan Women* (New York: State University of New York Press, 1998); Simone de Beauvoir and Gisèle Halimi, *Djamila Boupacha* (Paris: Gallimard, 1962); Djamila Amrane, *Les femmes Algériennes dans la guerre* (Paris: Plon, 1991); Anne Nivat (Récit recueilli par), *Louisette Ighilahriz. Algérienne* (Paris: Fayard/Calmann-Lévy, 2001); Fatima Zohra Saï, *Mouvement National et question féminine. Des origines à la veille de la guerre de libération nationale* (Oran: Editions Dar elGharb, 2002); Tahar Oussedik, *Lla Fat'ma n'Soumeur: Récit* (Alger: ENAG Editions, 2005).
49 See Labidi (2007)
50 See Marzouki (1993).
51 See Largueche and Largueche (1992) and Blili (1999).
52 Tunisia has what we might see as two generations of women filmmakers. Selma Baccar, Nejia Ben Mabrouk, and Moufida Tlatli can be situated in the first generation, marked by psychoanalysis; Nadia el-Fani, Raja Amari, and others of the second generation, often raise social issues.
53 AFTURD (Collective), *Tunisiennes en devenir*, vols. 1 and 2 (Tunis: Cérès Productions, 1992); CREDIF-ISHMN (Collective), *Mémoire de femmes. Tunisiennes dans la vie publique. 1920–1960* (Tunis: Edition Media COM, 1993).
54 Several women figures contributed to institutionalizing the urban women's movement. Nazli Fadil, daughter of Prime Minister Mustapha Fadil Bacha, who was involved in starting the "modernist" al-Khaldounia foundation in 1896 and also founded a literary salon; Manoubia Wertani, the first woman to remove the veil in public, in 1924, and Habiba Menchari, who repeated this gesture in 1929; Wassila Ben Ammar and Nejiba Ben M'Rad, who founded the Association des Femmes Musulmanes in 1932, led by Fatma Guellaty; Saida Ben Chedly and Zohra Bouhageb, who organized, starting in 1933, meetings on religious holidays during which they gave political speeches; Bchira Ben M'rad (the daughter of Shaykh Mohamed Salah Ben M'Rad, author of a pamphlet against Tahar Haddad's call for a reconsideration of the role of Tunisian women), leader of the Union des Femmes Musulmanes de Tunisie from 1936 on with her sisters and cousins Asma, Souad, Radhia and Fatma Belkhodja, who led the Union Féminine starting in 1938; from the 1940s, the Union des Femmes de Tunisie, a communist organization, led by Charlotte Joulain and, later by Nebiha Ben Miled; Souad al-Khattech, who led the women's section of *Shuban al-Muslimin* [Muslim Youth] from 1944 on; Bakhta Saddam, who founded the first women's section in the Scout movement in 1944; l'Union des Jeunes

Filles de Tunisie, women's sections in the Neo-Destour movement as well as in the Jeunesse Scolaire organization, that began to spread across the country in 1950; the Club de la Jeune Fille Tunisienne, begun in 1954; the Comités de Secours, directed by the princesses of the Bey's family, which expanded over this period; and the Union Nationale des Femmes de Tunisie, directed by Aicha Bellagha, founded in 1956. Many Tunisian Jewish women were involved in this struggle, among them Gladys Adda, Roberte Bijaoui, Beatrice Slama, Juliette Bessis, Gisele Halimi, and so on.

55 See Bornaz (1993), Haddad (1995), Bornaz (1999), Babbou (2002), Mabrouk (2001), and Nazli (2010).

56 See Ghanmi (1993) and Jrad (1996).

57 See Medimegh (2007).

58 Women from Sfax, Nabeul, and other localities have, with increasing frequency, documented the actions of women from their regions.

59 See Ben Miled (2005).

60 For example, I had collected Chedlia Bouzgarou's life history and she was in favor of publishing this, until the moment she returned to formal politics in 1986, after the divorce between Habib Bourguiba and his wife Wassila Ben Ammar (with whom Bouzgarou was often in open conflict). At this point, while Fatma Douik was head of the *Union nationale des femmes tunisiennes* (UNFT), Chedlia Bouzgarou was elected head of the Consultative Commission of Women Militants, which was reactivated.

61 Selma Baccar directed *Fatma 75* in 1975 for the United Nations International Women's Decade, a film that was for a long time censored by the authorities. In 2011, Sonia Chamkhi directed a film on the women who had been heads of political party election lists for the October 2011 elections, as well as on women active in civil society.

62 The public presentations of Master's and PhD theses of women researchers such as Meriam al-Gaied's *Discours psychiatrique dans le monde arabe. Le cas de la Tunisie* [treating the itinerary of Saida Douki, the first woman president of *l'Association Tunisienne de psychiatrie*; Tunis: Université de Tunis (Mémoire DEA), 2001], and the public discussion of the state thesis (*thèse d'état*) of Leila Blili showed the strength of opposition, in university circles, to the development of feminist research projects. A group of women researchers, which has submitted a formal request to create an association devoted to documenting women's history, has not obtained permission in 2005.

References

Al-Hamami, S. 2005. "AAna hazina hata al-maouet wa fi qalbi ghossat alam ismouha Aal-jazaer" [I Am Extremely Sad, and in My Heart There Is Pain Called Algeria]. *Al-Mar'aa al-Youm* 204:32–45.

Al-Munadjdjid, S. 1982. *Le concept de justice sociale en islam*. Paris: Editions Publisud.

Ammar, S. 1972. "Le suicide, problème de santé mentale." *Tunisie médicale* 2 (March–April): 99–120.

Amrane, D. 1991. *Les femmes Algériennes dans la guerre*. Paris: Plon.

As-Sulami, A. A. 1999. *Early sufi women: Dhikr an-Niswa al-Muta'abbidat as-Suffiyyat*. Translated by E. Rkia. Louisville: Fonsvitae.

Babbou, A. 2002. *Itinéraire*. Tunis: Apollonia.

Baker, A. 1998. *Voices of Resistance: Oral Histories of Moroccan Women*. New York: State University of New York Press.

Barlet, O. 2000. "Interview with Moufida Tlatli." Cannes, May. Accessed March 21, 2013. http://www.africultures.com/php/index.php?nav=article&no=5475&texte_recherche=interview%20with%20moufida%20tlatli.

Bartky, L. S. 1990. "On Psychological Oppression." In *Femininity and Domination: Studies in the Phenomenology of Oppression*, edited by L. S. Bartky, 22–32. New York: Routledge.
Belhassine, O. 2002. Mon père, cet éternel invité. *La Presse*, June 20, 5–6.
Ben Guiza, T. 2009. "De la philosophie des couples aux couples de la philosophie." *Réalités* 1202 (January): 8–14.
Ben Miled, E. 2005. "L'Islam ouvert à la rencontre de la modernité." *Réalités* 994 (January): 40–41.
Ben Sassi, L. 1989. Histoire de femmes. Aux dames bien nées, la valeur a attendu le nombre des années. *Tunis Hebdo*, August 21, 21–22.
Bergaoui, F. 2002. "Avez-vous entendu parler de Boujilda?" *La Presse*, June 20, 4–5.
Blili, L. 1999. *Histoire de familles. Mariages, répudiations et vie quotidienne, 1875–1930*. Tunis: Script Publications.
Bornaz, M. 1993. *Cétait Tunis 1920*. Tunis: Cérès Editions.
Bornaz, M. 1999. *Maherzia se souvient. Tunis 1930. Récit*. Tunis: Cérès Editions.
Brunschvig, R. 1975. *Encyclopédie de l'Islam*. Vol. 1. Paris: Maisonneuve et Larose.
Cudd, A. E. 2006. *Analyzing Oppression*. New York: Oxford University Press.
de Beauvoir, S., and G. Halimi. 1962. *Djamila Boupacha*. Paris: Gallimard.
Dessornes, C. A. 2008. "Les shahidas—Femmes kamikazes dans le monde arabo-musulman." *Geopldia*, October. Accessed May 29, 2013. http://www.geopoldia.org/index.php/fr/component/content/article/6-articles/22-les-shahidas.
Durrani, L. 1977. "Tensions and Role Conflict in the Tunisian Family." *Maghreb Review* 2, no. 3 (May/June): 13–17.
Dwyer, K. 2004. *Beyond Casablanca*. Bloomington: Indiana University Press.
Gamra, M. 2011. 111 cas de suicides, depuis le 14 janvier 2011, dont 69 par immolation par le feu. *Le Temps*, June 16, 7–8.
Ghachem, R., A. Boussetta, A. Benasr, and N. Oumaya, 2009. "Suicide et pathologie à Tunis: étude rétrospective sur 12 ans à l'hôpital Razi." *L'information psychiatrique* 85 (3): 21–23.
Ghanmi, A. 1993. *Le mouvement féministe Tunisien. Témoignage sur l'autonomie et la pluralité du mouvement des femmes (1878–1989)*. Tunis: Chama Editions.
Golley, N. A. 2003. *Reading Arab women's autobiographies*. Austin: University of Texas Press.
Haddad, R. 1995. *Parole de femme*. Tunis: Editions Elyssa.
Jrad, N. 1996. *Mémoire de l'oubli. réflexion critique sur les expériences féministes des années quatre-vingt*. Tunis: Cérès Editions.
Karoui, N. 1989. "ALe couple en Tunisie: du discours à la réalité." *Revue tunisienne de sciences sociales* 96–97:59–73
Khelil, H. 1990. "A Matière, 'mémoire et regard.'" *Sociétés: Revue des Sciences Humaines et Sociales* 28:27–30.
Khelil, H. 2003. Salah Abou Seif: entretiens de Hachem Nahhass. L'oeuvre passée au crible. *La Presse*, November 1, 6–7.
Krichen, K. 2008. "'La philosophie en Tunisie et ses adversaires' called the article a public 'lynching.'" *Réalités* 1196 (November 27–December 3): 11–12.
Labidi, L. 2007. "The Nature of Transnational Alliances in Women's Associations in the Maghreb: The Case of AFTURD and ATFD in Tunisia." *Journal of Middle East Women's Studies* 3 (1): 6–34.
Labidi, L. C. 1980. De la solitude des femmes du Sud. *Le Temps*, August 8, 11–12.
Labidi, L. C., and B. Hamza. 1983. "Evacuation sanitaire des enfants. Le cas de la Tunisie." In *Les transferts sanitaires d'enfants*, 73–81. Tunis: Publication of Institut national de santé de l'enfance de Tunis.
Largueche, D., and A. Largueche. 1992. *Mariginales en terre d'Islam*. Tunis: Cérès Publications.
Mabrouk, A. 2001. *Sombre histoire de cellules folles*. Tunis: Alyssa-Editions.

Marzouki, I. 1993. *Le mouvement des Femmes en Tunisie. Au XXème siècle. Féminisme et politique*. Tunis: Cérès Productions.
Medimegh, A. D., ed. 2007. *Lettres à Lili*. Tunis: Editions Carthaginoiseries.
Messadi, A., L. Louati, E. Mahjoub, R. Nouira, S. Dlimi, and F. Braham. 1988. "Contribution à l'étude des aspects épidémiologiques des brûlures suicidaires en Tunisie: A propos de 94 cas," *Annals of Burns and Fire Disasters* XI:29–35.
Nasraoui, N. 1994. "Les réactions des tunisiens non pauvres à la vue des pauvres." In *Les déterminismes socio-culturels de la pauvreté*. Série Sociologique No. 23, 241–58. Tunis: CERES Publication.
Nazli, H. 2010. *La princesse Nazli Fadhel en Tunisie, 1896–1913. Une figure moderniste*. Tunis: Sagittaire Editions.
Nivat, A. 2001. (Récit recueilli par), *Louisette Ighilahriz. Algérienne*. Paris: Fayard/ Calmann-Lévy.
Oussedik, T. 2005. *Lla Fat'ma n'Soumeur: Récit*. Alger: ENAG Editions.
Pruvost, L. 1973. *La prostitution des mineures, Mémoire en Sciences Criminelles*. Tunis: University of Tunis.
Rawls, J. 1997. *Théorie de la justice*. Paris: Editions du Seuil.
Saad, R. 1998. "Shame, Reputation and Egypt's Lovers: A Controversy over a Nation's Image." *Visual Anthropology* 10:401–12.
Saï, F. Z. 2002. *Mouvement National et question féminine. Des origines à la veille de la guerre de libération nationale*. Oran: Editions Dar elGharb.
Sen, A. 1999. *Development as Freedom*. New York: Anchor Books.
Sen, A. 2009. *The Idea of Justice*. Cambridge: The Belknap Press of Harvard University Press.
Taraud, C. 2003. *La prostitution coloniale. Algérie, Tunisie, Maroc (1830–1962)*. Paris: Payot.

7

WHAT FUTURE FOR WOMEN IN TUNISIA?

Khedija Arfaoui

This chapter is an analysis of the current situation in Tunisia, three years after the revolution that stirred the country, ousting a dictator—Zine El Abidine Ben Ali—who had ruled the country for twenty-three years with an iron hand. He privileged women's status, continuing his predecessor's policy of state feminism[1] as a significant factor in maintaining an image of a modern Tunisia. The status of the Tunisian women was well known the world over and was a source of admiration and envy for other Arab women. In a world that is constantly moving forward, bringing about change meant to improve the fabric of life in the home sphere as well as in the outer sphere. Habib Bourguiba, his predecessor and Tunisia's liberator from colonialism, believed a country could not develop without the participation of women, and hence his promulgation of the Code of Personal Status (CPS) in 1956. His vision of feminism can be traced back to an eighth century tradition of the Qayrawan[2] wedding contract that allowed a woman to demand that her husband does not take a second spouse. If he did, she would be entitled to divorce him. Bourguiba had thus abolished the major burdens that maintained women's subservient status: repudiation and polygamy. He also raised the marital age, established judicial divorce, and encouraged the establishment of co-educational schools and women's entry into the workplace.

Continuing the process of leading women to obtain full equality with men, Tunisia ratified the Convention on the Elimination of All Forms of Discrimination against Women (CEDAW) in 1985 but with some reservations.[3] It was the first Arab country to do so. Bourguiba meant to continue his women-friendly policy but his attempts to change the inheritance law more than he had already done[4] so that women inherited the same share as men (and not only half as it is still the case now) met resistance and were stopped almost immediately. He could not change what is clearly stated in the Qur'an. Ben Ali continued this policy by granting women more rights while ignoring women activists because they did not support his views. For example, women married to foreigners would not be able to give their citizenship to their children. But two amendments were made to strengthen equality of men and women: in 1993, the first amendment allowed a Tunisian woman to give her citizenship provided the father approved. A joint approval that their child is a teenager below age nineteen years had to be submitted. But the second amendment in 2002 corrected that, allowing a woman to obtain that citizenship upon request, without the father's approval.

When the revolution occurred, women activists had been working on having their government lift the reservations it had made to the CEDAW. To their utter dismay, they found that they had instead to fight to maintain the rights that they had had for over fifty years. The Islamists, who had won the elections of October 23, 2011,[5] had envisioned a total change in the country, in particular to the status of women. They claimed Bourguiba had de-Islamized the country by encouraging women to get rid of their veil and go to school when they should have been taught to be good wives and mothers. To change that, they made several attempts to introduce *shari'a* in the constitution being drafted at the National Constituent Assembly (NCA).

This research describes the turmoil and stalwart struggle against violence encountered by women activists who are insisting on equality and freedom in a country that is suddenly increasingly veiled and Islamized. It illustrates the resistance of the Tunisian people to this violent Islamization and the positive impact it had on the final draft of the new constitution.

Tunisian Women's Struggle against Threats to Their Rights

At independence, the Tunisian people, particularly in the North West and in the South, lived in utter ignorance, poverty, and superstition. Women, in particular, had been "for centuries under the veil relegated from life, like a motionless and breathless lung in the body of society"

(Ghorbal 2012, 58). In that context, Bourguiba transformed his battle against underdevelopment to a jihad:

> His combat against ignorance and poverty, he conceived it as the continuation and counterpart of his combat against the occupation. Once he had granted freedom to his people, he wanted to give them their dignity back by dragging them away from ignorance and poverty.[6] (Ghorbal 2012, 60)

It is interesting to know that the Arab Spring—during which women played a significant part—was also the outcome of utter poverty and that those who brought it about also claimed dignity and freedom from dictatorship, albeit a different kind of dictatorship. If women activists were not many before, either because they would not be authorized to organize or out of fear of being penalized,[7] the Arab Spring changed that. It brought fear to an end and made all women and men activists stand against dictatorship

Before the revolution, there were mainly two autonomous women organizations[8] that sought to inform women about their rights in the family and in the work sphere: the Tunisian Association of Democratic Women (ATFD) and the Association of Tunisian Women for Research and Development (AFTURD). People generally thought that they were courageous to challenge the government as they often did. However, many avoided any contact with them lest they had problems with the police. Ben Ali's departure changed everything.

The Aftermath of January 14, 2011

"No more fear" (*La khaoufa baada al'yaoum*) is the title of Mourad Ben Cheikh's documentary on the Arab Spring of January 2011. With Ben Ali gone, fear was gone too, and that notion created a much longed-for sense of freedom and connectedness. Indifference among pedestrians disappeared, and people felt drawn to one another as they never had before. They would stop by people they did not know and exchange their thoughts. Habib Bourguiba Avenue, the main thoroughfare in Tunis, became a sort of hive that drew people of all age groups together like bees, carrying the Tunisian flag, the flag that used to be associated with the dictator, and his hated party, the Constitutional Democratic Rally, known as RCD. That flag suddenly became the symbol of their recovered sovereignty, their dignity, and their citizenship, which were no longer in the hands of a corrupt dictator. Suddenly, ATFD and AFTURD were no longer the only women's organizations. A recent survey directed by Dr. Dorra Mahfoudh Draoui and funded by the United Nations Population Fund Agency (UNFPA) listed all the women-oriented organizations that were granted a visa after the revolution, all of them working on setting up programs meant to help the social and economic integration of women from disadvantaged backgrounds. The sample studied included 784 organizations,[9] 244 of which working especially on equality of chances between genders, 36% of them with members younger than thirty-five years of age (Haouari 2013). The information above is important because it shows that, although still limited, much is being done today and people have the freedom to organize and found organizations to help, where it is most needed, in the poverty-stricken regions. Under the dictatorship, only government-supported organizations could do that and, unfortunately, they could not do much. That was the real cause of the revolution. That is, while the coastline was thriving with its luxurious palaces, providing jobs in many sectors connected to the tourist sector, the northern and southern regions were starving. The revolution was ignited by the youth, women and men. It was spontaneous. No one had directed it, but the social networks were a great help in the matter to remain motivated, concerned, and always ready to stand up against anything that did not obey the real objectives of the revolution.

El-Nahda Islamization Project: A Religious Dictatorship

If everything had been prohibited by law and fear under Ben Ali, after January 14, 2011, everything became "haram" (prohibited by religion). The conservative forces that had disagreed with Bourguiba's modernist policy attributed all social evils to it. Women were the first targets and were confronted by violence: if they were on the street, they would be told to go home and dress decently, cover their arms and legs, and leave the outer world for men to put an end to men's unemployment. At times, they would be physically harassed. So were female professors who, for them should be examples as educators and dress as Islamists do: women were ordered to wear the headscarf, or hijab, have their arms covered, and wear long dresses. As to men, the Salafists who created this crisis situation at the university wore the kamis, a skirt over large trousers, as

Our Martyrs Did Not Die for a New Dictatorship.

men dress in Afghanistan. Tunisian men and women were expected to dress in that way.

The high divorce rate, men's unemployment, increasing numbers of single men and women, women's lower fertility, and delinquency were all said to be the consequence of Bourguiba's secular policy. Co-ed schools, which were considered contrary to Arab-Islamic culture, were set to be eradicated. Quranic schools were established throughout the country, separating boys from girls and having them wear an Islamic outfit as early as age 3. Crises at some universities, in particular at the Manouba University of Arts and Letters, disturbed classes. The campus was quickly overrun with radical Islamists known as Salafists,[10] many of them not even belonging to the university. Mass prayers would take place, with the Qur'an recited via the megaphone, making it impossible for anyone to teach or study; professors would be physically assaulted, particularly female teachers, on the grounds that they were "kufar" (non-religious or atheists) and not "decently" dressed. The Salafists asked for separate classes for boys and girls and for female teachers for girls and male teachers for boys. In addition, they wanted to impose the *niqab* on female students. At the sit-in organized by Salafists in December 2011, the sit-inners

> praised the virtues of the *niqab* and predicted hell and damnation not only to female students that "strip off" (in their lexicon, "unveiling one's face" has become synonymous with "stripping off!") but also to the faculty's teachers guilty of opposing the wearing of the *niqab*. (Mellakh 2013, 18)

All of these requests were met with strong resistance from the part of the Dean, professors, and students alike. The university's scientific committee, chaired by the Dean Habib Kazdaghli, refused absolutely to teach students wearing a *niqab*. Following that episode, a whole plot against the Dean Habib Kazdaghli took place: two students wearing a *niqab* entered into the dean's office and without waiting for authorization, they threw his files and documents everywhere. One of them claimed the dean had slapped her, and then pretended to lose consciousness. As a result, an ambulance came to take her to the hospital. That scenario was enough to allow the *niqab*-ed student to sue him. The dean had not touched her. A first in the judicial history of Tunisia, on July 5, 2012, the dean had to appear for the first time before the court, although "in the file of the facts, evidence, proofs, pleaded in favor of the innocence of the accused" (Mellakh 2013, 277). If the Minister of Higher Education had not been a Salafist, he would have immediately provided support of his ministry.[11] However, he never did. The dean had to appear in court several times, fortunately always with a strong support from his colleagues and from civil society. Salafists and girls in *niqab*s would also be present before the courthouse declaring everybody else was "kufar." As of early 2014, the case was still pending closure although the dean had won his case. This sudden reversal of the situation happened following a declaration made by Moncef Marzouki, the temporary President of the Republic, stating that female students should be allowed to attend classes wearing a *niqab*.

Are the Most Progressive Women in the Arab World Going to Adopt the *Niqab*?

Tunisian women had been gradually abandoning their modern, European looks since the early 1980s. Unlike the earlier days of independence when women of all age groups would gladly get rid of their traditional veil, today's Tunisian women, also of all age and social groups, have been wearing either a simple hijab, or the complete Islamic outfit, something similar to the Iranian chador. A few are wearing the *niqab*. Their appearance, however, remains intriguing for it is difficult for many to understand how a woman can enjoy becoming an anonymous self as such an outfit was not known in Tunisia.

State feminism may seem to have been imposed by both of the presidents who ruled the country for more than fifty years, yet their governments were quite progressive and called for an ever-modern Tunisia. It is not so with the present El-Nahda government, which is very conservative. If the resistance to Bourguiba's and Ben Ali's feminist policies was weak, the one against the conservatism of Islamist rule has been from the beginning strong and relentless.

Some Important Events in the History of Women in Tunisia

Tunisian women are proud to say that their country was founded in 814 BC by a Phoenician princess, Elissa or Dido, Pygmalion's sister, who had come from Tyr to found Carthage. The fact that Tunisia had a constitution drafted in 1861[12] and that it was the first in the whole Arab world is significant. It had repercussions on the fabric of life in Tunisia and will hopefully influence the new constitution that has been drafted and approved in January 2014. With the CPS, Bourguiba had been able to silence religious opposition and have women's rights embedded in the Tunisian fabric of life. Tunisia remains the only country in the whole Arab world that grants the most rights to women. However, this does not mean that Tunisian women have equal rights as they still inherit half a man's share. The inheritance issue remains a hard one as the Qur'an specifies that "Allah commands you as regards to your children's (inheritance); to the male, a portion equal to that of two females" [4:11].

The NCA was elected for one year to draft a new constitution and to prepare the new and final elections that would put an end to this temporary government. Consequently, since the elections of October 23, 2011, the Tunisian people have been eagerly watching and waiting for the final draft of the constitution. Expectations are high and the Tunisian constitution should be a model of perfection in terms of human rights but for the opposition coming from people using religion to justify their stand. Several attempts to introduce the *shari'a* in it have been avoided following fierce opposition from democrats, set on having a clear line drawn between religion and politics. Nevertheless, Islamists do not seem to be ready to abandon their goal. A Salafist slogan reads, "Shari'a is our path, and reform is our option" (Parker 2012).

Over three years since January 14, 2011, the Tunisian Youth Day (as decided after the revolution), celebrating the backbone of the Tunisian Revolution, stood up to oust their dictator, not much has been achieved to tackle the problems engendered by unemployment and poverty. On the contrary, much has been done to create and expand means and centers to Islamize the country through the use of mosques and foundation of Quranic schools. Much has been done to divide the country between Islamists and secular people.[13] The deteriorating state of the country since it has been in the hands of El-Nahda has weakened the Islamist movement, and El-Nahda decreased in popularity from 56% in January 2012 to 52% in February 2012. It is likely to decrease further. By contrast, the popularity of the Progressive Democratic Party (PDP) and Ettakattol increased slightly by 1% from 10% to 11% and 8% to 9%, respectively (Elali 2012). A survey realized by Zogby Research Services announces El-Nahda to get about 28% votes in the coming legislative and presidential elections. El-Nahda's support has declined because of wider distrust from the Tunisian people. This decline in popularity allowed Nida Tounis, the most popular opposition party led by Beji Caied Essebsi—former member of Habib Bourguiba's government and diplomat who was also prime minister in the first government that followed the revolution—to increase in popularity.

A strong tribute should be given to the civil society for the impact of its defense of human rights in general and women's rights in particular. Civil society has, indeed, been present each time El-Nahda and/or the other Islamist groups have threatened these rights. Feminist activists, mainly ATFD and AFTURD, had been working ceaselessly to lessen the threat and to reach their goal of securing women's full equality with men. Despite mounting Islamist radicalism, they succeeded in pushing the first interim government formed after the revolution[14] to lift most of the reservations against the CEDAW. That was achieved on August 16, 2011, giving women equality with men in marriage, divorce, and custody (Khalife 2011). It did not, however, lift one important reservation because it interferes with article 1 of the Tunisian constitution, which states that "Tunisia is a free, independent and sovereign state; Its religion is Islam, its language is Arabic and its type of government is the Republic." As a consequence, nothing was changed about parity in inheritance.

The lifting of some of the reservations was followed by a gender parity law (April 2011), which specified that no electoral list would be accepted if it did not have an equal number of men and women candidates in the election of the NCA on October 23, 2011. This law was accepted by all the parties and organizations, and was crucial in the women winning 23% of the NCA's seats. Of course, the possible percentage gain was limited because very few lists had women at the head of the list, particularly among the opposition parties, but El-Nahda had more women in the second names of their lists. The Tunisian authorities should also withdraw this declaration: no state should use its constitution to justify failing to comply with international legal standards. This is a statement that has been repeatedly used by democrats and by feminists in particular, that international conventions already ratified by Tunisia have to be respected as they have a priority over national laws. Islamist feminists disagree on this point.

Constitutional Developments

Tunisia's first constitutional charter can be traced back to the Fundamental Pact (1857) established by Mohamed Bey (1855–1859), following the decline of the Ottoman rule over the territory in the early nineteenth century. The Fundamental Pact proclaimed rules governing relations between the government, the people, and foreigners in an effort to solidify its rule and placate the European powers. However, this document was replaced in 1861 with a new constitution when Muhammad as-Sadiq succeeded Mohamed Bey as the Tunisian leader. This constitution weakened the Tunisian ruler in favor of European migrants who were given property rights and guaranteed equal protection of Tunisian law. Tunisia became a French protectorate in 1881. It remained under French rule until March 1956 when it gained independence, followed by the promulgation of a new constitution on June 1, 1959. The NCA, which was established on October 23, 2011, finished drafting a new constitution on January 26, 2014. It was ratified in January 2014; unlike the preceding ones and thanks to the new free and democratic media, the new constitution has been eagerly and passionately discussed by the people all over the country.

During the three years after the beginning of the "Arab Spring," not only has the Islamist-led government proven to be incompetent, but it has brought the country to a critical brink in terms of security and economy. Moreover, from the beginning, the emboldened radical Islamists used terror to deprive women of their rights. They did not succeed as evidenced by the huge marches on Tunisian Women's National Day (August 13, 2011, 2012, 2013), but each time there was a threat to women's gains and/or to universal freedoms. One such action came on

December 17, 2013, the third anniversary of the immolation of Mohamed Bouazizi in Sidi Bouzid, when a lone young woman challenged a meeting of contesting Salafists jihadists in Tunis, bravely holding the Tunisian flag all by herself. The jihadists were so stunned that their black flags disappeared (Horchani 2013). Islamists, whether from El-Nahda or from other radical Islamist parties, have not succeeded now that the articles of the draft constitution have been voted on one by one, and several articles show particular victories for women and for society at large.

In March 2012, *shari'a* was declared to become the main source of legislation, instead of article 1, which states that "Tunisia is a free, independent and sovereign state. Its religion is Islam, its language is Arabic and its type of government is the Republic." However, after fierce reactions from civil society, El-Nahda announced that the party committee had renounced implementing this change. In August 2012, a working group within the NCA proposed an article for the constitution indicating that women are "complementary" to men. Again, after much outrage, the proposed article was retracted in September 2012. Today, the articles related to human rights, and in particular women's rights, have been approved.

Articles 1 and 2 declared Tunisia a civil state based on citizenship, the will of the people, and the primacy of law. Both articles have not been amended. The fight between Islamists and secularists has been hard, but it has succeeded in rejecting amendments that make Islam "the main source of legislation." The danger remains, however, with article 6 that makes the state the "protector of the sacred" and the "guardian of religion." Harsh measures could be taken against citizens on such grounds. For example, in early January 2014, Sheikh Habib Ellouze, a Constituent member from El-Nahda, well-known for his extremely conservative stands, declared Mongi Rahoui an "enemy of Islam." Rahoui vehemently and pathetically complained that Ellouze's rhetoric had led Salafists to send him death threats. As a result of these threats, Rahoui's wife had to hide in another place, and his children were terrorized. Article 20 states that "[a]ll male and female citizens have the same rights and duties. They are equal before the law without discrimination" (Gaspani 2014). This article was passed by a vote of 159 out of 169 votes. Of course, there were strong voices against equality and parity on the part of men and women. El-Nahda female members of the NCA had already said "no" to the CEDAW. Four women said no to parity on January 7, 2014: Monia Ibrahim, Kawthar Ladgham, Sana Haddad, and Zohra

Smida. They voted against a law that was friendly to women, seemingly without acknowledging that they owed their elected position in the NCA to the April 2011 parity election ballot law. A few days later, article 45 was passed, which stipulated that equality of representation between men and women in elected institutions of the state is guaranteed. It was approved by 116 votes, 32 abstained, and 40 voted against. This vote has been considered a great news for secularists and for the Tunisian people at large because it makes clear, and has garnered support from the majority, that women have equal presence in public life, despite the most recent debates centered on religion as the foundation of state governance. The articles end with the statement that all necessary measures will be taken to eradicate violence against women. Article 45 states, "The State is committed to protect the rights gained by women and endeavors to sustain and develop them. The State guarantees equality of chances between men and women in the execution of various responsibilities and in all sectors. The State must strive to reach parity between men and women in elected councils. The State must take all the necessary measures to combat violence against women."

Another positive change in the new Tunisia outside the constitution processes is that identifying corruption among political leaders is gaining ground. One of the most striking examples is that of Rafik Abdesslam, Ghannouchi's son-in-law and former minister of foreign affairs, who has finally been recognized guilty of fraudulent money operations. Over one year after Olfa Riahi, a blogger/journalist accused him of (1) using state money to spend nights at the Sheraton Hotel (hence the name Sheraton-Gate given to the affair) and (2) receiving money from a foreign government. Initially, the Ministry of Justice challenged Olfa Riahi's report, claiming it was inaccurate, and she was harassed. She had to appear in court and for some time she was not allowed to travel. Recently, Abdesslam was accused of receiving a significant sum of money from China on his personal account when it should have gone to the central bank. This revelation was made in December 2012, together with the other charges. He is scheduled to appear in court in early February.

Tunisia has been going through very painful times, most particularly when the government offered dead ears to all warnings made about terror creeping throughout the country. Despite the difficulties, the Tunisian people have never lost faith that they will triumph. More will have to be done, in particular in the educational sector in which Islamists have been reinforcing Arabic and Islam among Tunisians, while marginalizing foreign languages and other cultures. Article 38 represents a real threat to democracy. It was voted for and is presently facing strong opposition from civil society and organizations. Threatening to radically change the Tunisian identity, article 38 states,

> Education is obligatory until age 16. The State guarantees the right to a public and free education in all its cycles, and makes sure to provide the means necessary for realizing the quality of teaching, education and training; it works at the way its Arab-Muslim identity is rooted, as well as the support of Arabic and the generalization of its use. (This was adopted by 141 votes, 4 abstentions and 9 against)

"Did we question our identity, our Arab or Muslim identity before the revolution?" Yadh Ben Achour, expert in constitutional law asked (Dhambri 2013). Clearly, those who brought about this article were up against the rich nature of the 3,000-year-old Tunisian identity!

Bourguiba had opened co-educational schools to help his country enter the world of modernity and join modern nations. Islamists are against modernity although they are using all the technology created by the West for their needs. It is for this reason that they have been striving to find ways to introduce their ideas—and make Tunisia an Islamist State. If one door is closed, they will try to open another one. Thus, for example, for Islamists, article 1 is not enough, they want Islam to be the religion of the State, for that is how they would be able to implement *shari'a* law. In September 2012, they had demanded that an "Islamic Supreme Council" be registered in the constitution. Such a body would reintroduce *shari'a* and therefore, it represents a clear danger for the democracy that the Tunisian people have struggled for so much. Fortunately, this law was not adopted; it is not enough to have adopted article 1 in the constitution. Other laws can introduce the *shari'a* and endanger freedom of thought, freedom of expression, and freedom of conscience, such as article 38 seen above.

Indeed, in the early days of the post-revolution, Rached Ghannouchi mentioned that the Tunisian people were afraid of *shari'a*, but they need not because there is nothing to fear from it. What he refused to consider was that *shari'a* was interpreted differently from one region to another. As a result, allowing *shari'a* to control the laws of a country is clearly a danger: as Horchani (2014a) declared: "it would be the end of co-education, probably the obligation for all girls to wear the headscarf, the end of art, philosophy, foreign languages." They had already been educating youth in this spirit, making them wear Islamic outfits, with a separation of the sexes. Voting on the draft constitution had been hard because of the conflicting ideals of Islamists and democrats. It is important though that articles on gender equality and parity have been approved. Once all of this is over, the country will have to prepare for its next elections. Not only will the eyes of the Tunisian people, the eyes of the entire world will be focusing there. Being the birthplace of the Arab Spring, Tunisia is bound to be the birthplace of democracy in the Arab world (Horchani 2014b).

Conclusion: The Arab Spring Is about Over, a New Era Is Beginning

Some would say that Tunisia has changed, but unfortunately not for the better. Violence continues to erupt in different sectors and in particular against women. Islamists have expanded Islamist centers for young children that provide them with a strict Wahabi education; they have been encouraging the *niqab, urfi* (religious unofficial) marriages, excision for girls, polygamy, and *jihad niqah* (brief marriage during war times) with poor young girls being sent to Syria to offer sexual services to jihadists. Several have come back, pregnant from they-do-not-know-who as they can marry several times in one single week (Zouari 2013). Despite the law condemning violence against women, they no longer feel safe when they are out, in particular at night. It is sad to hear that the police run away when they meet insurgents and need the help of the army. This was still happening as of January 2014, even around the city capital, Tunis, and also elsewhere in the country. Despite these difficulties, the Tunisian people never lost faith, and had high hopes, albeit with El-Nahda as a partner among the other parties.

Moreover, three years after January 14, 2011, El-Nahda finally agreed to step down. Islamist Prime Minister Ali Larayedh resigned to be replaced by Mehdi Jomaa, the Minister of Industry and an independent technocrat. He and the new independent government had the responsibility of helping the country organize the new elections. In the meantime, the new constitution was approved with 200 votes for, 12 votes against, and 4 abstentions, despite earlier attempts on the part of El-Nahda to introduce the *shari'a* law one way or another. A special tribute must be paid to the civil society for its presence and vigilance each time the Islamists tried to infringe on human rights and had religion monitor all the activities of the nation. As Beji Caied Essebsi, former prime minister in the early days of the revolution and leader of the strong opposition party, Nida Tounis, mentioned in his historic speech on January 14, 2014,

> Article 1 has finally been approved by the NCA. It includes everything:
>
> "Tunisia is a free, independent and sovereign state. Islam is its religion, Arabic is its language, and it is a republic. It is not possible to amend this article," nowhere will *shari'a* be mentioned. Nothing more is needed.

Notes

1 "State feminism" refers to a women-friendly policy adopted by the governments of Habib Bourguiba and Zinelabidine Ben Ali that granted women social and economic rights in order to benefit and build the state. While these rights benefitted all women, the National Union of Tunisian Women (UNFT, French acronym), created in 1956, was mostly composed of women related to the members of the government.

2 Founded around 670 by the Arabs, Qayrawan is a UNESCO World Heritage Site. It is famous as an Islamic cultural capital.

3 Tunisia formulated reservations against the following four articles: articles 9, 15, 16, and 29. Article 9, §2: the government did not ratify §2 that designated both parents equal rights in giving their nationality to their children. Article 15 §4: reservations were made as to the dispositions relating to women's rights to choose their residence and home that must not be interpreted in a meaning that would go against dispositions of articles 23§ 3 and 61§ 4 of the CPS that deal with the same issue. Article 16 (1) §c, d, f, g, h: Tunisia does not consider itself bound by §c, d, f, g, and h of article 16 (1) of the Convention that must not contradict the dispositions of the CPS related to giving the family name to the children and to the acquisition of property through inheritance means. Tunisia does not consider itself bound by the dispositions of §1 of article 29 on the grounds that differences of opinion of this kind cannot be submitted to arbitration or to the international court of justice without the consent of all the parties to the controversy.

4 Bourguiba improved inheritance laws to protect women's rights. For example, if a deceased man left only daughters, their uncle(s) or the latter's son(s) would inherit with them. The CPS changed that.

5 The 217 people elected at the Constituent Assembly (including forty-nine women, forty-two of them belonging to El-Nahda) were given one year to draft a new constitution. But it took them exactly one year and three months since they started giving the result of their work in early January 2014.

6 The translation from French is mine.

7 During the first and only free elections that took place on November 7, 1789, Islamists had realized about 30% of valid votes. Ben Ali countered the Islamist threat by a

merciless repression against Islamists. This repression extended afterward against a burgeoning civil society (Borsali 2012, 242). Borsali reports on the violence used by Ben Ali against Islamists at the end of the 1980s (Borsali 2012, 246). Islamist feminists used to "go around knocking on doors and go to hammams to meet women." This is to say that Islamist feminists were also fearful to speak against Ben Ali.

8 The National Union of Tunisian Women represented state feminism at its best.

9 For example, the Coalition for Women of Tunisia was founded in September 2012. The coalition now includes more than thirty organizations. They all work very differently. Some address women's problems in rural areas, where access to education and medical care is often scarce and quite poor. Women are especially affected by all these problems. Other organizations in the coalition provide political education or lobby for better laws. The gender approach and the universality of human rights in particular are used (Sabra 2013).

10 By contrast, El-Nahda had always pretended to be "moderate and democratic" although it had until recently been very lenient toward assassinations of political opponents. The leader of El-Nahda, Rached Ghannouchi, had even said that they were his children and that they reminded him of his youth.

11 The law stipulates that the ministry provides a lawyer to any civil servant prosecuted in the context of his responsibilities.

12 To ratify the Code of Personal Status on June 1, 1959, President Bourguiba had to silence all religious opposition. He succeeded to do so and made Tunisia a modern country. It is this modernity that Islamists see as *kufer* or blasphemy to replace it by the establishment of *shari'a* law.

13 Secular people are called atheists or non-believers by the Salafists.

14 The first government in the post-revolution period was led by Beji Caied Essebsi, currently the president of the most popular opposition party, Nida Tounis (the Call of Tunis).

References

Borsali, N. 2012. *Tunisie: Le défi égalitaire. Ecrits féministes*. Tunis: Editions Arabesques.

Dhambri, M. 2013. "Tunisie-Politique: Article 38 de la constitution: Yadh Ben Achour lance un cri d'alarm!" Accessed December 21, 2013. http://www.kapitalis.com/politique/20044-tunisie-politique-article-38-de-la-constitution-yadh-ben-achour-lance-un-cri-d-alarme.html.

Elali, A. 2012. "New Survey Points to Fluctuations in Popularity of Tunisian Political Parties and Leaders." *Tunisia Live*. Accessed December 21, 2013. http://www.tunisia-live.net/2012/03/23/new-survey-points-to-fluctuations-in-popularity-of-tunisian-political-parties-and-leaders/#sthash.Zgy9loKO.dpuf.

Gaspani, M. 2014. "Tunisia Enshrines Gender Equality in Draft Constitution-Reports." Thomson Reuters Foundation. Accessed December 22, 2013. http://www.trust.org/item/20140107164542-98nkf.

Ghorbal, S. 2012. *Orphelins de Bourguiba et héritiers du prophète*. Tunis: Cérès Editions.

Haouari, I. 2013. "Gender and Equality of Chances Observatory. A Database on On-line Organizations." *La Presse*, August 8.

Horchani, S. 2013. "Tunisie- Ma photo préférée de l'année 2013: seule contre tous." Accessed December 22, 2013. http://blogs.mediapart.fr/blog/salah-horchani/191213/tunisie-ma-photo-preferee-de-l-annee-2013-seule-contre-tous.

Horchani, S. 2014a. "Non à l'Article 38 et à l'Amendement no. 70 de la Constitution tunisienne en gestation!" Accessed January 15, 2014. http://horchani.blog.lemonde.fr/2014/01/13/non-a-larticle-38-et-a-lamendement-n70-de-la-constitution-tunisienne-en-gestation/.

Horchani, S. 2014b. "Tunisie: Sacrée Sharia! Chaque fois qu'on la pousse par la porte, les islamistes la font revenir par la fenêtre! (2/4)." Accessed December 22, 2013. http://horchani.blog.lemonde.fr/2014/01/03/tunisie-sacree-sharia-chaque-fois-quon-la-pousse-par-la-porte-les-islamistes-la-font-revenir-par-la-fenetre-24/.
Khalife, N. 2011. "Tunisia on Board with Women's Rights." Accessed January 15, 2014. http://www.huffingtonpost.com/nadya-khalife/tunisia-on-board-with-wom_b_981689.html.
Mellakh, H. 2013. *Chroniques du MANOUBISTAN*. Tunis: Cérès Editions.
Parker, E. 2012. "Tunisia's Salafist Political Party Calls for Implementation of Shari'a." Accessed January 15, 2014. http://confinder.richmond.edu/admin/docs/Tunisia constitution.pdf.
Sabra, M. 2013. "Interview with the Tunisian Feminist Saloua Guiga: Two Societal Projects on Collision Course." *Qantara*. Accessed January 15, 2014. http://en.qantara.de/Two-Societal-Projects-on-Collision-Course/21023c23341i0p9/.
Zouari, F. 2013. "Jihad sportif." *Jeune Afrique*, no. 2752:130.

8

THE MARGINALIZATION OF MOROCCAN WOMEN IN SOCIETY AND MEDIA

Fatima Sadiqi

Media, as a sum of graphic, visual, and textual images that television, newspapers, magazines, and radio advertisements vehicle, has a notorious manipulative power. Through subtle and glamorous messages, it acts on the subconscious of people, shaping their attitudes and behaviors, and interfering with their beliefs and values. The internalized images have a lasting effect on the media consumers in a world where images travel faster than ideas and where the development of new technologies is rapid in an unprecedented way.

In Morocco, a large portion of media targets women, making and unmaking their images in television, movies, magazines, newspapers, and so on. These images are often dictated by larger political and economic ideologies and "injected" in a society where tradition and modernity coexist and move in parallel. The combination of tradition, modernity, and fast technology has resulted in the gradual erasure of the *hududs* (space frontiers between genders and spaces on which Arab-Islamic patriarchy is based). The resulting media images affect women's position inside and outside the family, their self-confidence, as well as the attitudes toward them. In focusing on the traditional roles of women and neglecting the new roles that women have gained at a high price, the media in Morocco marginalizes women and their efforts.

In this chapter, I investigate the images and impact of media on Moroccan women. The methodology I used consists in questionnaires, interviews, and tape/video recordings. I also analyzed a sample of mainstream daily newspapers and weekly tabloids that constitute the major types of the print press. This was supplemented by an analysis of a sample of women's magazines, TV news, commercials, shows, and programs, as well as a sample of Moroccan films. Some of my findings are based on personal observation. The chapter is organized in three main sections. The first section provides an overview of the social status of women in Morocco. The second section presents the Moroccan media, and the third section deals with the interaction between the media and women in Morocco.

The Status of Women in Moroccan Society

From the early 1960s onward, the overall status of women in Morocco has unquestionably improved: the health standards for the entire population have increased, access to school has been democratized, paid work has been generalized, an increasing number of women are participating in the political arena, and the domain of public religion has become accessible to women. These improvements have been enforced by the requirements of economic development that the government in Morocco was determined to carry out, as well as by the feminist movement in the country.

Although these improvements broadened women's horizons beyond the domestic sphere, they have not really changed their social status, which remains largely defined by gender hierarchies (Ennaji 2005; Naamane Guessous 2001; Sadiqi 2003). Moroccan women do not constitute a homogeneous group. A dynamic interaction of various social variables such as the geographical origin, class, level of education, job opportunity, language skills, and marital status plays a central role in determining the choices and opportunities that Moroccan women have (Sadiqi 2003). Whatever their social prerogatives, Moroccan women live in a social order that is still controlled by a space-based patriarchy where the public sphere of power is still dominated by men and where women's cultural duties evolve around the private space (Belarbi 1993; Mernissi 1993; Sadiqi and Ennaji 2006). As a result of this, the changes that women have experienced have been more beneficial for their societies than for themselves, and their rights have remained largely fragile and liable to constant questioning, especially in periods of crises. For example, women in Morocco were the first victims of economic recession that hit the country in the mid-1980s, as well as the structural adjustment programs put in place to counter this recession (Ennaji 2005; Naciri 2003; Sadiqi 2003). Women who had the tools to do so voiced their anger through writings and activism, and their efforts bore fruit: today women's issues have become national issues and a lucrative project for the media.

The relationship between the Moroccan feminist movement and the state has not always been smooth and even; but on the whole, from the mid-1980s onward, women in Morocco started to play a new and "modernizing" role in the overall politics of their country. Theirs has become a "society" project. This project was not only supported but adopted by the state in an overall political and economic situation where the spectacular rise of political Islam constituted a real threat to both women and the state (Sadiqi 2008). Political Islam is the result of a combination of three deep-reaching events that took place at the international level at the end of the 1970s and the beginning of the 1980s and that greatly impacted the entire region of the Middle East and North Africa: the success of the Iranian Revolution, the downfall of the Soviet Union, and the emergence of the United States as the sole superpower. One of the major characteristics of political Islam is a return to the veil and the traditional roles of women.[1]

Although crippled by illiteracy, lower socioeconomic standing, and the weight of customs and traditions, a large portion of Moroccan women used education to conquer the public spheres of power and assume leading roles in the government, academia, and civil society. Today, Moroccan women participate actively in the production and development of their country. One field that was recently opened to women is religious clerical studies. Morocco has taken the lead in this area. In May 2006, 50 women graduated along with 150 men from *Dar al-Hadith al-Hassaniyya*—a religious seminar once just reserved for men—to become the first female *imams*, or clerics. These women do not lead prayers, like their male counterparts, but they are equipped to answer religious queries and teach Islam, often using Moroccan colloquial Arabic (*darija*) to reach the largest number of women from the lower sections of society. The efforts to promote women were pushed by the king as one of several ways to promote a liberal Islam.

So far as labor is concerned, women comprise 35% of the workforce, including one-third of all doctors and one-quarter of university professors.

With regard to political rights, in a public opinion poll included in the Arab Human Development Report (which canvassed participants in four sample Arab countries—Morocco, Egypt, Lebanon, and Jordan), 79% said women have an equal right to political activity. Indeed, women have been able to vote and run for office in Morocco in the mid-fifties.

Moroccan women's roles in the development of their country is better appreciated when the general context in which they evolve is understood. Morocco is a Muslim, developing, and multilingual country (Ennaji 1991). Being located at the westernmost part of the Middle East and North Africa region, Morocco is geographically situated at the crossroad between Europe and Africa; it is only seven miles from Europe and its southern region is a natural continuation of sub-Saharan Africa. The social organization in Morocco is based on patrilineal family and gender hierarchy. Patrilineal family is a structure where the father is the absolute head of the family whose authority over his wife (wives) and child (children) is culturally sanctioned. As a result, a gender hierarchy whereby males have authority over females is established at the onset of the basic cell of the society: the family.

Furthermore, having been colonized by France, Morocco is a country where two competing sets of paradigms co-exist: tradition and modernity. These two ways of thinking and praxis are not only reflected in scholarship and intellectual debates but also in most aspects of Moroccan life, such as language use, indoor decoration, clothing, and cuisine. This paradox is at the center of the still ongoing debates, sometimes opposing and sometimes conciliatory, toward the liberals (who defend the individual's rights) and conservatives (who place the family at the center stage of society). For example, while marriage is a social terrain that liberal feminists have been preparing for decades, strategizing and reconciliation with the state allowed them to rally the younger veiled feminists to defend their legal rights and dignity.

It is within this patriarchal system that an appreciation of women's endeavors to progress should be positioned. Today, Moroccan women have achieved a great deal. The ideological debate opposing Islamists (conservative) and non-Islamists (modernists), which dominated the Moroccan public discourses from the early 1990s to 2003, has been replaced by a more progressive thinking that seeks the improvement of society. The May 16 terrorist attacks on Casablanca marked a radical shift in this sense. Women have greatly benefited from this shift; their mobilization is increasingly impressive and the state response is equally impressive: a most progressive Family Law in 2004,[2] the Nationality Code in 2007,[3] and 12% of female representation in the June 2009 local elections. Furthermore, more and more civil society organizations encourage women's participation in the public sphere. As a result, many women have managed to become genuine role models and provide inspiration and leadership for the younger generations of both sexes.

Despite women's increasing visibility in the public sphere of power, the Moroccan media abounds with stereotypical images of women as subservient, docile, and weak. By so doing, it fails to recognize women's roles and instead of alleviating their problems, it reinforces and legitimizes them.

Moroccan Media Representations of Women

Today's Moroccan mass media, written or audio-visual, constitute a very complex domain where language, culture, and ideology inter-twine in very intricate ways. The media seem to be very powerful in the sense that the information they provide is construed within "in-built grids," to borrow Van Dijk's (1993) expression, that facilitate its absorption and transmission. Hence, ideologies, values, and stereotypes are easily enforced and sustained by the media, especially in a society where illiteracy is still very high.[4] The Moroccan media constitute an increasingly interesting aspect of the Moroccan cultural landscape; they both reflect and impact the overall sociocultural situation in Morocco. Besides using various channels of transmission, these media are multilingual[5] and vary in the quality of information, style, and the amount of background knowledge they do or do not expect from their audiences. For example, "serious" newspapers and TV programs co-exist with sensational tabloids and TV shows. Also, the Moroccan media outlets vary between national, oppositional, and other political parties. Whatever their mode of expression or scope, Moroccan media tend to feed on gender stereotypes.

Moroccan Media as a Gendered Space

Media and identity interact to create a space where individuals construct identities under the influence of the messages they are confronted with. Considerable literature has been allocated to the identity construction process and to relate it to media (Calvert, Jordan, and Cocking 2002, p. 57).

To understand the gendered aspect of Moroccan media, we need to assume that media in its globality can be conceived of as a space where the personal, social, economic, and political are brought together and made available for the public gaze, scrutiny, and judgment. As such, the media space has become increasingly instrumental in impacting behavior, attitudes, self, image construction, and decision making.

Another aspect of the importance of the media space is its association with Morocco's democratization process and opening. An increasing number of voices are expressing themselves through various media channels. From this perspective, the media is becoming a genuine mirror of how gender is handled in the public space. Indeed, there is more public recognition that genuine development cannot be achieved in Morocco without taking gender into consideration. As a result, some ministries started to integrate a gender approach in their budgets and a gender approach is being implemented in the policies of some public organizations. This is an area where Morocco is indeed ahead of many Arab and Islamic countries, if not among pioneers in this respect.

However, despite this, media is heavily biased against women. This state of affairs is linked to the social status of men and women in Moroccan culture as mentioned in the previous sections. Studies on the images of Moroccan women in the media are rather scarce. Most of the existing literature focuses on the contents of the broadcast sector, especially movies, TV series, and advertisements. Very little has been done on newscasts and serious programs such as political talk shows and documentaries.

The greatest bulk of studies paint a grim picture of women as they are portrayed in the media. In general, the studies confirm the idea that the roles given to women in the media largely fall short of potential. For example, insulting stereotypes still prevail and women are generally presented as victims, a tool to urge consumption or passive consumers. This is evidenced in the fact that women's bodies are used either as commodities or assigned a traditional role where they rarely appear as autonomous thinking individuals, and are often portrayed as illiterate, naïve, and stupid.

Such negative and demeaning images are unfair to women, who have been instrumental in promoting social and political change. For example, Moroccan women have historically fought for independence through media (Sadiqi et al. 2009). Women used the media to conquer the public space and make their voices heard.

As for magazines, although a few of them such as *Femmes du Maroc* (in French and Arabic) and *Citadine* have political and social sections that deal with women's consciousness-raising and social development, most magazines focus on women's traditional preoccupations, such as home decorating, cooking, cosmetics, and fashion, as well as family issues such as relationships between various members of the family and child-rearing. Women's achievements are often depicted as gains for the family and not for themselves as independent human beings, and their social realities and responsibilities are not treated in fair way. Women's conventional societal roles are more glorified than their roles as independent individuals with will and personal ambition.

A Note of Hope

In the midst of this rather negative picture of Moroccan women and the media there is hope. This hope can be sensed in the current transitional Moroccan media system that is more liberal and brings some change. The TV chain 2M, for example, attempts to portray positive images of women by underlining the social, legal, economic, and cultural bias against women. This TV channel also presents serious documentaries on sexual abuse and the harm caused by stereotypical gender role assignment.

On the contrary, topics such as gender equality, sexual harassment and abuse, criminal, and other legal provisions that confer more power on men than on women are given space in the daily newspapers *Al-Masaa* and the magazine *Tel Quel*. Furthermore, women's sports and health issues as well as the emotional, educational, and developmental issues of female teenagers are sometimes tackled, in addition to mature adult women at the pinnacle of their professional achievement. Also, various non-governmental organizations (NGOs) underline the fact that women are generally discriminated against in the field of journalism. They also call for the necessity of women owning their own newspapers.

In parallel, various academic and civil society voices continue to militate for women's political rights. It is relevant to remember that it was the efforts of organizations, governmental or non-governmental, that the "quota" system for women in the parliament and local municipalities is now a reality. However, and despite these positive aspects, we still need to portray Moroccan educated women significantly more often than illiterate women, and, thus, create role models for the future generations. This will allow women to appear in progressive roles that empower them. Despite the positive efforts on the part of the Moroccan media, one cannot help remarking that the women who benefit from positive and progressive images generally belong to upper classes. We still need more positive and progressive portraying of women as agents of change by underlining the various roles of lower class women, their participation in the economic field, their low wages, their exclusion from the decision-making process, and their overall marginalization.

If the Moroccan media, especially the daily press, continues its over-reporting of women in criminal news, of passive women, of women as sexual objects, stereotypes will easily be perpetuated and transmitted from generation to generation. To remedy this, a number of solutions can be proposed: incorporating media in the civil society agendas, encouraging serious fieldwork on the topic, engaging women in media decision making, and so on.

Radio

I notice a very high rate of radio listenership in Morocco: when driving cars, when selling in shops, in the kitchen, and so on. Gender-wise, one can think of working toward narrowing the gap between men at the level of reporting, topics, interviews, and so on. It is also important that the various gender equality programs that are devised by the Ministry of Women's issues and solidarity be aired on the radio and during the peak hours of listenership. There are also organizations that target the creation of networks of women working in and on the media across the Maghreb region. Such networks are excellent platforms for discussing issues and media-related problems, as well as ways to confront them. Another project to consider is the creation of women-led ethics committees that would deal with the Moroccan National Press and have links with international programs for gender equality in the media.

Such gender-based programs do not aim to empower women at the expense of men; they target equality between men and women in the media and, at the same time, underline the specific unequal conditions that harm women working in the media field or women as subjects of the media. Developing ethics of the visual and press media guarantees a fair treatment of men and women and combats discrimination, as well as safeguarding the right of individuals to free expression. Various experiences in the European countries can be taken into consideration while keeping in mind the fundamental cultural differences between countries.

Exercising the profession of a journalist is still a hard task for women in Morocco. The new Moroccan Family Law (*Mudawana*) ensures legal rights for women but a lot is still to be done at the level of changing mentalities and facilitating women's freedom of movement. The weight of tradition and a heavy space-based patriarchy are still in the way. The tasks involved in exercising the profession of a journalist often include forging professional relationships and meeting new people at various times of the day (and sometimes night) and in various public places such as hotels and cafés, which can be very difficult for women. These tasks are often seen as space-transgression for women and often constitute a source of constant stress and feeling of guilt. A woman's reputation is considered her family's reputation. Such encounters may also result in sexual harassment. The interviews I had with women journalists confirm these realities, which stay in the way of women having higher positions in the media enterprise. It is for reasons like these that women shun from choosing a media career.

Issues to Consider

In the absence of statistics, it seems that Moroccan women are rather few in the newsmakers in leading national and local news reports. Today, various driving forces are behind the image-construction of women in contemporary Moroccan media. Some of these forces are local and some are part of the global process. Combating and eradicating the existing stereotype of women as sex models in Moroccan mass media are still a challenge. Another important issue is that technology is not always gender neutral.

Conclusion: A Paradox

While the Moroccan feminist movement has scored spectacular results, and while the woman's issue has become part and parcel of Morocco's current transition to democracy, these highly positive scores and the evolution of women's social status are not accurately reflected in the media. A clearer strategy on women's issues should be a priority for the

Moroccan government. A government ministry study released Monday (April 14, 2008) in Rabat, under the title "Moroccan Media: Facts and Prospects," clearly underlines the fact that the images of women portrayed in television, the press, and advertising do not echo the political message of the government. The results of an analysis commissioned by the Ministry of Social Development, Family, and Solidarity show that the Moroccan media still associate women with household and family life.

Most advertisements perpetuate sexist stereotypes by showing women as housewives and men as directors, chairmen, executives, and businessmen. Both broadcast television and written press focus on topics that interest men such as politics, economics, and sports, and only rarely address issues such as violence against women or sexual harassment. Even horoscopes in mainstream newspapers address men only.

One particularly important season in the daily lives of Moroccans is Ramadan. During this season, viewers tend to watch the national channels especially Al-Ulaa and 2M. It is important to use this occasion to improve the image of women in the media. Various studies have used the Ramadan period to assess the attitudes toward women and the results indicate that these images are rather negative. For example, the role of women in reducing street violence is not highlighted despite the fact that sexual harassment and fighting violence against women are topics first brought about in the public sphere by women's NGOs.

It is true that some directors and scriptwriters are endeavoring to convey more progressive images of women. Moroccan society at large is increasingly conscious that women are assuming new roles in society and more and more institutional means of generating positive images of women are available. The National Union of Moroccan Press is calling for a "a more balanced image of women" in the Moroccan media. In fact, a media culture is badly needed in Morocco. Women's services to the nation, as well as their achievements at the social level, need to be valorized and acknowledged publicly. Multi-sector action plans, as well as awareness-raising campaigns, are badly needed. It is urgent to fill the huge gap between the negative images that the Moroccan media vehicle and the spectacular achievements that Moroccan women score everyday on the ground. Today's Morocco has launched many reforms, strategies, and schemes to effectively support women and improve their status; the media must sustain this reality.

Notes

1 The return of the veil and the traditional roles for women was perceived as a sort of "regression" by liberal women but as "progress" by the Islamists.
2 The major breakthroughs in the new Family Law are as follows:

(a) Wives and husbands are now jointly and equally responsible for their households and families; the previous duties of wives to obey their husbands will be abolished.
(b) Men and women may enter into marriage of their own free will and with equal rights. Brides no longer require the permission of a male legal guardian, but may have themselves "given away" if they so desire. Polygamy (the right of a man to marry up to four women) will be starkly restricted.
(c) A husband can no longer simply abandon his wife without consequences; divorce is being made easier for women. Simply uttering the ritual words for a divorce (repudiation, or *talaq*) is no longer sufficient for legal divorce, nor can a divorce be authorized by a notary public (*adul*). In all cases, the desire of a husband or wife for divorce must be authorized by a government family court.
(d) The minimum age at which women may marry will be raised to 18; exceptions may be made with a judge's permission.
(e) Couples will have joint custody of children conceived premaritally (during the "engagement"). If the husband refuses to recognize the child as his own, he can be forced to undergo a parentage test. This was not possible in Morocco up to now, leading many fathers to refuse to accept responsibility for children conceived out of wedlock, and causing the number of single mothers in Morocco to skyrocket.
(f) The Family Law needs to be enforced; it assigns a key role to the judiciary in upholding the rule of law and provides for the public prosecutor to be a party to every legal action involving the enforcement of Family Law stipulations.

3 Before 2006, Moroccan women married to non-Moroccans could not pass on their nationality to children.
4 The rate of illiteracy among Moroccans over ten years of age dropped to 38.5% at the end of 2006, from 43% in 2004.
5 The main languages of the media are written Arabic, spoken Arabic, and French.

References

Belarbi, A. 1993. *Le Salaire de Madame*. Casablanca: Le Fennec.
Calvert, S. L., A. B. Jordan, and R. R. Cocking. 2002. *Children in the Digital Age: Influences of Electronic Media on Development*. Westport: Praeger.
Ennaji, M. 1991. "Aspects of Multilingualism in the Maghreb." *International Journal of the Sociology of Language* 87:7–25.
Ennaji, M. 2005. *Multilingualism, Cultural Identity, and Education in Morocco*. Boston: Springer.
Mernissi, F. 1993. *Doing Daily Battle*. London: The Women's Press.
Naamane-Guessous, S. 2001. *Au Delà de Toute Pudeur. La Séxualité Féminine au Maroc*. Casablanca: Eddif.
Naciri, R. 2003. "The Women's Movement in the Maghreb: With Emphasis on Tunisia, Morocco and Algeria." *Al Raida* 20 (100): 20–28.
Sadiqi, F. 2003. *Women, Gender and Language in Morocco*. Leiden and Boston: Brill Academic Press.
Sadiqi, F. 2008. "The Central Role of the Family Law in the Moroccan Feminist Movement." *The British Journal of Middle Eastern Studies* 35, no. 3 (December): 325–37.

Sadiqi, F., and M. Ennaji. 2006. "The Feminization of Public Space: Women's Activism, the Family Law, and Social Change in Morocco." Special issue, *Journal of Middle East Women's Studies* 2, no 2 (Spring): 86–110.

Sadiqi, F., A. Nouaira, A. ElKhouly, and M. Ennaji, eds. 2009. *Women Writing Africa. The Northern Region*. New York: The Feminist Press.

Van Dijk, T. 1993. "Principles of Critical Discourse Analysis." *Discourse & Society* 4 (2): 249–83.

PART IV

WOMEN, COPTS, AND OTHER MINORITIES IN EGYPT

This part reveals that Islamist and Salafist parties harbored significant antipathy to Egypt's feminist and women's rights, especial during and after the revolution under the Morsi government. It argues that there is a sense of greater support for women and minorities under the new government, despite continuing political divisions.

The part also shows that the recent rise of the Muslim Brotherhood to power in Egypt sparked confrontation and tensions regarding religious minorities, among whom are the Copts who constitute the largest minority in the Arab World. The chapter provides a historical overview of the conflict between the Brotherhood and the Coptic community and explains why the relationship between the two continues to be one of mistrust, discord, and apprehension.

In addition to discussing the torment of religious minorities, particularly Christian Copts, Nubians, Bahai's, Berbers, and Blacks, this part explores their social and political circumstances after decades of exclusion, discrimination, and mobility restrictions. It underlines that liberal and democratic movements, among women and minorities, recognize that they must work independently as well as influence future governments.

9

EGYPT'S REVOLUTION RESHAPES WOMEN'S RIGHTS ADVOCATES AND THEIR AIMS

Sherifa Zuhur

Women's rights advocates in post-revolutionary Egypt have an uphill battle. Society's perceptions of women's rights remains limited—even with regard to the public abuse and violence against women euphemistically referred to as "*taharrosh*" (harassment). Women activists are factionalized in the wake of the January 25, 2011, and June 30, 2013, revolutions—some longtime supporters of women's rights have allegiances to the small youth group known as April 6, some of whose members defied a new protest law in November 2013. But many others believed women must seize the opportunity to obtain greater rights in a draft constitution finalized in the fall of 2013 and in the referendum in January 2014.

Women's rights activists are concerned that with regard to many indicators women still face very strong measures of discrimination in Egypt, and during the two and half years since the 2011 revolution, little progress has been made with regard to women's political participation, improving their status via legal reform, lowering the levels of discrimination and family violence, and fighting back against constrictions of women's rights promoted by Salafists, conservatives, and Islamists.

Women activists are more hopeful since the fall of Morsi's government on July 3, 2013. Many areas of reform have been obstructed by extremely conservative trends in the judiciary. It was of great significance that

Egypt's Mufti, Shawqi Allam issued a fatwa allowing women to be judges, opening the door for new judicial appointments (*al-Ahram*, October 23, 2013) There were only forty-two women judges (since 2007) because the state council had refused to appoint them, saying that since Egypt's law is based on Islamic *shari'ah*. Since the newly amended constitution still claims the *shari'ah* as a basis for law, this fatwa is also important in setting a precedent for other adjustments to inequality.

Under President Morsi, the opponents of women's rights were strengthened. Violent instances of *taharrosh* increased in this transitional period, with women's exclusion from the Islamist party leadership resulting in a slide in political representation. The Salafists were promoting enforced veiling and even vigilante-like moral regulation policing like Saudi Arabia's *mutawa'in*—an innovation Egyptian women rejected. After July 3, 2013, when the Egyptian military deposed President Morsi and installed former Constitutional Court justice Adli Mansour as president, Islamist supporters of President Morsi continued public and university protests aimed at disrupting the new government. The latter have little interest in women's rights and many women's rights supporters had opposed the Muslim Brotherhood, but were uneasy about the strong external support for Morsi by international Islamists and anti-military leftists. Those backing the Beblawi–Mansour government were divided into supporters and opponents of the military, supporters and opponents of revolutionaries who defied a November 2013 protest law, and Salafists, liberals, conservatives, and supporters of the former (Mubarak) regime.[1] A committee of fifty revised the 2012 constitution, and although only five women were on the committee (plus five women auxiliary members), they included within the constitution specific articles strengthening women's rights. Reintroduction of a women's quota in parliament was not included, but a 25% quota on local councils for women was made part of the draft.

Women's rights advocates are not shaped solely by their interactions with their opponents in Egypt. They learned under Mubarak to build annual campaigns through cooperation with non-governmental organizations (NGOs) and the media. Egypt's women's rights activists may be too small and divided to constitute a social movement; however, I find it useful to analyze them as such. Their opponents have grown in numbers, but so has a body of younger and older women who (a) use women's rights and gender as a category of analysis, (b) cooperate across political boundaries (and sometimes national ones, in regional endeavors), (c) make a living within the NGO communities, and (d) are media-savvy.

Charles Tilly reflects on social movements that enact successful action-oriented programs—creation of special-purpose associations and coalitions, public meetings, solemn processions, vigils, rallies, and demonstrations (Tilly 2004, 3). Egyptian women have done this, and although public demonstrations were once illegal, Egypt's demonstrations have now become so ubiquitous that the government sought to re-regulate them. Many restrictions on the use of public information constrained activists from working on certain issues, such as discussions of female genital mutilation (FGM) or harassment on public media, but a less regulated media has broken these boundaries. Women's activists also demonstrated Tilly's qualifiers of "worthiness" and "commitment" (ibid.).

Egyptian women sought to differentiate their movement(s) from international feminism and believed they could hold their own against religious adversaries by wielding examples of women's rights from Islamic history and Islamic counter discourse. Drawn into culture wars in the 1990s, some later acknowledged the futility in attempting to convince, or win arguments against these parties.

Egyptian women's advocates had long interacted with international women's rights advocates, for example, in comparing Egyptian feminist campaigns against legalized prostitution in the early 1920s with European anti-white-slavery efforts by Bertha Pappenstein. Badran explains that Egyptians were excluded in Egypt from the Committees for the Suppression of Traffic in Women and Children, until many Europeans left the country. Huda Shaarawi, leader of the Egyptian Feminist Union (EFU), spoke out at the Graz Convention of the International League for the Suppression of Traffic in Women and Children about the capitulatory treaties that granted Europeans special legal status and had been an impediment to an anti-prostitution law (Badran 1996, 193–200). Many other differences have arisen between the international funders of women's NGOs and the Egyptian activists working in these NGOs since.

However, given the political shifts of the 2011 revolution, women's rights advocates realized that state feminism linked to the Hosni Mubarak regime, and his National Democratic Party had been disabled under the government of Mohamed Morsi. Groups such as the National Council of Women were vulnerable to charges of former regime ties and being generationally irrelevant. These and other women's rights advocates had to combat a sidelining of women's issues, and somehow breach the long-standing gap between themselves and Egypt's "silent" female majority (reaching the "grassroots-base" in earlier language). They must also confront counter-feminist actions and discourse by Islamist and Salafist parties and organizations including the Muslim Brotherhood, religious spokespersons, for-hire street thugs, or ordinary Egyptians. And because some progressive groups like April 6 were averse to decisions by the Beblawi–Mansour government such as the new protest law, some women who might otherwise support the new draft constitution instead boycotted the referendum due to their political loyalties.

Feminist ideas or a "women's rights consciousness" have been iterated, published, and active in Egypt for more than 115 years. By the end of the twentieth century, they were being reinterpreted in Lila Abu Lughod's (1998) edited collection, which had multiple purposes: going beyond documentation to critique the Westernizing modernization project and universality of feminist movements. The Women and Memory Forum, one of the longer surviving feminist groups, organized in the 1990s, engaged in historical recovery of female figures largely absent from official or political accounts, and delineated the specifics of Egyptian women's lives, highlighting differences between Egyptian feminism and its Western counterparts. The Forum's direction allowed feminists to partially avert their opponents' charge that feminism is an invasion of foreign values.

Due to the practice of female segregation known as the "harem system" practiced by upper-class women from the eighteenth century, polygyny, early and arranged marriages, and limited support for women's education and employment, as well as their reduced rights under family law, scholars, politicians, and observers commonly regarded women's oppression in Egypt as a structural and cultural issue. However, they were also the object of imperialist versus nationalist controversy. Leila Ahmed saw Qasim Amin's argument over the liberation of women encapsulated into a colonialist-influenced discourse about the veil (Ahmed in Desai and Nair, eds. 2005, 315–16). Many observers subsequently view concerns over Egyptian women's threatened rights in an environment featuring much larger numbers of Islamists and less approval of women's choice of dress[2] to be likewise part of an externally driven discourse about the oppression of Muslim women, generally. Women's bodies, their visibility and violability, have remained a primary preoccupation of all discourses on Egyptian women, as it remains in campaigns against taharrosh and other forms of violence against women. Throughout, cultural features and class divisions indelibly imprinted themselves on women's efforts to obtain or study women's rights, and women's public participation.

Even as these women and others worked to expand women's rights, we may trace counter-movements of religious conservatives (men) and also women. Zainab al-Ghazali (al-Jabali) founded the Jama'at al-Sayidat al-Muslimat (Association of Muslim Women) in c. 1937, a female wing of the Muslim Brotherhood. Al-Ghazali had joined and then left the EFU, worked in support of an Islamic state, lectured at Ibn Tulun mosque to women, wrote in the Association's magazine, and in Ikhwan (Brotherhood) periodicals. Imprisoned along with many other members of the Muslim Brotherhood, she was tortured but survived. She upheld political activism for herself and other Islamic women leaders, but qualified that women must fulfill their domestic duties. When I interviewed her in 1988, she promoted an Islamic model for women's public participation, but it is not in many respects a feminist model. Women could work politically if their families permitted, so long as they wore modest clothes[3] and observed proper segregation from men in social and employment environments.[4] However, women—as men—in opposition to the government were often forced to compromise family ideals, given the repression of the state and their commitment to the *da'wah* (mission, program to spread the Muslim Brotherhood's ideals). I perceived the Al-Ghazali to be promoting a "new Islamic woman" (Zuhur 1992).

Egypt women were not granted suffrage or rights to stand for office—neither in 1922 with nominal independence from Great Britain, nor in 1952 by the Free Officer's. They obtained these rights at least in part, through the activism of Sorbonne-educated Durayya (Doria) Shafiq. Backed by the Bint al-Nil group (est. 1948), she "stormed" the parliament in 1951 by forcing her way into the chamber of deputies with a group of women, while some 1,500 women waited outside. Her demands included a reform of the personal status code and equal pay for equal work (Nelson 1996, 170–72). Egyptian officials agreed to consider her petitions, but then stalled. The Association of Sunnites' chairman complained to King Farouq that "The feminist movement is a plot organized by the enemies of Islam and the Bolshevik-atheists, with the object of abolishing the remaining Muslim traditions in the country . . . Your majesty, protect the Orient and Islam" (Nelson 1996, 173–74). It is interesting that such claims that women's rights threaten Islam's integrity are repeated by various Islamist women and men decades later, including under President Morsi. Women finally obtained suffrage following Shafiq's hunger strike in 1954 (Hatem in Joseph, ed. 2000, 46) The 1956 constitution granted women's political rights, although women had to "request" voting registration (pp. 49–50).[5]

Egyptian women addressed discrimination and oppression, especially of poor women, which others ignored. Among them, Nawal al-Saadawi (b. 1931) was removed from her governmental post as director general of public health when she wrote *Women and Sex*.[6] This and most of her subsequent forty-nine books were banned in Egypt. She was subjected to a fierce anti-feminist critique and academic disparagement to the extent that by the 1990s, younger women had never read any of Saadawi's works, but "knew" they opposed her approach[7] (Al-Ali 2000, 78). Yet Saadawi reached an international audience (through translation) thus shaming Egyptians to respond to questions about female circumcision, incest, prostitution, forced marriage, femicide, family violence, and exploitation of poor women.

The FGM Task Force, established in the 1980s and coordinated by Marie Assaad, was supported by President Mubarak, whereas Saadawi was anti-regime. Saadawi's Arab Women's Solidarity Association (AWSA, est. 1982) also inspired NGOs, such as Gama'at Bint al-Ardh, based in Mansoura. The government actually handed AWSA over to an Islamic women's group and Saadawi was subjected to an Islamist-initiated law suit to declare her an apostate and divorce her from her husband via third party in 2001 (Gallagher in Zuhur 2003). Saadawi along with many other feminists opposed the Egyptian government's stances vis-à-vis the United States, Israel, and Iraq in the first Gulf War. Positions on foreign policy divided the independent smaller women's activist groups such as those in the El-Nadim Center for the Rehabilitation of the Victims of Violence (est. 1993), NGOs such as the Egyptian Center for Women's Rights (ECWR; est. 1996), and the state feminism of presidential wives and the National Council of Women (est. 2000). Also important were the Lagnat al-Mar'a fi Ittihad al-Muhamiyin al-Arab (the women's committee of the Arab Lawyers Union), the projects of publisher Dar al-Mar'a al-A'rabiyya al-Nur, and the women's committees of political parties such as Taqaddum or the Nasserist party.

State feminism in the Middle East (Joseph 2000; Kandiyoti 1991) allowed certain women closely associated with national governments to advocate for others, but did not lead to equal citizenship. State feminism under Sadat and Mubarak predictably stood against Islamism while a counter-movement to reform for women coalesced within the Islamist opposition, or at least was one of its reference points. With the revolution of 2011, many expressions of concern over "rollbacks to women's rights" (or "winter following Arab spring") were based on the assumption that these rights had primarily been obtained through state feminism in Egypt—rights given, rather than those demanded.

In January of 2013, the ministry of education under the advice of Mohammad Sharif, a philosophy and educational consultant, moved to delete the picture of Durayya Shafiq and the women who had been killed in the January 25 revolution from the 2013–2014 editions of the public textbooks for grades 11 and 12. The reason given—which created a storm of protest—was that these women were not wearing the *hijab* and therefore their photographs must be deleted to avoid "provoking Egyptians' feelings" to appease certain Islamic satellite channels and please "al-Azhar, the Islamic Research Academy and the Endowments Ministry" (*al-Masry al-Youm*, January 13, 2013). Egyptian women were aghast, realizing that the question of dress and the image of Egyptian women activists were being subverted by opponents of women's rights in a climate of public ignorance.

Outside of Egypt, many wrongly believed that women were absent from the January 25 revolution because media photographs showed mostly young men. Street art movements such as the Noon al-Neswa and the Mona Lisa Brigades focused on women in their graffiti to show their place in the revolution (*Egypt Independent*, February 18, 2013). Doaa Eladl, a rarity, as a woman cartoonist, addressed the new religious betrayal of women's rights in her work and was promptly charged with blasphemy (Benjamin 2013).

State feminism had been an immensely important avenue for Egyptian women's rights because virtually no legal reform or other reforms could be accomplished in the authoritarian political environment without a wide and pervasive network of *wasta* (meaning social connections, and connective power, or "pull"). However, the state had never automatically nor consistently acted to advance women's interests; women activists had to cultivate and enlighten receptive governmental power mongers, educate women and men (who would further gender equality), and promote them as journalists, governmental representatives, and in international organizations. State feminism aided the coordination of campaigns on particular women's issues with the government and the state media and sometimes foreign media, as well, or foreign institutions located in

Egypt but that were exempt from some restrictions on speech or writing. As universities slowly drew on their connections with the state to promote the study of women and gender, many young women studied fields of development studies that incorporated *jandar* (gender theory).

Legal reforms referred to as Jehan's laws had been enacted in 1979 extra judicially—introduced during recess—rescinded and reissued in 1985. In 2000, an important package of reforms was signed into law, known primarily for the legalization of *khul'*, a form of divorce that allowed women to give up their deferred bride price (a gift of money at marriage) and leave unwanted marriages (Zuhur 2001). They also created family courts and the first opportunities for women to be instated as judges. These reforms would not have been possible without President Mubarak's support and cooperation between many varieties of women activists.[8]

Since the late 1970s, growing numbers of women in Egypt adopted a new style of Islamic dress that included a head covering, longer and more modest skirt, and sleeve lengths, which was referred to as *hijab* or *ziyy Islami* (Islamic dress). Some women who adopted this dress form had no political affiliations, but others were associated with the Muslim Sisters or other Islamist groups including the Takfir wa-l-Higra, who went underground, Islamic Jihad, and the Gama'at Islamiyya who began to violently oppose the government. A discourse about the virtues of Islamic womanhood and an alternative approach to gender theory and gender relations evolved. By the late 1990s, those wearing hijab represented a visible majority. Some women iterated an Islamic response to women's rights, by emphasizing the pre-Islamic, or extra-Islamic origin of customs harmful to women, describing a complementary relationship of gender roles instead of aspiring to absolute egalitarianism, and Ezzat, like some of my students and respondents, criticized those approaches that were "anti-men," anti-religious, or accepting of homosexuality (Karam 1998, 222, see also 231).

These women contrasted with the more recently emerging salafi groups that often demanded that women remain home as much as possible, not work if possible or if not in a non-segregated environment, not drive, not speak with men, and generally observe stricter sex segregation than is customary in Egypt. Under President Morsi's rule, Salafists created a new television channel for women and their influence visibly increased since 2011.

Egypt has a very large impoverished population, food subsidies cannot be abandoned, and privatization of a large and unwieldy public sector has squeezed many and increased inequities. Cairo and Alexandria are home to large *ashwa'iyat* or "unplanned" slums, often without electricity or water. As inflation and prices increased, larger numbers lived on slightly more than US$2 a day (the global poverty limit), but they could not subsist as readily as before. One million households live in Egypt's 1,000 poorest villages—the rural areas continue to be poverty-stricken than urban areas and women's situation with regard to female mortality, exposure to violence, and likelihood to matriculate from school or become employed is worse than men's. One in every four Egyptians is illiterate, and the illiteracy rate is increasing. In all, 69% of illiterates are female, many of them older women. However, in 2009, of the 11% of youth (18–29 years) who had never been to school, 81% were female. Also more poor youth are tracked into vocational education in high school and do not go on to college. There is strong social pressure to marry, but marriage is a costly and complicated bargaining process. Beginning in the 1990s, marriage costs had grown so sharply that lower middle class and lower class couples were waiting for years to marry, on average, for more than ten years. Men assume more than two-thirds of these costs (Singerman 1999, 2008), which tend to skew marriage in favor of older grooms who can meet the expenses. As women are expected to be virgins at marriage, they are pressured to marry while still young, often without finishing high school. Or they become engaged while in university, which decreases the possibility of their entry into the work force. People see these as general structural issues, but, in fact, the situation has led to marrying off of girls as an economic strategy for families, and not only in the traditional manner—to one husband, as early as possible for as hefty a bride price (mahr) as can be negotiated—but also to what amounts to trafficking of women, where they are forcibly married and then remarried. According to Zahra Radwan of the Global Fund for Women, "There are whole villages on the outskirts of Cairo and elsewhere where the bulk of economic activity is based on trafficking in women and forced marriages" (Boros 2013).

Three times as many young women as men were unemployed (*Egypt Human Development Report* 2010) since so many women are not in the work force. Of those who are, the rate is two and a half times that of men (*Egypt Facebook page, UNICEF* April 27, 2013).[9]

Therefore, even as conditions for educated women have improved, those less educated or illiterate continued to suffer from other aspects of sex-based discrimination, particularly in the years 2000 to 2010. The deterioration of conditions for some tended to diminish the impact of reforms for others (Tadros 2010, 89) who might have entered various professions. The pressure to maintain virginity until marriage and control women's behavior meant that family violence including honor killings continued in Egypt, as well as murder following incest, and other forms of violence relating to sexual control, or control over women's movements in public.

Rather than a large cohesive women's movement, many small legal or aid-oriented projects, such as the Centre for Egyptian Women's Legal Assistance, or the New Woman's Organization, assisted women with the social consequences of laws that need reform. In some cases, laws were reformed, but judges remained more lenient to men who batter or kill women (Fisk 2010), emotionally or psychologically abuse them, or compel the beliefs, dress styles, or control the movements of their wives and daughters.

At the same time, gender activists continued to protest in public in Egypt. Harassment and physical molestation of women in public in Egypt have been a problem for many years. Some claim these behaviors are new and represent a collapse in public morality. In fact, harassing women dates back to the nineteenth century. Political cartoons then and in the struggle with the British made reference to male harassment of females in public (Rifaey 1997; Rifaey and Zuhur 2001).

In the mid-1970s and early 1980s, harassment in public had already worsened, possibly due to greater numbers of women working in public and using public transport, and beliefs held by men and boys that unrelated women are fair game for harassment. In the 1990s, women were attacked in the *mulid*s (saints festivals), which tend to be densely crowded and on a daily basis in the streets and on public transportation; women began to discuss the issue of sexual harassment, although it was agreed that it was useless to expect police assistance. These were random attacks by men of all ages in the street, the Metro stations, and bus stops. State security agents and police also sexually attacked women and men in custody.

The Kifaya movement (est. 2004) emerged to counter President Hosni Mubarak's plan to run uncontested for a fifth term of office as president. Egyptians began to speculate that Mubarak might hand over the presidency to his son Gamal. Kifaya attracted supporters in public demonstrations, used social media, and was inspired by the Eastern European democratic movements such as those in Georgia and the Ukraine (Oweidat et al. 2008, 14). Demonstrators were detained by security forces, and often tortured or physically abused. The state security forces used sexual harassment and the media photographed security tearing off women's clothes in public (*Alarabiyya.net*, May 25, 2005). In an incident on May 25, 2005, police and "thugs" attacked four journalists and other women physically. The four journalists filed formal complaints and were refused justice, finally receiving a judgment from the African Commission for Human Rights in March of 2013 (Egyptian Initiative for Personal Rights 2013).

In 2006, as crowds celebrated the Eid al-Fitr, the holiday at the end of Ramadan, men violently mauled women along Talat Harb street in downtown Cairo (*New York Times*, November 15, 2006). Two years later, the same type of attack took place, and eight men were jailed. A young filmmaker, Noha al-Ostaz, was groped by a driver in 2008, but she jumped on his car and dragged him to the police. He was fined and received a three year sentence, a first for a molester (Otterman 2008) and many members of the public complained that the sentence was too harsh. The ECWR conducted a survey in 2008 on sexual harassment, concluding that all types of women, no matter if they were veiled or not complained of harassment at the rate of 40% for inappropriate touching. A total of 30% of those in the survey said harassment occurred daily (Barakat 2013). A regional conference on harassment was convened in Cairo, December 13–14, 2009, sponsored by United Nations Population Fund (UNFPA) and the Swedish Institute of Development, coordinated with the ECWR. The articulate national and regional spokeswomen gave the impression that their activities could solve the issue, but, in fact, such media and conference campaigns did not have much of an effect, if any, on the general public.

Revolution

The Egyptian revolution of 2011 was triggered by Tunisia's Jasmine Revolution, which had ignited in December of 2010, swiftly bringing an end to the rule of Zein Abedine bin Ali. Political activists in Egypt had succeeded over the years in holding larger public demonstrations to grieve national conditions, activating major strikes in the state-built factory cities of Mahalla al-Kubra and Kafr al-Dawwar, but there was no unified opposition to Hosni Mubarak until a cluster of events ignited revolutionary fever. In Sidi Gabr, Alexandria, Khaled Sa'id was beaten to death by the Egyptian police on June 6, 2010. Protests, use of social media, and a Human Rights Watch report made his death a cause celèbre to the younger activists. Demonstrations were held through fall, and after the Tunisian revolution in January 2011, protesters burned themselves to death outside the National Assembly building. Organizers invited others to protest Khaled Sa'id's death in a large demonstration on January 25, 2011 (Police Day), including Asmaa Mahfouz's video that went viral.

On January 25, the demonstrators called for an end to Mubarak's government, corruption, police repression, and brutality and mending of the economy. Unrest spread throughout Egypt, and finally, Omar Suleiman announced Mubarak's departure from the government on February 11, 2011, and a military council, the Supreme Council of the Armed Forces (SCAF) took over the government. Soon competition emerged over the formation of a new government. Demonstrations continued, especially against the substitution of military for civilian rule, and protesters were subjected to violence, including sexualized violence.

That support for women's rights was weak was evident as some Egyptians blamed this violence on women themselves for daring to attend demonstrations, forgetting that Egyptian women had protested, marched, and participated in political events since 1919. Due to the Islamist and Salafist ideas that men and women should be separated, there were many calls for women to absent themselves from Tahrir.

On March 8, 2011, International Women's Day, women had called for a Million Woman march. Only about 200 showed up. Men shoved and insulted the women demonstrators at Tahrir, telling them to return to their homes and wash clothes, or "make *mahshi* (stuffed vegetables), and that their presence was "against Islam." Men then jumped up and took over the women's platform (*Christian Science Monitor*, March 8, 2011). Women were shocked by these spontaneous, but strongly anti-woman sentiments. The day after International Women's Day, on March 9, 2011, military police set on a group of peaceful demonstrators at Tahrir square and detained some of them at the Egyptian museum. Some were tortured, and seven women were subjected to virginity tests to humiliate them, and prove they were not virgins (and so couldn't have been raped). The women were brought to the military court and some were given one year suspended sentences. Initially, the government denied conducting the tests. Comments were continuously made implying that women in public demonstrations were not respectable (Amnesty International 2011).

On International Women's Day of 2012, an event was held at the Cairo Opera complex for women, and sixteen women's groups also organized a march to the People's Assembly to demand equal representation for women. In 2013, women again marched, this time holding figures and banners representing Egyptian women in their history, including those who had been removed by figures in the Freedom and Justice-dominated government from Egyptian textbooks.

Sexual assaults also made headlines in the international media when Lara Logan of CBS was brutally attacked and beaten on February 11, 2011, and then spoke of her ordeal on *60 Minutes*. On December 17, military police beating a young woman protester in an *abaya* pulled her outer garment off to expose her chest in a blue bra and then stomped on her. The symbol of a blue bra spread through social media to represent the shamefulness of the military's response to protesters. Mona Eltahawy, an Egyptian journalist and feminist, told of a brutal sexual and physical attack she suffered in November 2011 to the *Guardian* (December 23, 2011). She went a step further and wrote "Why Do They Hate Us? The Real War on Women Is in the Middle East" in *Foreign Policy* (May/June 2012) unleashing a storm of counter-articles, angry with her diagnosis of misogyny, and labeling her an Orientalist, an exhibitionist. Eltahawy wrote, "Until the rage shifts from the oppressors in our presidential palaces to the oppressors on our streets and in our homes, our revolution has not even begun" (ibid.).

Meanwhile political struggle with the new Islamist government had polarized women. Some were left without a strong political base, as the weakened liberal parties splintered and a boycotting National Salvation Front mostly postured without effect. Newly elected Islamist women and men also blamed the women demonstrators for attending protests and thus encouraging, or deserving sexual attacks.

The process of creating a new civilian government was carried out by the SCAF and elections were held for the People's Assembly (the other body is the Shura Council) from November of 2011 through January of 2012 and presidential elections were held in May and June of 2012. A quota for women representatives was introduced under Sadat (in 1979), challenged and reintroduced under Mubarak. Egyptians were not supportive of reintroducing the quota, but a new rule in the electoral law required parties to put a woman on each list. The rule did not specify where they were placed on the list; if they are further down on the list, it is less likely they will be elected into office. The largest bloc of seats (37.5% of the vote) was won by the Democratic Alliance that included the Freedom and Justice Party representing the Muslim Brotherhood. The second largest bloc (27.8% of the vote) went to the even more conservative Islamist Bloc, containing the Salafist al-Nour Party.

The new People's Assembly under President Morsi contained fewer women than in most other world parliaments with ten women out of 508 or only 2%. This left Egyptian women far less represented than women in South Africa, Rwanda, Mozambique, South Sudan, or Kenya—and also less represented than Algeria, Tunisia, and Saudi Arabia (ECWR 2013). Only women in Oman and Yemen (with one representative each) or Qatar (zero women) are more poorly represented in parliament. The Shura Council of 2012–2013 had 12 women, 5 elected and appointed out of 270. However, the Shura Council was dissolved, and then with the fall of the government the People's Assembly was dissolved too.

Some were dismayed that under Morsi's government and during the elections, younger liberals expressed little interest in gender equality:

> Young activists and socialist parties are not sympathetic to gender as a political category, or as basis for rights and entitlements. The hundreds of frontline fighters in their midst who also happen to be women have attained their credentials as political leaders and foot soldiers without having to make claims based on their gender. They are keen to distance themselves from the language of gender equality and the recipes and prescriptions of old political and developmental paradigms. (Sholkamy, January 24, 2012)

And yet women are voting in large numbers. Women's involvement in the revolution and their importance as bloggers or organizers did not translate into more support for women's political or legal rights probably because voters are strongly prejudiced against voting for women in office.

It is also incredibly important to women's causes that politicians who back women's rights and prioritize them are elected. Manal Abu Hasan, an elected Freedom and Justice representative to the People's Assembly, opposed women's participation in public demonstrations and said that even if the (Morsi) parliament lacked women entirely, it would provide social justice. The 25% victory of Salafists within the parliament also supported this line of thought and the 2012 constitution. By then, the veteran female and male politicians who had been instrumental in Mubarak-era gains made by the Egyptian women were mostly gone from the political scene.

On the other issues of family violence against women, discrimination in the workplace, infringements on women's ability to operate in public space, and areas of legal discrimination and exclusion from the formal political sphere, women's activists would do well to coordinate given the nature of the counter-movement.

The Morsi government offended many women's activists when it reviled a draft statement by the United Nations Commission on the Status of Women (UNCSW), which had met from March 4–15, 2013, and was deliberating its agreed conclusions on violence against women (UNCSW 2013) The increase in violence against women in Egypt in public sexual harassment had not gone unnoticed and paired with international outrage over a rape in India, the Commission hoped to spur further reform. The Muslim Brotherhood claimed that supporting the United Nations' agreed conclusions would lead to the death of the family in Egypt, sexual freedom and homosexuality. Such characterization led Egyptians to see calls for changes in legal and social structures as a form of neocolonialist intervention and denied a gender element to social justice. The Freedom and Justice Party's leader then denied the party was anti-women and claimed to support their rights to demonstrate but complained that the United Nations declaration contradicted Egyptian law and invoked al-Azhar (*Ikwhan.web*, March 19, 2013). The Ikhwan (Muslim Brotherhood) position has been that women deserve no special help unless for their family roles, and that reforms should not countermand a traditionalist understanding of *shari'ah*. It has resurrected a xenophobic position against feminism, just as in conservative responses to the *khul'* legal reform of 2000 (Zuhur 2001), when ludicrous cartoons appeared depicting women abandoning their husbands and Egypt if they signed for their own passports (Rifaey and Zuhur 2001), and Islamists vowed to undo the legal reform package.

The presidential elections of 2012 had shown an Egypt divided between the Muslim Brotherhood and their allies, namely, the Salafists, liberals, and supporters of the military or the prior regime. Before the contest between Mohammad Morsi and Ahmad Shafiq, a former member of the previous government, the most popular Islamist candidate, Hazem Abu Ismail (disqualified due to citizenship rules) said that women who do not wear hijab are apostates, and wanted to prevent women from working after they have children and segregate working environments.

Several women pursued presidential candidacy, but did not gain strong support, including Bouthaina Kamel, a journalist, and Mona Prince, a professor of English (who was subsequently charged with defaming the Prophet; *Qantara.de*, December 16, 2011).

In the next presidential election, the Salafists still held some cards as they allied with the military and liberals of the Beblawi–Mansour government. They militated against appointments of some women to the 2013 transitional governments' cabinet such as Dalia al-Sadany, who was initially proposed for Minister of Scientific Research, because she is unveiled. Two women ministers were appointed by the SCAF and served under Morsi who appointed no women. Three women ministers were appointed in the Beblawi–Mansour government, and there are no women governors.

Under Mohammed Morsi, Egyptian women's rights activists faced two further setbacks: (1) the acceptance of the new constitution and (2) Muslim Brotherhood and Egyptian governmental statements countering the United Nations' Declaration on the Elimination of Violence against Women in its 2013 program. President Morsi had convened a meeting with women activists and representatives and announced a new initiative on behalf of women (Shalaby 2013) but what he intended was never clarified dismissed the initiative (Solovieva 2013). The Muslim Brotherhood and the Freedom and Justice Party—the former was banned in late December 2013 and the latter dissolved, had, like Salafists, mostly directed positions to women in their relationship to the family—as mothers, or widows, or, in the broader Muslim Brotherhood "family," as key supporters of the party, when following Morsi's removal, many male party leaders were imprisoned. The former position by some Freedom and Justice Party representatives that women should not demonstrate was overturned, as Muslim women members of the Ikhwan or supporters of Morsi actively protested at the two protest sites of Rabaa and al-Nahda, which were violently dispersed in August. After the protest law was passed, fourteen young women and seven teens in Alexandria organized an early morning protest, blocking traffic. They were charged with the possession of weapons and thuggery, and given harsh sentences of eleven years, before their sentences were suspended or dropped (CNN, December 9, 2013). Female students also participated in pro-Morsi demonstrations in eight Egyptian universities, in some cases attacking professors, staff, and offices. In one case, they stripped a professor, who they considered politically hostile, naked and filmed her. Perhaps this means women's "right" to protest is now more normalized.

Women and supporters of religious minorities had been very opposed to certain articles in the 2012 constitution and to the absence of any specific article to protect women's rights. Nothing in the 2012 constitution stated that Egypt's laws were to take into consideration international law with its important conventions to which Egypt is a signatory. The Morsi-appointed assembly, which voted to approve the constitutional draft, was insufficiently representative of the public, and its composition precluded viable opposition on behalf of women. The assembly's eighty-five persons contained only five women all of whom represented Islamist parties: four from the Freedom and Justice Party and one from the Wasat party. Five members were from al-Azhar, two from Hadara, four from al-Wasat, twenty-one Salafists (one representing Salafi youth and one representing the disabled), and thirty-four members of the Freedom and Justice Party or the Muslim Brotherhood were part of this assembly, totaling to sixty-four of the eighty-five. (Salah 2012) However, public approved the 2012 constitution in a referendum.

However, it was overturned along with Morsi and the 2013 constitutional draft is more favorable to women's rights than the previous version. Article 10 (2012) mentions women's rights in the family and says the state will endeavor to strike a balance between women's family duties and their work in society, but women need to be recognized as individuals and persons with rights distinct from their families (DW.DE, December 21, 2012). Article 6 grants Egyptian citizenship to the child of an Egyptian father or mother, meaning that Egyptian women married to foreigners may pass on their citizenship to their children. This equalizes the situation with men and prevents their children from being denied access to education or healthcare. Article 11 promises gender equality in every dimension. This had been denied in the 2012 constitution with an argument that the *shari'ah* disallowed it (Mahmoud 2014). Therefore, women's representation in parliament, senior governmental management, and on judicial bodies is ensured. The article also guarantees freedom against all forms of violence toward women and reconciling of family duties and work. Article 180 promises a 25% quota for women on local councils. Article 19 ensures rights to education making it obligatory to the end of high school (for the first time) or its equivalents (vocational schools). This is very important to girls who often drop out of high school to marry. Article 25 commits the state to end illiteracy. A total of 10.3 million Egyptian women are illiterate (only 65.8% of women are literate, CIA Factbook 2012]).[10] Article 53 promises equality under the law, and criminalizes discrimination, requiring the state to eliminate such discrimination; Article 9 declares equal opportunities for all. Article 89 disallows all varieties of slavery, sex trafficking, and human trafficking. Article 80 defines all below the age of eighteen to be a child, granting important rights to children and promising childcare. This definition upholds the reform of the Child Act that protects children against abuses of child labor and holds parents responsible for circumcising their daughters. Setting the age of adulthood at eighteen should also counteract Salafist or others' preferences for marrying girls off at the age of puberty. Article 93 commits Egypt to all international agreements and conventions ratified by Egypt on human rights. This would forestall a scenario like that of 2012 where Morsi's government decried the United Nations' resolutions for the year on violence against women. This article restates women's equality in all matters and their proper representation in parliament.

In the post-revolutionary period, violence against women has been visible (Eltahawy 2012; Sayed 2013) to all thanks to the media and social media. It is blamed on "Islamic culture," patriarchal influences, and hostility to women's participation in politics (El Sheikh and Kirkpatrick 2013), or conversely, but selectively, by the counter-movement, on women's public presence as when Member of Parliament (MPA), Reda Saleh al-Hefnawi asked, "How do [can] they ask the Ministry of Interior to protect a woman when she stands among men?"

As women require equal access to public space now more than ever, free of sexual harassment, the issue requires state intervention. Women's rights activists have also made powerful enemies of the evolving counter movements who seek to dominate Islamic space, and interpret *da'wah* as part of a continuing revolution.

External forces who call either for democratization on behalf of defeated President Morsi or complete secularization on the issue of women are seen quite differently from within or outside Egypt. During the revolutionary period, some were startled by the media attention given to Alia al-Mahdy, who had posed nude in stockings and shoes on her website under the title "Diary of a Rebel."[11] Liberals and secular activists inside Egypt including the April 6 youth movement swiftly disavowed al-Mahdy, as her blog received a million hits. She received death threats and left Egypt; reporters later claimed she would be killed if she returned, which seems offline to be an exaggeration. The Ukrainian group Femen adopted her, and she posed in December of 2012 with two Femen members with the Egyptian flag, to protest that now defunct Egyptian constitution in a video (Mourad 2013) entitled "Apocalypse of Mohammed."

But inside Egypt, public nudity (or professions of atheism) is not as pressing as the longstanding problems of inequality under the law and in the family. Coptic women are essentially excluded from family law protections and lack the right to divorce, because they are subject to Church law's restrictions and the process of Church-granted annulments. The right to nullification or divorce was limited to infidelity or religious conversion, and it was difficult to prove infidelity. Coptic women must receive second marriage permits from a clerical council. In August of 2011, the Right to Life movement threatened the Church, saying its 150,000 members would break away if not granted the right to divorce and demonstrated that autumn. These restrictions obviously impact Coptic men as well as women, and Egypt's small personal rights NGO, the Egyptian Institute of Personal Rights promoted, in response to the idea of civil marriage or divorce (Miller 2011). However, in the 2013 constitution, Christians remain guided by their own family law.

Christian women also face discrimination on the basis of their religion, and physical attacks, including displacement in areas of Upper Egypt, which were attacked by supporters of President Morsi. They have also, on occasion, been attacked for not wearing the hijab. Berber women face discrimination in that they have fewer opportunities to leave their home areas than men do, and where arranged marriages remain a norm. Bedouin women face a variety of persistent traditions from early marriage to family violence and problems coping with poverty and the absence of men, who go to other areas, to the coastal resorts in the Sinai, for example, to work. Migrants moving through the Sinai have been kidnapped and also trafficked, including women. As militants have defined the Egyptian army in the Sinai, sharp tensions between the

Bedouin communities supporting the jihadists and those opposing them have torn certain areas.

Women's rights advocates realize that Egypt's low ranking in 2013—worst of twenty-two countries—on a Thomson Reuters Foundation poll on conditions for women is no accident (Boros 2013). The extended period of political transition has prevented some changes from being sought. Women know they will not be granted these rights if passive. They must now rely on their own efforts and grassroots organizational talent, as has been true in the past.

A few recent efforts at effective television commercials against sexual harassment have been circulated. Another "take" rather than "wait" endeavor is the grassroots Operation Anti-Sexual Harassment group formed to physically combat harassers in November of 2012. They were in Tahrir Square when nineteen sexual assaults took place, and the volunteers themselves were attacked. They coordinate with other groups such as the Shuft Taharosh (I Saw Harassment) initiative of Fouda Watch, which encourages women to report instances of physical harassment; the HarassMap; the Nefssy Initiative; the Anti-Harassment Movement; and are supported by longstanding NGOs such as the Egyptian Initiative for Personal Rights, Nazra for Feminist Studies, and the Nadeem Center.

This reaction renders observers and activists hopeful that the revolution would finally recognize Egyptian women, despondent and outraged (Badran, February 2013; Badran, April 2013) by attacks on them and their exclusion, and awaken them to the fact they will wage a women's revolution on their own. Under Morsi, civil society was too weak to overcome the government's position (Elsadda 2013) but women now have a new opportunity. They must win seats on their own steam in 2014 elections without a quota. The parliament will be unicameral; there will be fewer appointed seats (which were sometimes allocated to women, or Christians in the past). Women will have to overcome the political parties' propensity to place their names lower on the electoral lists.

That post–Arab Spring feminisms must return to informal, opposition-aligned, even dissident structures is perhaps inevitable due to the strength of patriarchal privilege and given the growth of Islamist parties. The so-called moderate Muslim Brotherhood has been severely weakened, but the generalized ideas spread by conservatives that women's rights activists are anti-Egyptian, in pursuing a foreign philosophy (feminism) that will destroy the family and society, must still be combated by those who can point to the strong role played Egypt's women's rights activists in the country.

Practices deleterious to sex role expansion like the imposing of female segregation (as by Hamas in girls schools, Islah in Yemen, or the public norms in Saudi Arabia) have also been dealt blow with the banning of the Muslim Brotherhood, but such practices are regarded favorably by Salafists and other remaining conservatives.

International observers expressed valid and actionable concerns about women in the Arab Spring countries (Coleman 2012; Omar 2011). Women were not well served by an insulating patriarchal local government that ignored their rights while declaring a commitment to social justice. Feminism's image may have been wrongly tainted by Westernism or radicalism, and it may once again represent Egyptian women's best or only hope for obtaining gender justice.

Notes

1 Referred to derogatively as *feloul* (remnants).

2 According to a Pew study comparing Tunisia to other Arab countries, only 14% of Egyptians surveyed think that women should have the right to choose their own style of dress (meaning degree of covering up in public; 58), 52% thought women should wear hijab (54–55), and only 5% disagreed that a woman might not obey her husband (51). Mansour Mouadel et al. "The Birthplace of the Arab Spring: Values and Perceptions of the Tunisian Public in a Comparative Perspective." http://mevs.org/files/tmp/Tunisia_FinalReport.pdf.

3 Sherifa Zuhur, *Revealing Reveiling: Gender Ideology in Contemporary Egypt* (Albany: State University of New York Press, 1992).

4 Personal interviews with Zaynab al-Ghazali, Cairo, 1988.

5 Shafiq, however, confronted Nasser again over his authoritarianism and with other political demands and was placed under house arrest, which eventually may have broken her spirit.

6 Homa Khaleeli, "Nawal Saadawi: Egypt's Radical Feminist." *Guardian*, April 15, 2010, http://www.guardian.co.uk/lifeandstyle/2010/apr/15/nawal-el-saadawi-egyptian-feminist.

7 Al-Ali conducted her interviews with feminist figures and groups in Cairo in 1995–1996. Many of the same groups and individuals were present and active up to 2000 when American University in Cairo's Dean Cynthia Nelson drew on some of them to help establish a program in gender and women's studies. Many of my women students and contacts at this time reflected the same impatience with al-Saadawi and Western or "radical" feminists in general despite their concern with sexual harassment in the streets, gender discrimination, and interest in gender studies. Saadawi also recruited others into her al-Nahda al-Fikriyya lil-Mar'a Misriyyain 2000, a small group which met clandestinely. In this period, anti-regime activists were also responding to efforts by the state to control the cultural field even as they tried to withstand other types of attacks by Islamists or conservative Islamists (Mehrez 2010, 3–6, and also in the Appendices, 255–72).

8 The comprehensive discussions of laws requiring reform were supported by the World Bank and UNICEF in Mona Zulfiqar, *Women in Development: A Legal Study* (Cairo: UNICEF 1995).
9 See https://www.facebook.com/UNICEFEgypt, accessed Septmber 1, 2013.
10 See https://www.cia.gov/library/publications/download/, accessed March 11, 2015.
11 Her boyfriend, blogger Kareem Amer, had been charged with apostasy and insulting the president in the Mubarak period.

References

Alarabiyya.net, May 25, 2005.

Al-Ahram Weekly, October 10, 2013.

Aboul Enein, Ahmed. "Shura Members Condemn UN Declaration against Violence towards Women." *Daily News Egypt*, April 15, 2013.

Abu Lughod, Lila, ed. *Remaking Women: Feminism and Modernity in the Middle East.* Princeton: Princeton University Press, 1998.

Ahmed, Leila. "The Discourse of the Veil." In *Postcolonialisms: An Anthology of Cultural Theory and Criticisms*, edited by Gaurav Desai and Supriya Nair, 315–17. New Brunswick: Rutgers University Press, 2005 (reprinted from her book *Women, Gender and Islam*).

———. "Treacherous Sympathy with Muslim Women: Feminism, Colonialism and Islamophobia." *Qantara.de*, August 18, 2011. http://en.qantara.de/Treacherous-Sympathy-with-Muslim-Women/16963c144/index.html.

Al-Ali, Nadje. *Secularism, Gender and the State in the Middle East: The Egyptian Women's Movement.* Cambridge: Cambridge University Press, 2000.

Amnesty International. "Egypt: Admission of Forced 'Virginity Tests' Must Lead to Justice." May 31, 2011. http://www.amnesty.org/en/news-and-updates/egypt-admission-forced-virginity-tests-must-lead-justice-2011-05-31.

Badran, Margot. *Feminists, Islam and Nation: Gender and the Making of Modern Egypt.* Princeton: Princeton University Press, 1996.

Badran, Margot. "Hope for a Proper Revolution." *Qantara.de*, February 27, 2013. http://en.qantara.de/Hope-for-a-Proper-Revolution/20731c526/index.html.

———. "A Project of Patriarchal Extremism: The Muslim Brotherhood and Women's Rights in Egypt." *Qantara.de*, April 26, 2013. http://en.qantara.de/A-Project-of-Patriarchal-Extremism/20987c23300i0p163/index.html.

Barakat, N. "Defying Sexual Harassment." *Al-Ahram Weekly*, October 10, 2013. http://weekly.ahram.org.eg/News/4338/30/Defying-sexual-harassment.aspx.

Baron, Beth. *Egypt as a Woman: Nationalism, Gender and Politics*. Berkeley: University of California Press, 2005, 2007.

Benjamin, Medea. "Egyptian Female Cartoonist Pokes Fun at Fundamentalists." *Counterpunch*, March 29–31, 2013. http://www.counterpunch.org/2013/03/29/egyptian-female-cartoonist-pokes-fun-at-fundamentalists/#.UVemC96u2Oc.facebook.

Boros, Crina. "Egypt Is Worst State for Women, Comoros Best: Survey." *Reuters*. November 12, 2013. http://www.reuters.com/article/2013/11/12/us-arab-women-idUSBRE9AB00820131112.

Coleman, Isabel. "Women's Voices on the Arab Spring." Council on Foreign Relations, January 27, 2012. http://www.cfr.org/middle-east/womens-voices-arab-spring-isobel-coleman/p27209.

"Egypt Human Development Report." United Nations Development Program and Institute of National Planning, Egypt, 2010. http://www.arab-hdr.org/publications/other/undp/hdr/2010/egypt-e.pdf.

"Egypt PM Orders Police to Instate Sexual Harassment Hotline." *Al-Ahram Online*, March 28, 2013. http://tahrirsquared.com/node/3794.

Egyptian Initiative for Personal Rights. "Egypt Held to Account for Failing to Protect Women Demonstrators from Sexual Assault." Egyptian Initiative for Personal Rights, March 14, 2013. http://eipr.org/en/pressrelease/2013/03/14/1657.
El-Najjar, Mona, and Michael Slackman. "Silence and Fury after Sexual Attacks on Women." *New York Times*, November 15, 2006.
ElSadda, Hoda. "A War against Women: The CSW Declaration and the Muslim Brotherhood Riposte." *OpenDemocracy.net*, March 28, 2013. http://www.opendemocracy.net/5050/hoda-elsadda/war-against-women-csw-declaration-and-muslim-brotherhood-riposte.
ElSadda, Hoda, and Umaima al-Bakr, eds. *Zaman al-Nisa' wa al-Dhakira al-Badila* [Women's Time and Alternate Memory]. Cairo: The Women and Memory Forum, 1998.
El Sheikh, Mayy, and David D. Kirkpatrick. "Rise in Sexual Assaults in Egypt Sets off Clash over Blame." *New York Times*, March 25, 2013. http://www.nytimes.com/2013/03/26/world/middleeast/egyptian-women-blamed-for-sexual-assaults.html?pagewanted=2&_r=0.
Eltahawy, Mona. Why Do They Hate Us? The Real War on Women Is in the Middle East." *Foreign Policy*, May/June 2012. http://www.foreignpolicy.com/articles/2012/04/23/why_do_they_hate_us.
Fisk, Robert. "The 'Lie' behind Mass 'Suicides' of Egypt's Young Women." Part 3. *Independent*, September 9, 2010. http://www.independent.co.uk/voices/commentators/fisk/robert-fisk-the-lie-behind-mass-suicides-of-egypts-young-women-2074229.html.
Gallagher, Nancy. "Apostasy, Feminism, and the Discourse of Human Rights." In *Women and Gender in the Islamic World*, edited by Sherifa Zuhur, 121–30. Berkeley: University of California, International and Area Studies with University of California Press, 2003.
Hatem, Mervat F. "The Pitfalls of Nationalist Discourses on Citizenship in Egypt." In *Gender and Citizenship in the Middle East*, edited by Suad Joseph, 33–57. Syracuse: Syracuse University Press, 2000.
Joseph, Suad, ed. *Gender and Citizenship in the Middle East*. Syracuse: Syracuse University Press, 2000.
Kandiyoti, Deniz, ed. *Women, Islam and the State*. Basingstoke, Macmillan, 1991.
Karam, Azza. *Women, Islamisms and the State: Contemporary Feminisms in Egypt*. London: Macmillan, 1998.
"Katani: Freedom and Justice Party Supports Women, [sic] Right of Peaceful Demonstration" Ikhwanweb. March 19, 2013. http://www.ikhwanweb.com/article.php?id=30747.
Khaleeli, Homa, "Nawal Saadawi: Egypt's Radical Feminist." *Guardian*, April 15, 2010. http://www.guardian.co.uk/lifeandstyle/2010/apr/15/nawal-el-saadawi-egyptian-feminist.
Mahmoud, Tamer Nagy. "Egypt's Half-Full Cup of Egypt's Constitution." *Atlantic Council*, January 9, 2014. http://www.atlanticcouncil.org/blogs/egyptsource/the-half-full-cup-of-egypt-s-new-constitution#.Us8UUihhdZo.facebook.
Mehrez, Samia, ed. *Egypt's Culture Wars: Politics and Practice*. New York: Routledge, 2010.
Miller, David. "Egyptian Copts Demand Right to Divorce." *Jerusalem Post*, August 17, 2011.
Mouadel, Mansour, Zeina Mneimneh, Julie de Jong, Daniel Guzman Herrera, Stuart Karabenick, Tarek Bellaj, Mohamed Kerrou, John Boiney, Summer Allen, Marianne Abbott, Jill Egeth, and Mohamed Ikbal Elloumi. "The Birthplace of the Arab Spring: Values and Perceptions of the Tunisian Public in a Comparative Perspective." Pew Survey, 2013. http://mevs.org/files/tmp/Tunisia_FinalReport.pdf.
Mourad, Sara. "The Naked Bodies of Alia." *Jadaliyya*, January 1, 2013. http://reports.jadaliyya.com/pages/index/9291/the-naked-bodies-of-alia.

Nazra for Feminist Studies. "Joint Statement." March 12, 2012.
Nelson, Cynthia. *Doria Shafik: A Woman Apart*. Cairo: American University Press, 1996.
Omar, Manal. "Women and the Arab Spring." Testimony before the Senate Foreign Relations Subcommittee on International Operations and Organizations, Human Rights, Democracy, and Global Women's Issues and the Subcommittee on Near Eastern and South Central Asian Affairs. Washington, DC: United States Institute of Peace, November 2, 2011.
Otterman, Sharon. "In Cairo, A Groping Case Ends in a Prison Sentence." *The Lede*, October 23, 2008. http://thelede.blogs.nytimes.com/2008/10/23/in-cairo-a-groping-case-ends-in-a-prison-sentence/.
Oweidat, Nadia, Cheryl Bernard, Dale Stahl, Walid Kildani, Edward O'Connell, and Audra K. Grant. *The Kefaya Movement: A Case Study of a Grassroots Initiative*. Washington, DC: Rand, 2008.
Qantara.de. "The Revolution Is Not over as Long as the Military Rules." *Qantara.de*, December 16, 2011. http://en.qantara.de/The-Revolution-Is-Not-Over-as-Long-as-the-Military-Rules/18061c39/.
Rifaey, Tonia. "An Illustration of the Transitional Period in Egypt 1919-1924: Political Cartoons in Egypt's Revolutionary History." Master's thesis., Department of Arabic Studies, American University in Cairo, 1997.
Rifaey, Tonia, and Sherifa Zuhur, "Visualizing Identity: Gender and Nation in Egyptian Cartoons." In *Colors of Enchantment: Theater, Dance, Music and the Visual Arts in the Middle East*, edited by Sherifa Zuhur, 386–405. Cairo, Egypt and New York: American University in Cairo Press, 2001.
Salah, Fady. "The 85 People Deciding the Fate of Egypt." *Daily News Egypt*, December 4, 2012. http://www.dailynewsegypt.com/2012/12/04/the-85-people-deciding-the-fate-of-egypt/.
Salem, Sara. "Femen's Neocolonial Feminism: When Nudity Becomes a Uniform." *AlAkhbar English*, December 26, 2012.
Sayed, Diana. "Terror in Tahrir." *Egypt Independent*, March 2, 2013. http://www.egyptindependent.com/opinion/terror-tahrir.
Shalaby, Ethar. "Morsi Announces Initiative to Support Women's Rights." *Daily News*. March 24, 2013. http://www.dailynewsegypt.com/2013/03/24/morsi-announces-initiative-to-support-womens-rights/.
Sholkamy, Hania. "Egypt's Women Missing from Formal Politics." *Ahramonline*, January 22, 2012. http://english.ahram.org.eg/News/32349.aspx.
Sholkamy, Hania. "Why Women Are at the Heart of Egypt's Political Trials and Tribulations." *OpenDemocracy.Net*, January 24, 2012. http://www.opendemocracy.net/5050/hania-sholkamy/why-women-are-at-heart-of-egypt's-political-trials-and-tribulations.
Singerman, Diane. "Marriage and Divorce in Egypt: Financial Costs and Political Struggles." In *Les métamorphoses du mariage au Moyen-Orient*, edited by Dir. par Barbara Drieskens, 75–96. Cahiers de l'IFPO, 2008.
Singerman, H. 1999. *Art Subjects: Making Artists in the American University*. Berkeley: University of California Press.
Solovieva, Darla. "Activists Challenge Egypt's Views on Women's Status in Society." *Al Monitor*, March 29, 2013.
Tadros, Mariz. "Egypt." In *Women's Rights in the Middle East and North Africa. Progress amid Resistance*, edited by Sanja Kelly and Julia Breslin, 89–120. New York and Lanham: Freedom House; Rowman & Littlefield Publishers, 2010.
Tilly, C. *Social Movements 1768-2004*. Boulder and London: Paradigm and Publishers, 2004.
United Nations Commission on the Status of Women (UNCSW). "The elimination and prevention of all forms of violence against women and girls." E/CN.6/2013/L.5Draft Agreed Conclusions submitted by Ms. Marjon Kamara, March 19, 2013. http://www.un.org/ga/search/view_doc.asp?symbol=E/CN.6/2013/L.5.

Zuhur, Sherifa. "Claiming a Space for Minorities in Egypt after the Arab Spring." In *Multiculturalism and Democracy in North Africa*, edited by Moha Ennaji. New York: Routledge, 2014.

Zuhur, Sherifa. "The Mixed Impact of Feminist Struggles in Egypt during the 1990s." MERIA, March 2001, http://www.gloria-center.org/2001/03/zuhur-2001-03-06/.

Zuhur, Sherifa. *Revealing Reveiling: Gender Ideology in Contemporary Egypt*. Albany: State University of New York Press, 1992.

Zuhur, Sherifa, ed. *Women and Gender in the Islamic World Today*. Berkeley: University of California International and Area Studies and University of California Press, 2003.

Zulfiqar, Mona. *Women in Development: A Legal Study*. Cairo: UNICEF, 1995.

10

COPTS AND THE MUSLIM BROTHERHOOD: A HISTORY OF DISTRUST AND CONFLICT

Marlyn Tadros

One of the most iconic images from Tahrir Square, during the initial days of the January 25 revolution, was that of Muslims praying in the Square as Christians formed a human chain around them to protect them from any security forces' assault. Subsequent images of the cross and the crescent together filled the news and social media sites. An increased sense of optimism and unity permeated Egyptians from all walks of life, especially as it evoked the spirit of the 1919 Revolution, which coined the phrase "long live the Crescent with the Cross." It did not take long for misgivings and cracks in the unity to surface. On February 18, Islamist Sheikh Qaradawi returned from exile to lead Friday prayers in Tahrir, indicating a harbinger of what was to come. His return was, as Brownlee (2013) noted, like that of Iran's Ayatollah Khomeini in February 1979, which "gave an Islamist inflection to the first week of the post-Mubarak transition."

Furthermore, by July 29, 2011, Islamists organized a public demonstration in Tahrir Square in what came to be known as "Kandahar Friday"—a term denoting a Tablian-style Islamization. Thousands of Islamists, including the Brotherhood, Salafists, and others, descended upon Tahrir Square with banners that derided secularists and liberals and called for the application of Islamic *Shari'a.* They also raised the flags of both Saudi Arabia and Al-Qaeda, calling for a *jihad* against all infidels and against all "foreign imports" such as democracy and parties (Aref 2011). Copts once again felt alienated and excluded from political life, especially as rhetoric against them began to mount.

This chapter will review the political involvement of the Copts in Egypt from the turn of the twentieth century until today with special emphasis on the founding of the Muslim Brotherhood and its political implications for the Coptic minority. The first section reviews the Copts in the liberal period from the turn of the century to the end of the 1920s. The second reviews the rise of the Muslim Brotherhood and its impact on politics in pre- and post-1952 revolution period. The third discusses the post–Arab Spring period to the present day and reveals the continued fallout and mistrust between the Copts and the Muslim Brotherhood.

The Political Stage at the Turn of the Twentieth Century

A historical review of Coptic involvement in politics in Egypt shows that they had been at the forefront of the struggle for national independence from the British especially since the early twentieth century and until the pre-Nasserist era. With the secularization of laws and Westernization that began under Mohammed Ali and reinforced by Khedive Ismail in the late 1800s, the socioeconomic status of the Copts improved dramatically. They were, however, slower to Westernize than their Christian counterparts elsewhere in the Arab world (Hourani 1947). In spite of such slow progress, the Copts benefited a great deal, and the average Christian was "better educated and more affluent than the average Muslim, which resulted in social tension between Christians and Muslims" (Scott 2000).

The British continued what Mohammed Ali and Khedive Ismail had begun and, according to Hourani,

> They ensured greater freedom of religious thought and expression, greater equality before the law (although still far from complete equality) . . . But contrary to what might have been expected, they neither attempted to use the Copts as instruments of government nor gave them in any way a privileged position. Individual Copts cooperated with the British, like Butrus Pasha Ghali–but in general there were fewer Coptic officials under the British than there had been in previous periods. (Hourani 1947)

Nevertheless, the Copts constituted an important segment of Egypt's growing sector of civil society. Many were engaged as civil servants while a significant number were among the landed gentry and prominent merchant classes in the cities (Rizk 2001).

Relations between Copts and Muslims continued to be fraught with distrust, as Christian communities started to be associated with Western powers. They were accused of being collaborators and as a potentially disloyal community, which led to the view that they were "potential traitors, sources of weakness and instruments of European policy" (Hourani 1947). Tensions continued to grow because of what was perceived as excessive rights of Copts over Muslims, which culminated in the assassination of the first Coptic prime minister, Butrus Ghali, in 1910 by an Egyptian nationalist.

In the wake of the assassination, Copts decided to organize what came to be known as the 1911 Coptic Congress in Assiut seeking to redress problems Copts were facing and seeking to end what they perceived as religious discrimination. Pope Kyrollos V opposed the conference because of already existing tensions and believed that the British would "exploit [the conference] to sow discord in Egyptian ranks . . . [he] therefore, issued [a] proclamation urging the conference organizers to abandon the project" (Rizk 2001). Nevertheless, the Copts decided to convene. Among their demands was proportionate representation in parliament (Al-Bishri 1982). This deepened a rift that was emerging in an already fragile national unity.

Soon, however, the national struggle for independence superseded such demands and divisions. To ensure their inclusion in the struggle for independence and to prove their nationalism contrary to popular belief, the Copts joined the leader of the revolution Saad Zaghloul. Fakhri Abdel Nour, a prominent Copt in the early twentieth century, wrote extensively in his journal about their participation and how revolution leaders supported and welcomed Coptic participation (see Abdel Nour 1992). Such expressions of unity and nationalism brought Egyptians together, yet there were underlying issues that made some Copts wary of its ultimate goals. As Hourani wrote, "there was, however, a difference between the articulate leadership and the inarticulate spirit of the movement," the latter being much more Islamic than the former (Hourani 1947).

Nevertheless, the post-revolution (1920s) was a decade marked with friendly relationships and cooperation between Copts and Muslims, joined in a struggle for independence and of establishing a democratic secular state. Al-Wafd party, headed by Saad Zaghloul, prided itself on being the party of all Egyptians and therefore Copts found refuge within its politics: "The egalitarian and secular political beliefs of the party borrowed from Western thought, could be both demonstrated and reinforced by according a share of that power to minorities" (Carter 1986, 161).

There was one significant and important setback in this unity, namely, the introduction of religious rhetoric into political discourse (Carter 1986) and the rise of the Muslim Brotherhood:

> A natural accompaniment to the use of Islam was sectarian propaganda which was aimed at the new role the Copts were attempting to play in the society and polity. This auxiliary weapon was potentially extremely damaging to both opponents and the political system because it, too, relied on ancient and tightly-held prejudice for its firepower. Sectarian propaganda was used in the first parliamentary election in 1923 and was re-employed sporadically, if with increasing frequency, thereafter. It seemed to have little effect in that first election but it was, by the 1930s, reaching a much more receptive audience. (Carter 1986, 17)

The Perfect Storm

Following the fall of the puppet Caliphate system under the Ottomans, and the proclamation of an Egyptian independent monarchy, two new radical movements began to rise, and were formally established as the *Ikhwan al-Muslimun* (the Muslim Brotherhood) and *Shabab Muhammed* (Mohammed's Youth) in 1928. They were by no means the first. There had been several religious organizations prior to that period, but were more socially inclined than politically involved. The events that brought about their rise began prior to the 1911 Assiut conference. With the advent of the British colonialists, there came the concept of "people's organizations," or non-governmental organizations, and hence several such organizations burgeoned. Particularly prominent were the expatriate organizations. Soon, however, Coptic, as well as Islamic ones began to rise and were involved with community development rather than with any political activism. Moreover, missionary work increased, to the consternation of both the Muslim majority and the Coptic Pope.

The Muslim Brotherhood was founded in 1928, out of a need within the Islamic community for political involvement, and the restoration of an "authentic Islamic ruling system," perhaps even the restoration of the Caliphate system. Al-Bishri alleges that the rise of the Brotherhood was the direct outcome of several missionary incidents, and the upsurge of feelings that Islam itself was being threatened. One of the incidents he mentions, which had long-lasting consequences on Egypt's future and indeed freedom of belief, was the Zoymer incident in 1926. Zoymer was an American missionary minister who, out of missionary fervor, entered Al-Azhar, the largest Islamic institution in the Muslim world, and began distributing proselytizing brochures. The Al-Azhar's *ulemas* reproached him, and the incident passed without consequence. Zoymer, nevertheless, repeated the same action in 1928, this time entering the Al-Azhar with three foreigners, among them a woman. Exceedingly provoked, Al-Azhar students flared up. The *ulemas* sent messages to the then prime minister, Mustafa al-Nahas, asking him to prohibit missionary activities in Egypt. Zoymer formally apologized to the Al-Azhar, but the incident had long-lasting repercussions in Egypt.

Another incident was the convening of an international missionary conference in Jerusalem, in April of 1928. Rumors spread that Islam was being attacked in the conference halls and sessions, and Palestine reached a boiling point. Fiery telegrams were sent to Egypt, inciting public opinion. The government failed to take any action, because Egypt was still a protectorate, and the missionaries were safeguarded under British authority. Several other similar incidents occurred, until the termination of foreign occupation with the Mentro Convention in 1937, by which Egypt gained full sovereignty over its lands.

Other scholars add further reasons for the rise of the Islamic fundamentalist groups. Abu Seif Yussef cites the increase of imperialist pressure, and the violent methods practiced in Morocco and Libya to crush nationalist movements. Most of all, the spread of Zionist concepts and pressures in Palestine constituted an important factor in inciting feelings of rage and concern (Yussef 1987).

Additionally, 1928 witnessed the beginning of women's liberation after their participation in the struggle for independence, and women were finally acknowledged and granted the right to join universities.

In 1923, the first popular and secular Egyptian constitution was drafted, and the secular Al-Wafd party, which by then had included many

Copts in its leadership and membership, formed a short-lived government. That constitution guaranteed minorities

> that all Egyptians are equal before the law [article 3]; they have an equal enjoyment of civil and political rights, and are equally subject to public charges and duties, without distinction of race, language or religion. Article 12 guarantees absolute freedom of conscience; and Article 13 the free exercise of all religions or beliefs, in conformity with established usages and on condition that they are not harmful to public order and good morals. (Hourani 1947, 41)

All those events created a perfect storm, and enhanced the growing sentiment of a threatened identity, which eventually gave rise to the Muslim Brotherhood, and the more radical Mohammed's Youth. Both organizations accentuated the need for an "Islamic" community with an urgency to restore the Caliphate system. Both organizations also expressed belief in the *Umma*, which comprised all Muslims and Islamic nations, rather than either the "nation" or the subsequent "Arab nationalism" concepts. But where the Muslim Brotherhood called for a reformation of society, and discussed the role of Islam with regard to the minorities, ensuring their "appropriate" treatment and protection, the Mohammed's Youth group strongly emphasized that they would not deal with minorities in any form, shape, or manner (Yussef 1987).

Not surprisingly, from the outset, Copts were wary of the Islamist organizations because they stressed religious identity over national identity, which gave rise to even more radical organizations (Yussef 1987). Because the entire nation was just emerging from the liberal secular period of the 1919 revolution, the Copts were evidently disinclined to regress to the more constraining periods, in terms of either status or responsibilities. Moreover, Al-Banna, the founder of the Brotherhood, made no effort in forming a sound theoretical basis for inclusion of religious minorities that would reassure the Copts as to their position. Making nationalism synonymous with religion was, without a doubt, inadmissible to the Copts, and they continued to reject the Brotherhood. Particularly damaging was the fact that in spite of Al-Banna's constant verbal reassurances, his spokes-newspaper published articles that expressed virulent anti-Coptic sentiments (Al-Bishri 1988).

The Rise of the Muslim Brotherhood

The Muslim Brotherhood began as a social movement with the aim of changing society in such a way as to adhere to "authentic" Islamic teachings. Al-Banna set branches of his new organization throughout the country providing social services as well as Islamic teachings. In his speeches to his followers and inside mosques and schools, he constantly condemned what he termed the immortality of people—in their thinking, ideas, and actions. He condemned university research and university life in general and existing newspapers in particular (Mogheis 1997). Al-Banna dedicated an entire section in his autobiographical treatise in which he described the period between 1914–1918 as afflicted by a "wave of atheism and immorality in Egypt" (Al-Banna 1946) citing Westernization and the adoption of foreign concepts.

One reason for Al-Banna's popularity was his charismatic and his organizational abilities, building a sense of community around which they could be mobilized (Owen 2004). But another more important reason was, as Owen (2004) noted, that he "adopted . . . a distinctive concept of the 'comprehensiveness of Islam' in which the construction of mosques, schools, and clinics provided the framework which an urban Muslim could live much of his life with little contact with the Western and secular influences around him." Hence Al-Banna gave his followers what they were seeking, namely, a sense of self assertion and identity, an affiliation to a larger *Umma* [nation] of Islam.

Al-Banna's ideals resonated with many Egyptians, especially the working classes. In the beginning, he focused on the issue of British sovereignty over Egypt, where "Muslims and Arabs have no dignity and do not rise above being paid followers to those foreigners, and we own nothing except that blood which runs in our veins and those souls that are full of faith and dignity" (Al-Banna 1946). Those foreigners also brought with them an unwelcome secularization that was alien to Islam and its teachings.

As Hourani (1991, 349) noted,

> Although the Brothers did not at first claim that they themselves should rule, they would recognize as legitimate rulers only those who acted according to the *shari'a* and were opposed to a foreign rule which threatened the *shari'a* and the community of believers.

As their numbers grew and their power increased in the late 1930s, they had to formulate a political platform by which to counter the popular Al-Wafd party (Owen 2004). Toward the end of the 1930s and beginning of the 1940s, Al-Banna began making use of the conflict between the populist Al-Wafd party's opposition to the King and joined forces with him and other minor parties to undermine Al-Wafd. In 1938, he addressed his followers in the first issue published in May of *Al Nazeer* newspaper saying that now that their numbers have increased,

> In the past, our position regarding parties and political bodies was indifferent, but now you will become their severest adversaries inside the government and outside it, if they do not respond to you and take the Islamic approach. (Al-Banna 1938, quoted in Kherbawi 2013)

Al-Banna wrote,

> Dear brethren, I invite you to practical *jihad* after the *jihad* with words, and *jihad* has a price and sacrifice. Now that ten years have passed since our first calling, we must move from *daawa* by words to *daawa* accompanied by struggle and action. We will invite all organizations and institutions to Islam. If they respond to us we support them. If they are elusive we will resort to a relentless war until God conquers us all. (Al-Banna 1938, 3, quoted in Kherbawi 2013)

Al-Banna, therefore, specifically defined his approach in two steps: first, he would invite country leaders and politicians to join his beliefs and ideology. Second, he would become their most relentless adversary inside and outside leadership if they did not respond to his call to the extent that they would use violence if needed. In fact, as Kherbawi (2013) noted, because Al-Banna's words were not clear enough as to the extent the Brotherhood would go, Al-Banna's father, Sheikh Abdel Rahman Al-Saati, wrote an article in the same newspaper explaining their position:

> Prepare yourself, soldiers of Islam, and go gently with the nation and explain the medicine for it. If the nation refuses, tie its hands with chains, put weights of iron on its back, and feed it the medicine by force. If you found a tumor in it, cut it. Prepare, oh soldiers, for in this nation many have ears and eyes but they are blind. (Kherbawi 2013)

Al-Banna's ideology with regard to the relationship between religion and the state was clearly beginning to mature and to be more clearly defined. He believed in the revival of an Islamic state and wrote in his autobiographical treatise in 1946 that this consisted mainly of three premises: the first is the concept of a holistic Islam, where Islam is not just a religion and spirituality but is "worship and leadership, religion and state, spirituality, work, prayer, *jihad*, obedience, governing, the Quran and a sword." The second premise is the Caliphate principle that stipulates "the removal of parties and directing the nation to one way only" with the aim of bringing back the "lost Caliphate" system. The third premise is that of a review of the constitution to comply with Islamic teachings, and demanding that government review all its laws to comply with the same (Al-Banna 1946).

Egypt in the 1930s and 1940

Several skirmishes occurred during the late 1930s and 1940s in great part due to the religious propaganda used in elections—whether by Muslims or by Copts. As always, when religious propaganda and rhetoric is used in political campaigns, it eventually leads to violence: "Churches were stoned, priests abused, Copts beaten up and occasionally anti-Coptic demonstrations sparked" (Carter 1986, 272).

To aggravate matters, the king and his allies began using religious aberrations as an election weapon, spreading the rumor that the Wafd Party was, in essence, anti-Islamic, because it was controlled by the Copts (Al-Bishri 1988). They even claimed that the state's institutions should be reconsidered in light of the presence of minorities, and therefore a quota system should be introduced in parliament, as well as in employment positions (Al-Bishri 1988). This policy resulted in constraining employment positions against the Copts. Additionally, in 1934, the Minister of the Interior, al-Izabi Pasha, issued a decree in which he stipulated ten conditions for building churches, which made it literally and physically impossible to build any. Those conditions survive to this day and are erroneously named as the Hamayouni Decree.

In 1935, Farouk, King Fouad's son, succeeded him on the throne. Initially, all parties enthusiastically welcomed his ascension, especially as he was the first ruler to speak the Arabic language, and seemed to be a very promising change from his predecessor. Because he was very young, however, existing parties decided to utilize him to advance their own ends. Some of his advisors suggested that Farouk be crowned in a religious ceremony at the Al-Azhar, where he should be proclaimed Caliph, a return to King Fouad's unsuccessful attempt before him. Not surprisingly, the Wafd's enemies strongly supported the suggestion, whereas the then government of the Wafd vehemently opposed it. It was a renewed opportunity for the Wafd's accusers to sustain their attack against them, and accuse the Wafd of being controlled by the Copts.

The Constitutional Free Men Party, headed by Yakan, had repeatedly won the elections against the Wafd party through rigging them. Yakan changed his liberal ideas and concepts, into ones of radical support of the king and his policies. His party went as far as supporting the king in his wish to proclaim himself Caliph. King Fouad saw that the road was paved for the acceptance of such a move, since Egypt was the country of the prominent Azhar institution, which would ensure Egypt's religious, and hence preeminent, leadership in the Muslim world. Not surprisingly, the British supported the king in his endeavor, in order to conveniently weaken the Wafd's popularity, especially as the king was easily manipulated, and under their disposition. Fortunately, the attack against the restoration of the Caliphate system came from within the Al-Azhar itself, which immediately issued condemning statements. The more enlightened Azharites realized that the restoration of the Caliphate system essentially meant the revocation of the constitution, and a restitution of the exclusive one-man rule, albeit with a *Shura* council, which was a particularly vulnerable situation, given the presence of foreign occupation. The Wafd eventually succeeded in canceling the religious ceremony, but the entire period of the 1930s continued to be a difficult time for Egypt in general, and the Copts in particular.

In 1936, the Wafd Party attempted to introduce the Christian religion to Christian students in public schools, especially in those schools that had more than ten Coptic students per grade level. The attempt failed, particularly with the already prevalent accusations that the Wafd Party favored the Copts (Al-Bishri 1988). When the Copts began sending their children to private Coptic schools, their parents were penalized because, according to the law, mandatory primary schooling meant, in essence, "public" schools. This seemed to imply that the Copts were being forced to attend public schools, in order to study the Quran. To avoid those arising complications, Law No. 40 for 1934 was issued, placing Coptic schools under the supervision of the Ministry of Culture.

Significantly, among those who were against the introduction of the Christian religion in schools was the Muslim Brotherhood. According to Al-Bishri (1988), their opposition was not in order to provoke the Wafd, but was, in fact, an ideological belief, which they perceived as an encouragement of proselytizing and spreading heresies.

Another important controversy arose and necessitated the Pope's intervention, regarding the teaching of Quranic verses in the Arabic teaching texts of poetry and language. A flyer was sent to all schools regarding the mandatory studying of Quranic verses, in Arabic language classes. The Pope strongly protested, saying that Christian students should be exempt from studying the Quran. The government retracted its decision, and made it non-obligatory for Christian students (Al-Bishri 1988).

In 1940, another ministerial decree was issued, prohibiting Coptic teachers from teaching the Arabic language in schools, which left many unemployed (Yussef 1987). Copts were also excluded from many prominent positions, particularly in the army, police, and administration (Al-Bishri 1988). It was significantly noted that whenever the Wafd came to government, newspapers wrote that Copts were being employed more than Muslims in governmental positions, and that they were even being unjustly promoted. Such claims were proven false when other newspapers statistically proved otherwise (Al-Bishri 1988).

Misr al-Fatah—A Feeble Coptic Response

Another significant group that played an important role on the Egyptian political scene of the period was the Powerful Egypt Party (Misr al-Fatah), founded in 1933. Its agenda was a contradictory combination of secular and Islamic rhetoric, and its main strength was in opposing the Wafd Party. Among its members were a handful of Copts. It failed, however, to gain any significant popularity. Its motto was "God, the Nation, and the King," which clearly indicated its alliance with the much-despised palace. It tried repeatedly to ally itself with the Brotherhood, but the latter persistently refused. In 1940, the leader of the party, Ahmed Hussein, went as far as changing the party's name to the National Islamic Party, in order to court the Brotherhood, and gain the sympathy of its followers. This came at a time when Islamic sentiments were highly charged, and seemed to be louder than the secular discourse. Ahmed Hussein, the party's leader, was trying to win the "believers" on his side. The change in name also came at a time when the king was trying to establish himself as a Caliph, criticizing the Wafd Party's leaders for rejecting his suggestion, accusing them of Coptic infiltration and control (Al-Bishri 1988). Ahmed Hussein seized the opportunity to express his support of the king and show his Islamic inclination, and called for the restoration of the Islamic Caliphate system. To prove his point, he went as far as organizing attacks against nightclubs and liquor stores, in the name of Islam.

The Muslim Brotherhood's Al-Banna, perceiving Hussein's persistent attempts at courting him and the Brotherhood, rejected his advances and refused any joint collaboration, even though both were trying to undermine the Wafd party. Two months after changing the party's name, Hussein once again restored its previous name.

By the mid-1940s, a Christian party was formed in response to the Islamic movements, namely, the Christian Democratic Party, whose secretary general was Ramsis Gabrawi. By the early 1950s, yet another Coptic party was formed, namely, the Coptic *Umma*, headed by Ibrahim Hilal, a young, Coptic lawyer who believed in forming an armed and well-organized Christian party, very similar in extremism to the Muslim Brotherhood. The first party attacked the Wafd, and supported the King. Its main agenda called for the application of the Universal Declaration of Human Rights, and for writing the Arabic language in Latin transcription. The second party was formed in 1952, and called for the restoration of the Coptic language, and the founding of a Coptic broadcasting system. It also called for a "return to original Biblical words," from which stems all the sciences, a call that was essentially very similar to the Muslim Brotherhood's regarding Islam (Yussef 1987). They wore special clothes for their festivities, with the Pharaonic key of life, Ankh, drawn on the front (Yussef 1987).

In 1947, there was a confrontation between the Wafd and the Brotherhood in the Suez area, which resulted in the burning of churches, the attack against a Coptic school during which three individuals were burnt to death, as well as several other similar incidents (Yussef 1987). The Brotherhood, in essence, aimed at embarrassing the Wafd government, and the Royal Palace immediately seized the opportunity to demand its resignation. This demand was supported by the Christian Democratic Party (Yussef 1987).

Initially, the palace hoped to use the Muslim Brotherhood as a weapon against its opponents. Soon, however, that weapon seemed too powerful even for the palace:

> in the wake of a number of political assassinations [committed by the Muslim Brotherhood] and the discovery of the Brethren's secret paramilitary apparatus, the government finally acted by dissolving the society in December 1948. The Copts were relieved but the Brethren continued to operate underground and were implicate in the sacking of a Coptic church in 1949. They were also involved in a number of minor incidents, like removing crosses from the tops of churches. (Carter 1986, 277)

As of 1946, Coptic newspapers expressed concerns that the Brotherhood, especially in the provinces, had taken "aggressive attitudes" toward Copts. They also expressed fear of the creation of an Islamic state and spoke against increasing anti-Coptic sentiments exacerbated by the Brotherhood's rhetoric and behavior:

> The Brethren used both mosques and leaflets to spread their anti-Coptic message. So worried were the Copts by al-Banna's ambitions and so often did they hear themselves compared to the Jews in Europe, that they feared that they would meet a similar fate. (Carter 1986, 274)

Yet in 1952, elections took place and the Wafd Party won a majority of seats in parliament, headed by Mostafa al-Nahas as Prime Minister. He repealed the 1936 Treaty and the Sudan agreement of 1899, which led King Farouk to remove him from government. Anti-British demonstrations and riots erupted, and were ruthlessly crushed by the British army. A group of young, unknown officers, who called themselves the Free Officers, clandestinely organized, and eventually lead, a successful coup d'état. They deposed the king, dissolved the Wafd party imprisoning the prime minister and his wife, and soon thereafter abolished the constitution and the monarchy, and declared Egypt a republic.

One additional complication worthy of mentioning that strongly affected the Coptic–Brotherhood relationship arose during the late 1930s and 1940s prior to the 1952 revolution. This was the formation of the State of Israel in 1948, which was used as an excuse to accuse the Copts of wanting to create their own state. The Brotherhood, in particular, used this event as an excuse to blame the Copts:

> At a Brethren meeting in 1936, the Supreme Guide invited both Copts and Muslims to defend Palestine. When the audience voiced its objections to Coptic participation, he pointed out that fairness demanded this . . .: "If the Copts respond to the call, good; if they do not, we will see that they suffer for it." (Carter 1986, 108)

The political climate became so charged that in the 1938 election campaign a group of Azhari demonstrators "demanded that the Copts be expelled and sent to Palestine" (Carter 1986, 109).

The 1952 Revolution and the Rise of Sayyid Qutb

Following the 1952 revolution, there were repeated waves of Coptic migration from Egypt, some for political reasons and others for socio-economic reasons. The close relationship between the Muslim Brotherhood and the Free Officers alienated the Copts and raised their alarm. The Copts were also concerned about the confiscation of land in the revolution's agrarian reform because it primarily affected them given that much of the land belonged to some of the wealthiest families in Egypt. The revolution also exempted the Muslim Brotherhood from their decision to dissolve all old political parties and offered that they stay as a non-governmental entity dealing with social issues. Additionally, shortly after the revolution, unhappy with their non-governmental status, the Muslim Brotherhood issued a statement in which they condemned the current political system and demanded a new constitution whose principles were Islamic in all aspects of life.

Until 1954, the Brotherhood continued to be the only voice of Islamic opposition in Egypt. Some Brotherhood members joined the government in Egypt and others migrated to nearby Gulf countries for a better economic life (Ahmed 1989, 20). Nasser used their support to strengthen his power but soon began stressing the ideals of nationalism over religious identity, a position that displeased the Brotherhood. They eventually demanded that any decisions the Free Officers made should be given to the Brotherhood's Supreme Leader for approval, which of course angered the Free Officers. When the Brotherhood retaliated with an assassination attempt against Nasser in 1954, his regime began a relentless crackdown on Brotherhood members, outlawing the group, imprisoning its members, and hanging a few of its leaders (Mogheis 1997). After

Nasser strengthened his power even more, he began to gradually release Brotherhood members including the Supreme Leader. In 1958, a young Brotherhood member recently released from prison named Nabil al-Borai began calling for armed violence. He was later joined by Ayman Al-Zawahiri, the currently infamous Al-Qaeda leader, among others (Ahmed 1989, 33).

Also among those who were released was radical Sayyed Qutb, a Muslim Brotherhood leader, who had become even more radicalized during his prison years. Qutb is viewed as the "father of modern fundamentalism" (Zenishek 2013). He began hatching a plan in case the Brotherhood were arrested again. Qutb adopted violence as a legitimate way to gain power and did not rule out direct confrontation with the state. It was, for him, "authentic" Islam vis-à-vis the modern and mainstream state. His plan, therefore, included the destruction of buildings and assassinations of regime leaders. In 1965, the plan was exposed and Qutb arrested and hanged, but not before leaving behind him followers who were as militant as he was:

> Radical groups identified the regime with Qutb's concept of *al-Jahiliyya*, which literally means "period of ignorance," a term used by medieval Islamic historians to refer to pre-Islamic Arabian society. However, for Qutb, it refers to the belief that the Egyptian regime and Egyptian society had turned their backs on Islam. The radical groups also adopted Qutb's modern concept of sovereignty (*al-hakimiyya*), the belief that the right to legislate belongs only to God. (Scott 2000, 44)

During that period, the Brotherhood issued a monthly journal *al-Da 'wa*, which was edited by Umar Al-Tilmisani, the Brotherhood's Supreme Guide: "The journal focused on the four major enemies: 'Jewry,' 'the Crusade,' 'communism,' and 'secularism'" (Scott 2000). Other fringe groups emanating from the Brotherhood included the more radical and militant *Al-Jamaa Al-Islamiya* and the *Takfeer wal Higra* both of which were formed in the 1970s.

Qutb asserts in his writings that only

> first generation [Muslims] received the pure Quran; while later generations tainted by exposure to Greek, Persian, Jewish and Christian ideas, were never able to rise to the same level as the first generation.

> He advocated a new system in the form of an active, organized and distinct group emerging on the battlefield to abolish the Jahali system like Mohammad did in Mecca. (Zenishek 2013)

When Sadat gained power after Nasser, and because the socialists had been in control throughout the Nasserist era, he sought the assistance of the Muslim Brotherhood, their professed enemies, to eliminate them. Sadat promoted Islam at the expense of the minorities in order to secure their support, thus causing a serious deterioration in the relationship between the Copts and the state. He immediately released the Brotherhood members who had been imprisoned during the previous regime. Many of them returned from exile, having fled Nasser's regime to other Arab petro-dollar countries, amassing enough wealth to later strongly impact Egypt's economy. Sadat also arrested and imprisoned both the leftists and the Nasserists. Despite, or perhaps more accurately, because of, Sadat's Western orientation, the re-rise of the Brotherhood coincided with a rise in conservatism and fundamentalism, vehemently opposed to the West, no less than it had been with the Soviets, leading to the eventual assassination of Sadat in 1981.

Contrary to the politically secular Nasser, Sadat encouraged religious revivalism in all aspects of life. In 1971, he went as far as changing the constitution, whereby article 2, which stated that "Islam is the religion of the state," became more specific with the addition "and the Islamic Shari'a *one of the* main sources of legislation" [my italics]. In 1979, the constitution was once again amended, and the same article changed into the "Islamic Shari'a is *the* main source of legislation" (my italics). Even though the Church did not officially object to the wording, it remained, together with the Copts, wary of Sadat's policies. Their worst expectations came true when, in addition, Sadat released and pardoned the previously imprisoned Brotherhood members, encouraging them in order to counter the socialists, leftists, and the remnants of the previous regime. More significantly, Sadat adopted the slogan of Egypt as a country of "Science and Faith," and elevated an image of a "Believer President." To further promote a religious image, Sadat began giving an annual speech on the Prophet's birthday, as well as broadcasting himself with his government, on television, during Friday prayers.

By 1972, Sadat organized a meeting with the heads of the permanent committees of the People's Assembly, following student anti-government demonstrations, led by the leftists who had full control of the students' unions and leagues. The students were, in essence, protesting the autocratic rule, emerging from the frustration and disillusionment of 1967, demanding explanations for the defeat. Moreover, they wanted a change in the political ruling system, and demanded more freedoms and democracy. Sadat, according to eyewitnesses who attended the People's Assembly's committee meeting, was in favor of conducting a dialogue with the students, whereas some members suggested the founding of Islamic groups in all universities, to respond to them instead (G. Shukri 1991). Some of those present in the committee immediately offered donations for the founding and funding of such organizations. The suggestion was carried out immediately, but the government soon lost control, as different splinter groups began to burgeon. Among those groups were the groups already influenced by the radical teachings of Sayyed Qutb such as *Takfeer wal Higra* group, and the *Jihad*, both of whom believed in abandoning, and eventually attacking the *jahiliya* society, seeking a return to the Prophet's time. They also demanded the application of Shari'a. Ironically, though not surprisingly, they were against the government itself, which had originally helped in their birth, especially as Sadat's Western-oriented policy continued to provoke them. In essence, the government, which founded them, suddenly abandoned them, and left them to mushroom on their own.

Sadat initially encouraged both the Al-Azhar and the church, once again broadening the role of religious institutions in politics, as long as those institutions remained under his control. Coptic secularists' and laymen's roles continued to decrease, while the role of the clergy continued to increase. Copts who wanted to be politically active, or become "Coptic representatives," had to do so from within the church institution (Habib and Afifi 1994). Additionally, realizing the influence of the Copts abroad, and the potential of their economic power, Sadat formed a new ministry and called it the ministry of emigration, headed by a Coptic minister, to address the problems, prospects, investments, and issues of immigration. The ministry was dissolved soon after Sadat's death.

In 1977, the government announced its intention to "apply the Islamic Shari'a," concerning apostasy, in what it called the *Ridda* law (apostasy law). The Azhar presented a draft law to the parliament, stipulating for the execution of apostates and enforcing the *hudid* system. In response, the Coptic Church called for a Christian religious conference on January

17, 1977, the second in the history of Egypt, and the convening members issued a strong statement. Although the authorities prohibited the statement's publication and circulation, the grave impact of the conference was distinctly visible, and Copts circulated the document among themselves. The statement essentially discussed several aspects: freedom of belief and of exercising rites, the protection of the family and Christian marriages, equality and equal opportunities, and the representation of Christians in local councils. It also included warnings of the explosive fundamentalist trends and movements, and demanded the cancellation of the Ottoman laws that restricted the building of Churches and the freedom to publish the Christian history and heritage. One of the conference's resolutions was making the period between January 31 to February 2 a period of uninterrupted fasting. More importantly, it declared that the conference would remain assembled until the authorities complied with their recommendations.

Sadat grew increasingly angry at his loss of control of both the church and the Muslim Brotherhood and their allies. He ordered sweeping arrests of Coptic, Islamist, and secular leaders, a move that eventually culminated in his assassination by the very people he encouraged and funded, the Islamist radicals, and his successor Mubarak took power.

The Arab Spring

Copts have generally not fared well with revolutions in Egypt. The initial reaction to the January 25 revolution that ousted Mubarak though was that this was a different revolution because it was a people's movement in which all sectors of Egyptian society participated, standing against a common "enemy," namely, an oppressive military regime. It brought back the nationalistic spirit of the 1920s.

But Copts had been increasingly concerned long before the Arab Uprising. Time and again, during Mubarak's laissez-faire attitude, incidents against Copts went unpunished, from the very subtle to the overtly violent. Immediately prior to the Arab Uprising, there were several alarming incidents. Both 2010 and 2011 began with violence against Copts: in 2010, there was the Christmas shooting and murder of seven Copts (Hassanein 2010), and on the 2011 New Year's eve, a car explosion killed twenty-three Copts in the Saints Church in Alexandria (*BBC*, January 1, 2011).

In 2010 as well, there were massive Salafi demonstrations against the Pope (Girgis and Ali 2010), which were very unique for two main reasons: first, because no one had ever cursed the Pope so openly and in a public demonstration, and second, because it occurred in Cairo proper rather than in the outskirts or villages where most sectarian incidents occurred. The heavy-handed approach of the Mubarak regime toward the people, in general, and toward the Islamists, in particular, was no help either. It created even more resentment against Christians.

The official Coptic Church's position early on in the revolution expressed its support of the revolutionary youth, paying special tribute to the Supreme Council of the Armed Forces and expressing its support of a democratic Egypt through fair and free elections (February 2011). However, during the electoral process, once again, religious rhetoric was used in political campaigns. In order to undermine some secular parties that were formed, the Islamists, headed by the Muslim Brotherhood, claimed that those parties were "Copt-oriented" and were anti-Islamic, formed only to undermine or abolish Islam.

Copts participated in the elections process by trying to choose a candidate who would ensure protecting their rights. While many became members of the secular liberal Al-Kotla party, when the choice came down to either a Muslim Brotherhood-affiliated president or a former regime member, the majority chose to vote for the latter. Needless to say, they were accused of being anti-revolutionary traitors. When news circulated that Copts would definitely vote for the latter, the Muslim Brotherhood's members in different governorates threatened them, and many Copts were prevented from voting or even leaving their homes on election day (Ishak 2012), a fact corroborated by the Ibn Khaldun Center that monitored the elections (Ali 2012).

Following the election of the first Muslim Brotherhood–affiliated president, and throughout 2011, Copts continued to face a series of discriminatory policies and sectarian attacks. Minority Rights Group (MRG) cited over ten major attacks against Copts, "most of them involving disputes about whether they had permission to build or renovate a church" (Minority Rights Group International 2012).

Particularly vulnerable were the Copts outside of Cairo. Suffice it to say that all incidents ended with the Copts agreeing to reconciliatory terms that show there is no rule of law. From the acceptance of not showing crosses outside church building (see Saleh 2011; N. Shukri 2011) to not putting crosses or images inside churches (E. Maher 2012), and from eviction of Copts in Amereya, Alexandria, and others to the harassment of monks, and from firing warning shots at them to burning down their homes, and in at least one extreme case, after burning a Copt's home in Qena, Upper Egypt, the Islamists proceeded to cut his ear and the perpetrators were later acquitted by a court (*Al-Yom Al-Sabe'a*, April 22, 2012), the situation of the Coptic minority continued to be increasingly alarming.

Blasphemy cases were on the rise, used only against the Copts, the majority of which were based on hearsay and unverified rumors:

> From 2011 to 2012, the Egyptian Initiative for Personal Rights (EIPR) said there were 36 accusations of blasphemy that were dealt with extra-legally, sometimes with village residents forcing the accused Christians to leave their village. In Cairo, several cases against prominent figures ended in acquittals. But in southern Egypt, where Luxor is located, all recent cases that have gone to trial have ended in convictions, according to EIPR. Throughout Egypt, most cases are brought against Christians. (Chick 2013)

One of the worst attacks in the history of the modern Coptic Church was the attack on the main Orthodox Cathedral on April 7, 2013. Coptic Christians attending a funeral service for four Copts killed two days earlier in a remote village called Al-Khusus, in an anti-Christian rampage, were in turn attacked themselves by at least 200 Muslim rioters as they attended the service in the Cairo Cathedral. Two Copts were killed in the attack, eighty-four injured, including eleven police officers. Islamist President Mursi's statement that "Cathedral attack is like 'attack against me'" (*Al-Arabiya*, April 7, 2013) fell hollow, especially that videos of the attack and eyewitness reports showed police complicity (Elbaiady 2013).

Add to all of the above, the death of Pope Shenouda, in March 2012, which struck the general Coptic populace quite severely because he represented to them their last solace and support. They felt more vulnerable than ever before, given that the majority of the current Coptic population have not known another pope besides him in their lifetime. His death created a larger rift between the Islamists and the Coptic people when the Salafi parliamentarians decided not to stand in a moment of silent respect and mourning for the Pope during a parliamentary session, saying they would not "mourn" an infidel. Later, their spokesperson, Nader Bakkar, approved of their action and said it was "un-Islamic" to mourn a pope (Mohamed 2012).

On November 4, 2012, Pope Tawadros II was elected as the 118th Coptic Orthodox Pope of Alexandria. The immediate Salafi reaction was to refuse to congratulate him on his election and went as far as "inviting him to convert to Islam" (Said, 2012). Controversy continued regarding whether the president should or should not attend the seating ceremony, which was set on November 11, 2012. Salafis warned the Islamist president regarding attending the ceremony because it included non-Islamic rituals (Al-Hawari 2012). Eventually, the president decided not to attend but sent his prime minister and other official dignitaries instead. In a show of support, political leaders and intellectuals attended and congratulated the new Pope.

The new pope's first message was to reassure Egyptians that he would not be involved in politics and expressed his desire to work with the president if he was a "president for all Egyptians." He also said that he had voted for the current president's rival because he was familiar with his ideas and politics and knew him personally. However, he also directed a message to the Salafis and asked them to be more "moderate" and asked them to reassure the Copts regarding their safety (*Al-Fagr* 2012).

Copts continued to participate in the political process, and joined the much-contested Constituent Assembly tasked with drafting Egypt's new constitution. The Church had delegates in the Assembly to ensure Coptic rights were taken into consideration. Among their requests was that article 2 of the constitution regarding Islamic Shari'a remain unchanged. In addition, they wanted to ensure that they would be using their own laws when it came to family law. The church also objected to article 220 of the draft constitution, which was an explanatory article of the term Islamic Shari'a found in article 2. This basically changed article 2 to making Islamic Shari'a the only source of legislation.

Eventually, when civil society and liberals began withdrawing from the Constituent Assembly because of its bias toward the Islamists, its working methodology, and its inclusion or exclusion of articles without consensus, the three Coptic Churches—the Orthodox, Evangelical, and Catholic—withdrew from the Assembly. Their withdrawal only resulted in more verbal aggression against the Copts and threats that their demands in the constitution will be summarily excluded (Ibrahim 2012).

In general, Copts continued to be excluded especially in the rhetoric of the Islamists and that of the Brotherhood in particular, beginning with denying their very existence (Nakeeb 2011) and ending with denying them full citizenship rights. Some Islamists called for the restoration of the Islamic Caliphate, and the application of Islamic Shari'a, and a more restrictive interpretation of Islamic law. The Brotherhood, which was more diplomatically inclined, said that the application of Shari'a should be a gradual process. The increased theocratization of the state eventually led to the migration of many Copts. While the numbers are contested, they range between 100 thousand to 300 thousand who are said to have left Egypt (*Masrawy*, August 24, 2012). Others continued to stay and said they would not leave their homeland. It needs to be emphasized that the hate-rhetoric was not only directed against the Copts but also against Muslim liberals and seculars, many of whom were accused of being anti-Islamic and "Copt lovers."

Post-Islamist Egypt

In the weeks prior to the second uprising on June 30, 2013, Pope Tawadros announced that Copts were citizens and had a right to choose to participate in the uprising if they so wished (*Akhbar Al-Youm*, June 20, 2013). The majority of Egyptians participated, including the Copts, and ousted the Brotherhood-affiliated president of Egypt. Many Copts received threats should they choose to participate in the protests, and leaflets were distributed with severe warnings against them (*Al-Mogaz*, June 29, 2013).

Egyptians rose again against the Muslim Brotherhood president for his myriad failures on the political, economic, and social levels, and on June 30, 2013, there was an uprising that overthrew him and the ruling Muslim Brotherhood party. An interim government was formed whose president was the head of the Constitutional Court. Three Copts were immediately chosen as ministers.

As was expected, Copts, even more than the liberals, were accused of being the primary instigators against a "Muslim" president, and there were further threats against them. In the first week following this uprising, at least ten cases of attacks against Copts had been reported. The ousted president's supporters attacked a church in a remote village called Abu Mowas, in Minya. They stormed the church, broke glass, and looted it. They also passed by Coptic homes and burnt them down (*BBC*, July 17, 2013).

According to the Egyptian Institute for Personal Rights (EIPR), "sectarian violence in Nagaa Hassan in the Luxor governorate left four Copts dead and several homes torched and looted in the wake of the killing of a Muslim citizen" (EIPR 2013). On July 6, a priest was shot dead by gunmen in an outdoor market in northern Sinai, and five days later, "the body of a beheaded Christian man was found in the same area, where Islamist militants have launched a string of attacks on security and military posts since Mr. Morsi's overthrow" (A. Maher 2013).

Human rights organizations, including EIPR, all urged the new interim government to protect Copts during those tense times. They stated,

> The way that state agencies, particularly the security apparatus, have dealt with these attacks is disturbing. These agencies have acted slowly and have not performed their legally mandated roles, failing to intervene to protect citizens and their property despite prior knowledge of the charged atmosphere and despite their presence on the scene during attacks. (EIPR 2013)

The ultra-conservative Islamic rhetoric by the ousted president's supporters continued to waver between extreme enmity to Copts with occasional attempts at appeasing them. While the situation remained tense, Copts were relieved that Egypt was on a path of recovery and open to what they believed was more freedom and hence continued to support the military that overthrew the Brotherhood.

On July 26, 2013, after the army chief's call for mobilization on the streets of Egypt to counter what he termed "terrorism," the Church decided to participate by fasting and prayers for Egypt all day with Muslims. It then ended the day with church bells ringing for the first time in Egypt in at least four decades. The ringing of the bells coincided deliberately with the Muslim call for prayers as a show of solidarity. The message was that of hope and unity in spite of the Brotherhood's attempts at dividing the country on a sectarian basis.

On August 14, 2013, when the army decided to break up two Muslim Brotherhood sit-ins, resulting in many deaths, the Muslim Brotherhood and their supporters went on a three-day rampage across Egypt, writing graffiti on church fences and doors and for the first time in Egyptian history, torching approximately sixty churches and church-affiliated establishments including orphanages (Tadros 2013). In addition, many homes and businesses belonging to Copts were also looted and torched. Islamists also marked Christian homes, businesses, and establishments with an "x" sign in preparation for attacking them (*Al-Masri-Al-Youm*, August 19, 2013). In the Muslim Brotherhood supporters' subsequent statements, threats against the Copts as the "traitors of the revolution" continued to escalate.

Conclusion

In 2011, before the election of the Muslim Brotherhood president Mohammed Morsi, political scientist Bassam Tibi (2012, 128) had accurately predicted that

> [The Islamist] agenda raises the likelihood that the Muslim Brotherhood will make pro-democratic noises but, if it gains power, will practice the kind of Islamic democracy; seen in Gaza and Iran. A hasty election in the post-Mubarak era could therefore be highly damaging. What Egypt needs more is a careful institutional preparation of a transition from authoritarianism to some kind of democracy.

Throughout their history and ever since the inception of the Muslim Brotherhood, there has been a sharp separation between their verbal claims and rhetoric on the one hand, and their actions on the other. Copts had been at the short end of that separation, hence the mutual distrust between the Brotherhood and the Copts. Although Islam is tolerant of minorities, the Muslim Brotherhood saw in them a people with an inferior status that they hoped to maintain. Carter points out that

> One reason for the Brethren's hostility, despite the tolerance recommended by their religion, was a belief that the Copts had acquired far more power than they had a right to have. All authority exercised by non-Muslims over Muslims was offensive and against the God-given order. (Carter 1986, 274)

The Brotherhood's use of religious propaganda in election campaigns always alienated the Coptic community. Al-Banna himself made great use of it and accused opponents of "love of Christians" and of "displaying hostility towards Islam" by supporting Copts (Carter 1986, 275). Additionally, according to the Brotherhood, Copts needed to assimilate and in many cases went as far as demanding a subservient status for them, with Copts paying *gizya*.

The Copts were not passive receivers of such propaganda throughout it all. They sometimes tried to allay the fears of their Muslim counterparts, countering the Brotherhood's accusations through displays of patriotism and participation in political life, and at other times taking counter hostile measures to the Islamists and the Muslim Brotherhood. One thing is clear, that they never saw eye to eye and mutual mistrust persisted regardless of the ruling regime. Because of their history with the Brotherhood, Copts recognize that their interests lie in a Muslim society that is civil, liberal, and secular. Their political participation and economic and social welfare had always thrived in such a society. Any other system with religious undertones will always raise their suspicion and mistrust. It was clear that Copts and other minorities would only thrive in a democracy that guaranteed equal citizenship and rights to all.

Resurgent nationalism and fundamentalism conflict by definition with minority identities and the dialectics of "multiculturalism." They create, ad nauseum, a fertile soil for conflict in diversity. While Copts have been able to negotiate their status through the different eras, it is clear that they support liberalism that provides them security socially, politically, and economically. It is easy for them to assimilate in a liberal society rather than succumb to "coercive assimilation" in a fundamentalist one whose very premise is built on excluding them. It is similarly true that the fall of the Brotherhood, and deposition of its leader, does not guarantee Coptic rights and, as Brownlee noted, "does not presage a golden age for Muslim-Coptic relations, but merely a return to the subtler, pernicious problems of the Sadat-Mubarak era" (Brownlee 2013).

However, according to the Copts, it is still a start.

References

Abdel Nour, F. 1992. *Mozakarat Fakhri Abdel Nour, dor Saad Zaghlool wAl-Wafd fi al Haraka al Wataniya* [Journal of Fakhri Abdel Nour, Role of Saad Zahglool and the Wafd in the National Movement]. Cairo: Dar el Shorook.

Ahmed, R. 1989. *Tanzeemat al-ghadab al-Islami fi al-sabeenat* [Organized Movements of Islamic Anger in the 70s]. Cairo: Madbouli Publishing.

Akhbar al-Youm. 2013. "Al Baba Tawadros yatrok lel akbat horreyet al mosharka fi tazahorat 30 yonyo" [Pope Tawadros Leaves Decision to Participate in 30 June Demonstrations to the Copts]. June 20. Accessed June 2013. http://bit.ly/1aDZNqD.

Al-Arabiya. 2013. "Cathedral Attack Is Like 'Attack against Me:' Egypt President Mursi," April 7. Accessed May 2013. http://english.alarabiya.net/en/News/middle-east/2013/04/07/Clashes-erupt-outside-Cairo-s-Coptic-cathedral-after-funeral-prayer.html.

Al-Banna, H. 1946. "Mozakarat al Daawa wal Daeya." *Al Ikhwan al Muslimoon* Newspaper Series. Accessed January 10, 2014. http://www.ikhwanonline.com/Data/2009/7/19/daawa.pdf.

Al-Bishri, T. 1982. *Al-Muslimun wa-al-Aqbat fi Itar al-Jama'ah al-Wataniyyah* [Muslims and Copts in the Context of Nationalism]. Translated by Samira Bahr. Cairo and Beirut. Accessed December 2013. http://ccdl.libraries.claremont.edu/cdm/ref/collection/cce/id/518.

Al-Bishri, T. 1988. *Al-Muslimun wa Al-Aqabat fi Itar Al-jama'at Al-wataniya* [Muslims and the Challenges Facing the National Groups]. 2nd ed. Cairo: Dar Al-shuruq.

Al-Fagr. 2012. "Tawadros: entakhabt shafeek wa zeyarat al akbat lel kods marhoona be zeyarat al muslemeen" [Tawardos: I Elected Shafeek and the Visit of Copts to Jerusalem Is Dependent on the Visit of Muslims as Well]. November 13. Accessed June 2013. http://new.elfagr.org/Detail.aspx?nwsId=221839&secid=1&vid=2.

Al-Hawari, D. 2012. "Al-salafeyoon yohazeroon al raees mosri men hodoor marasem tanseeb al baba" [Salafis Warn the President Regarding Attending the Papal Seating Ceremony]. *Al-Yom Al-Sabea*, November 10. Accessed December 2012. http://www1.youm7.com/News.asp?NewsID=841418&SecID=12.

Ali, F. 2012. "Ibn Khaldun lel derasat: rasadna mana akbat al saeed men al tasweet" [Ibn Khaldun Center for Studies: We Monitored Cases of Preventing Copts from Voting in Election Reruns]. *Al Balad*, June 24. Accessed December 2012. http://www.el-balad.com/200272.

Al-Masri-Al-Youm. 2013. "x kalimat al serr fi estehdaf manazel al maseeheyeen wal shorta totalebhom behemayet anfoshom" [x Is the Secret Letter for Targeting Christian Homes and Police Asked Them to Protect Themselves]. August 19. Accessed December 2013. http://www.almasryalyoum.com/node/2046306.

Al-Mogaz. 2013. "Al Irhabiyun yohadedoon al akbat: law nazel youm 30, letre benzene yowala fi beyotkom we mahalatkom we kanayeskom" [Terrorists Threaten Copts: If You're Going Down 30 June, One Liter of Gasoline Will Burn Your Homes, Your Stores and Your Churches]. June 29. Accessed December 2013. http://almogaz.com/news/politics/2013/06/29/982481.

Al-Yom Al-Sabe'a. 2012. "Baraet al motahameen fi kadeyet kate3 ozon kepti be qena" [Acquittal of All Defendants in the Case of Cutting the Ear of a Coptic Man in Qena]. April 22. Accessed December 2013. http://www3.youm7.com/News.asp?NewsID=659888&SecID=203&IssueID=0.

Aref, J. 2011. "Gomaat Kanadahar wa kadaya al amn al kawmi al masri" [Kandahar Friday and Egyptian National Security Matters]. Itijahat, August 21. Accessed August 2013. http://www.albayan.ae/opinions/articles/2011-08-21-1.1491005.

BBC. 2011. "Egypt Bomb Kills 21 at Alexandria Coptic Church." January 1. Accessed January 2013. http://www.bbc.co.uk/news/world-middle-east-12101748.

BBC. 2013. "Coptic Christian Church Destroyed by Egypt Looters." July 17. Accessed December 2013. http://www.bbc.co.uk/news/world-middle-east-23339788.

Brownlee, J. 2013. "Violence against Copts in Egypt." Carnegie Endowment for International Peace. Accessed December 21, 2013. http://carnegieendowment.org/2013/11/14/violence-against-copts-in-egypt/hrt3.

Carter, B. L. 1986. *The Copts in Egyptian Politics*. Kent: Croom Helm.

Chick, K. 2013. "In Brotherhood's Egypt, Blasphemy Charges against Christians Surge Ahead." *The Christian Science Monitor*, May 22. Accessed December 2013.

http://www.csmonitor.com/World/Middle-East/2013/0522/In-Brotherhood-s-Egypt-blasphemy-charges-against-Christians-surge-ahead.

EIPR. 2013. "Wave of Attacks on Copts and Churches: EIPR: Authorities Must Take Immediate Action to Protect Citizens and Houses of Worship, Bring Perpetrators and Inciters to Justice." Accessed December 2013. http://eipr.org/en/pressrelease/2013/07/15/1762.

Elbaiady, F. 2013. "Makate3 al video al raheeba allati aradnaha bel shura le fadh dor el dakhelya fel hogoom ala el katedraeya" [Video Clips that We Showed at Shura Council to Expose Role of Ministry of Interior in the Attack against the Cathedral]. April 18. Accessed December 2013. https://www.youtube.com/watch?v=ikwMa0f5vvk.

Habib, R., and M. Afifi. 1994. *Tareekh al Kaneesa al Misreya* [History of the Coptic Church]. Cairo: al-Dar al-Arabeya.

Hassanein, A. 2010. "Etlaq nar ala masseeheyeen fi kena yaktol 7 baynahom shorti moslim was yoseef 9 baad kodda al milad" [Christians Short in Qena, Killing 7 among Them One Muslim Policeman and Injures 9 after the Christmas Liturgy]. *Al Masri al Youm*, January 1. Accessed December 2013. http://www.almasryalyoum.com/node/9762.

Hourani, A. 1947. *Minorities in the Arab World*. Oxford: Oxford University Press.

Hourani, A. 1991. *A History of the Arab Peoples*. London: Warner Books.

Ibrahim, E. 2012. "Egyptian Copt Jailed for 'Insulting Islam, Morsi' on Facebook." Accessed November 3, 2013. http://english.ahram.org.eg/News/53201.aspx.

Ishak, G. 2012. "George Ishak: mana el akbat men al tasweet amr hakeeki" [George Ishak Says Preventing Copts from Voting Is a Fact]. YouTube video, June. Accessed December 2013. http://www.youtube.com/watch?feature=player_embedded&v=gfbD0Db6KpM.

Kherbawi, T. 2013. "Ini ara al ikhwan erhaban." [I See the Brotherhood as Terrorists]. *Al-Wafd*, December 30. Accessed January 2014. http://bit.ly/111kQtc.

Maher, A. 2013. "Egypt's Coptic Christians Pay Price of Political Tumult." *BBC*, July 17. Accessed December 2013. http://www.bbc.co.uk/news/world-middle-east-23337659.

Masrawy. 2012. "Beltafaseel: hekayet horoob 100 alf kepti men hokm el ikhwan." [In detail: Truth behind Escape of 100 Thousand Copts from Ikwahn Rule]. August 24. Accessed December 2013. http://www.masrawy.com/ketabat/ArticlesDetails.aspx?AID=177832.

Minority Rights Group International. 2012. "State of the World's Minorities and Indigenous Peoples 2012—Egypt." June 28. Accessed December 2013. http://www.unhcr.org/refworld/docid/4fedb40036.html.

Mogheis, K. 1997. *Al Haraka al Islamiya fi Misr fi al Asr al Hadith* [Islamic Movement in Egypt in Modern Times]. Cairo: Legal Research and Resource Center for Human Rights.

Mohamed, M. 2012. "Nader Bakkar yakol sabab 3dam wokoof al salafeyeen dakeeka hedad ala roh el baba" [Nader Bakkar Explains Why Salafis Did Not Stand a Minute in Mourning of the Pope]. *Masrawy*, March 20. Accessed December 2013. http://www.masrawy.com/moraselon/ArticlesDetails.aspx?AID=161935.

Nakeeb, A. 2011. "Hal yougad akbat fi masr al an?" [Are There Copts in Egypt Now?]. YouTube, April 30. Accessed December 2013. http://www.youtube.com/watch?v=nYa55IaDAhs.

Owen, R. 2004. *State, Power and Politics in the Middle East*. London and New York: Routledge.

Rizk, Y. L. 2001. "A Diwan of Contemporary Life (408)." *Al-Ahram*, September 20. Accessed January 2014. http://weekly.ahram.org.eg/2001/552/chrncls.htm.

Saleh, S. 2011. "Tahkeekat Al-Ahram tanshor tafaseel etefak hank al demaa fi ein shams" [Al-Ahram Investigations Publishes Details of Agreement to Avoid Bloody Conflict in Ein Shams]. November 25. Accessed May 29, 2013. http://www.ahram.org.eg/archive/Investigations/News/79778.aspx.

Scott, R. 2000. *The Challenge of Political Islam: Non-Muslims and the Egyptian State*. Stanford: Stanford University Press.
Shukri, G. 1991. *Al Akbat fi watan motaghayer* [Copts in a Changing Nation]. Cairo: Dar al-Shorouk.
Shukri, N. 2011. "Masai le enha azma fi Aswan besabab kebab al kanaes" [Attempts at Ending Conflict in Aswan because of Church Domes]. *Christian-Dogma*, 7 September. Accessed March 3, 2013. http://www.christian-dogma.com/vb/showthread.php?t=125068.
Tibi, B. 2012. *Islamism and Islam*. New Haven: Yale University Press.
Tadros, M. 2013. "Ikhwan et al's One Day Rampage." Hakawi from the East: A Commentary on Insanity, August 15. Accessed August 2013. http://hakawi.wordpress.com/2013/08/15/ikhwans-et-al-one-day-ramapage/.
Yussef, Abu S. 1987. *Al Akbat wal Kawmeya al Arabeya* [Copts and Arab Nationalism]. Cairo: Arab Unity Studies.
Zenishek, S. 2013. "Sayyid Qutb's 'Milestones' and Its Impact on the Arab Spring." *Small Walls Journal*, May 9. Accessed December 2013. http://smallwarsjournal.com/jrnl/art/sayyid-qutb%E2%80%99s-%E2%80%9Cmilestones%E2%80%9D-and-its-impact-on-the-arab-spring.

PART V

MINORITIES AND SOCIOCULTURAL CHANGE IN LIBYA

Part five analyzes the social, political, and cultural ramifications of the Arab Spring for minorities in Libya. It argues that the major challenge of post-Qaddafi Libya is to move from a political system where neither minorities within the country nor democratic principles were tolerated toward a new social system that will allow for diversity while promising inclusiveness, allowing for political rights for groups that had been kept on the margin for over four decades.

The part also focuses on the institutional deficiencies left by the Qaddafi regime, and argues that the creation of a new and more inclusive social democracy that can integrate the country's minorities will, for a number of historical and institutional reasons, prove extremely tough.

The democratic process launched in Libya through the first free and fair elections is irrefutably a very vital step in the long walk to democracy. While providing an analysis of the multiethnic fabric of Libya, which was oppressed and marginalized by the previous regime, this part explores the potential for the adoption of a multiculturalist approach in Libya after the revolution.

11

LIBYA AFTER THE REVOLUTION: IDENTITY AND NATION-BUILDING

Dirk Vandewalle

The election of Nuri Abu Sahmain as president of Libya's General National Council (GNC) in late June 2013 brought, for the first time since the country's revolution against the Qadhafi regime, an Amazigh to the highest political office in the country.[1] Somewhat surprising, the fact that Abu Sahmain was Amazigh merited relatively little attention within the country except among some of the Amazigh groups that have started to organize politically since the end of the civil war in October 2012. Abu Sahmain himself downplayed his minority identity—Libya's Amazigh, Tubu, and Tuareg minorities are estimated at roughly 5% of the population—stressing instead his more nationalist, Libyan credentials. A few weeks later, in mid-July 2013, the GNC approved a draft law for the country's Constitutional Assembly. Under the law, Libya's Amazigh would be guaranteed two seats within the Constitutional Assembly (out of sixty, equally divided between Tripolitania, Cyrenaica, and Fazzan), as would the country's Tubu and Tuareg minorities. The adoption of the law promptly led to the resignation of all Amazigh members of the GNC, based on the argument that the Amazigh (and the other two minorities) had been underrepresented.

The two developments, so closely together in time, provide a telltale indication of how Libya is dealing with the issue of minorities and of identity almost two years after the death of Mu'ammar al-Qaddafi. On the one hand, Abu Sahmain, as head of the country's most prominent national institution, can be seen as representing those for whom a national identity—particularly in light of the need to hold the country together in the wake of the civil war—needs to be accentuated, perhaps at the expense of minority identities and interests. On the other hand, the actions of the Amazigh GNC members indicate that minority and identity politics have become a highly politicized issue in the new Libya.

It should be noted that for many Libyans, memories of the early twentieth century, when the Amazigh from western Tripolitania were in the forefront of efforts to help create the Arab world's first modern republic, still resonate.[2] The question today is whether and to what extent Libya wants to acknowledge and accommodate minority rights and identities while those in charge of the new state search to develop a new, more general social contract with Libya's population as a whole—a social contract that during the Qaddafi era was imposed on the country's population, and which did not include rights for minorities.

As in many countries emerging from a civil war and from a long period of dictatorship that had been marked by a skilled and deliberate use of divide-and-rule politics meant to protect the regime, many of Libya's new rulers are not surprisingly accentuating the "center" and the "national" first and foremost while paying lip service to minority rights. The use of unifying, nationalist rhetoric has been an important (and growing) aspect of the search for legitimacy among the country's current policymakers. Second, Libya's minorities are small compared to other Maghrebi countries and, unfortunately, some (particularly the Tuareg and to some extent the Tubu) have been accused of disloyalty. An understanding of how the Libyan government deals and is likely to handle its relations with the country's minorities in the future can only be comprehended within the search for a more general social contract that has now started to unfold in earnest.

In this search, as hinted at above, the legacy of the Qadhafi regime looms large. For over four decades, Libya was subject to Qadhafi's notion that a modern state, with its impersonal mechanisms of authority, was inappropriate for Libya, and that only Arab identity could serve as a focus for Libya. The central concept of Qadhafi's *jamahiriyya*, elaborated in the volumes of his Green Book, had been that people should govern themselves, directly, without the intervention of state-controlled institutions. Indeed, such was Qadhafi's conviction about the inappropriateness of modern state institutions that he at one point declared that the modern conventions surrounding statehood should be abolished: hence Libya would have no borders and would impose no entry visas for fellow Arabs—a notion that would come to haunt particularly the Tuareg and the Tubu once the civil war came to an end.

Although many of the more quixotic aspects of Qadhafi's *jamahiriyya* philosophy were eventually abandoned, Libya's new rulers in the wake of the civil war had to confront some of the lingering, pernicious legacies of the previous regime that had allowed no one, except Qadhafi, from formulating a vision for Libya as a society that served simultaneously as a focus of national identity. During the Qadhafi period, ethnic problems; issues of citizenship, cultural identity, and minority rights; and the notion of a national identity disappeared from any political agenda—because, by the tautological explanation of Qadhafi's philosophy, Libya as a *jamahiriyya* had settled these issues decisively.

In the aftermath of the revolution, Libya must now again—more than six decades after its independence—start to deal with problems of identity, minority rights, greater autonomy of the country's different regions, and the emergence of ethnic conflict in southern Libya. Of all Maghrebi countries, these challenges are potentially perhaps most profound in Libya since it has not yet developed a political agenda nor an institutional framework through which these difficulties can be resolved—pre-occupied as the current government is with a larger number of challenges against which its capacity pales in comparison. The divide-and-rule policies and the use of patronage by the Qadhafi regime suspended the issues that are now assuming more immediacy and relevance.

In addressing these, Libya, as outlined above, faces particular difficulties. First, its challenge is to move from a political system where neither multicultural issues within the country nor democracy were tolerated toward a new social contract for the country's population that will allow for diversity while promising inclusiveness, allowing for political rights for groups that had been kept on the margin for over four decades. Second, social contracts in oil exporters like Libya are notoriously difficult to change, in part because long periods of entitlements tend to create constituencies that are not inclined to see their privileges challenged.

The remainder of this chapter first outlines the institutional deficiencies left by the Qadhafi regime, and argues that the challenges of Libya's current policymakers to create a new and more inclusive social contract that can accommodate the country's minorities will, for a number of historical and institutional legacies, prove very difficult. It then analyzes whether or not Libya—now engaged in a challenging period of state-building and nation-building—will have enough political energy and willingness to accommodate issues of sub-national identity.

Libya's Revolution

Of all the "Arab Spring" popular uprisings, Libya's rebellion that started on February 17, 2011, against the regime of Mu'ammar al-Qadhafi stands as one of the most idiosyncratic and unexpected in the region.[3] Few observers predicted that the country's citizens would prove capable and willing to stand up against a regime whose mechanisms of repression had been an inextricable part of the divide-and-rule policies of Qadhafi's rule, honed over forty-two years of arbitrary and highly exclusionary rule. By doing so, Libya's citizens broke an implicit social contract that had traded patronage for political quiescence during the decades of Qadhafi's rule.

Observers had long noted the severe deficiencies in the development of social and political institutions during the Qadhafi years, predicting both long-term chaos and enormous difficulties in reconstructing (or perhaps more accurately, constructing for the first time) a modern state in Libya. Despite this, during the first real test of trying to create a first step toward building that new state, national elections went forward without major incidents.[4] Regardless of enormous difficulties, and despite having a low sense of national identity, the July 7, 2012, elections, barely seventeen months after the uprising against the Qadhafi regime had started, took place in an almost euphoric atmosphere.[5] It quickly became clear that Libya—even though its provisional government and the National Transitional Council (NTC) that had guided the country during the civil war faced enormous challenges—would not implode as many had feared.

Observers may have been right in predicting that Libya would face lingering problems of state- and nation-building as a result of its oil-led development and because of the neglect of the state as a focus of identity that goes back to the creation of the country in 1951. But they certainly did not envision the relative success the country experienced during its initial months in power in starting to create a political system that promised greater accountability and transparency. There are, however, important caveats that must be taken into account. Libya's revolution is less than two years old. Many of the initial developments that indicated progress toward a more integrated and responsive political system may well be halted or even reversed as the country now finds its way in order to address issues that will inevitably deal with identity and minority. While much of what has taken place seemed to augur well for the future of the country as a political community, it was also clear that the national elections of July 7, 2012, marked the beginning of a new period in which many new challenges—including those of reconciliation, minority rights, and national identity—could not be postponed, at least not according to Libya's own minorities.

So far, however, many of the problems that are at the heart of how the country's new political community will be constructed, and what the duties and obligations of both the state and local society will be vis-à-vis each other, have only tangentially been touched upon in the euphoria and the chaos of the post-revolution period. Even today, Libya's leaders (both the earlier NTC and the current GNC) have, not surprisingly, been preoccupied with securing the country (an unresolved task that still leaves many of the country's militias as a potent force to be dealt with), by constructing or reconstructing a number of state institutions that had been badly neglected during the Qadhafi period and are needed to address the everyday challenges of keeping the country's administration running.

At the margins of all this activity has been a still somewhat stilted debate about the role of the state in the new Libya or, in particular, about the relationship between this new state, the country's citizens, and minority groups within the country. There remains a very vaguely defined understanding of how the newly emerging political realities within Libya will be formalized into a new social contract for a country where such a pact was traditionally determined without consultation by the state during the Qadhafi regime.

Until the country's constitution is written and adopted, those details will remain murky.[6] Oil countries, and particularly Libya with its checkered history of state-building (or perhaps better state avoidance) during the Qadhafi regime, tend to rely on highly skewed and imposed social contracts that leave citizens and minority groups alike simply as bystanders. The Libyan elections were of course all about making citizens active participants in the country's political future, but it remains unclear to what extent this will include groups that have traditionally been sidelined. In Libya, oil and the way the old social contract was implemented have left some debilitating legacies: among them a profound sense of political atomization that was partly reflected in the outcome of the elections, the fact that the state continues to be seen as an indispensable provider, the lack of interpersonal trust, and, most importantly, the use of extensive patronage via oil-fueled revenues that traditionally kept the social contract in place.

Libya's Social Contract under Qadhafi

As defined in this chapter, social contracts are implicitly or explicitly defined rules and arrangements that delineate the political and economic rights, duties, and obligations between those in charge of the state and individuals within the state subject to their governance. They are the most visible—but sometimes least formally institutionalized—of all institutions that mediate between the state and society. They formally or informally describe and prescribe, in Douglass North's classic definition, the rules of the game between ruler and ruled.[7] These rules may be made explicit or left deliberately opaque; they can develop through custom, or they may simply be imposed single-handedly by the ruler. No matter how they historically emerge, however, they tend to become rules or norms that, particularly in authoritarian states such as Libya under Qadhafi, clearly limit the political voice of a country's citizens while essentially leaving them depoliticized.

In the traditional European context, as a result of long periods of strife and compromises during the state-building process that sometimes lasted centuries, social contracts became carefully calibrated, under most circumstances minutely defined, and backed by guarantees and legal review. They became intricately woven into the fabric of local societies, often becoming part and parcel of a cultural and religious identity. They remain until today jealously defended by both organized and non-organized groups that benefit from their content.

Historically speaking, social contracts in Europe as well as in Latin America are at the heart of politics. As a result, they are most often modified through the political process, requiring a high degree of transparency by a number of regulatory and legal institutions that provide predictability to both sides. They are furthermore constantly subject to often acrimonious review and adjustment, particularly during periods of economic retrenchment and reform when the state and its "social partners" need to recalibrate their previous positions to achieve a common goal.

In Libya, the social contract has essentially been of a very different nature. During the Qadhafi period, Libyans were never—except rhetorically—consulted as it emerged, a result of a much more problematic process of state-building that made possible the systematic exclusion of some groups of citizens, particularly minorities that did not fit the national "Arab" narrative possible. This distinction between the construction of social contracts in the West and in countries such as Libya is important not only for gauging their strength and shape but also for measuring the maneuvering room they now provide to governments to actually reform their political and economic systems.

One could argue that, strictly speaking, it is erroneous to refer to the social, economic, and political arrangements that have emerged in countries such as Libya as social contracts. They never were bargains in the sense of involving two negotiating sides that achieve mutually acceptable or agreed-upon arrangements. In Libya in particular, minority and ethnic groups were summarily disregarded. Rather than giving voice and access to diverse groups within society, they have more often than not led to a striking, enforced political silence.

In all countries of the Maghreb, but particularly in Libya, the colonial powers' bureaucratic legacies did matter significantly for local institutional development, and hence for how states constructed themselves and their social contracts. Where local populations had been introduced to and incorporated (even at low levels) into bureaucratic mechanisms during the colonial period, and where the hinterland had been incorporated into a unified economy that made extraction possible, the seeds were sown for political, charity, and civil society organizations that would eventually serve as the torchbearers not only for independence movements but for articulated regulatory, extractive, and coercive organizations that legitimated the state as the meta-institution for the territory. Where the colonial powers had been content to create settler, landlord economies or had few economic incentives to incorporate local populations into economic frameworks, the notions of state and of the possibility of articulated institutions remained unknown. In Libya, the most extreme example of exclusionary politics during the Italian occupation, the notion of statehood, would remain suspect and contested both during the monarchy and after the 1969 Qadhafi coup.[8]

In addition, oil has played an important role in how the social contract emerged and took shape in Libya. When the rapid inflows of oil revenues shifted the function of the state almost exclusively toward the distributive (and the coercive), it also eroded the need for clearly articulated institutional development. It obliterated the usual bargaining between the ruled and the ruler that had marked state-building processes elsewhere into unilateral decisions by a ruler bent on perpetuating a stateless society, a *jamahiriyya*. That this process could be so contracted and provoke so little local reaction attests to the profound de-politicization that takes place in oil exporters, and to the fact that the emergence of rent in Libya preceded state-building.

An important corollary for the debate on social contracts concerns the kind of political community that is created under these conditions, and how this influences the ability for further reform in the post–civil war period in Libya. Although observers have often invoked—somewhat rashly—the "no taxation, therefore no representation" principle as the rationale for the exclusionary nature of politics in the region, there is little doubt that Libyans and particularly minorities within the country have endured a long process of political disenfranchisement that essentially consisted of gaining relative wealth at the expense of formal political voice.[9] As long as external rents can be generated, there is little need for individuals to influence public agencies and to help shape public policy to their material advantage. There is little incentive to actively engage the state to determine the contours of the social contract. And because Libyans did not contribute to the creation of wealth, they were hard pressed to argue for either a greater share of the state's distributive largesse or for reform. The atomistic tendency of this type of development in Libya, particularly at the popular level, was to create personal rather than group interests.

Furthermore, social stratification in an oil state like Libya resulted overwhelmingly from the distributive and spending patterns of the state. This stratification was linked to the need of the regime to create (admittedly small) coalitions of support among the population. Although data are exceedingly difficult to obtain, one remarkable social and economic phenomenon in Libya has been the absence of a distinct middle class with its own goals, tactics, and methods that could function as the catalyst for political and economic change. It was virtually impossible to discern during the Qadhafi period distinct class preferences and clearly articulated class goals—in part because the combination of welfare politics and weak institutions atomized populations. In a process familiar to institutional economists, the way to advance in a country like Libya was never to articulate interests in a common setting, but to pursue them individually.

Moreover, as a result of the emphasis on distribution, rulers like Qadhafi tended to spend inordinate amounts of time trying to promote their clients and to create supporting coalitions to stave off other claimants to the country's wealth and power. Much of this maneuvering was concealed by the way in which the country's revenues were shielded from public scrutiny. Decisions concerning economic policies, distribution, and investments are, as a control mechanism, kept to the purview of small coalitions, rather than assigned to the market. Distributive largesse was augmented with reliance on informal mechanisms linked to history, religion, or culture.[10] The enormous bifurcation between formal and informal politics—and the cynicism and apathy this provoked—became the single most distinguishing feature of Libyan politics.

In summary, oil wealth in Libya allowed for the creation of extensive patronage systems that vitiated pressures for political liberalization and fostered the creation of one-sided, top-down social contracts. In this peculiar set-up, the Qadhafi regime could survive for a very long time by relying on relatively small coalitions. Libya under Qadhafi demonstrated that the state in oil economies can easily prevent the consolidation of social groups that, in the European context, were a prelude to democracy.[11] Or, in Putnam's (1993) formulation, these states can prevent the accretion of social capital that would give impulse to collective action.

Reshaping Social Contracts in Oil Exporters

If the Libyan revolution that started in 2011 made one thing explicitly clear, however, it is that the country's citizens were no longer willing to be subjected to the very one-sided social contract that had increasingly created a visible bifurcation between regime elites and the general population during the latter years of the regime. Indeed, they proved willing to sacrifice an estimated 30,000 individuals to escape from what they collectively judged as a social contract imposed upon them that was no longer acceptable.

But what new social contract will emerge in light of the removal of the restraints of the Qadhafi regime? According to the pronouncements of the country's interim rulers, Libya will become more equal for all, a more transparent country, while its leadership will be subject to higher standards of accountability—those are the promises either implicitly or explicitly expressed in the various campaigns of the political parties and individuals who took part in the elections on July 7, and certainly those conveyed explicitly by the NTC and the interim government.

As outlined above, however, the social contract and the accompanying patronage patterns that sustain them in oil exporters are most often very tenacious and difficult to remove, even if one political system is replaced with another. Particularly, the entitlement aspects linked to both prove very hard to reform, and patronage patterns often reestablish themselves in post-revolutionary situations, manipulated by new elites who take over access points from their previous occupants. Moreover, social contracts develop over relatively long periods of time, reflecting the compromises those in charge of the state are willing to make to implement each ruler's vision of what a particular political community should look like. Even if these bargains prove minimal in what they provide—as one could argue in Libya—they are deeply ingrained, turned into sets of entitlements citizens come to take for granted in lieu of more tangible political representation. As we know from riots throughout the region, even small adjustments (or announcements of potential adjustments) to these entitlements can be highly dangerous, and governments are loathe to tinker with social contracts until pushed to the wall. Libya, even under the highly authoritarian rule of Qadhafi, proved no exception, as a history of its attempts at economic reform prove.[12]

One of the most striking features of the Middle East, and North Africa's oil exporters, has been the extraordinary economic largesse bestowed by states upon their citizens. This largesse has left both state and society, implicitly or explicitly, with a set of expectations embodied in vaguely defined, one-sided social contracts.[13] Of these expectations, job creation for local citizens and subsidies of a variety of goods have often been the most visible tip of an iceberg of entitlements and privileges that necessitated a whole range of public policies pursued by the region's governments.

In Libya in particular, these policies have normally included, in addition to employment, the cultivation of a dominating public sector that did not restrict itself to traditional government activities but also infiltrated private commercial activities; the provision of a whole array of welfare programs ranging from education to housing to health care; and the creation of a host of economic strictures, such as import bans and extensive licensing systems, which in effect insulated local enterprises and elite coalitions from exposure to world competition. In most cases in Middle East and North Africa (MENA), but particularly in Libya with its fractured sense of identity, private elite concerns (rather than social ones) fueled the construction of social contracts.

When thinking about this kind of social contract in Libya during the Qadhafi period, two distinct aspects must be considered. The first is purely economic: the volume and value of actual goods and services delivered to local citizens, ranging from employment, education, subsidies, free health care, and a whole array of services and economic interventions. The second dimension, however, is equally important. Social contracts advertently and inadvertently created overlapping social groups—primarily labor, the military, narrow coalitions of supporters, and the general public—that were targeted as an intricate part of a political management strategy carefully maintained by Qadhafi while in power. In effect, in Libya, the social contract became a powerful political instrument that through economic patronage was meant to ensure regime survival.

For Libya as for other oil exporters in the region, the two decades of the 1980s and 1990s represented the beginning of a period of difficult adjustments to a number of local, regional, and international economic realities that inexorably reshaped the role the Qadhafi regime would play, and, by implication, how the social contract would need to be adapted to new economic circumstances. What needs explaining is precisely why the country avoided, delayed, or abrogated these necessary reforms in favor of incremental adjustments or consumer *infitahs* (economic liberalization)—even when Qadhafi seemingly clearly understood the economic difficulties Libya faced, and, at least rhetorically, was willing to implement economic changes.

This conundrum—that a seemingly very powerful state that managed to regulate the minutiae of its citizens' lives could not muster the willingness, strength, or capability to successfully implement and sustain economic reforms—hints at the broader social and political structures within which its political economy was embedded, as well as at the future difficulties the country faces.[14] Libya's social contract was simply the most visible expression of such structures: they clearly show the compromises Libya's ruler felt he needed to make (or not make), and the dense networks of coalitions he created in pursuit of power and survival—compromises that in all cases left out Libya's minorities and ethnic groups. As in few other states in the world, economic reform and change in Libya were inextricably linked to recalibrating political power between ruled and ruler, that is, to changing existing social contracts that had been imposed by the ruler. Not surprisingly, therefore, the (cosmetic) economic and political reform efforts of Saif al-Islam after 2005 were doomed from the beginning.

Libya's Future as a Political Community

Two important, intertwined questions emerge at this point. First, to what extent can Libya's current rulers escape this "shadow of the past"? And, as it tries to create a more inclusive political community, what impact will the country's lingering difficulties have on the fate of Libya's minorities?

So far, we have relatively little evidence of how Libya's new rulers mean to address these challenges beyond the statements and actions of the NTC and the current General National Assembly. Clearly, profound upheavals such as the Libyan uprising against the Qadhafi regime in February 2011 and the resulting civil war change the contours of whatever social contract existed. But they leave unclear how previously ignored ethnic and minority issues will be addressed. Greater calls for political voice and for participation of all Libyans were part and parcel of Libya's revolution, and certainly the election of minority group members to the GNC, as well as their deliberate representation on the Constitutional Assembly were positive developments. But whether those sensitivities to minority representation will remain acute is still unknown: it is important to note, for example, that minority and cultural rights issues were not an important part of the national elections campaign in 2012.

It is clear, however, that Libya as a political community, irrespective of how inclusive it will be, is changing. For the first time in the country's history, Libyan citizens on July 7, 2012, were asked to participate in free, multi-party national elections that would provide them with a political voice they never possessed previously.[15] Many observers had expected Libya's elections to be messy and dominated—as in neighboring countries—by the Islamist parties. In the end, both predictions were proven wrong: the elections turned out exceptionally well run, and have brought Mahmoud Jibril's National Forces Alliance—a secular group—to power. Jibril at one point had been head (2007–2011) of the National Planning Council during the final years of the Qadhafi regime, and became prime minster of the transitional government that had been established during the civil war—a position he later abandoned in favor of the then interim Prime Minister al-Kib.

What has irrevocably changed in Libya in the wake of the civil war is how a now politicized society thinks of what the contours of the new social contract in Libya should look like. Outlined against the turbulent political history of the country, the Libyan elections have so far made a number of issues clear. First, Libya has been able to take a major step forward toward the construction of a modern state. The elections may not have been perfect in every aspect, but they were symbolically important in pushing the country as a political community away from the shadows of the Qadhafi regime. Second, Libya still very much represents a young and somewhat inexperienced political system. Party platforms were hardly articulated and often revolved around individuals rather than presenting clear presentations of differing political views—and contained very few specific references to minorities and ethnic issues beyond some generalities.

Third, on a more cautionary note, the recent elections were only the beginning of what will undoubtedly be a very long, perhaps messy and drawn-out process that involves writing a constitution, creating a new government, and shaping a political community that all Libyans ascribe to. For a number of reasons described in this chapter, and dating back to the creation of Libya in 1951, this is bound to be a contentious process that will once more bring into focus some of the traditional divisive issues within the country. Violent incidents in eastern Libya, centered around the longstanding issue of the relative power of Cyrenaica versus Tripolitania and on Tubu versus local Arab tribes as well as focusing on Tuareg rights and citizenship indicate that national cohesion and consensus will remain important issues to be dealt with.

In contrast to much of the West where a gradual build-up of a unified national identity coincided or preceded a move toward electoral democracies, in Libya, this process was reversed. The recent elections therefore are only the beginning of a much larger construction project: for a new state and for a new identity. Libya's relatively inexperienced new rulers will have to create the political structures and processes needed to make a democratic process find traction within a nation where, according to recent polls, national identity is still weak.

How the country's new rulers design and develop these mechanisms of inclusion and create a consensus to entice the different and particularly minority groups to "buy into" this national project and into a new social contract is the major challenge ahead. This is especially so in a country where important issues such as the role of government, of regional versus national power, of national identity, of minority rights, and of the role of religion have been held in abeyance during the country's civil war and virtually so during the elections.

Conclusion: Identity, Social Contracts, and Libya's New State

The construction of a new social contract in Libya in the wake of the country's civil war has started in earnest. The recent national elections were the first tangible sign of a consultation process that hints seductively at a possibly new understanding of how the state and the country's citizens will interact. Certainly, looking back at what has been accomplished in so little time, the inclination is to see the glass half full. And rightly, Libyans are proud of what they have managed to construct so far out of the unpromising political and social ruins of the Qadhafi regime.

But there remain innumerable difficulties ahead. By mid-2013, the political mood in Libya had noticeably darkened, even as the country had very slowly started to develop some of the necessary institutional mechanisms to govern itself. It was perhaps this bifurcation—between a very slowly developing political, administrative, and bureaucratic institutional framework and a growing suspicion of those in charge of developing them, the GNC in particular—that described the country's most acute dilemma a year after the country's first post-Qadhafi national elections had taken place.

In Libya, these normal growing pains of a young political system continue to be exacerbated in important ways by a number of historical and more contemporary developments described within this chapter that continue to cast a shadow on the country's political way forward. The most important of these relate to the lingering uneasy relationship between Libya's different provinces—mostly between Cyrenaica and Tripolitania, but also increasingly between southern Libya (where the Tubu and Tuareg continue to raise important issues related to citizenship, identity, and cultural rights) and the two northern provinces—that continues to fuel debates over federalism and de-centralization. The unilateral announcement by Zubair al-Sanusi, leader of the country's most visible (but politically very weak) federalist party of a Transitional Council of Barqa (the Arab name for Cyrenaica) on June 1, 2013—to be outfitted with its own Congress, Senate and provincial government—hinted further at what will undoubtedly be very difficult and prolonged negotiations over the country's future constitution once the Constitutional Assembly is elected.

The country's lingering difficulties almost two years after the conclusion of the civil war continue to flow from the impact of the civil war that effectively kept military and political power fragmented at the expense of a Tripoli-based centralized government, pitting a revolutionary sector against the government, with civil society, including minority groups, emasculated in between. The government, as a result, still without a monopoly of coercive power, remains reduced to slowly, with great determination but with relatively little capacity, convincing the different militias and opposition groups to incorporate under the aegis of national institutions (such as the army, police force, different bureaucracies, and ministries). While there have been some successes in this regard, it has remained an arduous and slow process.

Admittedly some of the convulsions the country's young political system continued to experience were not substantially different from those of any country trying to lay down new political guidelines barely two years after the end of a long-term dictatorship: different factions trying to capitalize on the lingering weakness of the central government whose capacity to govern effectively remained overwhelmed by the sheer number of challenges it faced and by its inability to enforce national directives; a growing confusion over the implementation of decisions made by mostly inexperienced political actors whose interests more often than not remained local, tribal and regional rather than truly national; fiery rhetoric both by political parties and by individuals that had not yet been tempered over time to reflect compromise and political accommodation.

Unfortunately, in this process of muddling through, the country's formal political institutions, particularly the GNC, have not fared very well. Born out of the political energy of the civil war, and formalized through the July 7, 2012, elections, the GNC as a political bureaucracy has failed to generate much enthusiasm for its record—in contrast to its institutional predecessor, the Transitional National Council, which, despite its weak legislative record and its own infighting, was viewed by many Libyans as a credible national institution during the transitory phase of the civil war and beyond.

As always, the transition from a charismatic (TNC) to a more bureaucratized and regularized national political institution (GNC) is bound to bring disappointments—particularly in a country like Libya where patronage was used for over four decades as an effective mechanism of, simultaneously, instant economic gratification and political exclusion. And, in its defense, the GNC has tackled some almost intractable problems—of national security, reform of the security sector, efforts to fold the militias into centrally controlled institutions, providing greater mechanism for accountability and transparency of the country's financial and banking system, among others—with somewhat halting and limited success. Others, like transitional justice and gender equality, have barely been addressed.

By mid-2013 it was clear that although there is a slow process of bureaucratization and institutionalization taking place within Libya, the capacity to make national political institutions work effectively and according to their intended purposes remains lacking, and political control continues to be fragmented. Central issues—of de-centralization, construction of a national security sector, the role of civil society, gender issues, the debate over the use of the country's financial resources—are expected to remain to some extent in limbo until the adoption of a constitution has taken place. As always, the creation of a centralized state is a race against time: the construction of viable state institutions and the implementation of agreed-upon rules of the game before the centrifugal forces that dispute those rules can overwhelm the forces of centralized control.

In light of all this, it remains unclear at this point what the country's new social contract will look like—and what specific provisions will be made to incorporate minority and ethnic groups into the country's social fabric in light of the large number of problems the country's rulers face. Social contracts develop in response to a number of conditions and challenges that usually develop across years or decades: physical resources, the initial political, intellectual and social riches states possess or lack, the vision of their leaders, the slow accretion of rules, regulations, and reputations that start to permeate the daily lives of the state and society alike and, finally, the real or perceived threats of outside actors.

In the wake of Libya's civil war, neither the importance of creating nor implementing the underlying conditions that rethinking of these social relationships between the ruler and ruled implies should be underestimated. If social contracts are part and parcel of strategies that can promote growth and reform, whether or not countries will actually pursue such strategies remains a complex question. Rulers or decision makers of all oil exporters often have multiple options they can pursue.

Some of these choices involve risks and uncertainties its future government may not be willing or able to take, for a wide variety of political, social, or economic reasons. The uncertainties over how much political turmoil pursuing the rights of minority groups would engender, for example, is only one among a plethora of possible obstacles. Attempting to reform social contracts by creating more finely tuned participatory institutions opens up this creation and pursuit of such social contracts to public discussion and debate—a debate that in Libya has not so far been strongly supportive (beyond some campaign rhetoric) of the rights of minorities and ethnic groups. It is clear that Libya's new political system and, in particular the country's national elections, have opened up a new political arena where previously suppressed issues of political rights and state–society duties and obligations have now appeared as viable political issues.

To what extent the country's rulers will actively focus on a broader multicultural agenda that will bring all the country's diverse groups under the protection of the state is still an open question. Until now the lingering chaos has precluded a systematic attempt to elaborate on these concerns. The passage of the Constitutional Assembly law in mid-July 2013 indicated once more that Libya is, institutionally speaking, moving forward. But the fact that the Tuareg, Tubu, and Amazigh minorities immediately withdrew from the GNC in protest against what they considered inadequate representation within the Constitutional Assembly indicated as well how alienated the country's minorities feel from what has essentially been a nationalist revolution that, they argue, has paid scant attention to their needs and sensitivities.

As this chapter has pointed out, rewriting social contracts, particularly after violent upheavals such as Libya's civil war, is a difficult and prolonged process where the interests of elements of the political community are often compromised by the realities of the patronage politics and management of an oil economy. Pursuing minority rights and advocating broader multicultural sensitivities under such circumstances will require political will and a long-term and consistent hand on the political tiller to advocate and implement what to many Libyans may not look like pressing issues in light of the country's other and perhaps more fundamental challenges.

Notes

1 Part of this chapter was adapted from an earlier paper that focused on the more general topic of the changing social contract in Libya, appearing in Mehran Kamrava and Zahra Babar, *The Changing Social Contract in the Middle East* (New York: Columbia University Press and Hurst Publishers, 2013).
2 For a quick recall of that history, see, in particular, the earlier part of Lisa Anderson's, *The State and Social Transformation in Tunisia and Libya, 1830-1980* (Princeton: Princeton University Press, 1987).
3 Some Libyans and some outside observers somewhat uneasily refer to what happened in Libya as a revolution. Similarly, there is much disagreement over whether what took place in Libya qualifies as a civil war. Without endorsing or denying the validity of the use of these concepts, I use both throughout this paper as an expedient shortcut.
4 For background on Libya and the problems associated with oil-led development, see Dirk Vandewalle, *Libya since Independence: Oil and State-Building* (Ithaca: Cornell University Press, 1998). For an update of events, including the country's civil war in 2011, see Dirk Vandewalle, *A History of Modern Libya*. 2nd ed. (Cambridge: Cambridge University Press, 2012). Consult also Alison Pargeter, *Libya: The Rise and Fall of Qaddafi* (New Haven: Yale University Press, 2012), and Ethan Chorin, *Exit the Colonel: The Hidden History of the Libyan Revolution* (New York: PublicAffairs, 2012).
5 Polling in Libya is a new phenomenon. However, in one of the first polls after the 2011 uprising, Libyans overwhelmingly identified themselves as Muslim, while being "Libyan" came in a very distant third after tribal/regional identification.
6 At the time of writing this chapter (July 2013) the GNC had just approved a Constitutional Assembly draft law that provoked opposition within Libya's minorities since they felt underrepresented. The Constitutional Assembly now needs to be elected, after which the Constitution needs to be approved—a highly laborious process that will undoubtedly take much more time than originally envisioned in the TNC's Constitutional Declaration of August 2011.
7 Douglass C. North, *Institutions, Institutional Change and Economic Performance* (Cambridge: Cambridge University Press, 1990) and Douglass C. North and Robert P. Thomas, *The Rise of the Western World: A New Economic History* (Cambridge: Cambridge University Press, 1973).
8 See Lisa Anderson (1987).
9 There are two principal objections to this longstanding claim. The first has been succinctly elaborated by Waterbury (1998) who not only questions the assertion that

Middle East and North African (MENA) economies are under-taxed, but also rebuts the more general assertion that taxation in MENA has "evoked demands that governments account for their use of tax monies . . ." He adds furthermore that "there has been no translation of tax burden into pressures for democratization." The second is that popular demands for some sort of representation often derive from entitlements based either physically on earlier distributive largesse by governments during boom times, or are based on shared (often international) norms about what constitutes good governance.

10 The invention and re-invention of tradition as a means to greater legitimacy has not surprisingly become virtually a national industry in particularly the Gulf Cooperation Council (GCC) countries, where rulers heavily sponsor events that are deemed in line with the country's *turath* (heritage), a word that is invoked again and again in public discourse. For the United Arab Emirates (UAE), see Christopher Davidson (2005) and Vandewalle (2007).

11 For applications to the MENA region, see Shambayati (1994) on Iran; Crystal (1995) on Kuwait and Qatar; Entelis (1976) and Crystal (1996) on the UAE.

12 Libya attempted to reform its economy during at least three distinctive phases: in 1987, in the 1990s, and after 2003, the latter in part guided by Saif al-Islam al-Qadhafi who, in cooperation with the then Prime Minister Shukri Ghanem, brought in Western expertise to help design the necessary reforms for the country's highly inefficient economy.

13 Strictly speaking, in MENA one needs to distinguish between two different groups of oil exporters in the region: (1) the GCC countries and Libya, where oil revenues have provided the overwhelming share of government revenues, and (2) Iraq, Iran and Algeria, which have more diversified economies.

14 A conundrum Nazih Ayubi (1996) brilliantly analyzed in his *Over-Stating the Arab State: Politics and Society in the Middle East*, where he distinguished between fierce states—that rely overwhelmingly on coercion—and strong states that have clearly delineated institutions that allow them to take on a number of state tasks.

15 In 1952, shortly after the Kingdom of Libya was created, political parties were disbanded. Although there were elections (without parties) for the country's parliament in subsequent years, last week's elections can be considered the country's first multi-party elections in six decades since 1952. And taking into account that Libya in 1952 hardly resembled a political community, last week's elections can for all practical purposes be called the truly first competitive multi-party elections the country has ever witnessed since it was created in the wake of World War II.

References

Anderson, Lisa. 1987. "The State in the Middle East and North Africa" *Comparative Politics* 20 (3): 1–18.

Ayubi, Nazih. 1996. *Over-Stating the Arab State: Politics and Society in the Middle East.* New York: I.B. Tauris.

Chorin, Ethan. 2012. *Exit the Colonel: The Hidden History of the Libyan Revolution.* New York: PublicAffairs.

Crystal, Jill. 1995. *Oil and Politics in the Gulf: Rulers and Merchants in Kuwait and Qatar.* Cambridge: Cambridge University Press.

Crystal, Jill. 1996. "Approaches to the Study of Civil Society in the Gulf." In *Civil Society in the Middle East.* Vol. 2., edited by Richard Augustus Norton, 260–85. New York: Brill.

Davidson, Christopher. 2005. *The United Arab Emirates: A Study in Survival.* Boulder: Lynne Rienner.

Entelis, John P. 1976. "Oil Wealth and the Prospects for Democratization in the Arabian Peninsula: The Case of Saudi Arabia." In *Arab Oil: Impact on the Arab Countries and*

Global Implications, edited by Maiem A. Sherbiny and Mark A. Tessler, 77–111. New York: Praeger.

North, Douglass C. 1990. *Institutions, Institutional Change and Economic Performance*. Cambridge: Cambridge University Press.

North, Douglass C., and Robert P. Thomas. 1973. *The Rise of the Western World: A New Economic History*. Cambridge: Cambridge University Press.

Pargeter, Alison. 2012. *Libya: The Rise and Fall of Qaddafi*. New Haven: Yale University Press.

Putnam, Robert. 1993. *Making Democracy Work: Civic Traditions in Modern Italy*. Princeton: Princeton University Press.

Shambayati, Hootan. 1994. "The Rentier State, Interest Groups, and the Paradox of Autonomy: State and Business in Turkey and Iran." *Comparative Politics* 26 (3): 307–31.

Vandewalle, Dirk. 1998. *Libya since Independence: Oil and State-Building*. Ithaca: Cornell University Press.

Vandewalle, Dirk. 2007. *A History of Modern Libya*. 1st ed. Cambridge: Cambridge University Press.

Vandewalle, Dirk. 2012. *A History of Modern Libya*. 2nd ed. Cambridge: Cambridge University Press.

Waterbury, John. 1998. "The State and Economic Transition in the Middle East and North Africa." In *Prospects for Middle Eastern and North African Economies: From Boom to Bust and Back?* edited by Nemat Shafiq, 159–77. London: MacMillan Press.

12

MINORITIES AND CULTURAL GROUPS IN LIBYA: THE CASE FOR MULTICULTURALISM

Youssef Mohammad Sawani

This contribution is grounded in the tradition of multiculturalism. As a policy and approach, multiculturalism involves comprehensive responses to cater to contexts of ethnic and cultural diversity (Inglis 2003, 8). This chapter, while providing an account and analysis of the ethnic composition of Libya, is also an attempt at understanding why multiculturalism was not considered or employed as an approach to recognizing and managing diversity in contemporary Libya. It further explores the potential for the adoption of a multiculturalist approach in Libya. Given that the country underwent a bloody and violent confrontation with Gaddafi's authoritarian rule, it is interesting to explore how cultural and ethnic dynamics will feature in the building of the new political system. The main argument presented here is that social rifts developed within the fabric of Libya's society because multiculturalism was not embraced, and hence it offers the best policy options for structuring (or may be reinventing) Libya's politics after decades of authoritarian dictatorship and exclusion.

Given the consequences of Libya's revolution, civil war, and the ensuing tribal, ethnic, and regional clashes, the suitability of multiculturalism as a policy approach should not be overlooked in any future restructuring of state–society relations. The rifts and the levels of polarization along tribal, regional, and ethnic lines caused by the revolutionary process are a true reminder that equal rights should be recognized and protected through an effective resolution and/or reduction of social or political tensions or conflicts (Sawani 2012, 21). This is a requirement contributing to the enrichment of society while employing the politics of recognition that caters to all cultural and ethnic constituencies of the Libyan society.

Ethnic Realities in Libya

Studies on ethnicity and cultural groups in Libya are scarce. Existing literature seldom discusses these in more than a descriptive fashion. Some early studies actually question the existence of a distinctive Libyan identity and nationalism prior to the country's independence in 1951 (Golino 1970; Rivlin 1949). Such identity is presented as emerging only as a consequence of the formation of the Libyan state by virtue of a United Nations General Assembly resolution in 1951. In order to revisit this depiction, the next section will first provide a description of the ethnic landscape in contemporary Libya, identifying the various cultural and ethnic groups that make up today's Libya.

Ethnic and cultural minorities

Although Libyans may be largely considered ethnically homogeneous, distinguishable ethnic groups or communities do exist. Alongside his policy of Arabization, Gaddafi rejected the existence of any non-Arab ethnic identity, considering the notion a mere colonial invention. Since Libya's official population census and government statistics deemed all Libyans to be Arabs by definition and hence made no ethnic classifications, it was almost impossible to determine the real size of minorities. However, there is sufficient evidence to establish that the Berbers constitute the largest single group after the Arabs. The Berbers refer to themselves as Amazigh and the terms are sometimes used interchangeably, though Amazigh is also used as a collective designation for Berber, Tuareg, and Tibu, even though the exact identity of the latter is a source of contention. In any case, the Tuareg and Tibu are next in number to the Berbers in the overall population. They are considered Libyan, Arab, and African simultaneously (see Tempelhof and Omar 2012). It is also the case that the numbers of minorities of African origins, particularly the Tibu, have risen in the last decade. In addition to the traditional movement of these people across the borders of neighboring countries, Gaddafi's open door pan-African policy has had the effect of encouraging Africans to migrate and settle in the country for various reasons.

Berbers

The Berbers (or Amazigh) are the largest ethnic and cultural sub-group and second only to the dominant Arabs (Dagher 2011). It is difficult, however, to determine their actual size. Estimates vary but generally they likely constitute between 5% and 10% of the population, numbering between 236,000 and 590,000 (Moseley 2012). The Berber–state relationship has received little or no real scholarly attention. Aisha al-Rumi (2009, 2) notes that Gellner and Micaud (1973) did not even mention Libya in their study on Arabs and Berbers. Berbers may be categorized by what Kymlicka (1995) has termed a "national minority" (Inglis 2003, 36). Most Berbers live in the northwestern parts of the country in and around the Nafusa Mountain, otherwise known as the western mountain. They have, to a great degree, maintained their cultural and linguistic distinctiveness and preserved their identity, while Berbers in the eastern part of the country have been almost entirely assimilated into the Arab-speaking majority. Berbers seem to be the essential minority or cultural community that is seeking more recognition and power-sharing arrangements. Although discrimination has always been extra-legal, Berbers are eager to upgrade their position and gain more power even as their assimilation with their Arab fellow countrymen is increasing, particularly in urban areas and major cities.

Tuareg

The next main cultural and linguistic minority group, also related to the Berber, is the Tuareg. They are Berber-speaking (Tamahak or Senhaja dialects) and are Sunni Muslims of the Maliki School of jurisprudence (*fiqh*). They live in small scattered communities in the south east of the country. They basically inhabit the towns of Ghadames, Ghat, Sabha, and Murzuk. Their exact numbers are also difficult to determine but they are estimated to number anywhere between 17,000 and 560,000 (Moseley 2012). The Tuareg have been deprived of sufficient levels of social services, and unemployment among them has always been high. For long, they lacked any proper identity cards and no nationality was ascribed to them when they were issued with Libyan IDs. It is sad to discover that because they had no proper identification or official birth registration of their children, the latter have been hindered from attending schools as birth certificates are a requirement for this (Tempelhof and Omar 2012, 9).

However, determining who among them is Libyan or has Libyan origins remains a serious challenge for the authorities. This is particularly cumbersome to those who have no official identification, thus rendering them more vulnerable to discrimination. Many Tuareg organizations that have sprung up in post-Gaddafi Libya have raised the alarm that unless resolved and attended to by the authorities, the situation is bound to explode, causing yet more rifts in the country's already fragile social peace. The Tuareg organizations focus their activities on advocacy and the protection of those Tuareg who have been the target of much reported discrimination.[1] This has been particularly evident in the widely reported case of Tawergahans Tuareges who have been displaced from their town on the coast near Misurata.[2] During the uprisings against Gaddafi in 2011, the rebels of Misurata claimed that Tawergahans integrated in large numbers in government forces had committed crimes that ranged from theft and vandalism to rape and large-scale killings, the victims of which were purported to be the inhabitants of Misurata who rose against Gaddafi. Once the regime was liquidated, Misratans were keen to take revenge. The obvious result was indiscriminate displacement of the inhabitants of the whole town and the arbitrary arrest, torture, and killing of Tuareg who now pay a heavy price and are being widely persecuted because of the color of their skin.

Tibu

The third most significant minority is that of the Tibu (otherwise spelt, Tobou, Tebu, or Toubou), who are of African origin and who occupy some oases and villages in south-central Libya. The Tibu language is related to a Nigerian language. Those in Libya are Arabic speakers of West African ancestry and they have long suffered impoverishment. Their livelihood deteriorated following the demise of the camel and caravan trade across the Sahara. They are centered in the Tibesti Mountains and parts of southern Libya. Their territorial origins and reach are not clearly confined or restricted to one African state. They are generally considered Muslims who were converted by Sanusi preachers of the nineteenth century and that conversion helped nourish their links to Libya to some degree. They live now mostly in the southern towns of Sabha, Kufra, Gatroun, and Murzuq. They number but a few thousands and represent 0.02% of the overall population. They are also connected to their fellow Tibu in Chad, Niger, and the Sudan. Scores of them had fled to Libya in large numbers following the civil war in Chad between 1974 and 1994.

The Tibu are an example of an ethnic group that lacks any proper legal entrance status that determines their relationship with the state and other groups. The fact that the Gaddafi regime denied them citizenship or the right to permanent resident status made it difficult for them to gain viable access, if any, to social services and employment. As a minority, they have had no established right to political participation nor any access to the legal system. Their family members, including their locally born children with no right to permanent residency, have revolted against these and other conditions of deprivation and exclusion on many occasions.

The southern part of the country is rich in natural resources, especially oil and gas, but the realities of the living conditions in this region where the Tibu live are such that they have been subject to neglect and suffer from underdevelopment, discrimination, and all kinds of deprivation. The law that forbids them from obtaining Libyan citizenship is still in place. Given these conditions, the Tibu have had to resort to illegal trade activities for their survival. However, this has been the source of further agony and suffering that is bound to continue, since the strong Arab tribe of Zawi, the Tibu's powerful competitor, seeks monopoly over the activity (Martin, Weber, and Carment 2012). During Gaddafi's era the Zawi had the support of the regime, and their influential tribal leaders were Gaddafi's supporters. Consequently, the Zawi maintained a superior position vis-à-vis the Tibu, who were relegated to the status of underdogs with Gaddafi's consent and approval. Once the regime was overthrown, the Tibu took the opportunity to challenge the Zawi hegemony, and tribal and ethnic clashes ensued with casualties inflicted on both sides.

The Tibu's central demand was for basic services and fundamental rights, in the absence of tolerance of their distinctive culture or language under the Gaddafi regime. The latter offered them nothing while refusing to acknowledge the legitimacy of ethnic minorities. Libya's government had no room for the multiculturalism that would have allowed for their incorporation without losing their identity and distinctiveness or being denied or excluded from participation. Gaddafi employed the principle of *ius sanguinis* depriving Tibu born on Libya's soil from the exercise of most of the rights associated with citizenship.[3] Even the potential for naturalization was not open for Tibu. Only those integrated within the regime had the benefit of national identity cards that in fact did not identify them as Libyans but rather as Tibu. This belied the assimilation model that Gaddafi was practicing in an ideological–normative fashion.

Tibu were harshly repressed in 2009 following their protest against the Libyan government's discriminatory policies. They were forcefully evacuated and displaced from their homes in Kufra. In 2007, a violent confrontation took place when militias led by the Tibu leader Isa Majid of the Tibu Front for the Liberation of Libya attacked the Zawi tribe. Gaddafi's government intervened and crushed the Tibu uprising, and Tibu were subject to yet more deprivation and exclusion. In 2012, further violent confrontations took place between Tibu and Zawi tribesmen that left dozens of people dead and many wounded. In an angry reaction to what he saw as the apathy of Libya's interim authority, Isa Majid called for the international community to intervene and shoulder its moral duty to protect the Tibu from ethnic cleansing. He also threatened secession and the establishment of an independent Tibu state in the south of Libya (Martin, Weber, and Carment 2012).

Gaddafi's Policies: From Pan-Arabism to Pan-Africanism—A Tale of Contradictions

The Gaddafi regime was known for its adventurism and extravagance in both internal and external affairs. It started with the adoption and active practice of pan-Arabism, following in the footsteps of Gaddafi's mentor Gamal Abdul Nasser. In this context, Libya was characterized as the land of all Arabs, who were invited to work and settle regardless of where they came from in the greater Arab homeland. Libyan nationality was granted to scores of Arabs and in many instances Libya had non-Libyan Arab ministers in its government. For Libyan Amazigh, Tibu, and Tuareg, it was inexplicable and frustrating to see non-Libyans take advantage of their country's wealth while their ethnic or cultural status was denied.

Gaddafi's love affair with pan-Arabism was, however, short-lived and short of any serious achievements, as all his attempts at uniting Libya with other Arab states failed completely. He became frustrated and more ambivalent toward the Arabs who left him alone in his confrontation with the West following the Lockerbie disaster. He took a very sharp

U-turn in the direction of championing pan-African unity, and Libya became identified as an open territory for fellow Africans. Thereafter, Libya's borders witnessed a large influx of African migrants who worked and settled in the Jamahiriya of the "Brother Leader"!

Although they lived in misery and deprivation and many lost their lives in their attempts to cross the sea hoping to reach Europe, African migrants in Libya were officially welcome. It is ironic, however, that while Libyans of African or Berber origins lacked recognition and rights, African migrants were praised and hailed in state propaganda. Libya was a state that welcomed foreigners at the expense of its natives.

Gaddafi's regime adopted and implemented a policy that was in line with the inclusive all-encompassing ideology of Gaddafi's "Green Book"—"the Great Jamahiriyan" society—that had no room for multiculturalism. This was also part and parcel of its pan-Arabist policies and orientation. Therefore, the policy of Arabization implied that Arabism acquire the position of a superior model wherein Arab identity functions as a superior frame of reference for all. Arabism was the format that all non-Arab elements of the populace must conform to in a framework of assimilation. In the process, non-Arab elements were supposed to acquire Arab qualities in order for them to eventually become part of an Arab fabric.

The educational system during the rule of Idris Sanusi was focused on eradicating any impact Italian colonialism may have had on culture, language, and identity. Therefore, a policy of asserting and maintaining an Arab and Islamic national identity dictated that Arabic was the only language of instruction in schools. Minority issues or considerations were not a concern. Given the dominant international or global trends of the post-Imperial era, such a policy could be pursued without objection. The Gaddafi regime that came to power after a coup d'état in 1969 simply continued the same policy, though its approach had a more pan-Arab orientation. From its early days, Gaddafi's regime was determined to preserve and maintain an Arab identity. The regime also sought to liquidate traditional tribal leadership in its quest for legitimacy. Therefore, it played down any tribal, regional, or cultural distinctiveness by the employment of a pan-Arab policy that was strongly echoed in education and the media. Once the regime had consolidated its power and authority, it pursued this line with more stringent measures.

Libya's system of education during the Gaddafi era did not pay any heed to multiculturalism, citizenship, and democracy. School curricula were void of any material related to such concepts, and their teaching was disallowed. Instead, the regime embarked on a process of ideological indoctrination of students at various educational levels. This meant that students were only taught topics and subjects in an ideological fashion, as outlined in Gaddafi's Green Book. In this regard, democracy, for example, was only as the Green Book described it. Citizenship in Gaddafi's Jamahiriya society meant simply being loyal and faithful to the regime and its leadership. Any demand for multiculturalism or the recognition of minority rights was akin to sin and a danger that had to be quelled and kept at bay. Furthermore, according to the Green Book, all humanity will remain backward until it speaks one language, "Man is still backward because he is unable to speak one common language." [4] Therefore, there was no chance that education or the media would play a role in enriching or even in debating important issues and concepts other than in a dogmatic fashion advancing a mono-cultural approach. Berber language has never been introduced into school curricula or recognized as a national language. It has been banned from any public or governmental use. Berbers have only been able to teach their children their mother tongue prior to their joining school where Arabic has been the *Lingua Franca* (al-Rumi 2009, 4).

It was through the agency of the educational system in particular, however, that Gaddafi's policies of Arabization sought to impose Arabic language on the minorities, thus making it the *lingua franca.* While this achieved the goal of language standardization, it has not led to the assimilation of Berbers and other minorities into Arab identity. It is worth mentioning here that despite such a policy, Libya has not witnessed or suffered from any serious backlash from Arabization in any violent form. Arguably, it was thanks to Islam, that unifies all Libyans, that the country was saved from the adverse results of the assimilation policy. Gaddafi meanwhile realized that the issue was far more complicated than he had initially thought. His policy or desire for assimilation was not paying off the way he sought. So he moved toward adopting the more stringent and discriminatory policy or model of "the melting pot" whereby minorities had to be forced into conformity with Arabism.

The melting pot model, conceived originally by Robert Park (1950), implies the formation of an entirely new cultural community with a new identity. However, Gaddafi's strategy failed to produce any such environment. The only modality by which this might have been achieved was through intermarriage, but even this was accorded no more than the lip service. Among the Amazigh in general, and more explicitly in and around Jabal Nafusa and Zawarah, there was open opposition to the idea of inter-ethnic marriage. The communities kept intact their long held practice of intra-communal marriage and the regime had no way of forcing anything to the contrary. Although many Berbers, particularly those living in urban areas, broke away and married non-Berbers, they faced social penalties and exclusion from their tribes and extended families. The same applies to the attempt by the regime to impose Arab names on Amazighs. A law was introduced that made it illegal to adopt non-Arab or non-Muslim names. Berbers, however, kept their indigenous names for use at home and on their private social occasions.

Thus, during the Gaddafi era, not only was an opportunity lost to embrace multiculturalism and multilingualism as the bases for an inclusive notion of citizenship but also the regime failed in its attempt to (re-)define and unite the whole society under the banner of Arabism. Notwithstanding what has been demonstrated in other contexts about the connection that can be made between group-specific rights and citizenship, and despite the ideological or theoretical claims made in the Green Book about the importance of respect for the rights of minorities to achieve equality and justice, official recognition of such rights was still lacking. The Provisional Constitution issued by the Revolutionary Command Council (RCM) in December 1969, the Declaration of the People's Authority of March 1977, and the Great Green Charter of Human Rights of 1988 made no reference to minorities and in fact all constitutional documents had provisions wherein Libya was said to be an Arab state and Arabic was the language of its people.[5]

Contrary to its ideological claims, the Gaddafi regime acted in such a manner as to ignore, combat, and violate minority rights, while banning any expression of minority culture. Gaddafi's rule was characterized by a denial of Amazigh or Berber, Tibu, and Tuareg rights to exercise their cultural and linguistic identity. Gaddafi, for example, banned the practice of giving Amazigh names to the newly born. In fact, Gaddafi maintained that the Amazigh people were ancient Arab migrants from the Arabian Peninsula.

The report of the Committee for the Elimination of Racial Discrimination summarizes the situation:

> Texts dealing with Libya's history do not even refer to the country's Berber origin, or the Berber origin of North Africa in general. Such texts falsify history since they refuse to acknowledge that the first inhabitants of the country were Berbers; a fact which is hard to deny since all historians pinpoint the presence of Berbers on these territories since time immemorial. For the Libyan state, the Berbers, their history, language, culture and civilization had never existed. Libyan history school books refer to the original Berber inhabitants of the territory as "ancient Arabs." This is a deliberate will to deny the existence of the Berber characteristics and a part of the state's Arabicization policy which aims to bury all signs of the country's Berber identity.[6]

The first decade of this century did, however, witness a kind of openness and liberalization in Libya's politics, thanks to the initiatives of Gaddafi's son Saif al-Islam. As a result, some Berber rights and demands were accommodated by the state. These came about in response to changes in the local and global contexts. Gaddafi's regime was seeking the renewal of its political strength and legitimacy at home and abroad, and reforms seemed unavoidable. Global interest in and concern about minority rights had achieved a level of salience that went beyond the kind of awareness that United Nations Educational, Scientific, and Cultural Organization (UNESCO), for example, had hitherto advocated (Abdellah 2014). International attention to these issues was manifest in a new discourse that went far beyond the acknowledgement of the cultural and linguistic heritage of minorities to identify recognition of minority rights with strategies for achieving security and development. Libya simply had to accommodate to changes that were further consolidated by the impact of globalization. Thus, a new policy orientation was adopted, but it was rather limited in scope, given that Saif's initiatives were foiled and frustrated to an extent that eroded the impact of any achievements.

It was in this context that the World Congress of Amazigh was born in 1995 and it set in train developments that included a new Libyan Berber activism. Their focus was on three main courses of action: the first of which reflected, and was associated with, their belonging to the Ibāḍi tradition. Berbers in Libya set about advancing their sect and making it the vehicle or catalyst for establishing their distinctiveness and disparity from the dominant Arab Sunni majority. The second course of action was more of a cultural revival of Berber traditions and folklore wherein they celebrated their cultural and social occasions and ethnic/cultural distinctive symbols. The third track was more political and included activism expressive of a Berber opposition to Gaddafi in the diaspora. However, the major initiative was the formation and activity of the League of North Africa and other entities eventually leading to the establishment of the Libyan Amazigh Conference in London in September 2000 (Abdellah 2014). It was obvious that both Gaddafi's oppression and then the easing of restrictions during the period of Saif's reforms were instrumental in arousing Berber activism. However, the more Gaddafi adopted harsh approaches toward Berbers, the more they reacted in activism and vigilance, particularly in the diaspora. Oppression and exclusion backfired, and the discreditation campaign against Berbers played the role of a free publicity campaign that led to their predicament becoming a national issue.[7]

The revolution and the active participation of Amazigh

The 2011 revolution against Gaddafi saw the active participation of the Berber tribes in the western mountains, while the Tibu remained reticent with regard to joining the revolution.[8] The Tuareg fighters, by contrast, represented an essential component of the Gaddafi regime forces in the face of popular revolt, and as a result, the Tuareg became the target of much of the violence and discrimination during the revolution and beyond. The Berbers of Zawarah participated in the early stages of the uprising against Gaddafi but suffered harsh suppression. Most inhabitants of Zawarah actually abandoned their town and moved to Tunisia until the fall of the regime. The Nafusa (Western) Mountain towns such as Yefrine, Al- Qal'a, Kabao, Jado, Kiklah, and others actively participated in the armed struggle and produced some of the most famous rebel battalions. They became known for their courage and devotion to the national cause as opposed to personal greed, opportunism, revenge and/or reprisals. Once liberation was declared, most Berber fighters returned to their towns and villages and resumed their normal life, except for a tangible presence in Tripoli. They were willing to give up most of the facilities they controlled, and their battalions were largely receptive to calls for evacuating Tripoli.

Ethnic struggle and confrontations in post-Gaddafi Libya

Libya did not witness a struggle between its Berbers and Arab citizens except for competition for resources among Arab rebel militias from Zintan and Berber rebel militias from neighboring areas. Hot conflicts between Arabs and Berbers only occurred between the rebel gunmen from the town of Zawarah and pro-Gaddafi forces from Arab cities nearby. But these clashes were not primarily for reasons that had to do with cultural or ethnic distinctions, but as a consequence of the polarization wrought by the revolution between supporters and opponents of the Gaddafi regime. After Gaddafi's fall, some of the incidents were related to conflicts of interest over the smuggling of goods, drugs, alcoholic beverages, arms, and fuel across the border with Tunisia.

Today, however, there are multiple facets of confrontation to do with ethnic divisions. Clashes and violent confrontations have taken place between Amazighs and their Arab neighbors, particularly in Zawarah and the western mountain. In Kufra and Sebha in the south, bloody confrontations were quite frequent in late 2011 and in 2012 involving Tibu and the Arab tribesmen of Zawi (Wehrey 2012). The inaction and/or inattention of the interim authorities led Tibu leaders to threaten secession. The coastal town of Tawergah has become a ghost town, as its Tuareg inhabitants have been forced to flee their homes and to become displaced in many parts of the country. Such bloody confrontations are but some of the manifestations of the fissures along ethnic lines. Berbers in Zawra, for example, are suspicious of their Arab neighbors in Rigdalin, al Jmeel and Zultin, who they accuse of being Gaddafi loyalists. Such charges and the overall fragmentation may sound curious, given that Gaddafi was killed and his regime was liquidated. But they are an indication of the negative repercussions of the violent and bloody civil war/revolution and the divide it created between winners and losers typical of internecine conflicts. Arabs, for their part, accuse Berbers of opportunism and the desire to impose their hegemony in the broader region, thus abusing the status, strength, and armory they accumulated during the uprisings to conceal their real intention of driving Arabs out of their lands. The animosity is nonetheless an echo of previous confrontations that had taken place between the two groups. One such conflict involved the famous and large scale clashes that took place in 1958 (year of revolution for Zawra Berbers) when a violent confrontation or small-scale war occurred between the two groups because of land ownership disputes.

Amazigh in Post-Gaddafi Libya: From "Berbers Are Arabs" to "Libyan Arabs Are Berbers"!

After long decades of suppression of the Amazigh (Berbers, Tuareg, and Tabu) by Gaddafi, the current state of political fluidity and the absence of any strong political authority have opened the doors to all forms of expression among the Amazigh of Libya. The revolt against Gaddafi in the region of Jabal Nafūsah was characterized by clear assertions of its Amazigh components. Tripoli witnessed the convening of the Amazigh Conference. This conference is an indication of the commonalities of demands with the Amazigh of North Africa in general. Despite the fact that it was the first such conference to take place in Libya, its organizers were keen on linking it to non-Libyan Amazigh conferences initiated in neighboring countries. This may be explained by their desire to link themselves with the Amazighs of North Africa and thereby garner their support as well. This indication of a pan-Amazigh movement has been a cause for resentment among many non-Amazigh commentators.

The demands expressed by Libya's Amazigh range from enforcing identity and culture to upgrading the Amazigh language to the position of an official or at least a national language in addition to Arabic. The highlight was, perhaps, the convening of the "National Congress of the Libyan Amazigh" on September 26, 2011, which focused on the issue of enshrining the Amazigh language in the constitution. This conference was an indication of the common demands among the Amazigh of North Africa in general and the main point of concern was expressed in the conference logo and slogan of "constitutionalizing Tamazight . . . and support for [Libyan] national unity."[9] The conference adopted a number of steps for the promotion of Amazigh demands. The "organizers agreed to form committees representative of the various Berber towns and villages to follow up their demands and recommendations that were presented to the NTC [National Transitional Council] regarding assigning the Berber language an official status within the constitution, and called for Berber lawyers to assist in formulating provisions and legislation in a legal document which then can be presented to the interim Justice Minister for consideration for inclusion among the temporary provisions until the full constitution is drafted."[10]

Although questions about the written script for the Amazigh language (whether this should be Tifināgh, Arabic, or European/Latin) remain unanswered (Sawani 2012). the fact that the conference was connected to foreign conferences raises questions. There may be concerns as to the suitability of this with respect to the Tuareg and Tabu, though a similar gathering (the Second Gathering of the Libyan National Amazigh) connected to the conference was held in Ubari in the southwest on November 1, 2011, with representatives from both Berber and Tuareg making similar demands.[11]

The Amazigh felt that the National Transitional Council (NTC) ignored their demands and began to organize protests and sit-ins in Tripoli. The last three months of 2011 saw a number of such protests, the most notable of which was a large demonstration in Tripoli on December 6, 2011. They demanded respect for the Constitutional Declaration and the application of its provisions related to democratic government, freedoms, equal opportunities, equality, and respect for cultural and linguistic diversity.[12]

The response of the NTC and its government to the demands of the Amazigh was lukewarm, and they paid only lip service to such demands. The NTC and the interim government did not enter into a constructive dialogue aimed at integrating the Amazigh in the political process. Leaders of political movements and parties also took positions similar to those of the NTC. Some Islamist leaders considered the demands of the Amazigh unacceptable, endangering national unity while pronouncing that Arabic is the language of the Qur'an, that Arabs and Berbers belong to an Arab-Islamic culture that does not discriminate between its various components and that an Islamic state accommodates and best serves the demands of the Amazigh.[13]

For some Amazigh activists, it became obvious that their calls fell on deaf ears and they were bound to be excluded and neglected because Arabism is engrained in the consciousness of both Libyan liberals and Islamists. Some Berber authors suggested the government's lack of attention to the needs of the wounded and sick Amazigh rebels was only a reflection of such policies of exclusion. The response of the NTC and government failed to go beyond the speech that Mustafa Abdjaleel gave in the Berber town of Nalut on December 6, 2011, which only gave verbal assurances to the Berbers that "Tamazight culture and language are respected by all Libyans and that the Berbers need to *integrate* into the

Libyan society and avoid *exclusion.*"[14] This prompted other protests and manifestations of outrage. The most prominent was what happened on May 8, 2012, when Berber gunmen attacked the headquarters of the prime minister in Tripoli expressing the growing frustration, sense of marginalization, and demands for fair treatment.[15]

Their concerns were best expressed in the writings of Amazigh activists. Among the most powerful and visible examples was Fathi Ben Khalifa, a Libyan national and president of the World Amazigh Congress. Ben Khalifa demanded that the NTC listen and act on the demands and rights of the Amazigh or the latter would boycott the elections and refuse to accept its outcome. He also called on Amazighs to withdraw from the NTC and other state institutions. In what appeared as an ultimatum, he indicated that, given the failure of the NTC to engage and include the Amazigh, their next step would be to go directly and officially to the United Nations and international organizations and call upon them to address the Amazigh cause.[16] It was the inability of the NTC to respond to Amazigh demands that generated these counterproductive actions. If such issues remain unattended to and no clear-cut policy is adopted to address the demands and expressed aspirations of the Amazigh, the result may be to open up questions about ethnicity in the widest possible sense. The Amazigh may then move toward demanding their own political entity, threatening the national unity of the country. This is particularly significant since the Tuareg on the Malian border announced their "Azawad Republic," a Tuareg state with indications of support from Libyan Amazigh and a statement of support from the World Congress of Amazigh.[17]

As this suggests, there are wider implications for the region, extending from Egypt to Mauritania, where Amazighs have a presence. Reports have indicated the desire of some Amazigh activists to establish a Berber confederation. The idea is that this confederation (Tamazgha) should include all Berber-speaking peoples in North Africa and the Sahara in addition to Arabized elements of Berber origins. The territorial boundaries of this would-be confederation extend from the oasis of Siwa in Egypt in the east, to Darfur, Tibu areas, and the Azawad region in the south, and to the Atlantic in the west.

In the Libyan context, many tribes, such as the Qabaiel in Zawia, Hawrah in Elmaia, and Janzour on the coast, and Warfallah, have Amazigh origins and have been mentioned on many occasions by

Amazigh activists, thus potentially widening the scope of any Amazigh call for self-determination to include areas populated by Arab speakers.[18] The demands of the Amazigh were powerfully expressed in an article written by Ibrahim Grada, a prominent Amazigh politician, in the form of an open letter he addressed to the chairman of General National Council (GNC). In his letter, Grada warned of civil war unless the noble objectives of the revolution were served, including the attainment of Amazigh rights.[19]

Implications of Amazigh activism and demands

The revolution against Gaddafi has allowed Berbers and other ethnic groups to openly express their culture, heritage, and language to an unprecedented degree.[20] After decades of repression and oppression, the revolution lit the flames of culture, language, and diversity in Libya. The country is now thriving with festivals, radio stations, newspapers, seminars, and conferences that give expression to the Amazigh, Tibu, and Tuareg minorities. They are obvious beneficiaries of the revolution and at a minimum they are attempting to consolidate these gains and to link them to what other Berbers have achieved in countries like Morocco. Yet the slowness of the NTC, the government, and other interim authorities to take any serious policy initiatives contributes to increased tensions between the Berber activists and the government.

The local councils of the cities of Mount Nafusa issued a statement on the inclusion of Tamazight language in basic and elementary education curricula forcing the local administration of education authorities to comply.[21] This begs the following question: Will Berbers' claim and insistence on making Tamazight a national language and enshrining it in the constitution lead to its becoming part of school curricula only in Berber areas or, by virtue of being the national language, will it be universally taught and become a learning requirement for all Libyans? Teaching Arabic and Tamazight simultaneously is a political choice in the first place, but its effects will be profound on the issues of citizenship and participation, diversity, and its democratic management. Arab Libyans may accept Tamazight language teaching in schools in Berber areas and might acknowledge its universal teaching in all schools. Yet despite any advantages this may have for the democratic administration of diversity, it does not appear that the Berbers are ready to accept their language being learnt by everyone given the impact on privacy issues and cultural differentiation.[22]

The Provisional Constitution included state guarantees for cultural rights for all components of the Libyan society and confirmed in its first article that all languages will be considered national languages.[23] However, many questions still need to be answered. Although Berbers do not agree on a unified and coherent concept of identity, some of their extremists are trying to promote Tamazight in confrontation with Islam, while some Berber activists have launched a campaign to convince the rest of the Libyans that they are all, in fact, Berbers.[24] It is doubtful that such a campaign is likely to have a chance of success. Berbers have inhabited North Africa since before the Arab-Muslim conquests, but the process of Arabization was associated with that of Islamization. Islam and Arabism became the primary basis of the Arab identity. There is therefore reason to question the extent to which Berber activists want to refer back to history, if they are serious about establishing their claim to recognition or primacy on the basis of genetics, and thence the implications, given that North Africa has experienced the mixing of diverse ethnic groups throughout history.[25]

Future Challenges: Concluding Remarks

In the current circumstances, where no effective authority exists in the whole country, the Berber and Tibu and indeed the Tuareg have resorted to arms. This is no doubt to be expected, since, in an environment of insecurity and lack of central authority, suspicion arises, and minorities have become more aware of the potential and perceived threats. Continued marginalization and lack of any government policy that accommodates the aspirations of minorities will lead to their reluctance to give up arms, thus further endangering the process of post-conflict healing and reconstruction. The revolution against Gaddafi made it possible for minorities to arm and they had to mobilize in response to widespread violence and become involved in it. The need for security and self-defense amid civil war led ethnic groups and indeed all Libyan tribes and regions to arm for communal security. In these circumstances, the state was no longer able to command obedience, and its capacity, and legitimacy, eroded, generating yet more security threats and perceptions of vulnerability.

It is important and vital that new Libya adopts a new approach toward minorities. Such an approach should be based on the fact that Libyan society is multicultural and as such requires a new vision for building citizenship and assuring participation at large. This imperative is at any rate in keeping with the effects globalization has had on how the concepts and realities of multiculturalism and identity are understood. The full participation of Libyans in the revolution that put an end to Gaddafi's authoritarian rule serves as demonstration that citizenship need not be confined to the constraints of any exclusivist ideological design. The fact that all Libyans took part in the revolt is a reflection that this is possible. The sense of national unity that sustained the uprisings and the success of popular sentiment in avoiding the trap set by Gaddafi's divide-and-rule tactics serves as a strong indication of the potential for multiculturalism to define Libya's future.

Critics say that multiculturalism is a divisive strategy that threatens social cohesion and may lead to the disunity of society (Inglis 2003, 8). This criticism is partially based on the fact that the argument for multiculturalism, as a policy response to ethnic diversity, is based on evidence from a few, still contested, international cases. Yet Gaddafi's regime never explored what it may have to offer. Acknowledging minorities was associated with widening and deepening the divides in a society that Gaddafi's ideology sought to protect or preserve as exclusively Arab. If the new government adopts policies that award appropriate respect to minorities' rights and accord them constitutional rights, this will serve as the vehicle for future stability. Furthermore, upgrading the educational system to cater for multiculturalism will play an instrumental role in paving the way for building a new democratic and inclusive Libyan polity that will save the country from division and fragmentation.

Although multiculturalism involves embracing the plurality of cultures and their distinctive values, customs, and attitudes, since all Libyans, including minorities, are Muslims, who all suffered during Gaddafi's regime, Libya manifestly has the potential to build on this great unifying component of its culture and identity. The experience with dictatorship can be a very positive factor that creates opportunities. Libya is a multicultural society, with some qualifications, and in the normative sense, a multiculturalist approach to building the new polity may prove very constructive. Here multiculturalism does not mean simple integration but preserving diversity, with the education system geared toward inculcating inclusive citizenship. This imperative derives not only from the lessons of the past but also the need to devise programs and policies to deal with the arrival of new ethnic minorities resulting from population movements across the Sahara, many of which are illegal African migrants.

The case for multiculturalism as defined and advanced here is prescient, since the country is now busy composing the founding principles of its polity and political system. The establishment of viable political structures that permit the evolution and implementation of new forms of relationships among ethnic communities is a precondition for the success of the new state and its stability. Libyans need to value the instrumental functions of multiculturalism in its ability to resolve any existing problems and pave the way for the pre-emption of the potential for social or regional strife by employing the democratic features of multiculturalism.

Notes

1 Middle East Online (2012), accessed December 12, 2013, http://www.middle-east-online.com/?id=132021.
2 "LIBYA: Rocky Road Ahead for Libya's Tawergha Minority," accessed December 15, 2013, http://www.irinnews.org/Report/94455/LIBYA-Rocky-road-ahead-for-Libya-s-Tawergha-minority.
3 More on this model in Christine Inglis, *Multiculturalism: New Policy Responses to Diversity*, p. 27, accessed February 3, 2015, http://www.unesco.org/most/pp4.htm.
4 M. Gaddafi, *The Green Book*, Part Three, p. 50, accessed January 12, 2012, https://archive.org/details/TheGreenBookMuammarGaddafi.
5 A comparison with Morocco may be useful here; see, Moha Ennaji (2009).
6 "The Berbers of Libya," A Report Submitted to the Committee for the Elimination of Racial Discrimination, CERD, United Nations Economic and Social Council, accessed February 3, 2015, http://www.scribd.com/doc/49544721/The-Berbers-of-Libya2004.
7 "Libyan Berbers," accessed February 3, 2015, http://www.temehu.com/imazighen/berberism.htm.
8 For an analysis of the revolution against Gaddafi's regime, see Ali Abdullatif Ahmida (2012)
9 http://chaabpress.com/news5214.html, accessed January 11, 2013.
10 http://www.temehu.com/imazighen/berberism.htm#libyanberbers, accessed January 11, 2013.
11 http://ossanlibya.org/?p=22618, accessed January 11, 2013.
12 http://www.bbc.co.uk/arabic/middleeast/2011/11/111127_lybia_demostration.shtml, accessed May 3, 2012; and for the statement issued see, http://www.ahewar.org/news/s.news.asp?nid=745414.
13 http://libyafirst.blogspot.com/2012/04/blog-post_14.html, accessed May 12, 2012.
14 http://www.temehu.com/imazighen/berberism.htm#libyanberbers, accessed May 13, 2012.
15 http://ossanlibya.org/?p=26041#more-26041, accessed May 13, 2012.
16 Fathi Ben Khalifa, "Amazigh Libya ila ain wa ila matta" [Libya's Amazigh: where to and until when?], accessed May 12, 2012, http://ossanlibya.org/?p=25771.

17 http://www.rif7.net/details-2251.html, accessed May 13, 2012.
18 Amareer, "Is There Really an Arab Homeland?" accessed May 12, 2012, http://www.libya-watanona.com/adab/amarir/am03047a.htm.
19 Ibrahim Grada, "al-muhafadah ala al-thwrah wa illa fa harb ahliah talouh fi al-oufouk" [Preserving the revolution first or a civil war glooms a head], accessed August 12, 2012, https://www.facebook.com/igrada.
20 Best summarized in the founding manifesto of the Libyan Tamazight Congress, issued on September 17, 2000, accessed January 12, 2013, https://www.temehu.com/imazighen/berbers.htm.
21 See this Arabic link, accessed January 12, 2013, http://www.amazighworld.org/arabic/human_rights/index_show.php?id=2833.
22 Demands of the Amazighs triggered huge reactions. Samples of the commentaries and views may be viewed in readers' commentary on an article published online by the Amazigh activist Fathi Ben Khalifa. This may be viewed at, http://libyafirst.blogspot.com/2012/04/blog-post_14.html, accessed January 12, 2013.
23 For the text of the Constitution, see https://www.constituteproject.org/constitution/Libya_2011.pdf, accessed October 20, 2011.
24 Aymen Jamal Al-Tamimi, "Libya: Assessing the Berber Prospect," accessed January 12, 2013, http://www.meforum.org/3223/libya-berbers.
25 Ibid.

References

Abdellah, B. 2014. "Al-mas?ala al-amazighia wa thawra al-libiya" [The Amazigh Question and the Libyan Revolution]. *Electronic Al-Ahram*. Accessed February 12, 2014. http://digital.ahram.org.eg/articles.aspx?Serial=813874&eid=6015.

Ahmida, A. A. 2012. "Libya, Social Origins of Dictatorship and Challenges for Democracy." *The Journal of the Middle East and Africa* 3 (1): 70–81.

al-Rumi, A. 2009. "Libyan Berbers Struggle to Assert Their Identity Online." *Arab Media Society*, Issue 8, Spring. Accessed June 11, 2011. http://www.arabmediasociety.com/?article=713.

Dagher, S. 2011. "Camels, Minority Rights Spur Battle in Libya." *The Wall Street Journal*, October 12. Accessed May 29, 2012. http://online.wsj.com/article/SB10001424053111904563904576585920346901758.html.

Ennaji, M. 2009. "Multiculturalism, Citizenship and Education in Morocco." *Mediterranean Journal of Education of Studies* 14 (1): 5–26. Accessed February 22, 2012. https://www.um.edu.mt/__data/assets/pdf_file/0004/77053/MJES_141-all.pdf.

Gellner, E., and C. Micaud, eds. 1973. *Arabs and Berbers: From Tribe to Nation in North Africa*. London: Duckworth.

Golino, F. R. 1970. "Patterns of Libyan National Identity." *The Middle East Journal* 24, no. 3 (Summer): 338–52.

Inglis, C. 2003. "Multiculturalism: New Policy Responses to Diversity." Accessed May 21, 2013. http://www.unesco.org/most/pp4.htm.

Kymlicka, W. 1995. *Multicultural Citizenship: A Liberal Theory of Minority Rights*. Oxford: Oxford University Press.

Martin, P., C. Weber, and D. Carment. 2012. "Ethnic Conflict in Libya: Toubou." June 21, 2012. Accessed December 15, 2012. http://www4.carleton.ca/cifp/app/serve.php/1394.pdf.

Middle East Online. 2012. Accessed December 12, 2013. http://www.middle-east-online.com/?id=132021.

Moseley, M. 2012. "Libya's Ethnic Minorities and Upcoming Elections." Civil-Military Fusion Center. Accessed December 15, 2013. https://www.cimicweb.org/cmo/medbasin/Holder/Documents/i016%20CFC%20Med%20Basin%20Review%20INFOCUS%20%2805-Jun-12%29.pdf.

Park, R. E. 1950. “Culture and Civilization.” In *Race and Culture*, edited by E. C. Hughes, C. S. Johnson, J. Masuoka, R. Redfield, and L. Wirth, 15–23. Glencoe, IL: Free Press.

Rivlin, B. 1949. “Unity and Nationalism in Libya.” *The Middle East Journal* 3, no. 1 (January): 31–44.

Sawani, Y. M. 2012. “Post-Qadhafi Libya: Interactive Dynamics and the Political Future.” *Contemporary Arab Affairs* 5, no. 1 (January): 21–26.

Tempelhof, S. T., and M. Omar. 2012. “Stakeholders of Libya’s February 17 Revolution.” Accessed May 29, 2013. http://www.usip.org/files/resources/SR%20300.pdf.

Wehrey, F. 2012. “The Struggle for Security in Eastern Libya.” Carnegie Endowment.org, September 19, 2012. Accessed January 23, 2013. http://carnegieendowment.org/2012/09/19/struggle-for-security-in-eastern-libya/dvct.

PART VI

DEMOCRATIZATION, RACE, AND CULTURAL DIVERSITY

This part discusses the issues of authoritarianism, exclusion, and cultural diversity in North Africa. It addresses the questions why and how some authoritarian regimes still discriminate against minorities and exclude Blacks in the region.

This part argues that the construction of race in the region is different from that of its American counterpart and analyzes how racial segregation became not only an ideology of enslavement but also a structure based on patterns of color and cultural prejudice.

It provides a historical overview of the Black presence in this vast African territory and debates the impact of race and color on national identity and on the struggle for democracy. Through a focal analysis of the linguistic and political context, the section strives to highlight the crucial shifts in Morocco and Mauritania from dictatorship to democracy-friendly political systems that guarantee, in their constitutions at least, freedom of expression, and minority rights.

The part equally investigates the deep-seated bias through immigration and citizenship laws against Blacks in general, and sub-Saharan African people in particular.

13

BLACKS AND THE MAKING OF THE ARAB MAJORITY IN MOROCCO

Chouki El Hamel

Blacks in Morocco have been marginalized for centuries with the dominant Moroccan culture defining this marginalized group as 'Abid (slaves), Haratin (a problematic term that generally meant freed black people or formerly enslaved black persons), Sudan (black Africans), Gnawa (black West Africans), Sahrawa (from the Saharan region), and these and other terms refer to the fact that these people were Black and/or descendants from slaves.[1] Morocco has traditionally been described in local historiography as a racially and ethnically homogenous nation, defined religiously by Islamic doctrine and linguistically and politically by Arabic nationalism. Written history is generally silent regarding the recognition and conditions of minorities such as blacks and Jews. The culture of silence about the history of race and slavery had located black Moroccans either outside the community or completely absorbed in it. Yet, the most revealing testimony of slavery and its legacy in Morocco comprises the living experiences of the descendants of enslaved people living in major Moroccan cities, as well as in the rural south of Morocco such as in the Tafilalt region and Tata and Aqqa oases. Another crucial testimonial is the existence of the Gnawa: a spiritual order of a traditionally black Muslim people who are descendants of enslaved sub-Saharan West Africans. Initially, the institution of slavery in Islamic societies and those influenced by Islam was not legally drawn along racial lines. I argue, however, even though Islamic law explicitly prohibits the enslavement of other Muslims, Muslims did enslave other Muslims, particularly if they were black. In this essay, I analyze how racialist ideas and positions became not only an ideology of enslavement but also a structure based on patterns of color and culture prejudice. I discuss how this process preserved old Arab social relations at work in the creation of a "nationalist" Moroccan Arab majority and at the same time subjugated black ancestry.

Defining Blackness in the Moroccan Historical and Ideological Context

One of the few Muslim Africans who attempted to explain the dilemma of understanding race in Arabized Africa is the renowned Africanist scholar Ali Mazrui who argued that "The Arab lineage system permitted considerable racial co-optation. 'Impurities' were admitted to higher echelons as new full members, provided [that] the father was [an] Arab." (Mazrui 1986, 90). Thus, in the Arabized societies, one is either an Arab with a continuum from light complexion (like Syrian Arabs) to dark complexion (like black Arabs in Mauritania), or simply black; there is no specific category of a mixed group such as Mulattoes, Mestizoes, or creoles in the Americas. Ali Mazrui judged this system of race-mixing against "a system of descending miscegenation like that of the United States, [. . . because it] pushes 'impurities' downward into the pool of disadvantage."(Mazrui 2000, 113). He sees the Arab system as inclusive and tolerant. But in reality the dominant Arab culture had double standards in their treatment of non-Arabs such as black Africans, Egyptian Copts, and Berbers of the Maghreb (see Ennaji, this volume; Tadros, this volume). The Copts and Berbers were accepted into the Arab society with less prejudice than black Africans, but blacks in Morocco remained the "other within." Another example of racial distinction involves the Berbers, who were classified in the early Islamic period as children of Ham, but when power relationships changed and Berbers produced scholars and rulers, negative racial overtones diminished in the ensuing accounts of their achievements, which also gave their genealogy greater respect.

Indeed, on the surface, following Ali Mazrui's perspective, one does not find much in the way of a discourse valorizing racial purity in Moroccan society. To illustrate Mazrui's argument, I cite a typical example of some Moroccan rulers: the Sultan Mawlay Isma'il (1646–1727), whose mother was a black slave (*umm al-walad*) and who nonetheless perceived himself a descendant of Muhammad and therefore not black. Given that Morocco is a patrilineal and patriarchal society, the father gives to his son his *nasab* (ethnic kinship) and his religion regardless of the mother's status, whether non-Muslim, Berber, black, or a slave. The Moroccan definition of race accepted the other or blacks in the Arab family as long as they possessed Arab blood seemingly ignoring their other ethnic or racial affiliations. The Moroccan system of racial definition was clearly "racialist" and was in fact a curious inversion of the Western racist model. Whereas in the Western model "one drop" of black blood identifies one as black, in the Moroccan model, "one drop" of white blood identifies one as Arab (i.e., privileged). This process helped create a "nationalist" Moroccan Arab majority and at the same time subjugated black ancestry (i.e., those without the "one drop" of Arab blood), seen as having more bearing on the historical antecedents of slavery. Therefore, this process of assimilation camouflaged the dismissal of the natural affiliation of the "other" and manufactured Arab hegemony and political unity by insisting on the sacredness of the language of the Qur'an: Arabic. Hence, even people who descended from mixed marriages did not see any ambivalence in claiming one identity, namely, their Arab lineage. This racialist discourse is deeply embedded in the assimilationist process and culture and successfully concealed or silenced other elements that were a part of the construction of one's identity.

The Diverse History of Blacks

Moroccan Arabic sources assert that all the black people in northwest Africa were originally slaves who had been freed under different circumstances through time. However, one group of black people—namely, the Haratin—might not have been of slave origin from sub-Saharan Africa, but rather were native to Southern Morocco. The available written sources from antiquity to Jewish documents confirm that the natives of the area were black. The authors of ancient sources called the Haratin the "Ethiopians of the West;" and late Jewish sources, from some rabbis who lived in the Draa region, called them "Kushites" or black descendants of Ham (Jacques-Meunié 1972, vol. 11, no. 1: 140). The French Catholic priest Charles de Foucauld (1858–1916) who sojourned in the Sahara (in Tamanrasset) remarked that the inhabitants of the oases of Bani in southern Morocco were mixed Berbers and Haratin suggesting that the Haratin may have formed a majority in southern Morocco; he estimated that the Haratin in some areas in southern Morocco were nine-tenths of the population (de Foucauld 1988, 122).

The ancestral form of the term "Hartani" derives from the Berber word *ahardan*, which is connected with skin color. It means "dark color," and the earliest known usage of the term was among the Berbers of Sanhaja and Zanata before the great Arab migration of Banu Hassan in the thirteenth century. The Berber-speaking Tuareg people inhabiting the western and central Sahara and Sahel use a similar word to designate a person of both black and white parentage: *achardan*. Among the mountain-dwelling Berbers of Sanhaja origin, the term designates a person with a black skin "*Ahardan,*" in contrast with the white "*Amazigh.*" In fact, the Berber term *ahardan* (plural: *ihardin*) was used by Berber-speaking people not only in Tafilalt but also in the High and Middle Atlas and in Mauritania. Hence, the term Haratin was in use long before the arrival of the Arabs (especially the Banu Ma'qil) in the region in the thirteenth century. The Arabic-speaking population of Tafilalt used the term Hartani to designate "black slaves." Although the term Haratin has no significance in the Arabic language, it has produced diverging interpretations: for some it is an Arabic word of two possible meanings. Certain scholars suggest that "hartani" is a combination of two words: "*hurr*" and "*thani*," literally "the second free man," but more likely meaning "a free person of a second class." It has also been suggested that it derived from the Arabic verb "*haratha*" that signifies "to cultivate." The reason for the latter meaning could possibly be applied to the Haratin who were known to be cultivators in the south of Morocco, mainly in Draa region, thus lending credence to this inaccurate etymological argument. Incidentally, this fact alone rebuts the commonly held opinion that the nature of slavery in Morocco was mainly domestic in nature. The Arabic sources accepted the first meaning that the word Hartani meant in the common Moroccan language, namely, "freed," in opposition to a person of a free origin, hence connoting a legal status. There is also a commonly used term, *asuqi* (black), especially among the Berbers in the Souss valley region in southern Morocco. Berbers generally used three terms to designate black people: *asuqi*, *ismakh*, or *ismag*, and *aharadani* (Hartani). Each term was associated with regional Berber dialects in the Moroccan south, but at times and currently they are all used interchangeably, especially with the increase of rural exodus to metropolises, such as Marrakesh and Casablanca, in the recent decades. It is clear that by the seventeenth century, there was a differentiation between *hartani* (a black person or a free black) and *asuqi* or *ismakh* (a black slave).

Many anthropologists such as Denise Jacques-Meunié and Gabriel Camps confirm that the first inhabitants of the Moroccan Sahara were of a dark complexion but distinct from the so-called blacks of the Sahel or Savannah regions, emphasizing the diversity among blacks in the region (see Camps 1970, vol. 7, no. 1: 44–45; Jacques-Meunié 1982, tome I:180–81).[2]

The story of their displacement goes back to the Roman era. With the advance of the Romans into the Moroccan interior, the Jazula Berbers may have been forced to move toward the south and compete with the blacks in the oases of the Draa. Using the camel and other advantageous weapons, the Berbers most likely conquered the native populations of the Sahara and assumed for themselves a superior status, placing the natives in lesser, subordinate status. Trans-Saharan trade developed essentially with the spread of the camel in the Sahara. It is largely accepted that camels were introduced into North Africa (and by extension to Western Sahara) by the Romans during the first century. They may have entered into an interdependent or clientele relationship with the Haratin, with the Berbers assuming the patron's role (Gsell 1929, tome V:3). This claim is also congruent with the local oral traditions of Tata area in southern Morocco: that the Haratin were in the region as natives and had been free. The Haratin claim precedence in the region, that is to say that they were in this region long before the coming of the Berbers and later the Arabs, who were the real outsiders, and who consequently further altered the social and political structure of the southern oases. The Arabs added the *sharif* status (descent from the Prophet Muhammad), another layer, to the racial prejudice and the economic privilege in the social hierarchy, hence increasing the otherness of the Haratin. Indeed, like the Berbers, the Arabs ridiculously supposed themselves superior and came to own most of the land in the Moroccan oases and forced the Haratin to work for them in a system similar to social systemic strata found in western serfdom (Mezzine 1987, 269). They all lived in a separate walled rural community called *qsar* (plural: *qsur*) in a quasi-caste system.

Slavery and the Homogenization of Blackness

In addition to the lack of good sources documenting the history of the indigenous Haratin and the black people in Morocco, blackness was homogenized, obscuring the origin of the Haratin and undermining the diverse origins and historical migration of black Africans. The change in the meaning of *Hartani* into the synonym of "ex-slaves" could have developed with Mawlay Isma'il's project to create a royal army by enslaving all black Moroccans either by purchasing those who were already slaves or enslaving those who were ex-slaves or free. This new meaning was, at the very least, certainly reinforced as a result of the enslavement of the Haratin. It became a legal and an ideological construct to justify the subjugation of the free blacks. Official documents were written to prove that the Haratin were of slave origin. I cite the example of the *fatwa* (legal opinion) of Ibn an-Naji,[3] which represents the official opinion of the Makhzan (central authority) during the reign of Mawlay Isma'il against the opinion of the Fez learned men or "ulama." Fez was the most important intellectual center in Morocco thanks to its famous university al-Qarawiyyin. The Islamic scholars of the city were the ones who kept the ruler under scrutiny. It was these religious scholars who challenged the order of the sultan to enslave the Haratin. Registers of slaves were meticulously written to document the legality of the steps taken in buying the slaves and enslaving the Haratin. The official documents report that the total of all blacks acquired from all Morocco exceeded 221,320 (Jany al-AzharwaNur al-Abhar 1860). They also state that some scholars delivered their testimony and approval of the operation. The documents state that the sultan wanted to create a loyal and a strong professional royal army from this operation.

When he came to power in 1672, Mawlay Isma'il had to face a fragmented society and a political instability in many areas of Morocco. Traditionally, the strength of the royal power was negotiated and relied on a "clientele system" that is the political support of tribal or Sufi groups who would get in return royal favors. The sultans used to get their soldiers from some specific tribal groups or rural Sufi groups in return for tax breaks and rights in land. Mawlay Isma'il was convinced that this "clientele system" was not reliable in maintaining a strong central state. The soldiers provided to the state by a certain tribe were not completely freed from their obligations toward their tribes. Az-Zayani, a Moroccan chronicler (nineteenth century) reported that Sultan Isma'il gave the order to collect all black people. No black person was spared whether this person was slave or freed black or Hartani. (Ahmad az-Zayani, D 1577, 31–32). There the color of the skin was reason enough for a person to be enslaved and enrolled in the army of the sultan.

There are only a few documents that could give us a clear description of the Haratin protest but this protest did not amount to a consistent movement. We know of one learned man, ‘Abd as-Salam Jassus, who issued his *fatwa* (a legal opinion) against this operation, but he was imprisoned soon. When the sultan could not win him over, he ordered that Jassus be killed (Ad-Du‘ayyif 1986, 83–86).

Mawlay Isma’il's decision to enroll all black people in his army by force seems to be political in motivation. However, it is clear that his policy drove the image of the blacks in Morocco. His operation gave rise to cruel practices and racial conceptions that affected how Islam was heard and interpreted with regard to the situation of black people. He did not use the ideals of Islam to create a diverse army in a truly diverse society but he manipulated the Islamic law to serve materialistic needs to increase his power. He needed people whom he could trust in the military, soldiers who owed their allegiance solely to him and not to another "tribal" or lineage or Sufi solidarity as well. However, the decision to favor certain black individuals in the palace, some of whom had indeed reached a very high status in power, surpassing that of some Arab dignitaries, caused many tribes to envy them. Arabs and Berbers were furious out of envy and all kind of popular literature was written to downgrade the black "race" to delegitimize their growing political position. The practice of Islam did not transcend ethnic ties, and political loyalty was sometimes based on ethnic lines. This backlash against the blacks by Arabs and Berbers increasingly enforced the stereotypes and the racial attitudes against blacks.

Mawlay Isma’il spent twenty-four years of his reign pacifying Morocco and fighting the unsubdued populations who did not accept his regime (Ahmad an-Nasiri 1997, VII:71–88). The black army was a central force in unifying Morocco; without whom Mawlay Isma’il would not have succeeded to impose unity and peace in all of Morocco. The black army became the provider of the most powerful members of the society politically and economically; they became sultan makers. But this political stability was soon threatened by the rivalry of the Mawlay Isma’il sons. In 1757, a new Sultan Sidi Muhammad Ben ’Abd Allah came to the throne and decided to put an end to the political instability presumably created by the black troops; so, he dissolved the black army and substituted for them Arabs; only few of the blacks remained in the army throughout the 'Alawi dynasty.

In the end, the black army and their families separated themselves from the Makhzan (the old executive apparatus in the Moroccan political system) and reclaimed their original status of freedom, as a great number of them (such as the Haratin) were indeed free before their enslavement by Mawlay Isma'il. When the majority of the army left the Makhzan, they scattered all over the country and settled near and among different tribes. At times, some people raised questions about the status of the black army and their descendants wondering if they were still slaves, but religious scholars affirmed that all members of the black army were free. It was custom that some of them continued to be in the service of the government until after the French protectorate (1912–1956). In rural areas, and especially in southern Morocco, blacks and particularly the Haratin provided the crucial labor in agricultural production. These Haratin tended Berber and Arab-controlled oases and were often forced into a caste system working as sharecroppers called *khammasin*. They got one-fifth of what they produced and were prohibited, according to customary laws, to own land. The French occupation imposed a new capitalist mode of production in Morocco. The capitalist system altered the Moroccan social structures by transforming local human labor power into a class of wage earners. The creation of a wage-earning system influenced the migration of blacks from southern Morocco to the big cities, within the rural exodus, resulting in the eventual emergence of slums. Consequently, the number of slaves continually dwindled and the institution eventually died a natural death.

Conclusion

The conflation of the meanings of the term "Haratin" could have developed with Mawlay Isma'il's project. At the very least, the definition of the Haratin as "descendants of slaves," "former slaves," or "freed slaves" was certainly reinforced at that time and the belief that they were originally free and autochthonous was diminished. At the present time, all terms designating black people such as *Haratin* and *kuhal* (plural of *khal* "black color") are used interchangeably in most of the country. Hence, the repeated wounds of the horrors of servitude have been perpetuated to the present day as a result of the persistent racial contempt against the Haratin and black people in general, who have been stigmatized not only by virtue of being descendants of slaves but by being "black." It is true that many black individuals have climbed the social strata and practiced all kinds of professions, as well as others who migrated to Western countries and were able to send money home and purchase important estates or manage businesses in different parts of Morocco, but the majority is still struggling on the margins of an unjust society. Sa'dbuh, a Hartani from the Saharan city of Laâyoune, declared in a recent newspaper article "that the best status any Hartani could achieve in the Moroccan Sahara is a camel herder" (*Almassae* 2013, 17). According to a report written by Sulayman ar-Raysuni and Mawlay Idriss al-Muwaddin, published in the Moroccan journal *Almassae*, there are some entire villages that are still considered as outcaste groups deprived of basic social and administrative services, such as the black families who live in the area of Khadaqar-Rayhan in the northern area of Chefchaouen in the Rif region. The Moroccan government has been unable or unwilling to intervene and restore the wrongs against this community although the Moroccan Center for Human Rights, an independent organization, has provided information on the marginalization of the black families and the continuous implementation of discriminatory custom laws that inhibited the Haratin's claim to a proud identity and social justice (*Almassae* 2013, 16).

Notes

1 Most of this essay and its major points are taken from my book: Chouki El Hamel, *Black Morocco: A History of Slavery, Race and Islam* (Cambridge: Cambridge University Press, 2013).

2 Interestingly, even presently black people of Draa region are called Drawa (plural of Drawi) in northern Morocco from Marrakesh to Casablanca to Fez, and Drawi is often used pejoratively and interchangeably with black. See Remco Ensel (1999, 19).

3 I own a copy of this document of 48 pages which came from a private collection in Rabat. It is cited in the catalogue of Muhammad al-Mannuni, *al-Masadir al-'Arabiyya li-Tarikh al-Maghrib* (Rabat: Publications de la Faculté des Lettres et des Sciences Humaines, 1983), 212.

References

ad-Du'ayyif, Muhammad ibn 'Abd as-Salam. 1986. *Tarikh ad-Du'ayyif: Tarikh ad-Dawla as-Sa'ida*. Edited and Annotated by Ahmad al-'Ammari. Rabat: Dar al-Ma'thurtat.

Ahmad an-Nasiri. 1997. *al-Istiqsa' li-Akhbar Duwal al-Maghrib al-Aqsa*. Casablanca: Dar al-Kitab.

Ahmad az-Zayani. D 1577. *al-Bustanaz-Zarif fi DawlatAwladMawaly 'Ali ash-Sharif.* Rabat: Bibliothèque Royale, ms.
Almassae, Moroccan Arabic newspaper. 2013. 2098, Saturday-Sunday, June 22 and 23.
Camps, G. 1970. "Recherches sur les origines des cultivateurs noirs du Sahara." *Revue de l'Occident musulman et de la Méditerranée* 7 (1): 35–45.
de Foucauld, C. 1988. *Reconnaissance au Maroc 1883-1884.* Paris: Challamel.
El Hamel, C. 2013. *Black Morocco: A History of Slavery, Race, and Islam.* Cambridge: Cambridge University Press.
Ensel, R. 1999. *Saints and Servants in Southern Morocco.* Leiden: Brill.
Gsell, S. 1929. *Histoire ancienne de l'Afrique du Nord.* tome V. Paris: Librairie Hachette.
Jacques-Meunié, D. 1972. "Notes sur l'histoire des populations du sud marocain." *Revue de l'Occident musulman et de la Méditerranée* 11 (1): 135–50.
Jacques-Meunié, D. 1982. *Le Maroc saharien des origines à 1670.* Tome I. Paris: Librairie Klincksick.
Jany al-AzharwaNur al-Abhar. 1860. *The Gathering of Flowers and the Dazzling Light.* Rabat: Bibliothèque Royale, ms.
Mazrui, A. 1986. *The Africans: A Triple Heritage.* Toronto: Little, Brown.
Mazrui, A. 2000. "Africa and Other Civilizations: Conquest and Counter-Conquest." In *Africa in World Politics: The African State System in Flux*, edited by John W. Harbeson and Donald Rothchild, 96–145. Boulder: Westview Press.
Mezzine, L. 1987. *Le Tafilalt, contribution à l'histoire du Maroc au XVII et XVIII siècle.* Rabat: Publications de la Faculté des Lettres et des Sciences Humaines.

14

MULTICULTURALISM AND MINORITIES IN MAURITANIA

Madina Touré

On the geopolitical level, and in its recent history, Mauritania is part of the Arab Maghreb Union (UMA), an organization that it shares with Morocco, Algeria, Tunisia, and Libya. By its human geography, Mauritania is multiethnic: it is composed of an Arab-Berber population in the North, a black Arab group commonly called Haratine, and a multilingual and multicultural population further south.

This spatial distribution is not homogeneous in the sense that one finds here and there these different groups away from their natural environment. Reflection on multiculturalism in Mauritania is justified by its multiethnicity and by differences that are inherent to such diversity.

Arab-Berber culture and its territory (Trâb el Bîdhân) benefited from several studies by many specialists, but the Black culture (Negro and Haratines of Mauritania) is neglected and less known.[1]

However, because Mauritania is a huge country, the discussion will focus on the Arab-Berbers whenever it seems necessary, especially in their relations with the other populations of Mauritania.

The objective of this chapter is to contribute to a better understanding of these populations. I will give, in the first part, a historical overview of the Black presence in this vast North African space, called the Maghreb. This journey into the past will focus on the relationship between the empires and the kingdoms of Sudan and the territory that came to be called Mauritania. The aim is to see the impact of this relationship on its population. The second part will attempt to study the different ethnic groups that were inherited through these exchanges and their minority status as a result of their country's joining of the Maghreb.

A Historical Overview of Black Minorities in North Africa

The Negroid populations of North Africa

The works of Ki-Zerbo (1978) and Camps (1979) provide some insight into the human component of North Africa. They focus on a population of a Black majority in the Nile Valley, the Sahara, and the Maghreb.

Ki-Zerbo (1978, 76) advances that in Paleolithic age, the black population spread into Europe and beyond. Camps (1979, 14) confirms this thesis and argues that until the Neolithic age, with the exception of one or two cases, all human remains collected from numerous deposits of Central and Southern Sahara are Negroid. He adds that it is only from the sixth to the second millennium BC that the Sahara was divided into two ethnic families:

- Negroid "Bovidian" groups, weakened or fleeing to the south in search of better pastures for their herds.
- White people "Equidian" groups, better armed and more mobile than the first because of their horses.

Camps (1979, 16) thinks these newcomers had to push Blacks to leave their territory and go south. But the gradual desertification of the Sahara is, in itself, a sufficient reason to push Black pastors to travel for the welfare of their animals. The Phoenicians made their appearance in the twelfth century BC, the Greco-Byzantines in the sixth century BC, the Romans in the second century BC. The Vandals arrived in the fifth century AD, the Arabs in the seventh century AD, the Turkish-Ottomans in the sixteenth and seventeenth century AD, and the Imperialist Europeans in the nineteenth century in the Senegal River Valley and in the twentieth century in the Moorish country.

The White element gradually reversed the first tendency of a predominantly Black population in North Africa. The Black element has not disappeared despite the new rule, because according to Camps, "the existence of a Black population in the current Oases cannot be explained by only a strong mixing and a constant supply of Sudanese blood due to commerce and slavery throughout history." He thinks that the Hartani or Chouchan of Algerian and Fezzani Oases are descendants of the ancient Ethiopians, just like the Tuareg are sons of Garamantes and Regeïbat sons of Gétules. Jacques-Meunié argues in the same direction and claims that sedentary Blacks in Mauritania are "descendants of an ancient Black population that formerly probably occupied Africa until the shores of the Mediterranean" (Jacques-Meunié 1961, 16).

While the Black population was reduced in Northern Africa, probably because of interbreeding, it significantly increased over the centuries as one moved to the south. Indeed, the Sudanese kingdoms came to join or be confused with the Trab el Bidan (Moorish country).

Empires and Kingdoms of Sudan and the Trans-Saharan Trade

In his writings on the Northwest of Black and White Africa, Al-Bakri (Cordoba 1068) talks about the different Sudanese empires and kingdoms specifying the route that leads to them and the journey's span.[2] He mentions the Sudanese city, which is closest to the Banu Godâla (six days of walking), called Sunghâna, and lies by the Nile (the Senegal River). After this city, he cites successively from west to east the following:

- The kingdom of Takrur (which is Muslim)
- The kingdom of Silli (Sylla) on both sides of the river, whose inhabitants (Muslims) are involved in the trade of millet, salt, copper rings, loin cloths, and are rich in cotton and cattle
- The kingdom of Qalanbû (the NGalam), on the river, whose inhabitants are polytheists
- Taranqa and Zaqfawa Farawiyyin are other, less known, Sudanese kingdoms, which, according to al-Bakri, separate the NGalam of Ghana
- The empire of Ghana, with a Muslim city and another one that is pagan

Exchanges between North Africa and the Bilad-es-Sudan (land of the Blacks) put into perspective the role of slave traders from the southern Saharan states and Arab-Berber traders from North Africa. These exchanges were symmetrical and were not limited only to slaves. Sudanese countries provided the Maghreb, Egypt, and the Middle East with gold, ivory, agricultural products, or crafts, but especially slaves.

From North Africa the caravans carried not only capital and luxury goods (horses, blocks of salt, iron, copper) to the cities of the South but also some white slaves, artists, brought especially from Cairo for the rich Sudanese.

Slavery formed, with multiple usages, the base of Mediterranean societies. The rulers of Morocco, like Sultan Moulay Ismail in the fifteenth century, used African Blacks in large numbers in their army from the fifteenth to the eighteenth century (Chouki 2013). Inside the homes, the men were destined to domesticity, and women to the pleasures of the flesh. This resulted in a difference in price for the acquisition of such "goods." We observe here the following: higher prices for women than for men and higher prices for eunuchs than for un-castrated men.[3]

Slave states used several means to procure slaves; prisoners of war were sold by the winners, and methods of raids had two poles: the first was organized from the Mediterranean slave ports (Algeria, Morocco, Tunisia, and Tripolitania), and the second channel used the men of the desert who were true intermediaries between the Sudanese and Mediterranean countries.

To make an assessment of the trans-Saharan slave trade is certainly not an easy task. However, some authors have ventured and provided, through their investigations, an estimate of the number of slaves. M'bokolo (1995, 1:270) establishes a table of estimated trafficking between the eighteenth and nineteenth century.

M'bokolo (ibid.) cites the results of studies carried out by an American historian, Ralph A. Austen, on Arab-Berber trafficking during medieval times (700–1700). He claims that the range goes from 1,000 to 6,000 slaves per year arriving in North Africa during this period. He relied on the Libyan consular sources of the eighteenth century relating to such

Country of Slaves Destination	*Periods*	*Total*
Egypt	1700–1880	800,000
Libya	1700–1900	430,000
Tunisia	1700–1850	100,000
Algeria	1700–1890	70,000
Morocco	1700–1890	520,000

trafficking. These sources mention that 1,500 slaves reached North Africa per year. Then, in the early eighteenth century, the French ships carried away ten cargoes of slaves in seventy shipments from Libya to the east, with an average of 200 to 250 slaves per cargo. For the second half of the eighteenth century, the maximum number of caravans returned from Sudan, Ghadames, Fezzan (Libya), and Timbuktu.

Finally, François Renault, the French Consul in Libya, initiator of the counting of slaves in Libya, advanced an overall figure of 150,000 slaves trafficked in the fifteenth century (ibid., 272). Djibril Tamsir Niane considers that this trade, though having significant negative consequences, was not comparable to the Atlantic slave population whose harvest was incommensurate with the practices of Saharan and Mediterranean traders (UNESCO 1991, 32). He will even find a similarity in the political, sociological, and cultural aspects between Berbers and Sudanese who, according to him, have preserved the original acceptance of Islam without Arabization.

Charles André Julien (1980) draws attention to the difficulties resulting from interbreeding between the different components of the North African population. Thus, he embarks on a description of these races where the black or Negroid character is found here and there. He argues that the Arabs or whites get more "Negro" as one descends to the south.

Note here that the Blacks in North Africa, whatever their status, share the Muslim religion. When they are of servile status they end up losing their original culture in favor of that of their masters. They carry several names including Abd (plural: Abid) when they are still subject to captivity and Hartani (plural: Haratine) when they are released or freed; they are also called Sudani (plural: Sudan), common name for all Blacks.

Because of the absence of reliable figures, no one can speak with certainty about the number of this ethnic component in North Africa. Tunisia, for example, believes that Blacks are less than 1% of its population whereas Mauritania counts more than 40%.

The Blacks of Mauritania between Arab and African Identity

Modern Mauritania consists of five main ethnic groups. The Arab-Berbers (or white Moors) speak the Hassaniya language, an Arabic variety of the Beni Hassan, which they share with their tributaries, Haratines. They generally live in the north while Haratines are found throughout the country. The Haalpulaaren, speakers of Pulaar/Fulfulde, the language of Fulani/Fulbe live in the middle valley of the Senegal River, Trarza (provinces of Dimar and Toro), Brakna (the Law Yirlabé-Hebbiyabé), and Gorgol (the Bossea the Nguénar and Damga). The Soninke, who speak a different language (which extends to Mali, Ivory Coast, Guinea, Sierra Leone, through Senegal, Gambia, and Mauritania) live in the two regions of Gorgol (Kaédi and Djéol-Gori) and Guidimakha. The Wolof, with the same name for their language, are inhabitants of Trarza. The Bambara, who speak another language Mande (Bambara), are scattered in Brakna, Gorgol (Mbout) in Assaba, and in Guidimakha Hodhs. Many of them have lost the use of their language, but their surnames attest to their belonging to this ethnic group.

Haratines

Haratines, who are people of slave origin, speak Arabic. Their dependent status earned them the adoption of the language and culture of their former masters. They seem to be numerically a majority compared to other components of the Mauritanian population because of their massive presence in communities across the country and beyond its borders. Haratine tribes are attached to their former masters with whom they identify. They have traditionally lived around settlements dealing with fieldwork and domestic life in the oasis. It is a population that was highly marginalized both educationally and socially.

Moorish society, like all other Mauritania communities, is highly hierarchical with the hassanes on top of the pyramid:

- The hassanes (Arab-warriors)
- The Zouayas (marabouts, Tolba, clerics)
- The Zenagas (dependent Whites)
- The caste: Igâwounes—griots, Maalemines—blacksmiths, Nemadi—hunters, Imraguen—fishermen.
- Haratines, who constitute the base of the Moorish society. (Jacques-Meunié 1961, 25–30)[4]

The rapid urbanization of the country and the continuing rural exodus, as a result of droughts, increased the precariousness of their lives. Men and women earn their living doing odd jobs (babysitting, cheap labor, domestic work, etc.). Children in urban areas are often educated, but the large number of them who are found on the streets suggests that the attrition rate is very significant. This pushes them to work early in life, and as a result, they find themselves in the footsteps of their parents.

It should be noted, however, that there are exceptions to this in the sense that some of them have received quality education that led them, starting from the 1980s, to the highest positions of the state like lawyers, doctors, ministers, prime minister, president of the Assembly, and so on.

Wolofs

The kingdom of Wâlo, populated predominantly by Wolof, is located in the delta of the Senegal River. It is traditionally ruled by a king, called Brack, whose power extends to both sides of the river. Currently, the Mauritanian side is integrated into the Trarza region southwest of the country with Rosso as its capital. The Wolof Wâlo are historically linked to the Moors. The legend traces their origin to the union between Aboubekr Ibn Umar, the Almoravid movement, and a haalpulaar woman who gave birth to a person called Amadou Boubacar Ndiaye nicknamed Ndiadiane, paradoxically, eponymous ancestor of Wolof (Monteil 1968, 23). In the nineteenth century, another marriage will unite the queen of Wâlo, Njembëtte Mbodj Emir Mohamed Trarza Lehbib. This union gave birth to Emir Ely Njembëtte, who would play a big role in the pacification of the two territories.

Political and matrimonial alliances between the two groups remained fairly important to the extent that the surnames of Wolof tribes were adopted by Moors, blacks, and whites alike: Fall for Oulad Ahmed Ben Daman and Oulad Daymane, Diakhaté for Oulad Ebéri, and so on. The physical aspect (dyed black) of black Moors and Wolof (Haratines) is associated with both their common use of the Wolof language and their practice of fishing and agriculture.

Wolof society has a traditional structure that is scaled into different castes:

- The Guers at the top are the nobility
- The Gueweuls are griots, musicians, guardians of tradition
- The Teugues are blacksmiths, jewelers
- The Awdés are shoemakers, savatiers
- The Laobés are woodcutters, carpenters,
- The Diâmes are former slaves

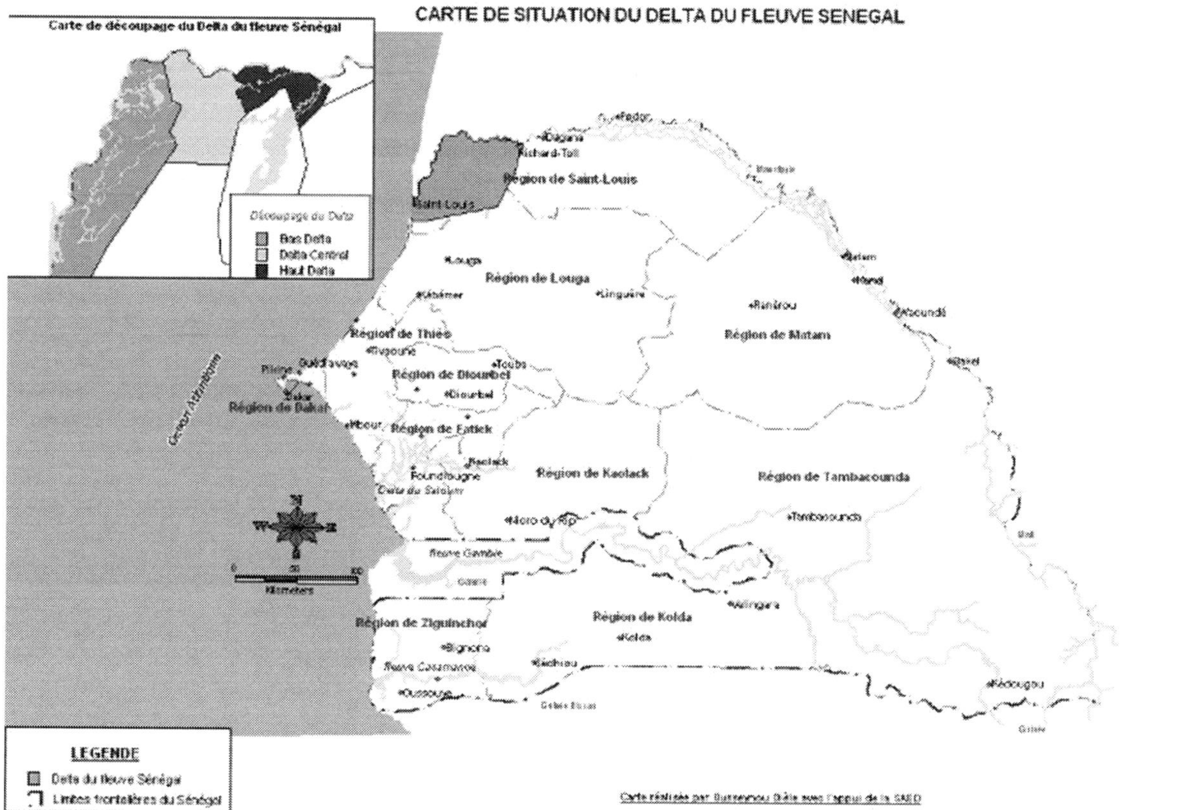

Carte du delta du fleuve Sénégal.

Source: http://www.memoireonline.com/01/08/871/maintenance-amenagements-hydroagricoles-delta-fleuve-senegal-perimetre-boundoum.html.

The Haalpulaaren

Fuuta Tooro, stronghold of Haalpulaaren and some Soninke in the middle valley of the Senegal River, is a large area divided into seven provinces that stretch from the west to east, as follows: Dimar, Toro, Law, Yirlabé- Hebbiyabé, Bossea, and Nguénar Damga. The country, which straddles both sides of the river, is largely inhabited by the Haalpulaaren (Wagué 2008/2009, 8–9).[5] Abdoulaye Bathily, Senegalese historian, quoted by Wagué, notes on this subject: "The Fuuta Tooro is regarded, rightly, as the country of Pulaaren Haal ('Toucouleurs' and Fulani). The reason is the numerical domination of the ethnic group in the middle valley of the Senegal which has marked its history to the extent that the roles played by other ethnic groups in the history of Fuuta and sometimes their existence in this country are ignored."[6] Lam (1992, 9–10) believes that the Fulani have occupied Mauritania "from the 2nd to the 7th century AD, when they began to leave the area to Fuuta Tooro, where they arrived between the late eighth and early ninth century."[7] Oumar Kane also made of Fuutaa the country of the Fulbe (deformed by the French and the Wolof to Peuls) and asserts that "they were more extended to the north and south of the river."[8] Wane (1969, 16) remarks the numerical superiority of Toucouleurs in Fuuta Tooro and states that its northern and southern borders "were respectively tens of kilometers on both sides of the Senegal River, bordering the Sahel and the Ferlo."

Just like its neighbors, the Haalpulaar society is based on caste and is divided into three major categories:

The Rimbés (Rimbe): free men, aristocrats

- Torobbés (TooroBBe) is the marabout class that has become the head of the country and society, probably with the theocratic revolution of 1776. They are holders of securities: Thierno (Marabout or Mrabet), Elimane/Almamy (Imam), Tapsirou (Tafsir Al Quran), Alpha (Alfahim), Elfekki (Alfâqih), and so on.
- Sébbés (Sebbe) is a generic term that refers to all black people different from Fulbe/Fulani/Haalpulaaren and are living with them: they are Sebbe Alambe (if they are of Soninke), Sebbe Jolfube (original Wolof/Djolfo) and so on. The Sebbe Haalpulaaren form the warrior class and are divided into Sebbe WurankooBe and Sebbe KoliyaaBe; they are run by Farbas and Diagarafs.

- Diawambés (JaawanBe) can be breeders, marabouts, counselors, or courtiers. They are known to be very intelligent, which earned them respect and fear. They are often the brains behind the leaders.
- Soubalbés (SubalBe) are fishermen living along the river. They are organized into strata headed by a chief, a teen, a JaaltaaBe, the Farbas, and so on.

The Gnègnbés (NyeenyBe): class of artisans/artists

- Maboubés (MaabuBe) are weavers and potters for men and women.
- Wayloubés (Waylube) are jewelers or blacksmiths, who were feared and respected for their power over fire and metal.
- Sakébés (SakkeeBe) are shoemakers or savatiers.
- Laobés (Lawbe) as in Wolof are woodcutters or carpenters.
- Wambabés (WambaaBe) and Awloubés (AwluBe) and MaabuBe-suudu-Paate are musicians or poets.

The Djiyabés (JiyaaBe): servile class. Note that there is no power from the master to the slave. These names are a legacy of the past.

- Mathioubés (maccuBe) were slaves.
- Dathianabés Alla (Alla DaccanaaBe) released by their masters.
- Sotibés (SootiiBe) bought their freedom.

Soninke

The Soninke live in two regions: the Futa in Gorgol and Guidimakha. Although there are a few minorities, Fulani and Bambara, this territory, which is situated in the upper valley of the Senegal River, is mostly Soninke.

It is a very ancient population that is implanted in the country, mainly in the north. Their long stay in the territory has left indelible toponymical traces in the sense that the name they had given to their locality remained intact and serves as a reference for all scholars of the Moorish country: Bilad Chinguetti (si-ngidi: wells or source of horses). The long cohabitation with the Berbers had also given birth to a common language, Azer or Azariya, a mixture of Soninke and Berber, which has been a living language until the 1960s (Jacques-Meunié 1961, 22).[9] In Guidimakha, Soninke's stronghold par excellence, there are many people of Bambara origin as evidenced by the name Bambaradougou or village Bambara bourg, Sélibaby district, the capital of the region.

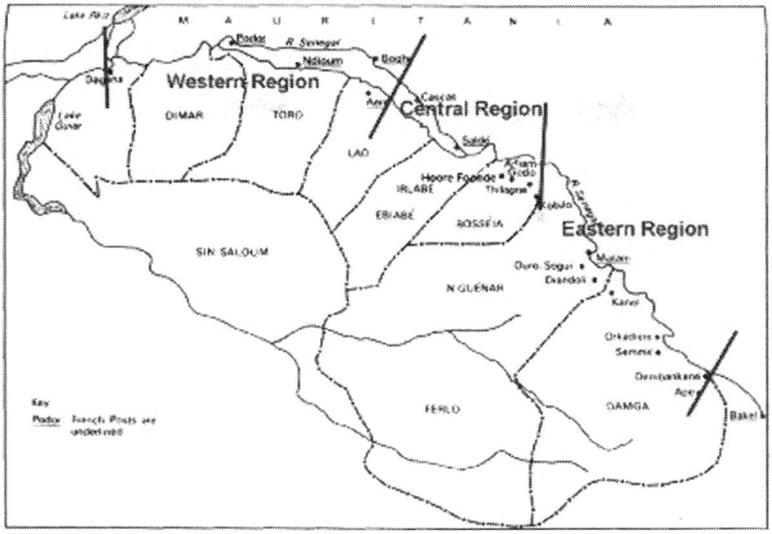

Map of Fuuta Tooro.

Source: http://www.google.fr/imgres?imgurl=http://www.suertenich.com/html/afriq/map_fouta.jpg&imgrefurl=http://blog.myheritage.fr/.

Like its neighbors, the Soninke society is based on caste, a social division giving each member a role complementing the other (Wagué 2008/2009, 180–218):

- The Hoore are the equivalent of Rimbe in Pulaar and Wolof Guers in the middle. They are the religious and political aristocracy at the top of society.
- The Gnakhamalos (Naxamalo) are socio-professionals including the Taago (blacksmiths/jewelers and potters for women), Garanko (shoemakers), the Sakko (equivalent Lawbe mid Pulaar), and so on.
- The Komo is an old servile class: It was the least favored class because of its submission, in the past, to the domination of all other classes.

Despite the upheavals associated with colonialism and changing attitudes, the social hierarchy persists in Mauritania's rural and semi-rural areas. Social barriers are less clear in the large urban areas, where the materialistic power of the individual often relegates to the background of his or her social origin. This is most striking in urban Wolof where contact with the colonists was earlier and more marked.

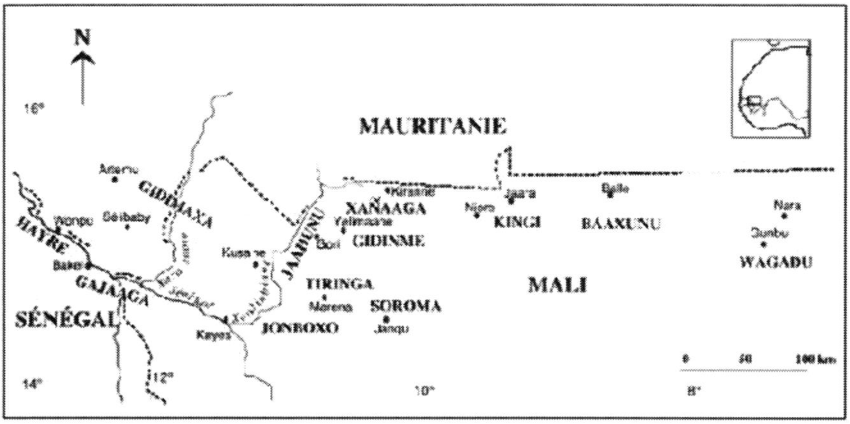

Map of Soninké Country.

Source: http://www.google.fr/imgres?imgurl=http://www.soninkara.com/images/stories/payssoninke.jpg&imgrefurl=http://www.soninkara.com/histoire-geographie/geographie/provinces-villes-et-villages-soninke.htm.

Status and Challenges of Minorities in Mauritania

The Encyclopedia Universalis (1996, Corpus 15) includes in the term "minority-only the non-dominant group of the population that owns and wishes to preserve ethnic traditions, religious or linguistic characteristics or significantly different from those of the rest of the population." A sociological view of international organizations cited in Corpus 15 takes into account four elements to define the concept of "minority":

- Community element : the members of a group must have characteristics that unite them and distinguish them from the rest of the national community.
- Quantitative element: a group must be large enough to have a digitally national importance, but also outnumbered in comparison to other national components to be qualified as minority.
- Psychological element: it requires that the minority has the consciousness of being; conversely the majority group should treat it as such to be qualified as a minority.
- Element related to minority–majority relations and oppression: without oppression, we can describe a given group as autonomous, but not a minority.

Statutes of minorities

- Ethnic minorities

In 2010, the total population of Mauritania was estimated at 3,459,773 people.[10] The Blacks of Mauritania fit in this definition of minority. Numerically, there are no reliable statistics on the ethnic composition of the population. However, some sources suggest the following estimates:

	Moors	*Haratines*	*Black-Africans*
ONS	40%	40%	20%
Marchesin (1992)	34%	26%	40%
Wikinews.org	30%	40%	30%
Lacoste et al. (1991)		20%	
MISOES	80% Moors		20%
Sounkalo (1995)	Hassaniya 2/3		1/3 or approx. 33%

A commission for a socioeconomic survey of Senegal was established in 1957 at the request of Senegal and Mauritania in order to "establish a human and economic inventory" of a well-defined portion of the valley of the Senegal River in Chemama (Ignegongba 1991, 8). Most of these estimates are based on the results of this investigation. The results, published in 1958, although partial, indicate that Blacks represent 20% of the population and that 80% are white and black Moors (Haratine). The Blacks of Mauritania are aware of this situation which stems from the fusion of their territory (Fouta Toro, right bank of the Senegal River) with the country called "Moorish" by the colonizer. The eve of independence and the creation of the young republic have marked the Mauritanian authorities. They were the first to adopt the colonial school system and receive training. The Moors had sent their servants or their tributaries (low-class persons).

- Linguistic minorities

Starting from the first decade of independence with the political will to Arabize the country, the situation was reversed. The linguistic policy of the country gave birth to the law of January 30, 1965, implementing a decree that mandated the teaching of Arabic in secondary schools. This gave rise to a strike in 1966 at the Normal School of Nouakchott and

Rosso High School. This protesting movement was supported by nineteen black Mauritanian seniors who published a manifesto denouncing "the monopoly of the Moors in the ruling of the country" (Leservoisier 1994, 189).[11] The nineteen protesters were imprisoned and, in retaliation, groups of Moors attacked the black people living in the city of Nouakchott. Official death toll was at six dead and seventy injured.[12]

In 1967, Arabic-French bilingual education was adopted in order to "resolve some of the issues raised during the ethnic unrest [. . .] and [. . .] to take into account the aspirations of Arabs and the fears of black African" (Sounkalo 1995, 37). An exclusive beginning class precedes the six primary school grades, which are bilingual. The position of Arabic in education increased in 1973 with a new reform that reserved the first two years of primary school to Arabic. Arabic language policy continued.

In 1979, Circular 002 "increasing coefficients of Arabic and Arabic subjects would confirm the government's commitment to take measures that are less theoretical, but more practical and applicable" (Sounkalo 1995, 38). "A new wave of strikes occurs, and the leaders are arrested, protests by African Negro rose to such an extent that the Military Committee of National Salvation (CMSN) decided to create an Institute of National Languages (ILN)" (Marchesin 1992, 342). The CMSN recommends to the government to "develop a national education system ensuring cultural independence where Arabic is the language spoken by all Mauritanians" (Sounkalo 1995, 39).[13] It states that Arabic is compulsory for all children whose mother tongue is Arabic, while those of other non-Arabic speakers have the opportunity to choose between Arabic and French. A year later, in 1980, two separate streams (one Arab and one French) accentuated the split in the community's secondary school.

> The 1991 constitution states that "the national languages are Arabic, Pulaar, Soninke, and Wolof; the official language is Arabic." French, the official language (since independence in 1960) and the training of Mauritanian Blacks are deleted from the Basic Law, thus, increasing the vulnerability of its users. But beyond the elimination of French as an official language, the concern of Mauritanian blacks is to see the dedication of "the primacy of Arabic over all the other languages spoken in Mauritania [. . .] and the result of a language policy that began over thirty years has managed to meet the aspirations of the Arabic community of Mauritania."[14]

Minorities challenge

On the eve of independence, Mauritania was administered from Saint-Louis, Senegal. In 1957, it received the agreement of France (Decree of July 24) to transfer the capital to Nouakchott. Mauritanian Negroes did not see it that way, fearing that this transfer calls into question their place in the future state. They were organized into two political parties: the General Union of Mauritania from the South (UGOMS), on the one hand, and the Democratic Bloc Gorgol (BDG), on the other. The latter went further to consider secession.

After independence in 1961, the Mauritanian National Union (UNM), consisting of black and Moorish UGOMS close to Saint-Louisians, claimed the annexation of southern Mauritania to Malian Federation.

In 1966, the founding congress of the Party of the People of Mauritania (PPM) became a social forum where blacks oppose the Arabization policy initiated by the government. The Mauritanian black officials in support of the students launched the strike, which led to the arrest of nineteen signatories of the manifesto as well as to ethnic clashes, as we noted above. Other strikes related to Arabization were triggered in 1979 in particular, but failed to halt the policy.

In 1983, several militant movements for the rights of Mauritanian blacks were grouped under the name of the Liberation Forces of Africans in Mauritania (FLAM) and launched in 1986, the "manifesto of Oppressed Black Mauritanians." In this manifesto "[t]he education system is defined as an iniquitous and assimilating system." Arabization is considered a "means of selection and elimination." As established in bilingual education, it can "give work to Bidan and block the paths of blacks" (Leservoisier 1994, 192).

The dissemination of this manifesto created a wave of arrests in different social layers of African Negroes. Imprisonment fell, and black African personalities were sent to the "prison-hospice" of Oualata, southeast of the country, where many lost their lives. Survivors were, for the most part, forced into exile for having lost their livelihoods, if not their dignity, after suffering degrading conditions of detention and humiliation.

In 1987, it was the turn of the Mauritanian military blacks to suffer the strike force of the state. An attempt to plot was attributed to them. Arrests were made, and a trial condemned three officers to death: they were executed. The lucky ones were imprisoned.

The year 1989 was the year of the painful events between Mauritania and neighboring Senegal. It was also an excuse to get rid of a lot of black Mauritanians, destroying their civil status documents and putting hands on their property. "These deportations led Senegal to enter the Security Council of the UN in July 1989. On August 22, diplomatic relations between Senegal and Mauritania were broken" (Leservoisier 1994, 220–21).

To celebrate the Day of Independence (November 28), twenty-eight young officers and soldiers were executed by their Moorish comrades in the early 1990s. This was followed by a purge of black elements, and those who were suspected of belonging to the movement of protest in the army were jailed.

The advent of the Internet contributes to a better visibility of movements and organization of human rights activists in Mauritania. Some have their own websites while others are known through social networks such as Facebook and Twitter. These organizations were created to help the victims of the old years called "Embers." Others came to assist them in the pursuit of justice, human rights, and peace.

As a case in point, the following are the major civil society organizations for the defense of minority rights in the country:

- EL HOR (the Organization for the Liberation and the Emancipation of Harratines): a "movement of Haratines in Mauritania committed to fight for emancipation, equality, dignity, and happiness of Haratines"[15]
- SOS Slaves: an association of general human rights for the promotion and protection of their defenders in Mauritania. It was created in February 1995 by descendants of slaves and masters, united by the same resolution to eliminate traditional slavery in Mauritanian space"[16]
- FLAM: African Liberation Forces of Mauritania, an organization created in 1983 to defend the rights of Blacks Mauritania
- OCVIDH or ODH: Organization against Violation of International Human Rights
- AVOMM: Assistance to Widows and Orphans of Mauritanian Military
- COVIRE: Association involving military survivors, widows, survivors, civilian political prisoners tortured persons, orphans, and the collective Sharing and Help
- Fléré: Front to fight against slavery, racism, and exclusion

- TPMN: do not touch my Mauritanian citizenship, a movement consecutive to the current enrolment/census problems
- Mauritania: struggles for a fair nation and republican spirit
- Harratine Negritude: defends Blacks' rights
- Birame Dah Ould IRA: "The Initiative for Resurgence of Abolitionist Movement in Mauritania (IRA) is a Mauritanian militant group whose objective is to fight against slavery, a practice that has become a crime since the act of August 8, 2007
- Awareness and Resistance: A network for raising awareness and resistance racism and discrimination[17]

Conclusion

Walo Brack, Futa Toro, and Guidimakha, like all colonial territories, suffered the colonial policy of division and separation. Indeed, to confirm their domination, the French colonizers destroyed all existing state entities and the delimitation process including new geographical boundaries during the nineteenth century. Colonial penetration in Africa has resulted in a general way in painfully experienced ethnic and political divisions related to arbitrary geographical splits. We witness the creation of new artificial boundaries, the dismemberment of the existing state or administrative institutions: it is the application of the colonial policy called "divide and conquer." This division was intended to avoid any major ethnic grouping in the same country, especially when the people in question are stubborn or unruly. This was the case of the theocratic regime of Fuuta Tooro (the regime Almamy: deformation of the Arabic "al Imam"), whose breakup in two stages took place in the second half of the nineteenth century. Its provinces were separated from each other before they were divided around the axis of the river that became the boundary line. Finally, the left bank was placed under the authority of Senegal while the right was given to the Moorish country. Other states suffered the same fate: Walo and Gadiaga/Guidimakha were also divided into two new territories for the benefit of Senegal, Mauritania, and Mali. The areas on the right bank of the country were annexed to the Moor country (Trarza and Guidimakha), while the portions on the left bank were incorporated in Senegal (Saint-Louis, Bakel) and Mali (Mali Guidimakha).

Thus, North Africa, composed of former Sultanates and Arab and Berber Emirates, living alongside the Black Kingdoms of the Senegal River Valley, were built on a new geopolitical map while the territories of the large Arab-Berber Maghreb retained their homogeneity (Algeria, Morocco, Tunisia, Libya). The territories south of the Sahara were annexed to the blacks' states of Mali, Niger, and Chad. Conversely, the black population of the valley (Wolof, Soninke, Bambara and Haalpulaaren) were geographically linked to new countries such as Mauritania.

To make matters worse, the social division of these communities has created a sub-caste of slaves or former slaves, based on the mass of the Mauritanian Black population, but difficult to classify into Arabic society. Movements of human rights endeavor to enforce the abolition of subsequent slavery and to enforce the law criminalizing these degrading practices.

To people who paid tribute to the first president, Moktar Ould Daddah, in the following words, "Mr. President, you have created Mauritania from scratch," he replied, "What nonsense! How can we forget the legacy accumulated over the millennia, many civilizations that have hatched here and there on the territory of the future Mauritania? Of course . . . with the independence, the story has changed direction: the colonial challenge—a strategic passage between Maghreb Mauritania and black Africa—was replaced by a national challenge—that Mauritanian history and geography were destined to be a link between the North and South of Africa . . . difficult inheritance. The only real wealth then, of today and tomorrow, is the men and women of Mauritania, with their energy and skills" (Ould Daddah 2003, 14).

But unlike its neighbors in Mali, Niger, and Chad, which are cited among the states of sub-Saharan Africa, Mauritania is making a choice that privileges its Arab status to that of a buffer state between white North Africa and black Sub-Saharan Africa, reflecting its ethnic composition.

Have the government authorities thought about the rich historical and social heritage that their country benefited from? Are they aware of the wealth that this diversity engenders? By adopting and accepting the role that nature has to offer, wouldn't Mauritania be reconciled with itself and its children? Wouldn't justice for all and equal opportunities for citizens of all races and languages turn this vast country—which Arab authors, in memory of its first Soninke inhabitants, call Bilad Chinguetti—into a nation-state worthy of a million poets?

Notes

1 Black culture was overlooked by colonial administrators, ethnologists, anthropologists, sociologists, historians, Islamologists, and so on.
2 Monteil, V. (traduction d'Al-Bakrî (Cordoue 1068)), 1968, 66 et s.
3 Eunuchs were reserved to guard harems and were safe for the concubines of Princes
4 According to Jacques-Meunié (1961, 25–30), Harratines are not a distinct race, but a social class, the free men of lower class, middle class between the slaves (Abid), and the free men of higher status. It would be a separate ethnic group "encysted among the whites."
5 Wagué, C. is a Mauritanian historian.
6 Idem, 12.
7 Lam, AM 9-10; Historian, Egyptologist Senegal, from the valley.
8 O. Kane, another Senegalese historian, 2004, 25–26
9 According to him, Azerbaijan was spoken at that time by Massena to Tichite but in Adrar as before.
10 World Perspective, University of Sherbrooke, Version 7.6 07-2011.
11 For more details, see Leservoisier (1994, 189).
12 Ibid.
13 The teaching of national languages will not receive sufficient resources, or strong political will. But a generation of children attended these courses in primary education before joining General Arabic and French. They had no difficulty adapting and succeeding. See Sounkalo (1995, 39).
14 Ibid.
15 Charter of the Organization EL HOR.
16 Note of presentation of SOS Esclaves29.
17 Source: Lawyers Without Borders, accessed February 3, 2015, http://www.asf-network.org.

References

Camps, G. 1979. *Les relations du monde méditerranéen et du monde sud-saharien durant la préhistoire et la protohistoire*. Recherches Sahariennes, cahier no. 1. Paris: CNRS.

Chouki, E. 2013. *Black Morocco: A History of Slavery, Race, and Islam*. Cambridge: Cambridge University Press.

Ignegongba, K. 1991. *La fécondité en Mauritanie*. Paris: CEPED.

Jacques-Meunié, D. 1961. *Cités anciennes de Mauritanie*, 194, illustrations 80. Paris: Librairie Klincksieck.

Julien, Ch. A. 1972. *L'Afrique du Nord en marche: Nationalisme musulman et souveraineté française*. Paris: Edition Julliard.

Kane, Oumar. 2004. *La première hégémonie peule: Le Fuuta-Tooro de Koli Tenella à Almaami Abdul*. Paris: Karthala / Presses universitaires de Dakar.

Ki-Zerbo, J. 1978. *Histoire de l'Afrique Noire*. Paris: Hatier.

Lacoste, Y., and C. Lacoste. 1991. *L'Etat du Maghreb*. Paris: Ed. La découverte.

Lam, A. M. 1992. *De l'origine égyptienne des Peuls*. Paris: Editions Présence Africaine/ Khepera.

Leservoisier, O. 1994. *La question foncière en Mauritanie*. Paris: L'Harmattan.

Marchesin, P. 1992. *Tribus, Ethnies et Pouvoirs en Mauritanie*. Paris: Karthala.

M'bokolo, E. 1995. *L'Afrique entre l'Europe et l'Amérique: la place de l'Afrique dans la rencontre des deux mondes*. Paris: UNESCO.

Moneteil, Vincent. 1968. *(Traduction) Al-Bakri (Cordoue 1068), Routier de l'Afrique blanche et noire du Nord-Ouest*; *BIFAN*, sér.B, n°1, 39–116.

Ould Daddah, M. 2003. *La Mauritanie contre vents et marées*. Paris: Karthala.
Sounkalo, J. 1995. "La situation linguistique en Mauritanie." *Notre Librairie*, numéro 120–121 (Janvier-Mars): 36–43.
Wane, Y. 1969. *Les Toucouleur du Fouta Toro (Sénégal): Stratification sociale et structure familiale*. Dakar: IFAN-CAD.

BIOGRAPHIES OF CONTRIBUTORS

Mathew Andrews is a graduate from Yale Law and Yale College. His work focuses on the intersection of language, religion, and ethnicity in creating and sustaining regional conflict. His main research areas are North Africa and the Middle East with a focus on minorities and women. Andrews intermittently teaches courses on social movements and human rights in the Center of Middle East Studies at Yale University.

Khadija Arfaoui taught English, American Studies, Women's Studies, and Human Rights at the Higher Institute of Languages of Tunis until her retirement. She was also a Teaching Assistant at George Washington University. Her interest has always focused on women and human rights. She joined civil society in the early 1980s, founding first Association for the Development and Protection of the Environment (ADPE), an environmental organization. In the meantime, she also joined Association of Tunisian Women for Research and Development (AFTURD) and Tunisian Association of Democratic Women (ATFD), Amnesty International, and more recently, CSID (Center for the Study of Islam and Democracy) and TAUN (Tunisian Association of the United Nations). She is a feminist researcher and lives in the Tunis area. She has published several articles.

Abderrezak Dourari, holds a doctorate on discourse analysis from the University of Sorbonne, France (1993). He is now professor in language sciences at the University of Algiers, and appointed head of the National

Pedagogical and Linguistic Center for the Teaching of Tamazight. He published many articles in magazines as well as a few books in Arabic and French, the most recent of which are *L'Aménagement de Tamazight* (ENAG, 2011), *Les malaises de la société algérienne, crise de langue, crise d'identité* (CASBAH Editions, 2003), and *Cultures populaires, culture nationale* (l'Harmattan, Paris, 2002).

Kevin Dwyer, an anthropologist, has carried out research in Morocco, Tunisia, and Egypt. He is the author of *Moroccan Dialogues: Anthropology in Question* (1982), *Arab Voices: The Human Rights Debate in the Middle East* (1991), and *Beyond Casablanca: M. A. Tazi and the Adventure of Moroccan Cinema* (2004), as well as articles on anthropological theory, human rights, and Moroccan cinema. He has been a fellow at the Woodrow Wilson International Center for Scholars, Washington, DC, and, most recently, was professor of anthropology at the American University in Cairo (2001–2008) and a visiting professor at the Columbia University.

Abderrahman El Aissati is a lecturer at Tilburg University. He holds a PhD degree from the Radboud University of Nijmegen (1996), on language loss and language attrition among speakers of Moroccan Arabic in the Netherlands. His research interests cover language and communication in general, including theoretical linguistics (phonology and language contact), sociolinguistics, and language and identity. More recently, he has been working on culture, communication, and globalization, and on Moroccan languages and computer-mediated communication, with focus on the use and social meaning of Amazigh on the Internet. A list of his publications can be found at: https://www.tilburguniversity.edu/webwijs/show/?uid=a.elaissati

Chouki El Hamel's research interests focus on the intellectual history of Islam and Islamic institutions in the Northwest and West Africa. What interests him most as a scholar is the culture of silence. He is particularly interested in investigating the subaltern relationship of servile and marginalized communities to ruling institutions, power, race, and gender politics within Islamic culture. He received his doctorate from the University of Sorbonne. He has taught courses on Islam and African history at Duke, North Carolina State University (NCSU), and Paris and was a Schomburg scholar before he joined the history department at the

Arizona State University. He is the author of *Black Morocco: A History of Race, Slavery and Islam* (Cambridge University Press, 2013).

Moha Ennaji is one of Morocco's leading academics with research interests in multilingualism, multiculturalism, education, gender issues, and migration. He is the author and/or editor of numerous books and articles on language and culture. His most recent publications are gender and violence in the Middle East, co-edited with F. Sadiqi (Routledge, 2011); Women as Agents of Change in the Middle East and North Africa, co-edited with F.Sadiqi (Routledge, 2010); *Multilingualism, Cultural Identity, and Education in Morocco* (Springer, 2005); *Language and Gender in the Mediterranean Region* [*International Journal of Sociology of Language* (*IJSL*) issue 190, 2008); *Migration and Gender in Morocco*, co-authored with F. Sadiqi (Red Sea Press, 2008), *Women Writing Africa, the Northern Region,* co-edited with F.Sadiqi et al. (The Feminist Press, 2009). Moha Ennaji is professor at Fès University and a visiting professor at Rutgers University. He is the president of the South North Center for Intercultural Dialogue.

Lilia Labidi is an anthropologist and psychoanalyst, currently visiting research professor at the Middle East Institute, National University of Singapore. She is the author of many works on the Arab world, in subjects such as the history of the feminist movement, psychology and sexuality, the construction of identity, and attitudes toward death. She has been a fellow at the Woodrow Wilson International Center for Scholars, Washington, DC; visiting professor at the American University in Cairo; is co-founder and active member of the Association of Tunisian Women for Research and Development; and the Tunisian Association for Health Psychology. She was Minister of Woman Affairs in the Tunisian government of National Unity (January–December 2011), following the overthrow of the old regime.

Fatima Sadiqi is professor of linguistics and gender studies. She has written extensively on Moroccan languages and Moroccan women's issues. She is the author of *Women, Gender, and Language in Morocco* (Brill, 2003), acclaimed by many critics as the first book on feminist linguistics in the Arab-Islamic world. Her Harvard Fellowship allowed her to start her new book *Berber Women's Religious Expressions*. Fatima Sadiqi has also co-authored, co-edited, and co-translated a number of books and articles. She is editor-in-chief of *Languages and Linguistics*, an international journal, and serves on the editorial board of *Gender and Language*, the first international journal in the discipline. Her recent interest in gender and migration is part of her concerns with how language, gender, and mobility interact with culture in a fast-changing planet.

Youssef Sawani is professor of politics and international relations at the University of Tripoli in Libya. His recent publications include *Attitudes of Arab Public Opinion towards Democracy: An Analysis of Survey Results* (Beirut: CAUS, 2014), *Libya: Revolution and State-Building* (Beirut: CAUS, 2013), *Theories in International Relations* (Beirut: Al-Maaref Forum, 2013), "Dynamics of Continuity and Change" in *The Libyan Uprisings and the Struggle for the Post-Qadhafi Future* edited by Jason Pack (Palgrave Macmillan, 2013), "The February 17th *Intifada* in Libya: Disposing of the Regime and Issues of State Building" in *Revolution, Revolt, and Reform in North Africa: The Arab Spring and Beyond edited by* Ricardo Rene Laremont (Routledge, 2013), "Post-Qadhafi Libya: Interactive Dynamics and the Political Future" (*Contemporary Arab Affairs*, vol. 5, no. 1, January 2012, 1–26), "Prospects in a Post-Gaddafi Libya" (*World Policy Journal*, issue Nov. 2011).

Marlyn Tadros is professor of web development and interactive media at the Arts Institute of New England in Boston. She is a research affiliate at the Middle East Center at Northeastern University (NEU) and is managing editor of its new *Journal of New Media Studies*. She was also a visiting scholar in the women's department at NEU. She occasionally teaches human rights and Middle East studies in the political science department, and was also a visiting fellow at the Human Rights Program at Harvard University. Prior to coming to the United States in September 1998, she was deputy director of the Legal Research and Resource Center for Human Rights in Cairo, Egypt. She is also author of numerous papers on the Middle East, especially minorities' and women's rights, with several publications in both English and Arabic.

Madina Touré holds a degree in general university studies and a PhD in history from the University of Nouakchot (Mauritania), where she also studied law. Her long experience in the field of documentation and library earned her the title of director of the University Library. Along with that, she is a research associate at the Laboratory of Historical and Scientific Studies (LERHI) at the University of Nouakchott. Her research is primarily on the Senegal River Valley.

Dirk Vandewalle teaches in the Government Department and the Amos Tuck School of Business at Dartmouth College. He is the author of *Libya since Independence: Oil and State-Building* (Cornell University Press) and *A Modern History of Libya* (Cambridge University Press). He has studied Libyan politics and economic development since 1982, and is currently working on a manuscript, entitled "From the Ashes of History: Libya's Search for a Modern State, 1951-2013." He was political advisor to Ian Martin, the United Nations Special Envoy to Libya, in summer 2011, and the Senior Political Advisor to the Carter Center electoral mission in Libya in 2012.

Sherifa Zuhur is director of the Institute of Middle Eastern, Islamic, and Strategic Studies; associate editor for the Review of Middle East Studies; and a past president of the Association of Middle East Women's Studies. She is a research professor *emerita* from the Strategic Studies Institute of the US Army War College and was a faculty member at the American University in Cairo; University of California, Berkeley; the Massachusetts Institute of Technology; and other universities. Her research in Egypt has addressed contemporary Islamic movements, gender politics, political formations and activism, and minority rights, and cultural expression and includes the books *Revealing Reveiling: Islamist Ideology in Contemporary Egypt* (1992) and *Egypt: Security, Political and Islamist Challenges* (2007). Her most recent book is *Saudi Arabia* (2012). She has published 17 books and monographs and 150 articles and book chapters.

INDEX